BLUEPRINT FOR MODERN AMERICA

BLUEPRINT FOR MODERN AMERICA

NONMILITARY LEGISLATION OF THE FIRST CIVIL WAR CONGRESS

Leonard P. Curry

VANDERBILT UNIVERSITY PRESS *Nashville*

Vanderbilt University Press

Nashville, Tennessee

Library of Congress Catalogue

Card Number 68–10827

Printed in the United States of America by

Kingsport Press, Inc.

Kingsport, Tennessee

TO M. P. C.

Acknowledgments

Every historian owes his first debt of gratitude to the librarians who make his research possible. Although space does not permit a full listing, I am greatly obligated to the staffs of all the libraries mentioned in the manuscripts section of the bibliography. Special thanks must be extended, however, to the staff of the Margaret I. King Library of the University of Kentucky, where the basic research was undertaken, and to the staff of the Library of Congress.

I also wish to acknowledge, with great appreciation, the financial assistance given me at critical stages in the progress of this study by the Southern Fellowships Fund, the American Philosophical Society, and the Arts and Sciences Faculty Research Fund of the University of Louisville.

I am personally indebted to Professor Thomas D. Clark and Professor Holman Hamilton of the University of Kentucky for their careful reading of an earlier draft of this study. I have further profited from Professor Hamilton's criticisms of a later version of the chapters dealing with congressional dominance. I have benefited, too, from the comments regarding the chapters on finance and currency made by Professor John C. Thompson of the University of Connecticut. My greatest debt is to my wife, Mary Prichard Curry, whose judicious criticism of this study at every stage of its development has been invaluable.

Finally, my sincere thanks go to Miss Mary Lee Tipton of Vanderbilt University Press, who has skillfully and tactfully shepherded this work through the publishing process.

This books owes much to all of these people and institutions but, obviously, the responsibility for any faults and errors is entirely my own.

Contents

BLUEPRINT FOR MODERN AMERICA

Introduction

Among the games historians play is one called "contemporary parallels." Usually this game is a variety of academic solitaire, or (what is almost the same thing) a desperate attempt to generate a spark of interest in a captive classroom audience. Occasionally, however, such analogies possess a degree of relevance to our better understanding of some historical problem. The similarities between some of the conditions existing in the early 1860s and some of our current circumstances are sufficiently close to suggest, at least, that our generation is peculiarly (and unfortunately) well equipped to appreciate the problems and accomplishments of the earlier era.

It was inevitable that most of the nation's attention, concern, and resources should be concentrated on the war—a war in which many citizens were surprised to find their government involved. Even more Americans were astonished that the battle should be so prolonged and victory so elusive. Many in this latter group charged the executive with inefficiency, or worse, and demanded that the military activity not be inhibited by political considerations or concern for public opinion. A few, however, declared the victory to be unattainable—or attainable only at a cost far too great to be borne—and called for negotiations with the enemy. These proposals were met with cries of treason, demands for the suppression of dissent, and the assertion that negotiations would result in the abandonment of the friends of the United States government in the theater of war to the none-too-tender mercies of their opponents. To many persons, the President seemed to be walking a tightrope between the two extremes. He spoke of his desire for peace, but only, his pro-negotiation critics noted, on terms wholly unacceptable to the enemy.

The President's personality and background—as well as his policies—were sources of discontent. He was a crude and vulgar westerner whose accent grated harshly on eastern ears. His reputation as a political manipulator inspired little confidence among many members of his own party. Not a few, in fact, regarded him (despite his electoral victory) as more or less an accidental president—the result of an unfortunate convention decision based on the political necessity of carrying certain critical states in a narrowly divided election. Springing from humble stock, he was poorly educated by contemporary standards, and his formal speeches—though frequently gracefully and imaginatively written—were better read than heard. His unfamiliarity with foreign affairs and his lack of understanding of the importance of world opinion, it was suggested, were losing friends for the United States abroad.

Domestic problems, too, plagued the nation. One of the most critical (as well as one of the most divisive) of these problems was racial in nature. Simply stated, the question was: What were white Americans prepared to support as a description of the current and future role of the Negro in national economic, social, and political life that Negro Americans were willing to accept? This question was inseparably connected with an allied one: To what extent could or would the national government override state and municipal authority, overturn state statutes and municipal ordinances, and undermine state and local practices? Only a limited area of consensus (mostly legal in nature) on these matters existed within the party which controlled both the executive and legislative branches of the national government. For residents of one region of the nation—on whose support the majority party depended for continued control of the federal governmental structure—had a long heritage of anti-Negro sentiment, no small part of which had been institutionalized by legal enactments. The presumed leaders of the Negro population made their pilgrimages to the White House at the invitation of the President. They listened to his pleas and proposals but found them generally inadequate to the existing needs. Indeed, some white and Negro leaders of the cause distrusted the Chief Executive's commitment because of his past statements and actions and his southern nativity.

Many Americans considered it essential that the federal government address itself to other domestic problems as well. They maintained that there existed a national crisis in the field of transportation correctable only by massive federal support for new transportation works. The cities, the states, and private corporations were declared to be incapable of dealing with the crisis alone. There was much support—especially in the northern states east of the Mississippi—for some measure of federal support for education in the states. Both major parties had pledged themselves to use the resources of the federal government to underwrite American development. But as the costs of the war created mounting federal deficits, voices were raised demanding that such expenditures be delayed. A series of ridiculously low estimates of war costs by cabinet officials, necessitating the passage of numerous supplementary appropriation acts, further aggravated the situation.

The war, in fact, created many economic problems. New tax measures had to be devised, but numerous special interests had to be placated, and neither the executive nor Congress appeared willing to come to grips with the realities of the situation. There were numerous debates on general monetary policy, and federal officials struggled to devise a program which would secure the support, or, at least, the acquiescence, of the financial community. Meanwhile, the prices of government securities declined, and bankers complained of the continuing gold drain. Moreover, a war-fed inflation sent living costs spiraling upward and produced widespread, if muted, discontent.

It was charged that civil liberties were being infringed and the freedom of the press endangered. Accounts of federal governmental pressures on newspaper owners and editors were commonplace. The administration was accused of managing the news; reporters were harassed to reveal their sources within the government. At the same time, it was unquestionably true that—both visually and verbally—the war was being given much fuller coverage than had been accorded to any previous conflict. Federal officials castigated and harried vigorous dissenters from the government's war policy, and in some instances federal troops were employed to police the civilian population. It was frequently charged that the Constitution was being subverted.

As voluntary enlistments proved insufficient to supply the manpower needed in the expanding military operations, the draft act came under attack. Not a few persons opposed the draft in principle and many more complained of its inequity—especially of the possibilities for evasion that were available, primarily, to the more affluent segment of society. This opposition reached riot proportions in a very few instances.

The abnormal situation that existed exacerbated the traditional power struggle between the executive and Congress and, partly because of the President's overriding concern for the war effort, the legislative branch was able to extend its power and influence. The Chief Executive's problems with Congress were compounded by a significant rift within his own party—a split frequently reflected in congressional roll calls. This party division was so severe as to produce, both within and outside of Congress, a movement designed to deny the President renomination and to replace him with a more cultured man of New England birth and education. This latter leader had both cabinet and senatorial experience and was regarded as the leader of the more radical elements of the party. He declared his loyalty to the Chief Executive, but many people thought him to be giving surreptitious support to the party rebels.

Economic and political problems created or intensified by the existence of war; a backlog of domestic legislation on which influential segments of the population would apparently countenance no further delay; a racial problem which had assumed crisis proportions—these were the hallmarks of the 1860s.

If (by virtue of this game historians play) there seem to be many similarities between the problems of this earlier period and the conditions existing today, many significant differences could also be adduced. Certainly no historian in full possession of his faculties would suggest that the history of the early years of the Civil War presents us with any specific guidelines for solving the problems of the present. However, at least two very general observations of more than antiquarian interest might be made. In the 1960s, despite the existence of a major armed conflict, a political commitment has been made (verbally, at least) to the modification of the present social and economic patterns by the passage of sweeping nonmilitary legislation. In the 1860s, despite the existence of a major armed conflict, the existing social and economic patterns *were* modified by the passage of sweeping nonmilitary legislation. Hence, it cannot be asserted, axiomatically, that a governmental structure burdened with the necessity of sustaining a major military undertaking *must* hold in abeyance important domestic legislation of novel and controversial nature. Indeed, it is theoretically possible to make creative use of wartime tensions and war-spawned administrative machinery in the social and economic spheres. Moreover, policy formulation and bold ventures are not necessarily the exclusive prerogative of the executive branch. For it was the Congress, far more than the President, which was responsible for the measures of the 1861–63 period that constituted the new blueprint for the social, economic, and political development of the nation for at least the next third of a century. It would seem, consequently, that much might be gained from a fuller understanding of the shaping and the shapers of this new America of the post–Civil War era.

The view that the Civil War was, in fact, a turning point in the historical development of the United States has gained almost universal acceptance. The emancipation of the slaves, the destruction of the political control exercised by the South, the emergence of the Republican Party as the dominant political force in the nation, and the death of federalism in its narrowest sense come quickly to mind as consequences which obviously justify such a conclusion. The role of Congress in these events, however—and in many other less readily recalled actions which contributed to the redrawing of the political, social, and economic blueprints for America—is too frequently relegated to a distinctly secondary position or, indeed, ignored.

The legislative branch of the national government has not as yet received its fair share of attention from American historians. Only recently—with the application of computer techniques to legislative analysis—has there been evidence of a continuing interest in one dimension of congressional history. Such quantitative studies, though frequently of great significance, reveal little or nothing about the evolution of legislation and its impact. Some might unthinkingly conclude that, in the absence of an extensive number of rare personal documents, no accurate concept of these aspects of congressional operations can be obtained. An intimate acquaintance with the debates and documents of a given Congress will almost inevitably produce a categorical declaration that this assumption is not correct in the case of any mid–nineteenth-century Congress.

It is probably less true of the Thirty-seventh Congress than of any other during this period. Shortly after the first Civil War Congress came to an end in early March 1863, one of its most influential members wrote that "The Senate has become a laborious committee where bills are drawn as well as discussed."[1] To a lesser extent this was true of the lower house as well. Measure after measure can be seen taking shape on the floor of the House or the Senate, and few indeed were the important bills of a nonmilitary nature which passed both houses without meticulous

1. John Sherman to William T. Sherman, March 20, 1863, quoted in Rachel S. Thorndike (editor), *The Sherman Letters,* p. 194.

explanation and, generally, extensive amendment. Time and again, members insisted on bringing to the floor proposals which had been rejected by committees of which they were members, and frequently committee deliberations were aired in the House and Senate. Consequently, the official records of this Congress, judiciously supplemented by other sources—newspaper accounts, diaries, memoirs, personal letters, and special studies—can reveal to the earnest inquirer a valid picture of this remarkable legislative body in action.

The accomplishments of the Thirty-seventh Congress, it could be argued, were a direct result of the extraordinary capabilities of its membership. Assuredly, men of great ability are found in every Congress, but perhaps the Thirty-seventh Congress had more than its share: the editors of the *Dictionary of American Biography* included sketches of fifty-six of the senators and sixty-seven of the representatives from this body in the initial twenty volumes of that work.

Some might say that the Thirty-seventh Congress had greatness thrust upon it. Impelled by the struggle for national survival, inspired by the battle for human freedom, possessed of a greater degree of sectional and political unity than any previous Congress: could the Thirty-seventh Congress possibly have been insignificant?

In any event, this Congress did exert a molding and impelling force on the course of national development by enacting numerous measures of lasting importance. This study will not deal with the legislation designed to create and support the military establishment necessary to prosecute the war. These were measures of great immediate consequence, but their primary significance—in the long run—was that they made possible Union victory. But it was the long-range, nonmilitary legislation of this first Civil War Congress and the enduring impact of this legislation on the social, economic, and political structure of the nation during the remainder of the nineteenth century that made this body historically significant.

The many legislative acts that dealt with the destruction of slavery and the status of the Negro defined, within broad limits, the role of this racial minority group in American life for many years to come. There were subsequent fluctuations and modifications, but what was done—and what was not done—by the Thirty-seventh Congress was of enormous consequence. The congressional efforts to frame and pass confiscation legislation had important implications for the future. For, though moral distinctions were made regarding various types of property interests, "morally acceptable" property interests were hedged about with stringent safeguards. The measures dealing with the public lands and national support for public improvements were of far-reaching social and economic significance. The gigantic transportation works and the colleges and universities—good, bad, and indifferent—which were built in the years that followed, left nothing that they touched unchanged. The tariff and internal revenue acts modified the structure of national finance and, together with the legal tender and national banking acts, had tremendous effect on the American economy. With the exception of the act establishing a national banking system, these measures did not represent legislative response to executive demands. They were, on the contrary, clear examples of congressional initiative. Furthermore, continued pressure by shrewd and powerful legislative leaders undermined presidential power and accelerated the trend toward congressional dominance of the national government.

Late in the final session of the Thirty-seventh Congress, a New England representative observed:

> The calmness of the nation while the war of the rebellion in all its strongholds rages with the greatest fury, will be noted as one of the most remarkable features in the history of the times. . . . The nation itself, through its executive, judicial and legislative organs, exhibits no renunciation of minor duties while unflinchingly prosecuting a task unmatched in magnitude or in possible results. Here there is no trace of any purpose to abandon enterprises which might, even in times of peace appal [*sic*] statesmen and legislators less bold in the assumption of the perpetuity of our Government, and less reliant upon the solid resources of our people.[2]

There was, indeed, "no renunciation of minor duties;" but there was something more affirmative as well. These men repeatedly demonstrated their willingness and their determination to meet the challenges presented and to seize the opportunities offered to come to grips with some of the most critical problems in American life. For it was the members of this Congress—sometimes by accident and sometimes by design—who drew the blueprint for a new America.

2. *The Congressional Globe,* 37th Cong., 3rd Sess., p. 297. The speaker was Justin S. Morrill of Vermont.

CHAPTER I

The Thirty-seventh Congress: Issues and Alignments

The Senate

The presiding officer's gavel rapped, and the Reverend Byron Sunderland offered a prayer of thanksgiving and supplication. It was Independence Day, 1861; but, standing with bowed heads listening and not listening to the words of the minister, was no group of local politicians met to indulge in spread-eagle oratory praising the glorious and everlasting union. The gavel rested in the hand of Hannibal Hamlin, Vice President of the United States, and the men facing him were American senators, called into special session by the President of the United States in time of gravest crisis. Surveying the chamber, as the voice of the acting secretary droned out the words of the presidential proclamation that had summoned them, the vice president's gaze rested on many men of commanding presence, national renown, and great abilities. Probably the most striking sight in the entire panorama, however, was not any one or all of the senators at their desks, but the vacant seats which ringed the hall.[1]

Twenty-one unoccupied desks starkly symbolized the deadly threat to the nation's existence which had brought these men together. From the eleven states now arrayed in rebellion against the national government there remained one lone representative in the Senate of the United States—Democrat Andrew Johnson of Tennessee. Long a bitter opponent of the "cotton aristocrats," Johnson had no intention of allowing them to dictate his course of action now; and until he became military governor of Tennessee eight months later, his was the vital voice of a submerged people—the unionists of the South.[2]

1. *Cong. Globe,* 37th Cong., 1st Sess., p. 1.

2. Brief biographical sketches of all members of Congress can be found in *Biographical Directory of the American Congress, 1774–1927.* With one or two

But those concerned for the present emergency and future national policy naturally turned their eyes to the Republican side of the chamber; for the withdrawal of the southern senators had given the Republicans an overwhelming majority in the upper house. Here, in consequence, sat the men who would lead the Senate and significantly influence the nation's course during this period of national crisis. Congressional leadership functions were rather widely dispersed in the mid-nineteenth century. Probably two thirds of the Republican senators played quite active roles on the Senate floor and in committee; but some eight or ten can be singled out as having assumed or having been accorded positions of authority and influence.

At this time, the office of majority leader did not exist. The titular head of the Senate majority, and consequently of the Senate itself, was the chairman of the Committee on Finance, who, by controlling the course of taxation and appropriation bills, exercised great influence on all matters before the upper house. In the Thirty-seventh Congress, this position was held by a rigidly scrupulous New Englander of Whig antecedents, William Pitt Fessenden of Maine, a seven-year Senate veteran. Though morose, unsociable, and irritable, he was industrious, conscientious, and extremely able. "There was," George W. Julian later recalled, "a sort of majesty in the figure and brow of Fessenden."[3]

Many persons considered the leader of the more radical Senate Republicans to be Benjamin Franklin Wade of Ohio, a former Whig. He was, a contemporary observed, "a man of uncommon downrightness. There was even a sort of fascination about his profanity." In this Congress he served as chairman of both the Senate Committee on Territories and the powerful Joint Committee on the Conduct of the War.[4]

---

exceptions, all of the senators and representatives discussed in this chapter are also the subjects of biographical accounts in Allen Johnson and Dumas Malone (editors), *Dictionary of American Biography.* In addition, there are one or more full-length biographies dealing with most of these individuals, and memoirs published by several congressmen. Those which have been used are listed in the bibliography. Reference to these items in the footnotes to this chapter will not be made unless material is quoted from them.

3. Noah Brocks, *Washington in Lincoln's Time,* pp. 26–27; George W. Julian, *Political Recollections, 1840 to 1872,* p. 356; *Biographical Encyclopedia of Maine of the Nineteenth Century,* pp. 21–33.

4. Linus P. Brockett, *Men of Our Day,* pp. 243–262; New York *Herald,* January 22, 1863. The quotation is from Julian, *loc. cit.*

Wade's colleague from Ohio, also an ex-Whig, was John Sherman. He was only thirty-eight years old and beginning his first Senate term, but because of his distinguished career in the House, he was already a powerful figure in his party and in the national capital. Recognizing Sherman's great abilities, the Republican Senate leadership took the highly unusual step of placing this freshman senator on the all-powerful Committee on Finance. A close friend of both Secretary of the Treasury Salmon P. Chase and Jay Cooke's brother Henry, Sherman played an important role in shaping Civil War financial legislation.[5]

Perhaps no senatorial colleagues were at once more powerful and more ill-matched than were the senators from Massachusetts—Charles Sumner and Henry Wilson. Sumner, chairman of the prestigious Committee on Foreign Relations, was polished, arrogant, oracular, vain, and totally devoid of a sense of humor. Estimates of his character and personality ranged from "the purest man in the Senate" to "cowardly, mean, malignant, tyrannical, hypocritical, and cringing and toadyish to every thing, and every body that had the odor of aristocracy." Many years later, one of Sumner's biographers was to sum up the senator's contributions by saying, "But his great work was not in the framing of laws. His was, rather, the role of an ancient Hebrew prophet—the kindling of moral enthusiasm, the inspiring of courage and hope, and assailing of injustice."[6] Ex-Whig Henry Wilson—"the Natick cobbler"—headed the important Committee on Military Affairs. Unlike Sumner, he sprang from laboring stock and was poorly educated—his lack of polish was apparent in both his speeches and his appearance. Though not so elegant as his senior colleague, Wilson was certainly a more constructive legislator and probably a more valuable senator *in toto*.[7]

5. Wilhelmus B. Bryan, *A History of the National Capital,* II, 491; Carl F. Wittke (editor), *The History of the State of Ohio,* IV, 377.

6. Brooks, *op. cit.,* pp. 23–25; Carl Schurz, *The Reminiscences of Carl Schurz,* II, 312; George F. Hoar, *Autobiography of Seventy Years,* I, 214. The quotations are from Julian, *loc. cit.;* Orville H. Browning, *The Diary of Orville Hickman Browning,* edited by Theodore C. Pease and James G. Randall, (November 28, 1862), I, 588; and George H. Haynes, "Charles Sumner," *DAB,* XVIII, 213, respectively.

7. Brockett, *op. cit.,* pp. 367–385; Brooks, *op. cit.,* p. 23; Josiah B. Grinnell, *Men and Events of Forty Years,* p. 78; Alexander K. McClure, *Colonel Alexander K. McClure's Recollections of Half a Century,* p. 288.

From Michigan came millionaire Zachariah Chandler, another former Whig. Grim and jocular by turns, Chandler was somewhat given to overindulgence in liquor and was often violent in debate. He served as chairman of the Committee on Commerce and was an influential member of the Joint Committee on the Conduct of the War.[8]

A former Democrat—Lyman Trumbull of Illinois—was chairman of the vitally important Committee on the Judiciary. He was a man of strong political conscience whose deceptively mild and frail appearance belied his industry in committee and his vigor in debate. Time and again during the Thirty-seventh Congress, proposals of more ardent and hot-blooded senators foundered on the rock of Trumbull's stern and unbending legalism.[9]

The most important spokesman for the Republican conservatives in the Senate was Jacob Collamer of Vermont, the oldest member of the upper house. His chairmanship of the Committee on the Post Office and Post Roads was a potentially important patronage post, but his influence in the Senate was primarily the result of an exhaustive attention to legislative details especially remarkable in a man in his seventieth year. He was an ardent and rather narrow-minded legalist, frequently buttressing his arguments with citations, detailed analyses, and carefully reasoned analogies. A contemporary observed that Collamer "was the impersonation of logical force and the beau ideal of a lawyer and judge."[10]

Two other Republicans of Whig heritage—Henry B. Anthony of Rhode Island and Solomon Foot of Vermont—occupied posts which should have automatically placed them in positions of authority, but neither seems to have wielded great power. It is quite possible that Anthony was named chairman of the Senate Republican caucus because he was a man of great personal charm and of moderate views. He was

8. Brooks, *op. cit.,* p. 27; Floyd Streeter, *Political Parties in Michigan, 1837–1860,* pp. 254–257; Edward Bates, *Diary of Edward Bates, 1859–1866,* edited by Howard K. Beale, American Historical Association, *Annual Report* (1930), Vol. IV (June 4, 1862), 260; Otis E. McCutcheon, "Recollections of Zachariah Chandler," *Michigan History Magazine,* V, Nos. 1 and 2 (January, April 1921), 142.

9. Brockett, *op cit.,* p. 389; George O. Seilhamer, *Leslie's History of the Republican Party,* I, 105.

10. The quotation is from Julian, *op. cit.,* p. 356.

notable primarily as a vigorous supporter of protective tariffs and an ardent defender of private property rights. Foot was probably selected president pro tem of the Senate because his ten successive years in the upper house constituted a period of continuous service surpassed by no Republican and equaled by only two—Sumner and Wade—neither especially well qualified for this post. Foot, on the other hand, had served as speaker of the Vermont House of Representatives and was considered to be exceptionally well versed in parliamentary law.

The Senate majority these men led was, if anything, even less unified than its leaders' divergent views would indicate. To speak of the Republican Party in the Senate as being composed of two wings—one radical and the other conservative—is a gross oversimplification. Within this group were senators of almost all shades of opinion, and alignments constantly shifted as different issues came before the Senate. Nevertheless, it is possible (and helpful) to categorize the Senate Republicans broadly under three rather general headings—radicals, moderates, and conservatives. These terms are, of course, entirely relative and intrinsically meaningless. They are used here only as labels to facilitate the classification of the Republican senators, though they can be said to represent (in the order listed) diminishing enthusiasm for the proposals of the radicals.

The radicals vehemently opposed all efforts to find a compromise solution to the sectional crisis of 1860–61 and peremptorily rejected all proposals for negotiation (either formal or informal) with the leaders of the disaffected section. They considered "coercion" not only the undeniable right and imperative duty of the nation, but also a welcome opportunity to reshape the American union and change the structure of southern society and politics. The radicals demanded that the national government, acting under the "war power," emancipate all slaves in the rebel area; and they expended much energy in devising methods for undermining the "peculiar institution" in the border states. They vigorously urged the enlistment of Negro troops and supported proposals for removing some of the legal and substantive disabilities laid upon the Negroes in the loyal states. They advocated the passage of stringent confiscation legislation enforceable by military tribunals. In acting to find solutions to the problems presented and to take advantage of the opportunities offered, the radicals did not consider the Constitution binding in detail (in either the loyal or the rebel areas) and insisted that the existence of a state of war (and, concomitantly, of the "war power") had legitimatized broad areas of extra-constitutional action.

It is doubtful that any two radicals could have been found who held identical views on all of these issues, but they were in general agreement with the positions outlined above. Wade, Henry Wilson, Chandler, Sumner, David Wilmot of Pennsylvania, Samuel C. Pomeroy of Kansas, Morton S. Wilkinson of Minnesota, and Lot Morrill of Maine supported the radical position with such fervor and consistency that they might be called advanced radicals. Others who were clearly radicals were Preston King of New York, James H. Lane of Kansas, John P. Hale of New Hampshire, and James W. Grimes of Iowa. A few generalizations can be made about these men. Though half of them represented midwestern states, only one was born beyond the Appalachians; two thirds of them were natives of New England. Their political antecedents were much less Whiggish than those of the Republican senators as a whole. Most of them seem to have come from mobile middle-class families, though their ranks included a Boston Brahmin and the son of a common laborer. They ranged in age from forty-two to sixty with a median of forty-nine, and two thirds of them were serving their first Senate terms.

The moderate Republican senators refused to associate themselves with any proffer of sectional compromise—though some of them might well have acquiesced in a compromise solution emanating from another source, provided such a proposal did not include constitutional protection of slavery in the territories. They viewed "coercion" as a painful duty which would, of necessity, produce some reshaping of both the Union and southern society. They were convinced that the institution of slavery in the rebel states would be an inevitable casualty of the war, and they desired that a program of gradual emancipation be immediately initiated in the border states. The moderates worked earnestly for the passage of a confiscation act as sweeping in nature as they believed could be enforced through the federal courts, though there was some difference of opinion as to what this meant in terms of practical legislation. They were uncertain about the wisdom of enlisting Negro troops (though they favored the employment of Negroes in quasi-military support units), and they doubted the expediency of agitating for the removal of restrictions imposed on Negroes in the loyal areas. The moderates generally held that the constitutional limitations on Congress were still in effect, but they were inclined to think that the President, as commander-in-chief, was not so circumscribed in dealing with the areas in rebellion.

Probably a wider divergence of views existed within the moderate bloc than among the radicals. Trumbull, Sherman, Henry S. Lane of Indiana, James Harlan of Iowa, and Jacob M. Howard of Michigan, for instance, leaned toward the radical position on some issues and hence might be termed advanced moderates. All represented midwestern states; three were born west of the Appalachians, and two were natives of New England. Fessenden, Foot, Anthony, Daniel Clark of New Hampshire, Samuel G. Arnold and James F. Simmons of Rhode Island, Lafayette S. Foster of Connecticut, and Ira Harris of New York were also moderates. All of them were born in, or within a few miles of, the eastern states which they represented. Almost all the members of the moderate bloc (including the advanced moderates) were former Whigs, ranging in age from thirty-seven to sixty-five, with a median age of fifty-one. Almost two thirds were serving their first Senate terms. More than half came from upper- or upper-middle-class origins and only two or three could definitely be called mobile, either geographically or socially. Thus, the primary differences between the radicals and the moderates seem to lie in the areas of social origin, political antecedents, and personal and family mobility.

The views of the conservatives on the questions of compromise, negotiation, and "coercion" differed little from those held by the moderates, except that the conservatives saw no reason for believing that a reshaping of the Union would or should result from a war which existed (in their view) for the sole purpose of preserving that Union. They did contemplate with equanimity the prospect of some societal changes in the South. They were entirely willing to see the institution of slavery undermined in the rebel area but doubted the wisdom of the national government's taking any official action to achieve this end. Though they opposed the expansion of the area of slavery, the conservatives considered that any interference with that institution in the border states would be the height of folly. They opposed any confiscation legislation that was not narrow and highly selective in its application and judicial in its enforcement (e.g., the confiscation through judicial process of the slave property of rebels-in-arms). They opposed the enlistment of Negro troops and any significant attack on Negro disabilities. The conservatives considered the

Constitution to be binding on all branches of the federal government and rejected the doctrine of "war powers," either legislative or executive.

Two of the Republican senators—Orville H. Browning of Illinois and Edgar Cowan of Pennsylvania—were so adamant in their opposition and so rigid in their constitutional views that they might be styled ultra-conservatives. Collamer, James Dixon of Connecticut, Timothy O. Howe and James R. Doolittle of Wisconsin, and John C. Ten Eyck of New Jersey could also be classified as conservatives. All but two of the members of the conservative bloc were born either in the state they represented or in a contiguous state. Though they ranged in age from forty-five to sixty-nine, five of them were less than forty-seven years of age. All but one were serving their first Senate terms. With one exception, all were of Whig or Know-Nothing political antecedents and more than half of them later aligned themselves with the Democratic Party. They tended to come from upper- and upper-middle-class origins and apparently were not highly mobile socially.[11]

On the minority side of the Senate, few remnants of the old Democratic leadership were to be seen. Moreover, neither the Democrats nor the Unionists created any structure of institutional organization in this Congress. Indeed, no individual or group seems to have been either capable or desirous of exercising any leadership function among the non-Republicans, but a few actually or potentially influential minority senators might be mentioned.

Though most of the Democratic senators had been Breckinridge sup-

11. Because of their limited service, no attempt has been made to categorize Edward D. Baker of Oregon, Kinsley S. Bingham of Michigan, and Richard S. Field of New Jersey. The reader is warned that: (1) all of these generalizations are subject to qualification in individual cases; (2) the categories are established and labeled *solely* on the basis of issues significant in this Congress; (3) the categorization of senators is based *solely* on my evaluation of the senators' positions in *this* Congress and does not take into consideration earlier or later actions; (4) some degree of subjectivity is unavoidably involved in determining what measures and views are to be labeled "radical," "moderate," and "conservative;" (5) the general comments about blocs of senators, though perhaps suggestive, are intended to describe the persons included and not to provide explanations for their views; and (6) any attempt to extrapolate this information on thirty-two senators so as to make it applicable to either the leadership or the membership of the Republican Party as a whole would be extremely hazardous.

porters in 1860, Stephen A. Douglas, had he survived, might have exercised some considerable degree of leadership, for he had long been a power in his party and in the Senate. An ardent unionist, his support of Lincoln in March and April of 1861, his defense of what he conceived to be presidential policy, and his general course of action both before and after the fall of Sumter did much to unify the country behind the President's leadership and especially to prevent unrest—and perhaps uprisings—in the Middle West. His party, the Senate, and the nation sustained a staggering loss when, barely a month before the first session of this Congress convened, he died of typhoid fever in Chicago.[12]

The titular head of the other wing of the Democratic Party, John C. Breckinridge of Kentucky, was a freshman senator. His assignment to two major committees indicated recognition of his potential importance. But for all his aristocratic heritage and statesmanlike appearance, Breckinridge may well have lacked the abilities essential to legislative party leadership. In any event, his extreme position on "southern rights" had separated him from most of his party colleagues even before he "went south" in the fall of 1861 to accept a Confederate military commission.

Probably the most prominent of the remaining old-line Democratic managers was James A. Bayard of Delaware, now nearing the end of his eleventh year in the Senate. For five years, this skillful political manipulator had played an active role in the direction of his party. Ardently proslavery in sympathy, he was in the South when Sumter fell and summed up his views in a letter to his son two weeks later, in which he declared that "if the people of Delaware when the time comes choose to submit to Northern despotism, it is no state for you or I to live in."[13]

Closely associated with Bayard in managing the party was Douglas's bitter enemy, Jesse D. Bright, who had represented Indiana in the Senate

12. New York *Herald,* March 7, 1861; Wood Gray, *The Hidden Civil War,* pp. 56–59; *Cong. Globe,* 37th Cong., 1st Sess., pp. 27–31, 32–40.

13. Roy F. Nichols, *The Disruption of American Democracy,* pp. 5, 13, 294–309, 314–322, 397, 504–505, 511; James A. Bayard to Thomas F. Bayard, April 16, 17, 22, 26, 1861, Thomas F. Bayard Papers, Library of Congress. I have found no evidence to corroborate the assertion of Charles A. Lincoln ("James Asheton Bayard," *DAB,* II, 66–67) that Bayard preferred Lincoln to either Breckinridge or Douglas in 1860 and that he became a Republican during the war and only gradually returned to the Democratic fold.

for fifteen years. A shrewd political operator of a rather crude type, Bright had played an important role in denying Douglas the Democratic presidential nomination in 1856 and preventing his endorsement by a united party in 1860. He owned a slave-operated plantation in Kentucky and was thoroughly southern in his outlook.[14]

The Democrat with the longest Senate service (since 1843) was James A. Pearce of Maryland, a former Whig. He was a brilliant conversationalist and an accomplished legal scholar noted primarily for his effective committee work. Despite his conservative views, he was universally respected by his colleagues. In a Senate overwhelmingly dominated by Republicans, Pearce was the only Democrat to hold a committee chairmanship—in deference to his scholarly qualities, he had been retained as head of the Committee on the Library.[15]

In addition to Breckinridge, Bayard, and Bright, only one other member of the Democratic inner circle was still present in the Senate—Henry M. Rice of Minnesota. Despite his ardent support of the Union cause, he was clearly destined for an early departure from the national scene. Though Rice was gracious, tactful, popular, ambitious, talented, and shrewd, he labored under the insurmountable difficulty of being a Democrat in a Republican state.[16]

Although never a member of the Democratic managerial group, Andrew Johnson, had he been less bitter, might have become the figure around which Senate Democratic pro-Union sentiment could have coalesced. Johnson was by nature poorly suited to a role of legislative leadership, however, and his acceptance of the military governorship of Tennessee removed him from the Senate before the midpoint of the second session.

One of the ablest and most energetic of the new Democratic senators was James A. McDougall of California. An ardent Douglasite and a close personal friend of Lincoln, McDougall had just been elected to the Senate by a coalition of Douglas Democrats and Republicans. In the Thirty-sev-

14. Kenneth M. Stampp, *Indiana Politics During the Civil War*, p. 16; Nichols, *op. cit.*, pp. 4, 5, 13, 15, 88, 294–309, 314–322.

15. *Cong. Globe*, 37th Cong., 3d Sess., pp. 292–294, 298–302; Bernard C. Steiner, "James Alfred Pearce," *Maryland Historical Magazine*, XVII, No. 1 (March 1922), 41.

16. Nichols, *op. cit.*, pp. 419, 421, 446, 487, 511.

enth Congress he repeatedly demonstrated his attachment to the Union cause and his support for stringent action to suppress rebellion and treason. The fact that he was frequently inebriated tended to diminish his influence and led many of his contemporaries to minimize his quite-considerable abilities.[17]

Among those Democrats who entered the Senate during the Second Session of the Thirty-seventh Congress, John B. Henderson of Missouri was probably the most able and influential. A bitter opponent of secession, he took a strongly pro-Union stand throughout his Senate career and by the end of the war was affiliated with the Republican Party.[18]

Of the eight Unionists who sat in the Senate at one time or another during the Thirty-seventh Congress, John S. Carlile of Virginia was probably the most energetic. Carlile, who claimed both Whig and Democratic antecedents, took an active part both in pressing for the enactment of war measures and in resisting what he considered to be violations of the Constitution (including attacks on slavery).[19] It is possible, however, that his closer connections with the Republican leadership gave the other Virginia Unionist, Waitman T. Willey, greater influence. Willey, a former Whig who later became a Republican, was a precise and methodical lawyer and a polished orator.[20]

Though the views of the Democratic and Unionist senators, with a few exceptions, did not, perhaps, diverge as widely from an area of common agreement as did those of their Republican colleagues,[21] various shadings

17. Hubert H. Bancroft, *History of California,* VII, 273–274; Harvey W. Scott, *History of the Oregon Country,* V, 39; John W. Forney, *Anecdotes of Public Men,* pp. 147–148; John Hay to John G. Nicolay, April 16, 1862, in Tyler Dennett (editor), *Lincoln and the Civil War in the Diaries and Letters of John Hay,* p. 42; Russell Buchanan, "James A. McDougall: A Forgotten Senator," *Quarterly of the California Historical Society,* XV, No. 3 (September 1936), 199–212.

18. *Cong. Globe,* 37th Cong., 3d Sess., p. 1197; Henry C. McDougal, "A Decade of Missouri Politics—1860 to 1870: From a Republican Viewpoint," *The Missouri Historical Review,* III, No. 2 (January 1909), 135.

19. *Cong. Globe,* 37th Cong., 2nd Sess., pp. 626, 3312; William P. Willey, *An Inside View of the Formation of the State of West Virginia,* pp. 207–210.

20. Willey, *op. cit.,* pp. 181–194.

21. For an analysis of the views and actions of both the Democratic senators and the Democratic representatives, see Leonard P. Curry, "Congressional

of opinion are nevertheless discernible. These variations are, perhaps, most clearly dealt with by classifying the non-Republican senators as moderates, conservatives, and ultra-conservatives. These terms, like those applied to the Republicans, are purely relative. They do represent, in the order listed, increasing opposition to the radical proposals, but a fuller description of these positions is essential if they are to have any utility as bloc labels.

In personal characteristics, the Democrats and Unionists in all these categories were a remarkably homogeneous group. Every Democrat but one had given unbroken allegiance to that party and all but one of the Unionists had Whig political antecedents (though two or three others could also claim some Democratic connections). The non-Republican senators seem to have sprung almost entirely from middle- and upper-middle-class roots. They ranged in age from thirty-three to sixty-four, with a median age of forty-nine; and with three exceptions, each was serving his first Senate term. There are virtually no observable differences in the backgrounds of the conservatives and the ultra-conservatives, but the moderates differed from their party colleagues in a few respects.

Among the Democrats, Henderson, Andrew Johnson, McDougall, Rice, and John R. Thomson of New Jersey frequently leaned toward the majority Republican position and thus might be classified as advanced moderates. The same designation could be applied to several Unionists—Willey, Thomas H. Hicks of Maryland, Joseph A. Wright of Indiana, and Benjamin F. Harding of Oregon. Other moderate Democrats were James W. Nesmith and Benjamin Stark of Oregon and Milton S. Latham of California. Garrett Davis of Kentucky and Robert Wilson of Missouri were moderate Unionists.[22]

The moderates' views on the questions of compromise, negotiation, and coercion were, after Fort Sumter, essentially identical with those held by the Republican conservatives, though some of the more advanced Democrats and Unionists leaned more toward the position of the Republican

Democrats—1861–1863," *Civil War History,* XII, No. 3 (September 1966), 213–229.

22. It should be noted that Davis came to the Senate a very advanced moderate and by the end of the Thirty-seventh Congress had become solidly conservative. He is here placed with the moderates on the basis of his over-all performance *in this Congress.*

moderates. Most of the non-Republican moderates, however, had favored compromise during the winter of 1860–61. On the question of limiting the further expansion of slavery, they were either neutral or mildly favorable. In general, they believed that emancipation, in both the loyal and the rebel states, could be accomplished only by constitutional amendment, though a few were of the opinion that the President had certain limited powers in this field. The moderates held that the Constitution was still binding on the Congress, but not, in every case, upon the President. With minor exceptions, they were willing to support confiscation legislation only if such legislation would be enforced by judicial process, but their views on this matter were not quite so restrictive in nature as those of the Republican conservatives. The moderates were reluctant to authorize the the enlistment of Negro troops and unwilling to interfere with the current status of the Negroes in the loyal areas. Thus, the Democratic and Unionist moderates occupied a position somewhere between the Republican conservatives and moderates and perhaps should be placed somewhat closer to the latter than to the former.

The moderate bloc contained all of the Democratic and Unionist senators from the nonslave states and all but one of the "replacement" senators[23] from the border states. They tended to be slightly younger than their more conservative colleagues, including in their ranks all but two of the Democrats and Unionists below the age of forty-five. They seem to have been somewhat more mobile socially, and much more mobile geographically, than the conservatives and ultra-conservatives. Undoubtedly the most significant observation to be made, however, is that more than two thirds of all the Democrats and Unionists who are listed here can be classified as moderates.[24]

The non-Republican conservatives—Democrats Pearce of Maryland and Lazarus Powell of Kentucky and Unionists Carlile of Virginia and

23. That is, those senators who replaced sitting senators who had either died or joined the Confederacy.

24. Because of their short periods of service, no attempt has been made to categorize Breckinridge, Bright, Trusten Polk and Waldo P. Johnson of Missouri, William A. Richardson of Illinois, David Turpie of Indiana, and James W. Wall of New Jersey. If they should be included, the above figure would have to be modified somewhat, for Breckinridge, Polk, W. P. Johnson, and Bright were clearly of ultra-conservative bent.

Anthony Kennedy of Maryland—advocated a general announcement of proposed constitutional guarantees for the institution of slavery and did not oppose unofficial negotiations with representatives of the seceded states. They considered coercion legal but highly undesirable. They opposed as unconstitutional all emancipation legislation and any attempt to limit the spread of slavery. The conservatives considered the enactment of any confiscation legislation extremely unwise and strenuously resisted the passage of all legislation to authorize the enlistment of Negro troops or to diminish Negro disabilities in the loyal areas. They considered constitutional limitations to be totally unaffected by the existence of civil war.

The ultra-conservatives were the two Delaware Democrats—James A. Bayard and Willard Saulsbury. They probably would have preferred to see a recognition of the Confederacy, followed by diplomatic negotiations leading to reunion on the basis of constitutional concessions acceptable to the South. The ultra-conservatives held that all constitutional limitations were still in effect and declared emancipation, the exclusion of slavery from the territories (or the District of Columbia), coercion, and confiscation to be clear transgressions of these limitations. They were violently opposed to any attempt to modify the Negro's position in the North or to enlist Negro troops. In the face of growing hostility, the ultra-conservatives rarely advocated the most unpopular of these views publicly after the summer of 1861.[25]

An examination of the origins of the senators who served in the Thirty-seventh Congress indicates the extent to which American political life had succumbed to rigid sectionalization. Although more than half the senators were born in states other than the ones they represented, in only four instances did natives of slave states represent free states. In no case did a senator born in a nonslave state represent a slave state. In an era of great frontier expansion, state boundaries obviously presented few obstacles to aspiring politicians; but by 1860, the line between the slave and nonslave areas had become an impassable barrier to all but a very few seekers after elective office.

The Senate chamber contained a remarkable aggregation of political leaders and spokesmen—representives of the political order that was

25. All of the warnings in footnote 11, above, must be reiterated here in regard to the Democrats and Unionists.

dying and of the political order even now being born; men of mature years and political fledglings; former and future cabinet members, former and future vice presidents, one future president, and state officials without number. Certainly there was no absence of talent. But could any amount of talent be expected to deal successfully with a crisis unprecedented in the nation's history and probably as grave as that ever faced by any legislative body? This was to be not only a period of preservation but also a period of construction, for this Congress laid the foundations of a new nation. The Senate, of course, did not act alone—there was the President, who need not for the moment concern us, and there was the House of Representatives.

The House of Representatives

In the chamber at the other end of the Capitol on that July 4, the scene was less orderly than that in the Senate. Here, too, the chaplain prayed—an interminable prayer—and the clerk of the last House read the President's proclamation and called the roll of representatives. But there the similarities ended. The Senate is a continuing body; the House is not. From this difference arose the purposeful disorder in the lower house. The roll call of the yet-unsworn members was occasionally interrupted by protests and notice of contests to be filed. But when the clerk announced the presence of a quorum and declared the next order of business to be the election of a speaker, the House was ready to take the first step toward organizing itself into a legislative body.[26]

The contest for the speakership had been a heated one. For more than a month, candidates had been actively campaigning for votes; during the last days before the convening of Congress, the canvassing had been frantic. Feeling was so intense that the Republican caucus had made no nomination for the position. In fact, *no* caucus nominations were made, for neither the Democrats nor the Unionists bothered with this empty formality.[27]

26. *Cong. Globe,* 37th Cong., 1st Sess., p. 2.

27. Henry L. Dawes to Mrs. Henry L. Dawes, July 3, 1861, Henry L. Dawes Papers, Library of Congress; Galusha A. Grow to Edward McPherson, July 12, 1861, Edward McPherson Papers, Library of Congress; New York *Herald,* July 3, 1861; Nichols, *op. cit.,* p. 511.

The three leading Republican candidates for the post were Galusha A. Grow of Pennsylvania, Francis P. Blair, Jr., of Missouri, and Schuyler Colfax of Indiana. Grow was a former Free Soil Democrat who, though only thirty-seven years old, had spent ten years in the House. He had played a prominent role in the establishment of the Republican Party and received the caucus nomination for speaker in 1857. Lincoln was rumored to favor Grow's candidacy because he thought that the Pennsylvanian's homestead bill (which Buchanan had vetoed) had made an important contribution to the Republican victories in the Midwest.[28]

"Frank" Blair—another ex-Democrat—was the son of Francis Preston Blair, Sr., and the brother of Lincoln's Postmaster General. One of the founders of the Republican Party in Missouri, Blair was a vigorous young man whose major drawback as a candidate for legislative leadership was a known propensity for overindulgence in liquor. By the end of this Congress, he was already out of sympathy with his more radical constituents, and before the end of the war, he was again aligned with the Democrats.

The third Republican aspirant to the speakership was Schuyler Colfax, a former Whig who had been active in the formation of the Republican Party in Indiana. A member of the House since 1855, a ready debater, a clever manipulator, and a dependable partisan, he was viewed as the compromise candidate to whom the members of the majority would turn in the event of a deadlock between Grow and Blair. Colfax had entered the lists late and allowed his name to be used until the day before Congress convened. At that time, apparently convinced that he could not succeed, he withdrew from the race, reiterating this withdrawal on the floor of the House just before the balloting for speaker began. Colfax's withdrawal from the contest was generally viewed as a victory for Grow, for it was thought that this meant additional Midwestern votes for the Pennsylvanian.[29]

After Colfax's statement, John Hickman of Pennsylvania placed Blair's name in nomination, and Thaddeus Stevens, also of Pennsylvania, nominated Grow. No nominations were made by the members of the minority parties.

28. Philadelphia *Inquirer,* July 4, 1861.

29. Brockett, *op. cit.,* pp. 220–228; Philadelphia *Inquirer,* July 4, 1861; Galusha A. Grow to Israel Washburn, May 30, 1861, Israel Washburn Papers, Library of Congress.

The decision not to make a Republican caucus nomination probably favored Blair, who might be expected to attract more Democratic and Unionist votes than Grow. He did so. Six Unionists and five Democrats favored him on the first ballot, while a single Unionist joined the Republicans supporting Grow. The Grow forces could easily afford to make this concession, however, for the first ballot quickly revealed the Pennsylvanian's strength. Of the eighty votes needed for the choice, Grow had seventy-one. Even with non-Republican support, Blair was able to secure only forty votes. Since the decision against a caucus nomination had been made on the basis of a tacit agreement that the candidate with the largest number of votes on the first ballot would receive united Republican support, Blair withdrew and urged his supporters to change their votes; Grow was thus elected speaker.[30]

So, for only the second time in the last four Congresses, a speaker was elected without a lengthy contest. The Blairs (for the whole family had been involved in the canvass) were, of course, bitterly disappointed; but the choice was probably a wise one. Grow proved an able and remarkably fair presiding officer. At the end of the Congress, the traditional vote of thanks to the speaker passed unanimously—a tribute with but a single precedent in the entire history of the House.[31]

Next to the speakership, the most important leadership position in the House was, of course, the chairmanship of the Committee of Ways and Means, for this post carried with it the powers later exercised by the majority leader. Grow offered this berth in turn to Francis P. Blair and to Schuyler Colfax, but Blair demanded the chairmanship of the Committee on Military Affairs and Colfax preferred to retain his control of the Committee on the Post Office and Post Roads—one of the most powerful pork-barrel and patronage committees of the House. This narrowed the field to Thaddeus Stevens of Pennsylvania and Justin S. Morrill of Vermont. Grow preferred Morrill. "I could have the Chairmanship of Ways and Means," Morrill wrote to his wife two days before the commit-

30. *Cong. Globe,* 37th Cong., 1st Sess., pp. 3–4; Montgomery Blair to Joseph Holt, July 3, 1861, Joseph Holt Papers, Library of Congress.

31. Montgomery Blair to Joseph Holt, July 3, 1861, Joseph Holt Papers, Library of Congress; Henry L. Dawes to Mrs. Henry L. Dawes, July 4, 7, 1861, Henry L. Dawes Papers, Library of Congress; Hubert B. Fuller, *The Speakers of the House,* pp. 149–157; New York *Herald,* March 5, 1863.

tee assignments were made public, "but I have declined it. The work is very great and I dursn't undertake it."[32] By threefold default, the post went to Stevens.

Stevens, at sixty-nine, was one of the oldest members of the House. He had long been powerful in Pennsylvania politics, first as an anti-Jacksonian, then successively as an anti-Mason, Whig, and Republican. Apparently motivated by a lust for political power, Stevens was bitter and uncompromising and, as a friendly contemporary later recalled, "rather adapted to the position of leader of the opposition, than to the conduct and control of the majority." John Sherman, who served with him, said that the Pennsylvanian "was not a very useful member of the committee."[33]

Stevens's true forte was running debate. When on the floor, he made few gestures, usually locking his hands loosely before him and speaking calmly and deliberately in a low but distinct voice. His words were often not in keeping with his delivery, however, for he made much use of biting sarcasm and personal invective. He paid relatively little attention to his role within the Committee of Ways and Means, devoting his energies instead to his position as floor leader. Even this is a misnomer: Thaddeus Stevens was never a leader—he was a commander.[34]

Morrill was not shoved aside. He too was placed on the Committee of Ways and Means and later made chairman of the subcommittee on taxation. In this position he exercised much greater control over committee activities than did Stevens, and he generally attended the conferences of committee chairmen. Indeed, in the Thirty-seventh Congress, one finds a virtual separation of the function of majority leader and developer of financial legislation. Morrill, a former Whig, was eighteen years younger than Stevens and differed from him in many respects. His appearance was

32. New York *Herald,* July 6, 1861; Justin S. Morrill to Mrs. Justin S. Morrill, July 6, 1861, quoted in William B. Parker, *The Life and Public Services of Justin Smith Morrill,* p. 125.

33. The quotations are from Isaac N. Arnold, *The History of Abraham Lincoln, and the Overthrow of Slavery,* p. 223, and John Sherman, *Recollections of Forty Years in the House, Senate and Cabinet,* I, 195. On the question of political motivation, see Richard N. Current, "Love, Hate, and Thaddeus Stevens," *Pennsylvania History,* XIV, No. 4 (October 1947), 259–272.

34. Brooks, *op. cit.,* p. 17; *Cong. Globe,* 37th Cong., 2nd Sess., p. 2076.

as kindly as Stevens's was forbidding; his manner was as urbane and courteous as Stevens's was rude and sarcastic; and his attention to the details of legislative business as meticulous as Stevens's was spotty.[35]

The third ranking Republican on the Committee of Ways and Means (and, as it turned out, a very important member indeed) was Elbridge G. Spaulding of New York—another ex-Whig. Twice treasurer of New York in the 1850s, he was well-grounded in the problems of government finance. His contribution to the drafting and enactment of the legal tender legislation of the Thirty-seventh Congress was probably greater than that of any other representative.[36]

In addition to Stevens, Blair, and Colfax, three other Republicans might be singled out as important because they combined personal influence with committee chairmanships. With a large number of delicate problems to be solved regarding qualifications, the Committee on Elections would be an active and important body. To head this committee, Grow named Henry L. Dawes of Massachusetts, a former Whig. Dawes was a serious and hard-working legislator, but he also possessed a keen sense of humor and, if the occasion demanded it, biting wit. He frequently refused to compromise his views for the sake of political expediency and consequently found himself from time to time in uncomfortable situations.[37]

Grow picked Elihu B. Washburne of Illinois, an old-line Whig and a long-time personal and political friend of Lincoln, to head the Committee on Commerce. Given to wild gestures in delivering magisterial lectures to the House, Washburne was known for his opposition to liquor, tobacco, and government land-grants. In private contacts, he was a delightful

35. Seilhamer, *op. cit.,* II, 40–42; Walter H. Crockett, *Vermont, the Green Mountain State,* III, frontispiece; New York *Herald,* December 13, 1861; Undated and unsigned memorandum (Mss. Nos. 1311–1312), Justin S. Morrill Papers, Library of Congress.

36. D. W. Manchester, "Banks and Bankers of Buffalo: Hon. Elbridge Gerry Spaulding," *Magazine of Western History,* V, No. 6 (April 1887), 795–802.

37. Seilhamer, *op. cit.,* II, 47–49; William S. Robinson, *"Warrington" Pen-portraits; a Collection of Personal and Political Reminiscences from 1848 to 1876,* p. 472. See also numerous letters in Henry L. Dawes Papers, Library of Congress.

person—intelligent, informed, and cultured—but when he clashed in political battle, he did not rely on charm.[38]

John A. Bingham of Ohio, a forty-six-year-old former Whig, was named chairman of the influential Committee on the Judiciary. A veteran of six years in the House, Bingham was an experienced stump speaker and an able advocate, whose addresses have been described as "overflowing with invective, rhetorical phrases, and historical allusions of varying degrees of accuracy." He was, above all, a dependable partisan.[39]

Probably the two most outspoken and influential emancipation spokesmen in the House were Owen Lovejoy of Illinois and George W. Julian of Indiana. Lovejoy—"the most impassioned orator in the House"—had devoted his life to the antislavery cause. Believing Lincoln to be the only man who could unite the Republican Party in Illinois, Lovejoy had been influential in persuading him to abandon the dying Whig Party and affiliate with the Republicans.[40] Julian, originally a Whig, had been a Free-Soiler during the early 1850s, occasionally obtaining some Democratic support. He was an outspoken foe of Know-Nothingism. Attached to the Republican Party solely because of the slavery issue, he was from the beginning unsympathetic toward other aspects of the Republican program—notably protective tariffs. Julian was an able, conscientious, vigorous, and incorruptible legislator who repeatedly demonstrated that, to him, ideological loyalties were more important than party loyalties.[41]

Classifying House members accurately according to ideology is much more difficult than is categorizing senators. Not only are there many more individuals to be considered (and hence more subtle gradations), but the institutional organization of the lower house tends to dominate the majority members far more than does its Senate counterpart. Using the same criteria established for the upper house, however, such representatives as

38. Julian, *op. cit.*, p. 367.

39. The quotation is from Thomas D. McCormick, "John Armour Bingham," *DAB*, II, 277.

40. Julian, *op. cit.*, p. 366.

41. Stampp, *op. cit.*, p. 6; *A Biographical History of Eminent and Self-made Men of the State of Indiana*, pp. 7–111 to 7–121; Grace Julian Clarke, "George W. Julian: Some Impressions," *Indiana Magazine of History*, II, No. 2 (June 1906), 57–69.

Stevens, Julian, Lovejoy, Bingham, Samuel C. Fessenden of Maine, Albert G. Riddle of Ohio, William E. Lansing of New York, and Albert S. White of Indiana could be numbered among the advanced radicals. The radical label could also be applied to such House members as Colfax; Isaac N. Arnold of Illinois; Elijah Babbitt and Samuel S. Blair of Pennsylvania; Fernando C. Beaman and Roland E. Trowbridge of Michigan; Harrison G. O. Blake, John Hutchins, and William P. Cutler of Ohio; Thomas D. Eliot of Massachusetts; Anson P. Morrill of Maine; Edward H. Rollins of New Hampshire; Aaron A. Sargent of California; Charles B. Sedgwick and William Wall of New York; John P. C. Shanks of Indiana; and William Windom of Minnesota.

Among the advanced moderates in the House were Washburne; Justin S. Morrill; Cyrus Aldrich of Minnesota; James M. Ashley, Sidney Edgerton, and John A. Gurley of Ohio; Jacob P. Chamberlain, Frederick A. Conkling, Alfred Ely, Reuben E. Fenton, Richard Franchot, Theobald M. Pomeroy, and Socrates N. Sherman of New York; John Covode, William M. Davis, John Hickman, William D. Kelley, James K. Moorhead, John Patton, and John W. Wallace of Pennsylvania; Thomas M. Edwards of New Hampshire; Luther Hanchett and John F. Potter of Wisconsin; Samuel Hooper of Massachusetts; Francis W. Kellogg of Michigan; Dwight Loomis of Connecticut; Frederick A. Pike and John H. Rice of Maine; Eliakim P. Walton of Vermont; and James F. Wilson of Iowa.

The moderate bloc also included Dawes, Spaulding, Francis P. Blair, Roscoe Conkling of New York, Martin F. Conway of Kansas, James T. Hale and Edward McPherson of Pennsylvania, Albert G. Porter of Indiana, and Alexander H. Rice of Massachusetts. Numbered among the Republican conservatives were Charles Delano, Benjamin F. Thomas, and Charles F. Train of Massachusetts; Alexander S. Diven of New York; William M. Dunn of Indiana; Bradley F. Granger of Michigan; Valentine B. Horton of Ohio; John T. Nixon and John L. N. Stratton of New Jersey; and William Kellogg of Illinois. Granger, William Kellogg, and Thomas were probably the most conservative Republicans in the House.[42]

The House Democrats and Unionists were at this time—and, except

42. Since no attempt is made to classify all the House members, descriptive generalizations about the persons composing various blocs will not be included either here or in the section dealing with the Democrats and Unionists.

for two or three truncated Democratic caucuses in the spring of 1862, remained—completely unorganized. Still, a few members of the minority parties might be singled out as more influential than most.

In the balloting for speaker, most of the Unionists cast their votes for John J. Crittenden of Kentucky. Although he entered the House of Representatives for the first time in 1861, Crittenden was no stranger to the national scene. Next to Clay and Webster, perhaps no name had been more intimately associated with American Whiggery than that of Crittenden. He had spent twenty years in the Senate and had twice served in the cabinet. Though the second-oldest member of the House, Crittenden still spoke with freshness and vigor; his utterances always commanded attention and respect. Hoping to bring Crittenden into the envisioned pro-Union political coalition, the Republican leadership took the highly unusual step of naming him Chairman of the Committee on Foreign Affairs.[43]

Another Kentucky Unionist active on the floor during this Congress was Charles A. Wickliffe. Only a few months younger than Crittenden, Wickliffe had both Whig and Democratic antecedents. He had a haughty and disdainful mien, an arrogant air, and a talent for vituperation which he managed to keep moderately well in check during this Congress.

A third political veteran among the Unionists was Francis Thomas of Maryland. Originally a close friend of Jackson, Thomas had left the Democratic Party in the 1850s, and his political affiliation in 1861 was somewhat vague—in 1860 he had spoken for Douglas but was thought personally to have favored Bell; and he was apparently supported in the congressional election by the friends of Douglas, Bell, and Lincoln. Thomas subsequently became a Republican.[44]

The two Democrats receiving the highest number of votes in the speakership election were John S. Phelps of Missouri and Clement L.

43. To further this same end, non-Republicans were named to head several other House committees. Unionist Robert Mallory of Kentucky was chairman of the Committee on Roads and Canals, and minor committee chairmanships went to another Kentucky Unionist—George W. Dunlap—and to five Democrats—John A. Logan and James C. Robinson of Illinois, Moses F. Odell of New York, William Allen of Ohio, and Jesse Lazear of Pennsylvania. Logan and Allen later became Republicans.

44. Charles B. Clark, "Politics in Maryland During the Civil War," *Maryland Historical Magazine,* XXXVI, No. 4 (December 1941), 390.

Vallandigham of Ohio. Phelps, a veteran of sixteen years in the House, had succeeded to the chairmanship of the Committee of Ways and Means —and consequent control of the House—late in the Thirty-fifth Congress. His relative lack of success in obtaining urgently needed financial legislation resulted less from any shortcomings of Phelps as a political leader than from the overwhelming complexities of the political and economic situation. His activities in raising and commanding Union troops in Missouri frequently prevented his attendance during the Thirty-seventh Congress.[45]

Vallandigham, newer on the national scene, had been elected to the House three years earlier and quickly established himself as an able and vigorous champion of the West. A nominal supporter of Douglas in 1860, Vallandigham's denunciations of the Lincoln administration became increasingly violent as the war continued, especially after he was gerrymandered out of his House seat in 1862.

From Ohio came two other able young Democrats—Samuel S. Cox and George H. Pendleton. Cox, though only thirty-six, was beginning his third term in the lower house. A moderate anti-Lecomptonite and a Douglas supporter in 1860, he had taken an active role in the 1860–61 attempts to find a successful method of compromising the differences between the North and the South. A ready debater and endowed with great wit, Cox was the acknowledged humorist of the House.[46]

The son of a distinguished lawyer and member of Congress, Pendleton was an able advocate, a polished speaker, and a cultured gentleman. He had been a wavering anti-Lecomptonite before the war, and during the conflict he gave unstinting support to essential military and financial legislation while vigorously opposing such things as confiscation, emancipation, and unlawful arrest.[47]

Another effective midwestern Democrat was William S. Holman of Indiana. Already he was acquiring a reputation for caution and conservatism in fiscal affairs which would eventually earn for him the nicknames

45. Nichols, *op. cit.*, pp. 223–242; Sherman, *op. cit.*, I, 194.

46. Nichols, *op. cit.*, pp. 174–175.

47. *Ibid.*, pp. 156, 161, 168–170; Sherman, *op. cit.*, I, 226; Sylvanus E. Johnson, "George H. Pendleton," in O. O. Stealey, *Twenty Years in the Press Gallery*, pp. 382–385.

of "The Watch Dog of the Treasury" and "The Great Objector." Often sharply criticized because of his penurious attitude toward federal funds, Holman nevertheless enjoyed both the affection and respect of his colleagues. "Though he was a member of several Congresses that were notoriously extravagant, if not actually corrupt, his enemies could not point to a single act that breathed the suspicion of dishonesty."[48]

Applying to the House non-Republicans the same criteria used to classify their colleagues in the Senate presents certain difficulties. Although the advanced moderates and the ultra-conservatives are fairly easy to identify, the issues which were permitted to come to a vote in the House were generally presented in such a form as to sweep the moderates and the conservatives into the same camp.[49]

Among the advanced moderates were found such Unionists as Jacob B. Blair, William G. Brown, and Kellian V. R. Whaley of Virginia; Samuel L. Casey of Kentucky; Richard A. Harrison of Ohio; William P. Sheffield of Rhode Island; and George P. Fisher of Delaware. Here, too, might be classified such Democrats as George H. Browne of Rhode Island, James E. English of Connecticut, Edward Haight and Moses F. Odell of New York, William E. Lehman of Pensylvania, and John W. Noell of Missouri.

No Unionists are clearly identifiable as ultra-conservatives, but this label could unquestionably be attached to Democrats John B. Clark and John W. Reid of Missouri and Henry C. Burnett of Kentucky, all of whom cast their lots with the Confederacy in the fall of 1861. Of the Democrats who remained, those most clearly of ultra-conservative bent were William J. Allen of Illinois, Henry May of Maryland, and Benjamin Wood of New York. With some reservations, Vallandigham might also be so categorized.

Falling somewhere in the conservative-moderate spectrum (and it must be remembered that this range was far narrower among non-Republicans than among members of the majority party) were such Unionists

48. Charles C. Carlton, "William S. Holman," in Stealey, *op. cit.*, pp. 318–322, quotation from p. 322.

49. The device of the previous question was used to prevent the introduction of amendments, and it is votes on amendments to major pieces of legislation that are most valuable in establishing gradations of opinion.

as James S. Rollins of Missouri; Charles B. Calvert, John W. Crisfield, Cornelius L. L. Leary, and Francis Thomas of Maryland; John J. Crittenden, Robert Mallory, George W. Dunlap, Charles A. Wickliffe, Henry Grider, James S. Jackson, and George H. Yeaman of Kentucky; Joseph E. Segar of Virginia; and Hendrick B. Wright of Pennsylvania. Here, too, could be found the great majority of the House Democrats, including such representatives as Cox, Pendleton, and William Allen of Ohio; Jesse Lazear and Joseph Bailey of Pennsylvania; Erastus Corning, Isaac C. Delaplaine, Edward H. Smith, and John B. Steele of New York; William A. Hall and John S. Phelps of Missouri; Aaron Harding of Kentucky; John Law, William S. Holman, and Daniel W. Voorhees of Indiana; William A. Richardson and James C. Robinson of Illinois; William G. Steele and George T. Cobb of New Jersey; and George C. Woodruff of Connecticut.

In addition to those representatives so briefly dealt with here, many others by their votes and their voices, their influence and their intelligence, their courage and their caution, aided in the direction of a war, the destruction of an old political edifice, and the design of a new nation. They constituted the rank and file of the House of Representatives of the Thirty-seventh Congress, which eventually consisted of 181 seats. Though political affiliations during this period are sometimes vague and confused, it is probably safe to say that, of these seats, the Republicans initially held 106 (eight fewer than in the Thirty-sixth Congress); the Democrats held 49; and the Unionists held 26. New England was almost solidly Republican, the only exceptions being a Unionist and a Democrat from Rhode Island and two Democrats from Connecticut. The Republicans also had slightly more than two thirds of the seats in both the New York and the Pennsylvania delegations, but only two of the five New Jersey seats. Kentucky, Maryland, and Delaware (with the exception of two Democrats from the first state and one from the second) were solidly Unionist. Eventually, four Unionist representatives were admitted from Virginia and two each from Tennessee and Louisiana, while Missouri sent one Republican, three Democrats, and three Unionists to the House. The Democrats had made a respectable showing in the older states of the Middle West, capturing five of nine seats in Illinois, four of eleven in Indiana, and eight of twenty-one in Ohio (a Unionist held one of the Ohio seats); but all of the other states of this section were solidly

Republican. From the west coast, California sent three Republicans and Oregon a single Democrat.[50]

The Thirty-seventh Congress included men of varied educational background, national stock, political experience, vocational training, and religious affiliation. It was, all in all, a fair sampling of American political intellect and conviction. And while there was no lack of stupidity and bigotry, neither was there any dearth of talent and vision. Seldom have conditions conspired to give so great a challenge to vision, so broad a stage to talent, and such inevitable and enduring consequence to action.

50. *The Tribune Almanac for 1862,* pp. 18–19; *The Tribune Almanac for 1863,* pp. 16–18. These lists, while not without a few small errors, are the most accurate ones readily obtainable.

CHAPTER 2

Congress and Slavery: The Loyal Area

Whether or not slavery was the major cause of the Civil War will undoubtedly remain a debatable question, but politically it was certainly one of the most vital and divisive issues of the American scene in 1861. Congress could not possibly have ignored the institution of slavery during the Civil War even if there had been a desire to do so. But the Republicans (especially the radicals) admittedly did not wish to ignore slavery. The only real questions were how long slavery could endure; in what fields Congress would act; what the nature of the congressional attacks would be; and what roles would be played by Congress and the executive.

Of all the problems concerning the Negro and slavery with which the Thirty-seventh Congress struggled, perhaps none presented more difficulties or was more certain to arouse determined opposition than the attempt to find some means of freeing the slaves in the areas still loyal to the Union. Against loyal citizens in loyal regions, not even the most ardent abolitionist could legitimately call for an enforcement of emancipation by the "war power." Both political realities and common justice demanded that emancipation in these areas be accompanied by compensation. Even granting this, however, there remained the widely held opinion that compensated emancipation could not be constitutionally imposed upon loyal states by congressional action.

Since the District of Columbia was under direct congressional control, it was almost inevitable that it should be the first point of attack. Restricted in its scope of operations by the Holman Resolution[1] and

1. *Cong. Globe,* 37th Cong., 1st Sess., pp. 24–25. On July 8, 1861, the House adopted a resolution introduced by Holman and subsequently amended by Hickman, which distinctly limited the propositions which could be considered by the Special Session of the Thirty-seventh Congress. The text of this resolution was as

inundated by the press of more urgent matters, the Special Session of the Thirty-seventh Congress found no opportunity to consider this problem. Scarcely had the Second Session convened, however, when Henry Wilson of Massachusetts introduced a resolution in the Senate referring the entire "black code" and fugitive slave laws of this area to the Committee on the District of Columbia, with instructions to "consider the expediency of abolishing slavery in the District with compensation to the loyal holders of slaves." Wilson followed this on December 16, 1861, by introducing a bill (S. No. 108) "for the release of certain persons held to service or labor in the District of Columbia."[2]

The matter was brought before the House by Republican John Hutchins of Ohio who, on the fourth and ninth of December, introduced two bills to abolish slavery in the District (one of which made no provision for compensation). In the Committee for the District of Columbia, the measures were placed in the hands of Unionist Representative Charles H. Upton of Virginia. A moderate on the slavery issue, Upton personally thought it "inexpedient to legislate upon the subject at this time." But being alive to political realities, he suggested that "if necessary to conciliate the anti-slavery extremists and stop their growling [we] could give them this bone." By mid-March, therefore, the committee had formulated a bill (H.R. No. 351) to abolish slavery in the District and reported it to the House.[3]

The bill was accompanied, however, by a minority report signed by Unionist Charles B. Calvert of Maryland and Democrat John B. Steele of New York, setting forth the objections of many representatives. Practically the entire document consisted of a reprinting of an adverse report of a House select committee on a similar proposal in 1836. Calvert and

---

follows: "*Resolved,* That the House, during the present extraordinary session, will only consider bills and resolutions concerning the military and naval operations of the Government, and the financial affairs therewith connected, and the general questions of a judicial character; and all bills and resolutions of a private character, and all other bills and resolutions not directly connected with the raising of revenue, or affecting the military or naval affairs of the Government, shall be referred to the appropriate committees without debate, to be considered at the next regular session of Congress."

2. *Cong. Globe,* 37th Cong., 2nd Sess., pp. 12, 89–90.

3. Charles H. Upton to Lincoln, January 16, 1862, Lincoln Papers, Library of Congress; *Cong. Globe,* 37th Cong., 2nd Sess., pp. 16, 36, 1192. The quotations are from the first source.

Steele proposed that, instead of passing the bill reported, the House adopt four resolutions declaring (1) that Congress had no power over slavery in the territories or in the District, (2) that Virginia and Maryland had not intended to convey such power when they had ceded the District to the United States, (3) that emancipation without the consent of the slave owners consituted a violation of the spirit of the Constitution, and (4) that emancipation in the District without the consent of the people of Maryland would be "in flagrant violation of public faith, an abuse of the trust conferred on Congress by the cession, and hazardous to the peace and security of that State, and particularly unfortunate at this time, as calculated to discourage many loyal citizens and strengthen the power of the rebellion."[4] It is doubtful that these views had much weight with the Republican majority, but the bill was not, in fact, considered by the House. This apparent neglect is probably explained by the fact that on March 12, 1862, the same day that the House report was printed, the Senate began consideration of a similar bill.[5]

Though some supporters of the Senate measure thought it unlikely to pass, there was an obvious determination on the part of Morrill of Maine, who had the bill in charge, to push it through the Senate without undue delay. The proposal was before the house on twelve of the next seventeen days during which the Senate was in session. The most vociferous and active opponent of the measure was Garrett Davis of Kentucky, though most of the border state senators spoke against it during this period.[6]

4. Committee for the District of Columbia, U. S. House of Representatives, *Minority Report* [*on Emancipation in the District of Columbia*], *Ho. Com. Repts.*, 37th Cong., 2nd Sess., No. 58, [1144]. The quotation is from p. 22.

5. *Cong. Globe,* 37th Cong., 2nd Sess., p. 1191. The bill was reported to the Senate on February 13, 1862. See *ibid.,* p. 785. The measure reported seems to have been almost entirely the work of Colonel Thomas M. Key, a Cincinnati lawyer-politician and intimate of Chase, who was currently in Washington serving as a member of McClellan's staff. See Salmon P. Chase to Thomas M. Key, April 18, 1862, quoted in J. W. Schuckers, *The Life and Public Services of Salmon Portland Chase,* pp. 434–435; James G. Wilson and John Fiske (editors), *Appleton's Cyclopedia of American Biography,* III, 530.

6. Detroit *Daily Advertiser,* March 15, 1862; *Cong. Globe,* 37th Cong., 2nd Sess., pp. 1191–1192, 1266–1268, 1285–1286, 1299–1303, 1319–1320, 1333–1339, 1350–1360, 1375–1380, 1446–1451, 1467–1479, 1496–1504, 1516–1526.

The Senate bill would abolish slavery in the District, limit to $300 the aggregate amount awarded as compensation for each slave freed, and create a board of three commissioners (to be appointed by the President, subject to Senate confirmation) to pass on all claims. Amendments were immediately adopted restricting compensation payments to loyal slaveholders only, and making re-enslavement punishable by imprisonment for from five to twenty years.[7] At the same time, Davis launched the border-state attack on the measure and introduced an amendment requiring the freed Negroes to be colonized outside the United States. He proposed a $100,000 appropriation for that purpose, declaring that emancipation without colonization would be resisted by the border states by all methods, including force, and would "inevitably and immediately introduce a war of extermination between the races."[8]

Some rather unexpected support for the colonization scheme came from James R. Doolittle of Wisconsin who, on March 18, presented an additional amendment restricting the operation of Davis's proposal to those Negroes who desired to emigrate. The next day Doolittle delivered a lengthy speech strongly supporting colonization and asserting that the Negroes would go voluntarily.[9]

A few speeches were made on the bill and some amendments were introduced during the remainder of the week, but no further action was taken by the Senate until March 24.[10] On that date, the Senate came to a vote on Davis's proposal and Doolittle's amendment. Although the Wisconsin senator's amendment passed easily (23 to 16), the division on the actual question of attaching a colonization clause to the bill was much closer. When the roll call of the senators was completed, the vote stood 19 to 19, and the vote of Vice-President Hannibal Hamlin defeated the colonization proposal. But Doolittle was undismayed. "I shall carry it in the Senate," he predicted, "by 6 or 8 majority. Colonization is our duty and our interest."[11]

Thirteen Republicans voted for the colonization amendment, and it

7. *Cong. Globe,* 37th Cong., 2nd Sess., p. 1191.

8. *Ibid.,* pp. 1191–1192.

9. *Ibid.,* pp. 1266, 1285, Appendix, 83–86.

10. *Ibid.,* pp. 1266–1268, 1285–1286, 1299–1303, 1319–1320.

11. *Ibid.,* pp. 1333–1334; James R. Doolittle to Mrs. James R. Doolittle, March 27, 1862, James R. Doolittle Papers, State Historical Society of Wisconsin.

was defeated, in part, by border-state votes: two border-state senators, Carlile of Virginia and Kennedy of Maryland, voted against the measure; and two others who were present earlier in the day—Bayard and Saulsbury of Delaware—were absent at the time of the vote. Perhaps these senators desired thus to make the District of Columbia emancipation measure as unpalatable as possible to the Republicans of the Northwest in the hope of attracting sufficient opposition to defeat the bill. If such was their hope, it proved illusory, for during the debate that occupied a considerable portion of the next nine days no Republican rose to protest the passage of the bill without a colonization provision.[12]

There was no doubt, however, that many persons, both in and out of the Senate, viewed the present bill as too radical. On April 1, a New York Republican paper commented editorially:

> Policy and clemency alike argue against immediate emancipation. Make it slow in its action; grant compensation to loyal owners; require the instruction of the freedmen during a proper period of tutelage; and provide some territory beyond the limits of the country, where the negroes may be settled by themselves; and Congress will give to every section of the country a gratifying assurance that its treatment of the black is not the dictate of fanaticism or the triumph of sectionalism, but the wise result of counsels, the justice of which can be recognized even in South Carolina. . . . The actual bill is ill-guarded and precipitate. If the florid logic of Mr. Sumner be not too potent, it may still be amended.[13]

On April 3, Doolittle again introduced his colonization amendment. It was adopted by a vote of 27 to 10—more than double the most optimistic majority the Wisconsin senator had ventured to predict. Now, fearful that the District of Columbia emancipation bill would pass, with or without a colonization provision, no border-state senator voted against the amendment, but five of them who were present both earlier and later during the day did not vote on the measure. At the same time, it was apparent that a number of the Republican opponents of colonization had come to doubt

12. *Cong. Globe,* 37th Cong., 2nd Sess., pp. 1333, 1350–1360, 1375–1380, 1446–1451, 1467–1476, 1496–1504, 1516–1523. For the attitude of the Northwest toward the Negro, see Jacque Voegeli, "The Northwest and the Race Issue, 1861–1862," *Mississippi Valley Historical Review,* L, No. 2 (September 1963), 235–251.

13. New York *Times,* April 1, 1862.

their ability to push through an unamended emancipation bill; for six members of the majority party who had earlier opposed the amendment —including such ardent radicals as Wade of Ohio, Wilmot of Pennsylvania, and Wilson of Massachusetts—now voted for the colonization proposal. The gratified Doolittle declared that the Senate's action would be supported by three fourths of the nation's voters and had saved the Republican Party.[14]

During these last days of debate on the District of Columbia emancipation bill, a number of substitutes were presented. Perhaps the most notable was a compromise measure introduced by Joseph Wright of Indiana which would have provided for gradual emancipation if approved by the residents of the District. This proposal was submitted on April 1 and supported by Wright in a speech of considerable force. It made no difference. All the substitutes were defeated—Wright's by a vote of 10 to 27. On the third of April, the bill was brought to a vote and passed. Supporting it were twenty-nine Republicans; opposed were fourteen Democrats and Unionists. "I have not the slightest doubt," exulted Doolittle, "my amendment *saved* and *carried through* the Bill."[15]

Press opinion was, naturally, divided. The Democratic Boston *Post* opposed the bill because it was not gradual in its operation and because there was no provision for submitting the question of emancipation to the voters of the District. But the radical Detroit *Daily Advertiser* declared, "The loyal people of the North . . . are becoming impatient at the

14. *Cong. Globe,* 37th Cong., 2nd Sess., pp. 1522–1523; James R. Doolittle to Mrs. James R. Doolittle, April 4, 1862, James R. Doolittle Papers, State Historical Society of Wisconsin. For evidences of widespread support for colonization, see *Cong. Globe,* 37th Cong., 2nd Sess., pp. 15–16, 36, 365, 1730–1731; Abraham Lincoln, "Address on Colonization to a Deputation of Colored Men" (August 14, 1862), in Nicolay and Hay, *Lincoln's Works,* VIII, 1–9; James Mitchell to Abraham Lincoln, July 3, 1862, Lincoln Papers, Library of Congress; Samuel C. Pomeroy to Orville H. Browning, October 27, 1862, Orville H. Browning Papers, Illinois State Historical Library. The San Francisco *Daily Alta California* had earlier (December 6, 1861) advocated the establishment of reservations within the United States for the free Negroes.

15. *Cong. Globe,* 37th Cong., 2nd Sess., pp. 1379, 1467–1470, 1473–1474, 1518–1520, 1522, 1526; New York *Herald,* April 2, 1862; James R. Doolittle to Mrs. James R. Doolittle, April 17, 1862, James R. Doolittle Papers, State Historical Society of Wisconsin.

unaccountable delay of Congress in acting definitely upon the bill to abolish slavery in the District of Columbia. All true men will admit that it is a national disgrace." As the measure was sent to the House, the Washington correspondent of a New York Democratic paper reported that Lincoln was opposed to any emancipation in the District without the approval of the residents and charged that the bill was being rushed through Congress not for the purpose of freeing the slaves, but to force Lincoln to take a stand on emancipation.[16]

Whatever their reasons, the Republican leaders obviously had no intention of allowing the measure to gather dust in the House. On April 9, the bill was taken from the speaker's table and referred directly to the Committee of the Whole. Vallandigham's motion to reject it without reference was defeated, 45 to 93. On the tenth, the House went into Committee of the Whole and began a two-day consideration of the measure. After several hours of discussion, Stevens was able to push through a resolution limiting further debate to one minute. Nor was any amendment allowed. Shortly before the Committee of the Whole reported the bill to the House, Kentucky Unionists John W. Menzies and Charles A. Wickliffe introduced two substitutes which would have provided for gradual, uncompensated emancipation, but both were decisively defeated. The Republican attitude had been baldly stated earlier by Elihu Washburne of Illinois when he said, "If gentlemen of the other side offer amendments, let us hear them, and then vote them down."[17]

The final vote came at about 5:45 on the afternoon of April 11, and the bill was passed, 92 to 38. The measure was supported by all of the Republicans and a handful of northern Democrats and Unionists.[18] Many years of agitation had finally resulted in the first real break in the southern slave system. It was a time of rejoicing for the Republicans, and one unfriendly observer reported:

> A few of the radical members indulged in excessive and quite undignified manifestations of delight, hurrahing in the corridors, and seizing every negro

16. Boston *Post,* April 7, 1862; Detroit *Daily Advertiser,* April 1, 1862; New York *Herald,* April 6, 1862.

17. *Cong. Globe,* 37th Cong., 2nd Sess., pp. 1589–1590, 1613–1623, 1629–1648, Appendix, 88–94, 101–105. Wickliffe's substitute would have compensated owners who freed their slaves immediately. See p. 1648. Quotation from p. 1644.

18. *Ibid.,* 1648–1649.

they met and overwhelming them with congratulations. These men exhibited more gratification on this occasion than they have ever shown over any of the Union victories.[19]

Some entertained hopes that Lincoln would veto the bill. He did, in fact, express regret that the measure had not provided for gradual emancipation. Furthermore, the President delayed action on the bill for several days to allow Representative Wickliffe to remove from the District two of his family servants who were ill, thus becoming, in Senator Sumner's words, "for the time being, the largest slave-holder in the country." "But," reported a Maryland Unionist, "he could not say it was unconstitutional, and he had come to the conclusion, after full consideration of all the pros and cons, that he would do less mischief by approving than by rejecting it; and he hoped that the people of Washington would see the difficulties of his position, and treat him with forbearance." On the sixteenth of April, the bill was signed. "That infamy," exulted a radical editor, "is wiped from the national escutcheon."[20]

In a message to Congress announcing that he had signed the measure, the President took occasion to praise the principles of compensation and colonization embodied in the legislation. These remarks, Senator Doolittle ventured to hope, would cause some radicals to "open their eyes at last to see that what I have been endeavoring for 4 or 5 years to show them, that the *question of race* is a more troublesome one than the question of condition is the truth."[21]

While Doolittle was gratified by the favorable mention of colonization, the President himself may well have been more interested in attracting additional congressional support for further legislation embodying the principle of compensation. Shortly before the District of Columbia eman-

19. New York *Herald,* April 12, 1862.

20. *Ibid.,* April 16, 17, 1862; Browning, *op. cit.* (April 14, 1862), I, 541; Charles Sumner to John A. Andrew, April 22, 1862, John A. Andrew Papers, Massachusetts Historical Society; John W. Crisfield to Mrs. Mary H. Crisfield, April 25, 1862, Crisfield Papers, Maryland Historical Society; Detroit *Daily Advertiser,* April 17, 1862. The slaves were, however, retained by their masters until the compensation was paid.

21. Abraham Lincoln, "Message of April 16, 1862," quoted in Roy P. Basler (editor), *The Collected Works of Abraham Lincoln,* V, 192; James R. Doolittle to Mrs. James R. Doolittle, April 17, 1862, James R. Doolittle Papers, State Historical Society of Wisconsin.

cipation bill had been reported to the Senate, a presidential message had given impetus to congressional action regarding compensated emancipation in another area. In December 1861, Lincoln had urged Congress to provide for compensation for slaveholders in states which passed emancipation acts. This recommendation, to the distress of some moderates, had gone unheeded. Undismayed, the President sent a special message to Congress on March 6, 1862, asking for the passage of a joint resolution (the text of which was included in the message), declaring that the federal government should give financial assistance to any state which adopted a plan of gradual emancipation.[22]

The communication was received with profound interest, and the Washington correspondent of the New York *Times* declared, "The friends of the Union's reconstruction are delighted and strengthened, while the radicals are proportionately distressed. . . . It is evident that a document of such an important character was not generally anticipated." Indeed, there was little doubt that the message took the legislators by surprise. In the House, it was referred to the Committee of the Whole; and the Senate referred it to the Committee on the Judiciary. It was reported that the Republicans, while openly expressing gratification, were preparing to oppose the passage of such a resolution. Border-state representatives, on the other hand, were said to be favorable to the President's proposal, but fearful of supporting it openly lest their position (opposing congressional interference with slavery in the states) be undermined.[23]

Though it was hardly politically feasible for the Republicans to do other than praise Lincoln's message, there were various reasons why some members of the majority party would be opposed to acting on it. Some were opposed to any further compensation to slaveholders; some probably feared that the adoption of the resolution would delay, if not forestall,

22. Abraham Lincoln, "Message of December 3, 1861," in *Cong. Globe,* 37th Cong., 2nd Sess., Appendix, pp. 1–4; George W. Riggs to James Buchanan, December 11, 1862, James Buchanan Papers, Historical Society of Pennsylvania; Abraham Lincoln, "Message of March 6, 1862," in James D. Richardson (editor), *A Compilation of the Messages and Papers of the Presidents,* VI, 68–69. See also Mss. Nos. 14810–14813, Lincoln Papers, Library of Congress, for Lincoln's draft of the message of March 6, 1862.

23. New York *Herald,* March 8, 1862; *Cong. Globe,* 37th Cong., 2nd Sess., pp. 1102–1103, 1112; New York *Times,* March 7, 1862.

the enactment of broader, compulsory emancipation legislation; and some undoubtedly opposed the passage of the resolution because it had been proposed (complete with text) by the President. At a time when congressional leaders were actively seeking to subordinate the executive to Congress, they certainly would not support any attempt by Lincoln to influence congressional action.

Lincoln did not intend to sit back and patiently await congressional action. On Sunday, March 9, he sent Postmaster General Montgomery Blair to ask Unionist Representative John W. Crisfield of Maryland to arrange a meeting with the border-state representatives on the following morning. At the conference, Lincoln, while denying any desire to interfere with the rights of the states, urged support for his proposal.[24]

On the same day, Roscoe Conkling asked unanimous consent to introduce the President's resolution and, when Democrat Benjamin Wood of New York objected, was able to muster the necessary two-thirds majority to suspend the rules. During the House debates on March 10 and 11, the Republicans in general and the Republican leaders in particular were not notable as ardent supporters of the measure. Only three members of the majority—Roscoe Conkling, Alexander S. Diven, and Abram B. Olin, all of New York—made remarks of any importance in support of the proposal, and Stevens went so far as to characterize the resolution as "about the most diluted, milk and water gruel proposition that was ever given to the American nation." Several postponement motions were narrowly beaten, and on March 11, 1862, the resolution was passed by a vote of 89 to 31. The plea of one of the Republican papers for "the moral sanction of a unanimous vote" had gone unheeded. The majority consisted of all of the Republicans, a handful of northern Democrats and Unionists, and a few border-state representatives.[25]

On March 20, Trumbull of Illinois, from the Committee on the Judiciary, reported the joint resolution (H.R. No. 48) to the Senate. During its consideration on March 24, 26, and 27, and on April 2, no

24. John W. Crisfield, "Memorandum of an Interview between the President and some Border Slave State Representatives," in Nicolay and Hay, *Lincoln's Works,* VII, 120–128.

25. New York *Times,* March 11, 1862; *Cong. Globe,* 37th Cong., 2nd Sess., pp. 1149–1154, 1168–1179, Appendix, 68–71. The Stevens quotation is from the *Globe,* p. 1154.

speech of any importance was made in support of the proposal. The opposition, which came mainly from the border-state senators and the two Democratic senators from California, was to no avail, and on April 2 the resolution was passed, 32 to 10. Voting in the affirmative were all of the Republicans present, plus Unionists Willey and Davis and Democrats Henderson and Thomson.[26]

This terminated the Senate's interest in compensated emancipation for the time being, but the House took another step. On April 7, on the motion of Republican Albert S. White of Indiana, a select committee of nine was created to consider a plan for gradual emancipation and to report the same to the House.[27]

The question of compensated emancipation now faded out of the picture until the President revived the issue some four months later. On July 12, 1862, he again met with the border-state legislators and again urged them to support a program of compensated emancipation. Lincoln added that the pressure from the abolitionists was increasingly difficult to resist. For two or three days after this meeting, the border-state men consulted among themselves as to the wisest course to pursue, but only nine of the twenty-nine congressmen responding to the appeal were willing even to recommend consideration of Lincoln's plan.[28] In the meantime, the President had taken a second step. On July 14, he sent to

26. *Cong. Globe,* 37th Cong., 2nd Sess., pp. 1298, 1332–1333, 1371–1375, 1390–1393, 1490–1496.

27. To this committee the Speaker eventually appointed Republicans Albert S. White of Indiana, Francis P. Blair, Jr. of Missouri, and James F. Wilson of Iowa; Unionists George P. Fisher of Delaware, Cornelius L. Leary of Maryland, Kellian V. Whaley of Virginia, Samuel L. Casey of Kentucky, and Andrew J. Clements of Tennessee; and Democrat William E. Lehman of Pennsylvania. *Ibid.,* pp. 1563, 1580, 1607, 1655.

28. Abraham Lincoln, "Appeal to Favor Compensated Emancipation," in Nicolay and Hay, *Lincoln's Works,* VII, 270–274 (see also, Mss. Nos. 17000–17003, Lincoln Papers, Library of Congress); New York *Herald,* July 13, 14, 15, 16, 18, 1862; Philadelphia *Inquirer,* July 18, 1862; Boston *Post,* July 21, 1862; Charles A. Wickliffe and others to Abraham Lincoln, July 14, 1862, Andrew J. Clements and others to Abraham Lincoln, July 15, 1862, Horace Maynard to Abraham Lincoln, July 16, 1862, all in Lincoln Papers, Library of Congress.

Congress a bill authorizing the distribution of six percent bonds to states which provided for emancipation, either immediate or gradual. The value of the bonds remitted would be proportional to the number of slaves in the state. Lincoln urged the passage of the bill "substantially as presented."[29]

In the Senate, the president pro tem, Solomon Foot of Vermont, treated the President's bill in the same manner as one introduced by a senator, and it was read twice by title and once at length. This brought immediate protests from Senators Powell, Grimes, and Sherman, all denying the right of the President to introduce a bill in Congress. Foot said he had no comment on this subject. The message and the draft bill were eventually referred to the Committee on Finance. In the House, both were immediately referred to the select committee headed by Albert S. White.[30] This committee had apparently not been idle during the period since its formation, for on July 16, White reported a bill (H.R. No. 576) authorizing federal aid to states adopting a program of gradual emancipation. The measure was accompanied by a thirty-three-page report which strongly supported the proposal, and a forty-nine-page appendix which dealt with possibilities for colonization in the West Indies and Central America.

Though designed to accomplish the same ends, this measure differed in its details from that proposed by Lincoln. It provided that "whenever the President of the United States shall be satisfied that any one of the States of Delaware, Maryland, Virginia, Kentucky, Tennessee, or Missouri shall have emancipated the slaves therein by law within and throughout such State," he should cause to be delivered to such state five-percent, thirty-year bonds in an amount equal to $300 for each slave freed. The entire amount of bonds delivered under this act was not to exceed $180,000,000, and $20,000,000 was to be appropriated to aid in colonizing the free Negroes in areas outside the borders of the United States. To avail themselves of the aid offered by this measure, the states must pass

29. Abraham Lincoln, "Message of July 14, 1862," in Richardson, *op. cit.*, VI, 84. On the same day that he sent this bill to Congress, Lincoln went to the Capitol for additional consultations with the border-state senators and representatives. See Philadelphia *Inquirer*, July 15, 1862.

30. *Cong. Globe*, 37th Cong., 2nd Sess., pp. 3322–3324, 3333.

emancipation acts within five years and must provide for all slaves to be freed within twenty years. A re-establishment of slavery would require repayment of bonds and interest.[31] But the Republican leadership remained unimpressed by Lincoln's proposal, and no further action was taken on the bill.[32]

In the meantime, Congress had been presented with an unparalleled opportunity to strike at slavery within a state. In late May and early June of 1862, a resolution of the Virginia legislature calling for the creation of a separate state of West Virginia was presented in the Senate by Willey of Virginia and in the House by Unionist William G. Brown of Virginia. In each house, the resolution went to the Committee on Territories.[33]

The bill which emerged from the Senate committee and which the upper house took up on June 26 was not exactly what the Virginians had had in mind. It was not a simple act admitting a new state—it also required the provisional government (prior to the admission of West Virginia as a state) to provide for the emancipation of all children born of slave parentage after July 4, 1863. Moreover, by some mysterious means, fifteen additional valley counties had been added to the area as outlined in the original resolution. This was a puzzling change, for those counties could not be expected to approve such a transfer.

The reasons for this alteration remain unclear. It may be that the ardent antislavery men on the Committee on Territories saw this as the quickest way to bring more slaves under some sort of emancipation scheme. Senator Willey, who fought vigorously for the statehood measure, apparently thought that it was a scheme to defeat the bill. It is possible that he was correct. Two Republican members of the committee —Orville H. Browning of Illinois and James H. Lane of Kansas—opposed the bill in committee; and the two Unionist members—John S. Carlile of Virginia and Robert Wilson of Missouri—voted against it in the Senate. This left only three unqualified friends of the measure on the committee, and under such conditions the possibility of unfriendly modifi-

31. Select Committee on Compensated Emancipation, U. S. House of Representatives, *Report, Ho. Com. Repts.*, 37th Cong., 2nd Sess., No. 148, [1145]. For the text of the bill, see pp. 32–33. See also *Cong. Globe*, 37th Cong., 2nd Sess., pp. 3394–3395.

32. *Cong. Globe*, 37th Cong., 2nd Sess., p. 3395.

33. *Ibid.*, pp. 2415–2419, 2526–2527.

cation of the bill for the purpose of killing it certainly cannot be discounted.[34]

As might be expected, Sumner of Massachusetts was opposed to the gradualism of the emancipation provision and quickly introduced an amendment requiring immediate emancipation. The West Virginia statehood bill was considered in the Senate on the first and fourteenth of July and provoked considerable discussion. Hale of New Hampshire approved the gradual emancipation feature, but Collamer of Vermont denied that Congress had the power to place any restriction on the admission of a state. Willey introduced a substitute (designed to answer the most obvious constitutional criticisms) requiring West Virginia to pledge gradual emancipation but not actually to provide it before admission. On July 14, the Senate began to vote on the bill, defeating Sumner's amendment by a margin of more than two to one. Carlile announced that he could not support any bill placing restrictions on a new state and moved an amendment requiring that the proposition be submitted to the voters in the area concerned. Willey, Wade, and Wilkinson violently opposed this suggestion; but, apparently sensing that he was on shaky ground, Willey subsequently modified his substitute to provide for a referendum, and in this form it was adopted.

After further discussion and amendment, Carlile attempted to strike all of the bill except a simple statement admitting West Virginia as a state; but his proposal was defeated by a vote of 11 to 25. The Senate then passed the West Virginia bill, 23 to 17. The majority consisted of twenty-one Republicans, one Democrat (Rice), and one Unionist (Willey), while negative votes were cast by seven Republicans, five Democrats, and five Unionists. At least four of the seven negative Republican

34. *Ibid.*, pp. 2941–2942; Willey, *op. cit.*, p. 106; Browning, *op. cit.* (June 13, 1862), I, 550. I am strongly inclined to believe that the addition of the fifteen valley counties was intended to secure the bill's defeat. Browning (who was in a position to know) reported that the counties were added "with the aid and under the direction of Mr. Senator Carlisle [*sic*]." This action, coupled with Carlile's later insistence on a referendum, clearly indicates a desire to defeat the measure. Carlile's views would appear to have been quite clear and simple. He desired the creation of a separate state of West Virginia without restrictions; he did not desire the creation of a separate state of West Virginia at the price of emancipation. See Orville H. Browning to Abraham Lincoln, July 1, 1862, Lincoln Papers, Library of Congress.

votes probably resulted from the fact that no provision was made for immediate emancipation.[35]

It was apparent that the House intended to waste no time before taking up the proposal. The bill was called up two days later, on July 16, and Joseph E. Segar's tabling motion was defeated by a vote of 44 to 70. Despite the restrictions now incorporated into the measure, most of the Virginia representatives still favored it—only Segar supported the motion to table, while Unionists Jacob B. Blair and William G. Brown voted with the majority, and Kellian V. R. Whaley was paired against the motion. But many representatives were sufficiently dissatisfied with the measure in its present form to make immediate favorable action unlikely. Consequently, Roscoe Conkling's motion to postpone further consideration of the matter until the second Tuesday in December was carried, 63–53. The majority consisted of a weird combination of extremists on the slavery issue (it is not often that one finds Henry May and Thaddeus Stevens on the same side on any issue), while most of the more moderate members of the House cast negative votes.[36]

The reason for the coalition of the radicals and conservatives on this issue is obvious. The ultra-conservatives opposed both statehood and emancipation. The radicals cared nothing for statehood (indeed, disliked the admission of a state which would add to the moderate strength in Congress). They were, however, willing to accept West Virginia statehood as the price to be paid for extending emancipation—but not if that emancipation was to be delayed for a generation. Hence, both groups of extremists opposed the measure in its present form.

By December, some of the reluctance to pass the West Virginia statehood bill had abated, both in conservative and in radical ranks. The conservatives were coming to accept emancipation as inevitable, and the radicals were somewhat chastened by the results of the recent elections. The measure again came before the House on December 9, 1862. Republican Martin F. Conway of Kansas spoke bitterly against the bill, declar-

35. *Cong. Globe,* 37th Cong., 2nd Sess., pp. 2942, 3034–3039, 3307–3320. Willey's substitute eliminated the additional fifteen valley counties. The seven negative Republican voters were Browning, Chandler, Cowan, Howard, King, Sumner, and Trumbull.

36. *Ibid.,* p. 3397. For a statement of Brown's views at this time, see Philadelphia *Inquirer,* July 8, 1862.

ing it to be merely the first of a series of propositions that would subdivide the southern states and create more than thirty additional electoral votes. Crittenden of Kentucky also attacked the measure, basing his opposition on constitutional grounds. Support for the bill came from Schuyler Colfax of Indiana and, reluctantly, from Republicans Abram Olin of New York and Thomas M. Edwards of New Hampshire and Unionist Horace Maynard of Tennessee. All declared the bill to be both constitutional and expedient.[37]

All this talk of the Constitution apparently irritated Stevens, who finally arose and flatly declared that the bill was, of course, not constitutional, but was permissible under the laws of war. "This talk of restoring the Union as it was under the Constitution as it is," he continued, "is one of the absurdities which I have heard repeated until I have become about sick of it. This Union can never be restored as it was." It would never be restored by his consent, he added, if slavery was protected by the Constitution. He favored admitting West Virginia as a state largely because of the emancipation clause which was attached to the bill. This apparently did not leave much to be said, and the House adjourned.[38]

On the following day, additional support for the bill came from Democrat John W. Noell of Missouri, Unionist William P. Sheffield of Rhode Island, and Republican John A. Bingham of Ohio, while Segar of Virginia continued his opposition to the measure. The bill was passed by a vote of 96 to 55. The majority consisted of eighty-five Republicans, eight Unionists, and three Democrats—one each from the states of New York (Haight), Pennsylvania (Lehman), and Missouri (Noell). Casting negative votes were thirty-two Democrats, twelve Unionists, and eleven Republicans. Some of the dissenting Republicans apparently opposed the measure because of the gradualism of the emancipation provision. Segar cast the only negative Virginia vote.[39]

Rumors of a presidential veto were now heard. This represented, to the bill's opponents, more of a forlorn hope than an expectation. Six months earlier, such a veto might have been a possibility, but not in December of 1862, for Lincoln's outlook, like that of the Congress and that of the nation,

37. *Cong. Globe,* 37th Cong., 3d Sess., pp. 37–39, 41–51. For favorable Republican press opinion, see Philadelphia *Inquirer,* December 10, 1862.

38. *Cong. Globe,* 37th Cong., 3d Sess., pp. 50–51.

39. *Ibid.,* pp. 53–59.

was constantly changing. Half of the cabinet, indeed, favored a veto; and one of the Virginia representatives is supposed to have worked vigorously to prevent such a contingency. It seems doubtful that a veto was ever likely. The bill was signed.[40] The President may not have preferred the method used by the supporters of the West Virginia bill, but he was deeply committed to the encouragement of gradual emancipation in the states. He may have been somewhat troubled by the failure to provide compensation for the slaveholders, but this was a minor point. For any general legislation along these lines passed by Congress could easily be made to apply to West Virginia and compensation thus be provided at a later date.

In his last annual message to the Thirty-seventh Congress, in December 1862, Lincoln had devoted almost half his message to one final plea for action in the field of compensated emancipation. He asked Congress to pass a constitutional amendment providing for federal aid to states which passed emancipation acts freeing all slaves before 1900. He also asked for the passage of a constitutional amendment authorizing Congress to appropriate money for colonization purposes.[41]

Though the proposition attracted some support in the Democratic press and among Unionist legislators, it is probable that the Republican congressmen did not wish to acknowledge that any such amendments were necessary, for this would have seemed to cast doubt on the constitutionality of many other appropriations. In any event, no action was taken for over a month, and even then it was not in the form recommended by the

40. New York *Herald,* December 26, 1862; Bates, *op. cit.* (December 30, 1862), p. 271; Willey, *op. cit.,* pp. 199–201; Abraham Lincoln to Cabinet, December 23, 1862, Montgomery Blair to Abraham Lincoln, December 26, 1862, William H. Seward to Abraham Lincoln, December 26, 1862, Edwin M. Stanton to Abraham Lincoln, December 26, 1862, Edward Bates to Abraham Lincoln, December 27, 1862, Gideon Welles to Abraham Lincoln, December 29, 1862, Salmon P. Chase to Abraham Lincoln, December 29, 1862, all in Lincoln Papers, Library of Congress. For Lincoln's opinion, see Mss. Nos. 20625–20628, Lincoln Papers, Library of Congress. Seward, Stanton, and Chase defended both the constitutionality and expediency of the bill. Bates and Welles declared the measure to be both unconstitutional and inexpedient. Blair held the bill to be inexpedient though he was vague on the question of constitutionality.

41. Richardson, *op. cit.,* VI, 126–142. See especially pp. 136–142. The texts of the constitutional amendments will be found on p. 136.

President. On January 6, 1863, Representative Noell, from the Select Committee on Gradual Emancipation, reported a bill (H.R. No. 634) to the House. This measure applied only to Missouri and authorized the President to issue to that state $10,000,000 in five-percent, thirty-year bonds if a plan of immediate emancipation should be adopted within a period of one year after the passage of the bill. The measure also pledged federal support for voluntary colonization. Only three short speeches were made on the bill. It was pushed rapidly to a vote on the same day and passed, 73 to 46.[42]

In the Senate, however, no such haste was evident. When the bill was taken up on January 16, the Committee on the Judiciary submitted a substitute. This proposal would have increased the compensation to $300 per slave (with a maximum of $20,000,000) and allowed gradual emancipation, with the Missouri slaves being freed by July 4, 1876. Senator Henderson of Missouri spoke at length in support of the substitute, and further consideration was then postponed.[43] After successive postponements, the bill was again considered by the Senate on the twenty-ninth and thirtieth of January. The debate at this time revealed considerable opposition from several northern Republicans either to the amount of money authorized or to the length of time allowed, or both. Also, many border-state senators objected on constitutional grounds. This opposition made it doubtful that the Missouri emancipation bill could pass in its present form. It was, therefore, recommitted to the Committee on the Judiciary on January 30.[44]

During the following week, the committee drafted another substitute and reported it to the Senate. On February 7, consideration of the Missouri measure was resumed. The new version authorized payment of up to $20,000,000 in the event that the state's slaves were freed by 1865, and up to $10,000,000 if they were freed by 1876. Debate on the seventh

42. Boston *Post,* December 5, 1862; Philadelphia *Inquirer,* December 15, 1862; *Cong. Globe,* 37th Cong., 3d Sess., pp. 207–209. Nine additional votes in favor of the bill and two against it were later recorded by unanimous consent. See *Cong. Globe,* 37th Cong., 3d Sess., pp. 222, 226, 235, 254.

43. *Cong. Globe,* 37th Cong., 3d Sess., pp. 351–357. Henderson had been working actively for the measure since the beginning of the session. See Philadelphia *Inquirer,* December 15, 1862.

44. *Cong. Globe,* 37th Cong., 3d Sess., pp. 586–597, 611–625.

and twelfth of February consisted (in addition to interminable opposition speeches) of the presentation of a number of amendments from both northern Republicans and border-state senators. With one exception, all amendments were defeated. On February 12, the substitute was adopted by a vote of 26 to 10, and the Missouri emancipation bill, as amended, was passed, 23 to 18. Only one non-Republican, Henderson of Missouri, voted for the proposition. The Democrats and Unionists were joined in opposition by five Republicans, including the titular leader of the party in the Senate, William P. Fessenden of Maine.[45]

The measure (still bearing the designation H.R. No. 634, but now an entirely new bill) was returned to the House and recommitted to the Select Committee on Emancipation. The session was nearing its end, and the passage of any Missouri emancipation bill was rendered even less probable when, on February 25, the select committee reported a totally different measure to the House. The bill was never considered, though three Missouri congressmen obtained permission to print remarks opposing it. On March 3, 1863, the last day in the life of the Thirty-seventh Congress, Albert S. White moved to suspend the rules and take up the bill, but (a two-thirds majority being required to suspend the rules) the motion went down to defeat when only sixty-two representatives supported it while fifty-seven cast negative votes.[46]

One other gesture in the field of compensated emancipation was made by the Thirty-seventh Congress. In the House, Bingham introduced a bill designed to free the slaves in Maryland, and on February 25, the measure was briefly reported and then recommitted to the Select Committee on Emancipation.[47]

One reason for the failure of Congress to pass legislation to compensate border-state slaveholders whose slaves were freed by state action lay in the considerable divergence between the views of the House and those of the Senate. On the question of emancipation, the Senate was by far the

45. Philadelphia *Inquirer,* February 9, 1863; *Cong. Globe,* 37th Cong., 3d Sess., pp. 776–805, 897–903. The other Republicans who voted against the bill were Cowan, Grimes, Harding, James H. Lane, and Ten Eyck. The one amendment adopted (proposed by Sumner) reduced the amount of money to be appropriated for each slave freed from $300 to $200.

46. *Cong. Globe,* 37th Cong., 3d Sess., pp. 1055–1056, 1294–1295, 1426, 1545–1546, Appendix, 137–138, 143–151.

47. *Ibid.,* pp. 381, 1293–1294.

more conservative of the two bodies. Immediate emancipation, to a majority of the senators, seemed too radical a step. To a majority in the House, the thirteen-year delay permitted by the Senate version of the Missouri bill undoubtedly appeared excessive. Many radical Republicans in both houses, in fact, probably considered any gradualism immoral. The Democrats and Unionists, on the other hand, were overwhelmingly opposed to any congressional action on slavery in the loyal states. Hence, only a compromise that would effectively unite the Republican majorities in both houses could secure congressional approval. But neither the radical Republicans in the House nor the moderate Republicans in the Senate were sufficiently interested in compensated emancipation in the loyal states to seek compromise very earnestly. It was, after all, a subject pressed upon them by the President and not one proposed by either the House or the Senate leadership. Lincoln might circumvent Congress, and he might, by threat of veto, force a modification of a measure which the congressional leadership had pushed through (as he did in the case of the confiscation bill); but he was unable to force his will upon Congress. Indeed, he was scarcely able to resist the counterpressure for congressional dominance of the executive.

In dealing with slavery in the territories, Congress was not hampered by the constitutional limitations which restricted its attacks upon slavery in the states. First priority, however, was given to the movement to free the slaves in the District of Columbia, and it was not until May 8, 1862—more than two thirds of the way through the second session of the Thirty-seventh Congress—that Lovejoy of Illinois, from the Committee on Territories, reported a measure (H.R. No. 374) dealing with the subject. This bill would have prohibited slavery not only in the territories but also in all areas acquired by the federal government (e.g., forts, dockyards, arsenals, and armories), on vessels on the high seas, on national highways, and in all other places where the federal government had exclusive jurisdiction. There was no mention of compensation for slaveholders in these areas.[48]

The measure was discussed in the House on May 9 and 12. Lovejoy repeatedly tried to push the bill through under the operation of the previous question, but the House would not support him. As it became obvious that many members objected to the measure as too broad, Love-

48. *Cong. Globe,* 37th Cong., 2nd Sess., p. 2030.

joy gradually pared the bill down to a bare prohibition of slavery in the territories. In this form, it was passed on May 12, by a vote of 85 to 50. No Democrats and only two Unionists (Richard A. Harrison of Ohio and William P. Sheffield of Rhode Island) supported the measure, and no Republicans opposed it.[49]

In the Senate, the Committee on Territories rephrased and simplified the bill, and it was passed with practically no discussion on June 9, by a vote of 28 to 10. Only one Democrat (Rice of Minnesota) supported the measure. No Republicans opposed it, but three found themselves conveniently absent, and three others opposed taking the bill up, though they supported it on the final vote. Of the seven senators absent, six would probably have cast negative votes.[50] On June 17, without discussion, the House concurred in the Senate amendment by a vote of 72 to 38, and that plank of the Chicago platform calling for the exclusion of slavery from the territories had been redeemed.[51]

The congressional attack on slavery in the loyal areas was not, however, wholly successful. In most of the border states, the "peculiar institution" remained, for a coalition of radical and conservative influences had prevented Congress from implementing Lincoln's sweeping proposals to encourage voluntary emancipation. Just what effect congressional agitation of the matter had on those states is difficult to determine. It is true that Missouri, Maryland, and Virginia later made either constitutional or legislative provision for emancipation, but it seems probable that later events had more influence on their actions than did the debates of the Thirty-seventh Congress. But the actual legislative accomplishments were considerable. Three successful attacks had been made on slavery in the loyal areas of the country. The slaves in the District of Columbia and in the territories had been freed, and gradual emancipation had been forced on the new state of West Virginia. For the first (but not the last) time, a mid–nineteenth-century Congress had come to legislative grips with the thorny question of the status of the Negro in America.

49. *Ibid.,* pp. 2041–2054, 2066–2069.

50. *Ibid.,* p. 2618. The measure would undoubtedly have been passed by a free vote in a full Senate, but the margin of victory would have been much closer, probably about 27 to 21.

51. *Ibid.,* p. 2769. For the Chicago platform, see Thomas V. Cooper and Hector T. Fenton (editors), *American Politics,* Book II, 41–43.

CHAPTER 3

Congress and Slavery: The Rebel Area

From the very beginning of the Civil War, many radicals viewed the conflict as a God-given opportunity to attack slavery in its citadel—the rebel states. Indeed, it was obvious that many of these antislavery men believed that the "peculiar institution" must be destroyed while military operations were in progress, if it was to be destroyed at all. They frankly and frequently expressed their abhorrence of the idea of a restoration of "the union as it was."

But on what ground and by what methods should the assault be launched? Against the armed enemies of the government they could, with some degree of legitimacy and with the expectation of considerable popular support, call for actions not strictly authorized by the Constitution. But even within Republican Party ranks there were many congressmen who opposed emancipation schemes on constitutional, social, economic, and political grounds. In addition, border-state men, however loyal, viewed such proposals with deep distrust.

Two major avenues of attack on slavery in the rebel states were available to the radicals. A direct legislative assault could be made by passing a general emancipation act, or the advancing armies could be utilized as instruments for the piecemeal elimination of slavery. Each alternative offered attractive features, and the emancipationists pressed for legislation in both areas.

The Army and Slavery

Given a war between two sections divided primarily over the issue of slavery, it was only natural that Congress should be immediately and continuously concerned with the relationship between the army and runaway slaves. Only four days after the first session of the Thirty-seventh

Congress convened, Lovejoy introduced a resolution declaring that the capture and return of fugitive slaves was no part of the duty of Federal troops. The proposal, however, contained several additional sections dealing with other aspects of the question and—probably for this reason—was tabled by a vote of 88 to 62. On the following day, Lovejoy reintroduced his resolution without these sections and it was passed, 93 to 55. "Our conservative people," Lovejoy caustically observed, "were timid & vexed, but they had to vote right at last."[1]

Press reaction to the proposition was mixed. The Washington correspondent of the New York *Times* merely found the situation confused. "The resolution is vague," he wrote, "and subject to misconstruction, and no doubt perplexed members as to the course proper to be pursued in disposing of it. . . . The issue is unfairly presented, and the vote will define the position of neither party accurately." The Philadelphia *Inquirer's* capital reporter, however, detected a plot. "There is a deep laid scheme on the part of the Abolitionists in Congress to commit this Administration to such a course of policy as will indeed make this war a war for the extermination of slavery and slaveholders. This is the first step in the programme. Others will be speedily taken."[2]

This prediction of further action was not fulfilled during the first session of the Congress. But border-state men continued to demand the return of fugitive slaves, and when Congress reconvened in December 1861, it was obvious that many of the more radical Republicans were much irritated by the continued assistance given by army commanders to slaveholders attempting to reclaim fugitives. The radicals' first target was a recent order of Major General Henry W. Halleck expelling slaves from his lines in the Department of Missouri. On December 4, Senator Sumner introduced a resolution calling on the President for copies of any orders issued in the Department of Missouri relative to fugitive slaves, acknowledging that this request was based on his opposition to Halleck's directive. On the following day, the resolution was passed without discussion and without division.[3]

1. *Cong. Globe,* 37th Cong., 1st Sess., pp. 24, 32; Owen Lovejoy to Charles Sumner, July 10, 1861, Charles Sumner Papers, Harvard University.

2. New York *Times,* July 12, 1861; Philadelphia *Inquirer,* July 15, 1861.

3. Charles B. Calvert to Abraham Lincoln, August 3, 1861, Lincoln Papers, Library of Congress; *Cong. Globe,* 37th Cong., 2nd Sess., pp. 9, 19.

In the House, more direct action was attempted. On December 9, Lovejoy introduced a resolution directing (later changed to requesting) the Secretary of War to revoke Halleck's order. Many moderate Republicans would have preferred to avoid an open clash with the executive on this issue, but for two days, Lovejoy did his best to push the resolution through under the previous question. The House, however, refused to support him and finally, irritated by the continual pressure, surprised observers by tabling the resolution by a vote of 78 to 64.[4] One representative explained the situation in this manner:

> The House is in a very bad frame of mind just now. Lovejoy and a few such have been undertaking to manage everything, the army in the field, and everything else, till yesterday, in perfect disgust of everything the House voted directly against its own sentiments, and laid on the table a resolution offered by Mr. Lovejoy disapproving of Gen. Hallecks orders in reference to slaves. So the Country will read that we approve of the order. Strange that every good cause is to be ruined by fanaticism and madness.[5]

No further action was taken by either house on this matter, and all in all, the agitation of the issue in Congress probably did more harm than good.

Even more galling to radical Republicans was the fact that on several occasions military personnel had returned fugitive slaves to their masters. As early as December 4, 1861, Lovejoy introduced a bill making it a penal offense for any member of the military to aid in the return of fugitive slaves. Consideration of this measure was postponed to December 10, and it was lost in the shuffle while the resolution regarding Halleck's order was under consideration.[6] On December 20, the matter was again brought to the attention of the House when Republican John P. C. Shanks of Indiana introduced a resolution declaring that any military order directing the return of fugitive slaves constituted a military infringement of strictly civil power. Vallandigham indicated that he wished to debate the resolution, and it went over under the rules.[7] Hardly had that matter been disposed of, however, when Wilson introduced a resolu-

4. *Cong. Globe,* 37th Cong., 2nd Sess., pp. 33–34, 57–60.

5. Henry L. Dawes to Mrs. Henry L. Dawes, December 12, 1861, Henry L. Dawes Papers, Library of Congress.

6. *Cong. Globe,* 37th Cong., 2nd Sess., p. 16.

7. *Ibid.,* p. 158.

tion requesting the Committee on Military Affairs to report a bill enacting an additional article of war forbidding military officers to use forces under their command to return fugitive slaves, with violation punishable by dismissal from the service. Though the House had just refused to adjourn, it was now found convenient to do so. A number of Republicans obviously preferred to avoid the issue, for eighteen of them joined with the Democrats and Unionists to pass the adjournment motion.[8]

But over the weekend the insurgent Republicans were apparently convinced of the error of their ways, for when the Wilson proposal again came up for consideration on December 23, it was passed without discussion. Though there was no division on the resolution itself, there was a test vote on a motion to table, which was defeated, 34 to 70. With the exception of William M. Dunn of Indiana, all the Republicans present (including thirteen of those who had voted to adjourn on the twentieth) opposed the tabling motion. The Shanks resolution, now superfluous, was referred to the Committee on the Judiciary.[9]

Nothing further was heard of this matter until February 25, 1862, when Francis P. Blair, Jr., reported a bill from the committee creating an additional article of war as outlined in Wilson's resolution. Many Democrats and Unionists opposed the proposal, and even Blair was not disposed to press it to an immediate vote. The same could not be said of other Republicans, however, and the measure was pushed through under the operation of the previous question and passed by a vote of 83 to 42. No Republicans opposed the bill, though ten were conveniently absent.[10]

The Senate had also been considering the problem of the relationship of the army to fugitive slaves. On December 18, Sumner secured the passage of a resolution directing the Committee on Military Affairs to consider the expediency of prohibiting the use of Federal troops to return fugitive slaves. A bill to accomplish this object was introduced by Henry

8. *Ibid.*, p. 159. The final vote to adjourn was 58 to 53. Republican opposition to the resolution seems to have centered in New York, Pennsylvania, and Ohio. Four Republican representatives from each of the first two states and three from the latter state voted in favor of adjournment.

9. *Ibid.*, pp. 168, 172.

10. *Ibid.*, pp. 955–959. Four affirmative votes and five negative votes were later recorded by unanimous consent. See *ibid.*, pp. 975, 999.

Wilson five days later and reported back to the Senate from the military affairs committee on January 7, 1862. The measure was discussed as in Committee of the Whole on the twelfth and reported to the Senate, but the press of other business prevented further consideration. The only test vote at this time came on a motion to postpone indefinitely, defeated 13 to 23.[11]

On March 10, the Senate took up the House bill (No. 299) creating the additional article of war. The border-state senators, realizing the futility of opposition, concentrated their energies on attempts to amend the measure. Amendments forbidding army personnel to harbor, detain, or conceal fugitive slaves and suspending the operation of the article in areas where federal authority was recognized were offered and defeated. A third amendment would have forbidden federal troops to entice slaves away from loyal masters, but this too was defeated. The measure was then passed, in the form that it came from the House, by a vote of 29 to 9. The support for the amendments and the opposition to the bill was exclusively Democratic and Unionist, though one Democrat (McDougall of California) and one Unionist (Wright of Indiana) voted for the measure.[12]

The mere nonreturn of fugitive slaves, however, was not enough for many Republicans—they desired that the army be made an effective instrument of abolition by providing for the enlistment (and consequent emancipation) of slaves. Secretary of War Cameron, in fact, advocated such a course of action in his initial report to Congress, prepared and circulated clandestinely in December 1861; but the President ordered the recall and modification of the paper. Moreover, some individual commanders enlisted Negroes before any legislation specifically authorizing such enlistment was passed by Congress. This brought them under attack by Democrats and Unionists, while radical Republicans castigated commanders who did not take this course. "I am uneasy," wrote Governor Israel Washburn of Maine, "that there are no (apparent) measures being taken to call out & organize the blacks. *They must be formed into*

11. *Ibid.,* pp. 110, 130–131, 161, 207, 358–359. Among the Republicans only Cowan cast an affirmative vote, but six members of the majority party were absent.

12. *Ibid.,* pp. 1142–1143. Wright also opposed the amendments, though McDougall supported them.

Regiments, officered & paid. Then, & only then, can we reasonably hope to see the Rebellion put down."[13]

Late in May 1862 in a speech before the House, Republican Charles B. Sedgwick of New York, after prior consultation with William Lloyd Garrison, defended the use of Negro troops. But not until the following July did the conflict first come to a head in the lower house. On July 5, Kentucky Unionists Wickliffe and Mallory launched strong attacks on Major General David Hunter for having enrolled Negro troops. In reply, Stevens insisted that Lincoln was the one to be condemned for his weakness in not having ordered such enlistments throughout the army.[14]

Some Republicans were privately even more violent in denouncing those who did not favor Negro enlistments. Senator Chandler, for instance, declared,

> McLelland [*sic*] is an imbecile if not a Traitor. He has virtually lost the Army of the Potomac & should in my estimation *Suffer* the *Extreme penalty of the Law.* I will neither relax or let up, on my position. Stanton is my Friend *& I will* Stand by him. Michigan has lost 4000 men in the Army of the East, 2500 of them *by the Spade.* McLelland will not take Negroes to dig ditches, Cut down timber & do hard work, but will *force* my brave boys to do this menial work *& die in doing it* rather than take Negro Slaves belonging to rebels & who only asks [*sic*] freedom in return. 40,000 brave men have been sacrificed to this Negrophoby [*sic*] & I will no longer keep quiet. It is wicked.[15]

On July 9, the Senate took up a bill (S. No. 384) to authorize the President to call out the militia for an indefinite term. To this measure, Grimes immediately introduced an amendment providing that there should be no exclusion from the militia on account of color. At the

13. Nicolay and Hay, *Abraham Lincoln,* V, 125–126; James S. Rollins to Joseph Holt, December 17, 1861, Joseph Holt Papers, Library of Congress; Israel Washburn to Hannibal Hamlin, January 16, 1862, Israel Washburn Papers, Library of Congress.

14. Charles B. Sedgwick to William L. Garrison, May 17, 1862, Anti-Slavery Letters, Boston Public Library; *Cong. Globe,* 37th Cong., 2nd Sess., pp. 2323–2327, 3121–3127. The subject of Sedgwick's speech was an amendment which he proposed to submit to the confiscation bill (H.R. No. 471) authorizing the enlistment of slaves. The amendment was never actually presented.

15. Zachariah Chandler to Mrs. Zachariah Chandler, July 11, 1862, Zachariah Chandler Papers, Library of Congress. I have slightly modified capitalization and punctuation.

suggestion of Sherman, the amendment was modified so as to authorize the President to enlist Negroes in the federal forces, but making no mention of Negro enrollment in the state militias. Grimes's proposal was immediately and strongly denounced by the border-state senators, especially since the amendment provided that the Negroes so enlisted, and their immediate families, should be free. The supporters of the proposal felt called upon to deny that racial equality was either desirable or possible. "I think the law of caste is the law of God," declared Sherman. "You cannot change it." Even Wilson denied that he favored Negro equality.[16]

The measure was considered as in Committee of the Whole on July 9, 10, and 11. On the tenth, the Democrats and Unionists, with the help of a number of Republicans, pushed through two amendments providing for compensation to loyal slaveholders whose slaves were enlisted and granting freedom only to slaves owned by disloyal persons. Several Republicans, notably Cowan and Browning, were also active supporters of the border-state position in debate. Cowan even went so far as to charge that this bill was designed to force Lincoln to do something that he did not desire to do and which the radical Republicans had not been able to persuade him to do.[17]

Apparently unhappy with the shape which the bill had assumed, the radicals, led by Henry Wilson of Massachusetts, suddenly shelved the measure and, on the fourteenth of July, took up another proposal. This bill (S. No. 394) empowered the President to call out the militia for any period up to nine months and authorized him to employ Negroes in any capacity. The Negroes so employed and their immediate families were to be free.[18]

If the radicals hoped to avoid the restrictive amendments, however, they miscalculated the temper of the Senate. On July 15, by a vote of 18 to 17, the Senate adopted an amendment which provided that only the slaves of disloyal owners would be freed upon enlistment. After other

16. *Cong. Globe,* 37th Cong., 2nd Sess., pp. 3197–3207, quotation from p. 3199.

17. *Ibid.,* pp. 3197–3207, 3227–3236, 3249–3254. Republicans Anthony, Browning, Collamer, Cowan, Doolittle, Foster, Howe, Henry S. Lane, Simmons, and Ten Eyck supported both amendments.

18. *Ibid.,* pp. 3320–3321.

modifications were made, the bill was passed on the same day by a vote of 28 to 9. All of the Republicans present voted for the measure, and they were joined by two minority members, Rice of Minnesota and Wright of Indiana.[19]

The session was rapidly drawing to a close, and the Republican leadership of the House had no intention of allowing the measure to die with the session. Consequently, on the following day, the House took up the bill and pushed it through under the operation of the previous question. No opportunity was given for amendment or debate, and the measure was passed without a division. The only test vote was on a motion to table, which was defeated 30 to 77.[20]

To the disgust of the radicals, however, few Negro troops were enrolled, congressional action notwithstanding. Additional legislation was obviously indicated. On January 12, 1863, Stevens introduced a bill (H.R. No. 675) which would have *required* the President to enlist 150,000 Negro troops. All regimental officers were required to be white, but company officers might be either white or colored, at the discretion of the President.[21]

When the measure came before the House on January 27, Stevens presented a substitute he had drafted. The new proposal authorized (rather than required) the President to raise as many Negro troops as necessary. The proposal included a section providing for compensation to

19. *Ibid.*, pp. 3337–3352. The closeness of this tally, as compared with the 22 to 16 vote by which the same amendment was attached to the earlier bill, might lead one to believe that the party whip had been wielded with considerable effectiveness. But this was hardly the case. Only two Republicans (Harris of New York and Howard of Michigan) who had voted for the amendment on July 10 voted against it on the fifteenth, and one (Fessenden of Maine, the titular leader of the Senate Republicans) who had not voted on the amendment on the tenth supported it on the fifteenth. The real reason for the decreased majority was the absence of three Democrats and a Unionist who had voted for the amendment on the tenth.

20. *Ibid.*, pp. 3397–3398.

21. *Cong. Globe*, 37th Cong., 3d Sess., p. 282. Stevens's bill apparently stirred the President to action, for two days later he wrote to General John A. Dix inquiring about the possibility of garrisoning Fortress Monroe and Yorktown with Negro troops. See Abraham Lincoln to John A. Dix, January 14, 1863, Lincoln Papers, Library of Congress.

loyal slaveholders whose slaves were enlisted. On the same day, Hickman also presented a substitute which contained several remarkable provisions —officers of Negro units were to be "of collegiate education" and were to receive twice the pay of officers in white units, and the government was to establish a line of semimonthly steamers to transport Negroes "dependent upon the United States for support" (i.e., "contrabands") to Liberia, apparently on a compulsory basis.[22]

Stevens's bill, significantly, had never been referred to the Committee on Military Affairs, and this matter was thoroughly threshed out on the following day. Sheffield and Olin insisted that the measure should be so referred. Olin, who was a member of the committee, said that such a proposal was under consideration and would soon be reported. The session thus far, he caustically observed, had been monopolized by the Committee of Ways and Means "with the aid of the Speaker." But Stevens and Hickman vigorously opposed such a reference, insisting that the committee would bury the bill.[23] When motions to table the bill and to refer it to the Committee on Military Affairs were defeated by large majorities, and the main question ordered by a small majority, the opponents of the measure proceeded to demonstrate that a minority was not completely powerless in congressional operations. By entering a series of dilatory motions and demanding the yeas and nays, the bill's enemies forced thirty-nine roll-call votes and four calls of the House. This was possible, as one observer commented on the following day, because the Republicans "acted without talent or concert. . . . Messers. Wickliffe, Cox, Vallandigham, Allen, Perry & Co., on the other hand, are leagued and confederated in scientific phalanx. Last night they relieved each other by alternate relays, rank after rank reinforcing, delivering fire, and dropping to the rear, with the condensed precision of a secession *corps d'armee.*" The House was thus kept in continuous session until 5:35 the following morning, when the majority capitulated and, by unanimous consent, the vote ordering the main question was declared to be reconsidered.[24] The filibusterers were probably under no illusion as to their ability

22. *Cong. Globe,* 37th Cong., 3d Sess., p. 557.

23. *Ibid.,* pp. 570–571.

24. *Ibid.,* pp. 572–583; New York *Times,* February 1, 1863. The quotation is from the *Times.* Vallandigham led the filibusterers, who consisted mostly of

to defeat the measure, but they did object to having such a bill forced through the House without discussion and without an opportunity to offer amendments. They believed, correctly, as it turned out, that the measure would not emerge unchanged from an open discussion in the House.

A full-scale debate on the measure followed on January 29, 30, 31, and February 2. The opponents of the bill were mostly Democrats and Unionists but also included Republicans Benjamin F. Thomas and Abram Olin. A number of other Republicans supported proposals to modify the measure. The most radical supporters of the bill were Stevens and Lovejoy, who bitterly assailed the Democrats for their opposition. The measure's most violent opponent, May of Maryland, incorporated into his speech a demand for federal recognition of the Confederacy. Though no amendments were officially received, Stevens, in response to pressure from the House, repeatedly modified his bill. The measure, as it finally came to a vote, contained provisions specifically prohibiting the placing of white troops under Negro officers, the enlistment of slaves of loyal masters, and the establishment of recruiting offices in the border states. The bill was passed in this form, 83 to 54. Five non-Republicans supported the measure, and five members of the majority party were numbered among the opposition.[25] It was claimed that "Several members who had promised to vote nay came over at the last moment, so that the relative majority was somewhat larger than was anticipated."[26]

Thus the measure was sent to the Senate. Border-state and Democratic

border-state and midwestern Democrats and Unionists, but several Republicans apparently co-operated with them.

25. *Cong. Globe,* 37th Cong., 3d Sess., pp. 598–607, 626–637, 649–664, 680–690, Appendix, 72–86, 91–94, 103–106. Among those Republicans supporting modification of the bill were William M. Davis of Pennsylvania, William M. Dunn and Albert G. Porter of Indiana, and Carey A. Trimble of Ohio. The five Republicans voting against the measure were Bradley F. Granger of Michigan, James T. Hale of Pennsylvania, Valentine B. Horton of Ohio, William Kellogg of Illinois, and Benjamin F. Thomas of Massachusetts. It will be noted that many of these Republican "deviationists" came from states having a common boundary with slave states and especially from the Northwest where anti-Negro sentiment was wide spread. Granger and Thomas were well known for their conservative views. The non-Republicans supporting the bill were Unionists William G. Brown of Virginia, Samuel L. Casey of Kentucky, George P. Fisher of Delaware, and William P. Sheffield of Rhode Island, and Democrat John W. Noell of Missouri.

26. New York *Herald,* February 3, 1863.

senators girded their loins for the battle and perhaps made filibuster plans. "We must defeat the bill," asserted Senator Richardson of Illinois. "Resistance to the collection of all Taxes & civil war in the North West is certain and inevitable." Such preparations were not needed, for on February 13, Wilson, from the Committee on Military Affairs, reported the bill back to the Senate with the recommendation that it not pass. The committee asserted that the twelfth and fifteenth sections of the act of July 17, 1862, granted sufficient authority to make the bill unnecessary. The Senate apparently agreed, for nothing further was heard of House Bill No. 675.[27]

The point made by the Senate military affairs committee had been repeatedly raised during the House debates by the opponents of the measure; but Stevens, Lovejoy, and the other radicals professed to be unconvinced. Actually, they were undoubtedly well aware that enlistment of Negro troops was possible under the earlier act, but their real purpose was probably to force Lincoln to do something that he did not desire to do —order the enlistment of Negro troops on a large scale. From the viewpoint of the radical Republicans, this was the frustrating factor. The President was the commander-in-chief of the army. The radicals had been unable to convert him to their views. And finally, though they could, through congressional action, cause the army to foster emancipation in a negative way, they were not sufficiently powerful to force through Congress any measure which would compel Lincoln to convert the army into an effective, affirmative instrument of emancipation.

Emancipation in the Rebel States

The ultimate aim of many radical Republicans was the emancipation of all slaves in the rebel states. This, they insisted, was possible by an application of the laws of war or the exercise of the "war power." Early in the second session, a conservative Republican observed, "The organization of a party designing either to rule the administration or to supplant it has *I* think already commenced. Emancipation . . . will be the watchword."[28]

27. William A. Richardson to [John H. George], February 3, 1863, John H. George Papers, New Hampshire Historical Society; *Cong. Globe,* 37th Cong., 3d Sess., pp. 923–924.

28. Timothy O. Howe to Grace T. Howe, December 13, 1861, Timothy O. Howe Papers, State Historical Society of Wisconsin. For a statement of the radical

During the winter and spring of 1862, the House had under consideration a bill designed to accomplish this purpose. Throughout this period, it was tied tightly to the confiscation bill, both in committee and on the floor, and for that reason its course up to May 26, 1862, is traced in the next chapter. But as the session wore on, and as moderate and conservative Republicans became increasingly irritated by the radicals' unrelenting pressures, the opponents of emancipation legislation became more confident of success. "I think too, the idea of the Ultras of emancipating all the slaves will fail," a Maryland Unionist had cautiously predicted in January 1862. A month later, Cox was able to declare exultantly, "I think we *have them beaten* in the House."[29]

When the confiscation bill passed the House, the emancipation bill coupled with it was defeated by four votes. This was accomplished by the votes of sixteen Republicans who joined all the Democrats and Unionists in the House in opposing the measure.[30] Foes of emancipation breathed a sigh of relief, and one northern Democratic paper asserted that the Republican opponents of the bill had "raised themselves to the rank of patriots and statesmen by their conservative course at this perilous crisis to the constitution and the Union."[31] The emancipationists had not given up the fight, however, and on May 27, the day after the rejection of the measure, Porter entered a motion to reconsider the vote by which the bill had been defeated. He further stated that he intended to offer an amendment to the measure.[32] The radicals began the furious struggle to secure the necessary votes to assure reconsideration.

Porter's motion came before the House on May 28, and the Indiana

---

position, see Charles Sumner to Parke Godwin, March 23, 1862, Bryant-Godwin Papers, New York Public Library.

29. William P. Fessenden to John A. Andrew, March 9, 1862, John A. Andrew Papers, Massachusetts Historical Society; John W. Crisfield to Mrs. Mary H. Crisfield, January 27, 1862, Crisfield Papers, Maryland Historical Society; Samuel S. Cox to Franklin Pierce, February 24, 1862, Franklin Pierce Papers, Library of Congress.

30. *Cong. Globe,* 37th Cong., 2nd Sess., p. 2363. For the Republican opponents of the bill, see below, p. 89*n.*

31. New York *Herald,* May 28, 1862.

32. *Ibid.; Cong. Globe,* 37th Cong., 2nd Sess., p. 2393. Porter said he had opposed the original bill because it had provided for wholesale emancipation. His substitute would free only the slaves of certain enumerated classes of rebels.

representative, noting that "a large number of the members of the House are going on an excursion, and . . . there will be a thin House," moved that further consideration of the motion be postponed to June 4. It is distinctly possible, however, that the real reason he desired a postponement was that the party whips had not been wholly successful in driving the insurgent Republicans into the fold. If the emancipationists really wanted a delay, their plans were thwarted when Holman moved to table Porter's original motion.[33] Faced with the necessity for immediate action if the bill was to be salvaged, the supporters of reconsideration entered three successive dilatory motions on which they demanded the yeas and nays as the pages scurried through the corridors of the Capitol in search of absent representatives. The strategy worked. When the vote on Holman's motion was finally taken, it was defeated by four votes.[34]

When the House resumed consideration of the question on June 4, it was obvious that the radical pressure on Republican representatives had been effective. A second tabling motion was voted down, 65 to 86, and the motion to reconsider the adverse vote on the emancipation bill carried by a vote of 84 to 64. Eleven of the sixteen Republicans who had originally opposed the bill now voted for reconsideration. Included in this group were seven who had voted to table the reconsideration motion on May 28. After some additional discussion, the measure was recommitted to the Select Committee on Confiscation and Emancipation, with instruc-

33. *Cong. Globe,* 37th Cong., 2nd Sess., pp. 2408–2409. The tabling of a motion to reconsider a measure was the method generally used to bury a proposal.

34. *Ibid.,* p. 2409. The vote on Holman's motion was 69 to 73. The supporters of reconsideration were obviously not very sure of their ground. During the time consumed by the delaying tactics, six supporters of the motion to table the reconsideration motion came into the House, and nine opponents of the motion appeared. If the vote had been taken immediately after the motion to table was made, the motion would have failed by a vote of 63 to 64. The eventual outcome on this question was rendered possible by a number of factors. Dawes and Porter, who had opposed the original bill, and Covode, who had been absent when the vote was taken on May 26, supported reconsideration. These changes would normally have been sufficient to reverse the four-vote majority against the measure, but four supporters of the emancipation bill were paired with opponents of the measure on the question of reconsideration. The real difference was made by the fortuitous (?) absence of five opponents of the emancipation bill (two of them Republicans) when the vote was taken on the tabling motion.

tions to report a substitute submitted by Porter. This proposal would have freed only slaves owned by persons in actual rebellion against the government of the United States and provided for voluntary colonization of the Negroes so freed.[35]

Some two weeks later, on June 17, Republican Thomas D. Eliot of Massachusetts reported the substitute to the House with amendments. The point of order was immediately raised, and sustained, that the committee had been instructed to report Porter's substitute and thus had no power to report a modified measure. Eliot thereupon reported the substitute measure unamended.[36]

"We hope today to pass the Emancipation bill," wrote abolitionist Owen Lovejoy, on June 18. In this hope he was gratified. After some debate, the substitute was somewhat modified, adopted as an amendment, and passed by a vote of 82 to 54. One Unionist (Fisher of Delaware) joined with eighty-one Republicans in supporting the bill, while six Republicans found themselves unable to stomach even this weaker measure and joined the Democrats and Unionists in opposition.[37]

And so, after much compromise and ardent labor, an emancipation bill was sent to the Senate. At first glance, the effort might seem wasted, for the measure never reached the Senate floor. There was, however, good reason for this. During late June, the Senate was involved in considering the confiscation bill. This measure was amended by the upper house to bear on slavery, and the final version (written by the conference committee) contained an emancipation provision somewhat broader than the House emancipation bill. This legislation satisfied the desires of many Republicans and blunted the demands of the still-unsatisfied radicals. For though all slaves in the rebel states were not declared free, the measure

35. *Ibid.*, pp. 2560–2561, Appendix, 294–297.

36. *Ibid.*, pp. 2764–2765.

37. *Ibid.*, pp. 2790–2794; Owen Lovejoy to [William C. Bryant], June 18, 1862, Bryant-Godwin Papers, New York Public Library. The Republicans opposing the bill were Charles Delano and Benjamin F. Thomas of Massachusetts, Alexander S. Diven of New York, Bradley F. Granger of Michigan, Valentine B. Horton of Ohio, and William Kellogg of Illinois. Noell made an adverse minority report from the Select Committee on Confiscation and Emancipation on the Porter substitute. See Select Committee on Confiscation and Emancipation, U.S. House of Representatives, *Minority Report, Ho. Com. Repts.*, 37th Cong., 2nd Sess., No. 120, [1145].

did provide for the emancipation of all slaves of rebels found within Union lines.[38]

There was, of course, another method by which the slaves of rebel masters could be freed—presidential proclamation. But until Lincoln issued his preliminary emancipation proclamation on September 22, 1862, his course in regard to slavery had earned him the strong support of the border state Unionists in Congress and, conversely, had called down on his head the bitter condemnation of the congressional radicals.[39]

The pressures being brought to bear on Lincoln were too great to be resisted for long, however, and despite the failure of Congress to follow his recommendations for the passage of a compensated emancipation act, delaying action any longer was politically impossible. As early as May 28, 1862, Stanton told Sumner that a decree of emancipation would be issued in late July; and on July 22, the President did, in fact, submit a draft emancipation proclamation to the Cabinet. Secretary of State Seward later recalled that the release of such a proclamation was strongly urged, not only by the Republican radicals, but also by foreign powers. Immediacy was the keynote of these protestations and one senator (a rather moderate one, at that) professed to believe that the Confederates would soon emancipate all their slaves, thus depriving the administration of the support of both the northern abolitionists and the European antislavery elements. On the advice of Seward, however, Lincoln withheld the proclamation until after the indecisive battle of Antietam on September 17.[40]

The preliminary emancipation proclamation was issued during the recess of Congress, and when (indeed, before) the Third Session of the Thirty-seventh Congress convened in December 1862, it was quickly evident that both the radicals and the Unionists had experienced a change

38. *Cong. Globe,* 37th Cong., 2nd Sess., pp. 2871 ff. For a discussion of the enactment of the confiscation bill, see Chapter 4.

39. E.g., *ibid.,* pp. 494–500.

40. Charles Sumner to John A. Andrew, May 28, 1862, John A. Andrew Papers, Massachusetts Historical Society; Nicolay and Hay, *Abraham Lincoln,* VI, 125–130; Abraham Lincoln, "Draft of Emancipation Proclamation," in Nicolay and Hay, *Lincoln's Works,* VII, 289–290; Browning, *op. cit.* (January 22, 1863), I, 618; Jacob M. Howard to [Lyman Trumbull], August 16, 1862, Lyman Trumbull Papers, Library of Congress. Senator Howard did not explain how he expected this emancipation would be accomplished.

of heart toward Lincoln. The session was barely begun when Clark introduced in the Senate a joint resolution approving the policy enunciated by Lincoln in his September proclamation. The resolution was ordered tabled and printed.[41] The House, apparently marking time until the Senate should send down the joint resolution, took no cognizance of the proclamation. Aside from a brief attack on Lincoln's policy by Richardson in his speech discussing the presidential message, no real attention was given to the matter for a week.[42]

Still the Senate took no action. The Unionist representatives launched their attack on the proclamation on December 11. George H. Yeaman of Kentucky introduced a joint resolution declaring the September proclamation unconstitutional and condemning the policy of emancipation as not calculated to restore peace, not well chosen as a war measure, and "an assumption of power dangerous to the rights of citizens and to the perpetuity of a free people." Lovejoy, the bellwether of the House radicals, quickly moved to table the resolution. This motion was carried by an almost straight party vote of 94 to 45. Only three Democrats (Haight of New York, Lehman of Pennsylvania, and Noell of Missouri) and two Unionists (Leary of Maryland and Casey of Kentucky) voted for the motion, and only two Republicans (Thomas of Massachusetts and Granger of Michigan) opposed it. By accident or design, however, thirteen northern Democrats, one northern Unionist, and eleven border-state men were absent when the vote was taken.[43]

As soon as this vote was recorded, Hutchins rose to defend the President's proclamation. Prefacing his remarks by the assertion that "Liberty is right; slavery is wrong," he declared that free government would have no hope unless slavery should be abolished. He then proceeded to defend the proclamation as both constitutional and advisable. "A State institution at war with the General Government," he asserted, "may be lawfully overthrown or destroyed by the national authority, if necessary to preserve the Government." Moreover, the proclamation was a military order and,

41. Preston King to Francis P. Blair, Sr., October 27, 1862, Blair-Lee Papers, Princeton University; John W. Crisfield to Mrs. Mary H. Crisfield, January 18, 1863, Crisfield Papers, Maryland Historical Society; *Cong. Globe,* 37th Cong., 3d Sess., p. 6.

42. *Cong. Globe,* 37th Cong., 3d Sess., Appendix, pp. 39–41.

43. *Ibid.,* p. 76.

Hutchins declared, "As a military order, the constitutional power to issue it cannot be seriously questioned, for it is the exercise of the war power by the President." As to the desirability of the proclamation, he argued, "it will weaken in a vital point the rebels, and powerfully strengthen the Government." Emancipation did not imply political and social equality, however. This, he insisted, was a matter for the states to decide. Hutchins's speech was answered by Menzies, an erstwhile defender of Lincoln, who launched a bitter attack on administration policies, including emancipation, confiscation, military arrest, and suspension of the writ of *habeas corpus*. He announced that, though he had never done so in the past, he would now support the Democratic Party as the party of union.[44]

Still the Senate took no action, and on December 15, Republican Samuel C. Fessenden of Maine introduced a House resolution (*not* a joint resolution) approving the September proclamation as constitutional and well chosen as a war measure. By large margins, a motion to table the resolution was defeated, and the proposal was passed. The vote adhered closely to party lines. Only two Democrats (Haight of New York and Noell of Missouri) and one Unionist (Fisher of Delaware) supported the resolution. Only two Republicans (Granger of Michigan and Thomas of Massachusetts) opposed the measure, but seven other members of the majority party who were present immediately before the tally did not record their votes.[45]

It was obvious that the radicals were fearful of bringing any such resolution before the Senate. Even if a favorable majority could have been

44. *Ibid.*, pp. 76–82. The administration was, of course, already committed to several of these policies when Menzies had made a speech defending Lincoln in January 1862. See *Cong. Globe*, 37th Cong., 2nd Sess., pp. 494–497.

45. *Cong. Globe*, 37th Cong., 3d Sess., p. 92. The seven nonvoters were John T. Nixon of New Jersey, John P. C. Shanks of Indiana, Thaddeus Stevens of Pennsylvania, John L. N. Stratton of New Jersey, Carey A. Trimble of Ohio, Burt Van Horn of New York, and John W. Wallace of Pennsylvania. All had voted against tabling the resolution and Stevens's hearty support of the measure was a well-established fact, but it is possible that the others, especially those from Indiana, Ohio, and New Jersey, were reluctant to go on record as favoring emancipation. All were present later in the day's session. Other nonvoters included nineteen additional Republicans, twelve northern Democrats, and eight border-state representatives. At least seventeen of these were present at some time during this day's session.

mustered (and this, in itself, seems somewhat doubtful) the vote would undoubtedly have revealed a considerable division within the Republican ranks. Some Republicans agreed with Samuel G. Arnold of Rhode Island, who feared that the passage of such a resolution would "draw out an opposition which would otherwise be latent." Others, such as Browning of Illinois and Doolittle of Wisconsin, opposed the proclamation itself. Browning, in fact, was active in an attempt to prevent the issuance of the final proclamation on January 1, 1863.[46] Under these circumstances, the House radicals were understandably reluctant to send a joint resolution to the Senate. Consequently, when Wilson introduced such a measure in the House early in January, it was referred to the Committee on the Judiciary, from which it never emerged.[47] After all, the Senate approbation would have meant little, and any attempt to obtain this approval might have resulted in a split in party lines or a conflict between the Senate and the Executive. This was too high a price to pay for an empty gesture. The matter was dropped.

By the end of the Third Session of the Thirty-seventh Congress, none could deny that congressional achievements in the field of emancipation were considerable. Slavery had been abolished in the territories and in the District of Columbia. As a result of congressional action, West Virginia slaves would ultimately be free. Legislation preventing the return of fugitive slaves by army personnel had been passed, and other enactments made it possible for the President to use the army as a positive weapon against slavery. Furthermore, it was theoretically possible for slavery to be almost entirely eliminated from the rebel states by the application of the emancipation provision of the confiscation bill. Radicals might lament the failure to pass a more stringent general emancipation act, and moderates might bemoan the lack of accomplishment in the field of compensated emancipation; but solid progress had been made. Congressional enactments plus the emancipation proclamation (influenced, at least in part, by pressures from congressional radicals) had charted the course of America's future development. The Negro would be free.

46. Samuel G. Arnold to Manton Marble, December 7, 1862, Manton Marble Papers, Library of Congress; Browning, *op. cit.* (December 31, 1862, January 12, 1863), I, 606–607, 613. Secretary of State Seward also seems to have opposed the proclamation in private conversation. See Browning, *op. cit.* (January 22, 1863), I, 618.

47. *Cong. Globe,* 37th Cong., 3d Sess., p. 281.

CHAPTER 4

Congress and Confiscation: Private Property

The Republican leadership in Congress early indicated a firm intention to pass some sort of legislation that would result in the confiscation of rebel property. The known reluctance of the more conservative elements within the majority party to support confiscatory legislation, however, forced the radicals to approach this subject cautiously. On the second day of the First Session of the Thirty-seventh Congress, Senator Chandler of Michigan gave notice of his intention to introduce a bill to confiscate the property of all military, executive, legislative, and judicial officers of the Confederacy and the Confederate states. Three days later, on July 8, 1861, Republican Dwight Loomis of Connecticut introduced a resolution in the House directing the Committee on the Judiciary to report a similar bill. This resolution was agreed to without a division.[1] The committee, however, never reported such a measure, probably because the Senate took action first.

On July 15, both Chandler and Trumbull introduced confiscation bills which were returned to the Committee on the Judiciary. Five days later, Trumbull reported his own bill from the committee. It was a far less rigorous measure than the one advocated by Chandler and Loomis and provided merely for the confiscation of property used for insurrectionary purposes. Trumbull also submitted an amendment emancipating slaves used for insurrectionary purposes, stressing that it did not come from the committee. Powell of Kentucky objected to its present consideration, and the bill was ordered to lie over.[2] The measure was destined to receive amazingly quick action, however. On July 22, the bill was briefly opposed by Breckinridge of Kentucky and Pearce of Maryland and supported with equal brevity by Trumbull of Illinois, Henry Wilson of Massachusetts,

1. *Cong. Globe,* 37th Cong., 1st Sess., pp. 11, 23.
2. *Ibid.,* pp. 120, 216–217.

and Ten Eyck of New Jersey. Trumbull's amendment was adopted by a vote of 33 to 6, with the senators from Kentucky, Maryland, and Missouri dissenting. The Senate, without a division, then passed the bill and sent it to the House.[3]

In the House the bill went to the Committee on the Judiciary, whence Bingham reported the measure on August 2. At the same time the committee reported an amendment which would have confined the operation of the bill to slave property only. Bingham announced that he was opposed to this modification and called the previous question. After the amendment was defeated, a discussion followed, waxing more bitter and violent with each passing minute. At the height of the furor, John J. Crittenden, the venerable representative from Kentucky, indicated a desire to speak on the subject. The effect was almost magical. William Kellogg of Illinois immediately appealed for, and obtained, unanimous consent for Crittenden to be heard, and the debate took on a totally different cast, with courtesy the keynote. The Kentuckian outlined several objections to the bill—Congress had no power over slavery, and the constitution forbade the punishment of treason by the forfeiture of property beyond the lifetime of the offender. He also feared that the measure would give the false impression that this was an antislavery war and thus stiffen resistance in the South.[4]

In the now-calm debate that followed, it became evident that Crittenden's arguments had had some effect and, at the suggestion of William Kellogg, Pendleton moved that the bill be recommitted. Not even the violence of Stevens could stir the House after Crittenden had quieted the storm. Though the vitriolic radical leader characterized those who objected to the confiscation bill as advocates of the rebels, no one even deigned to reply to him. The measure was recommitted. It seemed that the moderate Republicans had revolted against their party leaders and joined with the minority to defeat the measure.[5] This result was more apparent than real, however, for two factors still had to be considered. It

3. *Ibid.*, pp. 218–219. Three of the senators who opposed Trumbull's amendment were prosouthern in more ways than one. Waldo P. Johnson and Trusten Polk of Missouri and John C. Breckinridge of Kentucky would join the Confederacy before the Second Session of the Thirty-seventh Congress convened.

4. *Ibid.*, pp. 409–411.

5. *Ibid.*, pp. 411–415.

was true that the measure had been recommitted, but to a moderately friendly committee which had initially reported the bill. There was also the question of whether or not the moderate Republicans could resist the pressure of party discipline. The answer was not long in coming.

On the following day, the Committee on the Judiciary reported the measure back to the House with a minor clarifying amendment establishing the fact that the act would affect only slaves used for strictly military purposes. During the previous day's debate, Bingham had stated that he thought that the measure, as originally reported, was susceptible of a broader interpretation. Despite opposition from northern Democrats, border-state men, and a few moderate Republicans (notably Porter of Indiana and Edward McPherson of Pennsylvania), the bill was pushed to a vote under the operation of the previous question. It passed, 60 to 48. With the exception of two northern Unionists, only Republicans supported the measure, but seven of the majority party joined the Democrats and Unionists in opposing the bill. The members of the Committee on the Judiciary who were present split four to three in opposition to the measure, and one can only wonder how it was ordered reported from that committee.[6]

Since the House had amended the bill, it was now returned to the Senate. The lack of a quorum prevented immediate action, but on August 5, without debate, the Senate agreed to the House amendment by a vote of 24 to 11. Only one Democrat (McDougall of California) favored the bill, and only one Republican (Cowan of Pennsylvania) opposed it. Some of its supporters admitted that the measure finally passed, though relatively mild and partial, was indefensible on constitutional grounds. But, declared one approving journal, "constitutions are made for peace.

6. *Ibid.*, pp. 410–411, 430–431. Supporting the measure were Unionists Richard A. Harrison of Ohio and William P. Sheffield of Rhode Island. The Republicans who opposed the bill were Diven of New York, Dunn of Indiana, Hale of Pennsylvania, Horton of Ohio, McPherson of Pennsylvania, Porter of Indiana, and Stratton of New Jersey. Porter and Diven were members of the Committee on the Judiciary. The other committee members opposing the bill were Democrats Pendleton of Ohio and May of Maryland. Committee members favoring the bill were Republicans Bingham of Ohio, Kellogg of Illinois, and Thomas of Massachusetts. Twenty-one representatives who were present earlier in the day did not vote on the measure, and nine of these (seven Republicans and two Unionists) had been in the House immediately before the vote was taken.

We are at war, and we must make war and do it effectively, without regard to paper cobwebs."[7]

When Congress reconvened in December 1861, it quickly became apparent that many members, untroubled by constitutional scruples, viewed this confiscation act as entirely too limited in its effect. More sweeping bills, confiscating all property of rebels, were quickly introduced in both the House and the Senate, and Republican caucuses on December 9 and 11 endorsed this policy. "The general disposition among Congressmen," asserted the Washington correspondent of the New York *Times*, "is to pass a law making more certain and stringent the forfeiture of rebel property, while that of the Unionists will be more securely protected." This opinion was confirmed by another Washington resident who informed a friend that "It is fully taken here that congress will pass a law for confiscating property as broad as the confederate, which extends to all the interests of residents in the free states."[8]

In each house, the Committee on the Judiciary was given the task of examining the confiscation measures. On December 20, Lovejoy introduced a resolution directing the judiciary committee to report a bill confiscating the property and freeing the slaves of rebels. The representatives, however, were apparently not anxious to proceed hastily, for by a vote of 52 to 60 they refused to second the previous question. A series of rather complicated parliamentary maneuvers followed, and the House was finally treated to the spectacle of Lovejoy's unintentionally aiding in the tabling of his own resolution.[9] Unhampered by instructions, the

7. *Ibid.*, pp. 427, 434; San Francisco *Daily Alta California,* August 18, 1861. The vote on August 5 was the only Senate division on the passage of the measure.

8. *Cong. Globe,* 37th Cong., 2nd Sess., pp. 1, 7, 18; New York *Herald,* December 8, 9, 10, 12, 13, 1861; Philadelphia *Inquirer,* December 10, 12, 1861; New York *Times,* December 8, 1861; R. H. Gillet to Caleb Cushing, December 5, 1861, Caleb Cushing Papers, Library of Congress. It is interesting to note that even at this early date, Republican Theobald M. Pomeroy of New York (from Seward's home district) warned of the danger of a clash with the executive on the issue of confiscation legislation. See Philadelphia *Inquirer,* December 12, 1861.

9. *Cong. Globe,* 37th Cong., 2nd Sess., pp. 19, 158–159, 334. The opposition to the tabling motion was exclusively Republican. Nineteen Republican votes, however, were cast in favor of the motion. Of the six members of the Committee on the Judiciary who were present, only Bingham of Ohio opposed the motion. The other five voted to table.

House committee retained the confiscation proposal for three more months.

It was the Senate committee which first produced a confiscation bill. On January 15, 1862, Trumbull reported a measure (S. No. 151) which provided for the confiscation of the property, and the freeing of the slaves of persons in rebellion against the government. The bill was taken up for the first time on February 25. On the previous day, the New York *Times* had pointedly remarked, "There is a strong feeling everywhere that the *property* of every Southern rebel should be confiscated, and especially that his slaves should be set free."[10]

Trumbull of Illinois, as chairman of the committee reporting the bill, was first to take the floor in its defense. He declared that the rebels were subject to both domestic and international law, and that, viewed in this light, the measure presented was constitutional.[11] The bill also authorized the President to provide for the voluntary colonization of the emancipated Negroes; Trumbull, apparently realizing that this clause would be quite controversial, took this occasion to defend it. He was frank to acknowledge the Negrophobe feelings of midwesterners and seemed to consider this the main reason for the inclusion of the colonization clause. "There is," he stated, "a very great aversion in the West—I know it to be so in my State—against having free negroes come among us. Our people want nothing to do with the negro."[12] Pomeroy and Willey immediately rose to protest the colonization clause, Willey on the grounds of its great cost, and Pomeroy because the country could not afford to lose so many laborers. Ten Eyck, however, declared that he would oppose emancipation

10. *Ibid.,* pp. 334, 942–946, 1014–1015, 1040, 1049–1054, 1074–1077, 1136–1141, 1157–1162, Appendix, 60–68; New York *Times,* February 24, 1862.

11. This position represented a slight change in Trumbull's views. Earlier he had deprecated any appeal to either the war power or to the plea of necessity. In regard to the latter, he had said, "Necessity is the plea of tyrants, and if our Constitution ceases to operate the moment a person charged with its observance thinks there is a necessity to violate it, it is of little value." See *Cong. Globe,* 37th Cong., 2nd Sess., p. 18.

12. *Ibid.,* pp. 942–944; quotation from p. 944. Trumbull's statement must have pained the old abolitionist Gerrit Smith, who was present on the Senate floor during the day's discussion of the confiscation bill. See Philadelphia *Inquirer,* February 26, 1862.

without colonization and stated that the bill could not have been reported without such a provision.[13]

In the days that followed, McDougall, Cowan, and Carlile made lengthy speeches challenging the constitutionality of the measure. Only Morrill defended the bill, justifying it on the basis of the war power and the necessity to preserve the Union. The only other senator to speak on the measure during this period (February 25–March 11) was Browning, who opposed the bill but appeared to favor some of the ends to be accomplished by it.[14]

It was obvious to all concerned that the Republicans were far from united in support of the confiscation proposal. The bill itself was a compromise measure; many radicals considered it useless, while some of the conservative Republicans thought it both unconstitutional and unwise.

In several Republican caucuses during the second week in March, a number of the moderates had been urging that the bill and all amendments be referred to a select committee of the caucus for the framing of a measure that all the Republican senators could support. On March 14, however, the moderates were defeated when the caucus voted 11 to 10 against the formation of the committee.[15] Perhaps because of the closeness of this vote, the Senate occupied itself with other concerns (notably the District of Columbia emancipation bill) for almost a month.

The debates were continued in the nation's press, however. The Detroit *Daily Advertiser* declared itself "for a relentless confiscation of rebel property," and late in March demanded, "Why does the bill to confiscate the property of rebels so long hang fire in Congress?" The Democratic Boston *Post,* on the other hand, while admitting the right of confiscation

13. *Cong. Globe,* 37th Cong., 2nd Sess., pp. 944–946.

14. *Ibid.,* pp. 1040, 1049–1054, 1074–1077, 1136–1141, 1157–1162, Appendix, 60–68.

15. Browning, *op. cit.* (March 14, 1862), I, 534. In view of the widely divergent opinions on this issue held by various members of the majority party, it seems highly improbable that *any* measure could have gained the support of all of the senators. It will be noted that only about two thirds of the Republican senators were present at this caucus. It is my personal opinion that a full caucus would have supported the committee proposal.

in the abstract, opposed the enactment of such legislation in issue after issue.[16]

It was not until April 7 that Trumbull opened the second series of debates (which was to last for a month) by defending the bill and replying to earlier criticisms of it.[17] In the discussions of the following month (April 7–May 6) only four senators gave unequivocal support to the measure. These four were Trumbull, Howard, Henry Wilson, and Wade. A number of other important Republicans either voiced flat opposition to the proposal or indicated that extensive amendment would be required to gain their support. As would be expected, several border-state senators also took the floor against the measure.[18]

On April 10, Sherman of Ohio introduced an amendment (in fact a substitute) which restricted the operation of the confiscation bill to officers and employees of the Confederate government and required that judicial proceedings take place before the title to the property confiscated should finally rest with the United States.[19] This less stringent measure received considerable support, but general discussion continued for two weeks before the Senate came to a vote on the proposal. At that time, the amendment was adopted by a vote of 26 to 11. Seven Republicans, two Unionists, and two Democrats opposed the measure. The opposition was a conglomeration of diehard opponents of any confiscation legislation (e.g., Saulsbury of Delaware) and radicals who demanded a stronger bill (e.g., Wade of Ohio).[20]

16. Detroit *Daily Advertiser,* March 12, 26, 1862; Boston *Post,* March 12, 17, 25, April 1, May 1, 18, 1862.

17. *Cong. Globe,* 37th Cong., 2nd Sess., pp. 1557–1562.

18. *Ibid., passim.* Howard's speech, in particular, seems to have commanded close attention and attracted favorable comment. See *ibid.,* p. 1720; Philadelphia *Inquirer,* April 19, 1862. Among the Republicans opposing the bill were Browning, Collamer, Doolittle, Fessenden, Foster, Hale, Harris, Sherman, and Ten Eyck. Of the negative speeches, Collamer's was considered the most effective. See Timothy O. Howe to Grace T. Howe, May 6, 1862, typed copy in Timothy O. Howe Papers, State Historical Society of Wisconsin.

19. *Cong. Globe,* 37th Cong., 2nd Sess., p. 1604.

20. *Ibid.,* pp. 1808–1814. Those senators opposing Sherman's amendment, in addition to those named above, were Carlile, King, James H. Lane, Morrill, Pomeroy, Stark, Trumbull, Wilkinson, and Robert Wilson.

When consideration of the measure was resumed on April 29, Cowan moved the reference of the bill and all amendments to a select committee of seven. This proposal was hotly debated the following day, with the major opposition coming from Wilmot, Hale, Wade, and Clark, all of whom undoubtedly feared a weakening of the measure. Cowan, McDougall, and Carlile favored such action, but the opponents had their way and the motion was defeated, 18 to 22. One Unionist (Wright of Indiana) joined with twenty-one Republicans in opposing reference, while seven Republicans, seven Democrats, and four Unionists supported the motion. The defeat of the proposition seems to have been largely the result of an indiscreet speech (somewhat vitriolic in tone) which Cowan made against the bill on April 30. This apparently made the ardent supporters of confiscation unwilling to entrust the measure's fate to a committee which, in accordance with senatorial practice, Cowan would head.[21]

So the debate was resumed. The pending question was a substitute submitted by Collamer of Vermont requiring the individual conviction of rebels on charges of treason before their property could be seized. Even then, only property sufficient to pay the fine imposed could be taken. Slaves of such persons would be emancipated, and the President was also authorized (but not required) to declare free the slaves of rebels in areas where the rebellion continued for six months after the passage of the bill.[22]

Much of the opposition to the creation of a select committee had come from senators who favored more stringent measures than any yet presented to the Senate. As the debate proceeded, however, it became apparent that only a minority of the senators would support the radical viewpoint. Irritation mounted on both sides as the extremists found themselves unable to bend the Senate to their will.

Henry Wilson lashed out at the border-state senators with the assertion that "Slavery and treason this day and this hour in this country are one and the same."[23] Wade concurred, charging that those senators who

21. *Ibid.*, pp. 1856–1861, 1873–1886; Timothy O. Howe to Grace T. Howe, May 6, 1862, typed copy in Timothy O. Howe Papers, State Historical Society of Wisconsin. Among those supporting reference was the Republican Senate leader, Fessenden of Maine.

22. *Cong. Globe*, 37th Cong., 2nd Sess., p. 1895.

23. *Ibid.*

questioned the constitutionality of confiscation measures aided the rebels. Turning to the senators from the slave states, he declared,

You cannot escape from this war without the emancipation of your negroes. . . . I see the hand of God taking hold of your own delinquency to overrule for good what your rulers meant for evil. Pro-slavery men seem to suppose that the Ruler of the universe is a pro-slavery Being; but if I have not mistaken Him greatly, He is at least a gradual emancipationist. [Laughter.][24]

This provoked an intemperate reply from Saulsbury of Delaware, who condemned abolitionist agitation as the cause of the war and asserted that the Negroes, if freed, would be re-enslaved. Taking a strong white-supremacy line, he proclaimed:

We mean that the United States of America . . . shall be the white man's home; and not only the white man's home, but the white man shall govern, and the nigger [*sic*] never shall be his equal. [Applause in the galleries.][25]

But all senators were not as certain as Wilson and Saulsbury as to the proper course to pursue. "The confiscation bill," wrote Senator Howe, "has annoyed me . . . because . . . I have been painfully conscious it was charged with terrible consequences for good or evil. . . . I knew that to be wrong upon that subject was to be terribly wrong." Many of Howe's colleagues shared his agonizing indecision, and the immediate prospect before the Senate was a long and acrimonious dispute culminating in no confiscation bill at all, or one unsatisfactory to many senators. Consequently, there was amazingly little opposition from the floor when, on May 6, Clark of New Hampshire renewed the proposition to refer the entire problem to a select committee. The number of members was set at nine and the motion to create the committee carried by a vote of 24 to 14. The opposition consisted of thirteen Republicans and Unionist Wright of Indiana. Six Republicans who had earlier voted against raising such a committee now supported the motion.[26]

24. *Ibid.,* pp. 1918–1919.

25. *Ibid.,* pp. 1922–1923.

26. *Ibid.,* pp. 1954–1965; Timothy O. Howe to Grace T. Howe, May 6, 1862, typed copy in Timothy O. Howe Papers, State Historical Society of Wisconsin. The six who changed their votes were Anthony of Rhode Island, Clark of New Hampshire, Harris of New York, Morrill of Maine, and Sumner and Wilson of Massachusetts.

On the following day, Senator Foot, the President pro tem of the Senate, appointed Clark chairman of the select committee. Other Republicans on the committee were Collamer of Vermont, Cowan of Pennsylvania, Harlan of Iowa, Harris of New York, Sherman of Ohio, and Wilson of Massachusetts. The minority members were Democrat Henderson of Missouri and Unionist Willey of Virginia.[27] Henderson and Willey might reasonably be expected to oppose practically any confiscation measure; Clark, Collamer, Cowan, and Sherman had all urged amendments to make the original bill less stringent; and only Harlan, Harris, and Wilson were supporters of anything as strong as the bill originally reported from the Committee on the Judiciary. All in all, the raising of the select committee would seem to be a victory for the moderates.

This supposition was partially borne out when the confiscation bill (S. No. 310) was reported on May 14. The committee had taken Collamer's bill—the weakest proposal to come before the Senate—as a point of departure. To this proposition, the committee had added a section authorizing the forfeiture of all property upon conviction of engaging in or inciting an insurrection. The President was authorized to seize the property of certain classes of rebels and hold it until judicial proceedings were completed and judgments satisfied. Proceedings in rem and the forfeiture of property without the conviction of the owner were authorized only in certain specific and narrowly circumscribed instances. The committee had also incorporated Collamer's proposal authorizing the President to declare the slaves of rebels free after issuing a warning proclamation. Furthermore, the slaves of certain classes of rebels who failed to answer to an indictment were to be emancipated, and the return of fugitive slaves was forbidden except on proof of the owner's loyalty. A major sop to the radicals was the section permitting the President to enlist Negro troops.

27. *Cong. Globe,* 37th Cong., 2nd Sess., p. 1991. Foot appointed Trumbull to the committee, but he insisted on being excused and Harlan was appointed in his place. Trumbull may well have viewed the raising of the committee as a personal affront, for he had been the chairman of the committee which had originally reported the bill, and it was generally considered to have been largely Trumbull's work. The normal course in the event of a deadlock on the floor would have been to recommit the measure to the committee which reported it with instructions as to the desired changes.

All in all, the committee measure, while stronger than Collamer's bill, was still wholly unsatisfactory to the extremist senators.[28]

The fact that the radicals never intended to allow this bill to come to a vote was obvious from the first. While the border-state senators contented themselves with offering amendments and briefly defending them, the radical senators made lengthy speeches and supported any dilatory motion. Finally, on May 21, the bill was postponed indefinitely to take up other legislation.[29] The explanation for this action can be found in the proceedings of the House of Representatives.

Early in March, various rumors were heard regarding the status of the House measures. "The House Judiciary Committee, it is said, have abandoned all their confiscation and emancipation schemes, on the ground of their unconstitutionality," reported the Washington correspondent of one important eastern paper. This proved to be essentially correct. It was not until March 20, 1862, that the House Committee on the Judiciary made its report. When Hickman of Pennsylvania finally reported the five bills, six joint resolutions, and four House resolutions involved, it was with the recommendation that they not pass. Pendleton moved that they be tabled, but no action was taken at this time. More than a month later, on April 22, after some time spent in reading the measures, Pendleton's motion was defeated and the House took up the first of the bills.[30]

It was immediately apparent that the measures reported from the committee would have rough going in the House. The initial bill was completely changed and then postponed for a week. The second measure was then considered, entirely transformed by amendment, and tabled on the following day. Such actions irritated the radicals beyond measure and prompted Stevens to imply that "the rebels have a majority in this House."[31]

As soon as the second bill had been disposed of, Olin of New York moved that the rest of the measures be referred to a select committee of

28. *Ibid.,* pp. 2112, 2165.

29. *Ibid.,* pp. 2163–2173, 2188–2205, 2217–2230, 2250–2254.

30. *Ibid.,* pp. 1303, 1682, 1698, 1766–1767; New York *Times,* March 3, 1862. See also Philadelphia *Inquirer,* March 3, 1862.

31. *Cong. Globe,* 37th Cong., 2nd Sess., pp. 1767–1772, 1788. Quotation from p. 1770.

seven. This proposal attracted considerable support, but it also ignited violent attacks on the opponents of the confiscation bills by various radical Republicans. These assaults drew from Crittenden a speech, characterized by one observer as "his best effort during the session," in which he pleaded for unity of purpose and the avoidance of divisive issues.[32] However much Olin's proposal might enrage the radicals, it apparently offered the only avenue by which any confiscation legislation could be pushed through the House. Consequently, at a Republican House caucus that night (April 23), it was decided that the bills would be so referred.[33]

This decision may have been, in part, the result of a belief that public opinion in the North would not yet support sweeping confiscation measures. The New York *Times* was an excellent weathervane paper for moderate pro-Administration opinion and had earlier supported confiscation of rebel property in principle. A decidedly different tone was evident, however, when the *Times* commented editorially on the bills before the House:

> If the power of confiscation reside in Congress at all, and should be exercised, the time for its exertion has not yet arrived. . . .
>
> It is safe to say the feeling of the Northern people is strongly adverse to these premature, ill-considered and sweeping manifestations of resentment. . . .
>
> Let Congress leave the future to take care of itself. Let it give strength, efficiency and success to the army, and let it support the Executive and Judiciary in the enforcement of anti-treason statutes already existing, and it need waste no more time upon confiscation bills.[34]

On April 24, after the House had listened in resigned silence to a bitter attack on slavery by the ultra-radical Lovejoy, Olin's motion was passed

32. *Ibid.*, pp. 1788–1805; New York *Herald*, April 23, 1862. Republican John A. Gurley of Ohio had tried to raise such a select committee on December 9, 1861, but his attempt had failed. See *Cong. Globe*, 37th Cong., 2nd Sess., pp. 35–36.

33. New York *Herald*, April 24, 1862; Washington *National Intelligencer*, April 24, 1862. Roscoe Conkling denied the next day that the caucus had considered the matter, but the subsequent activities of the Republicans in the House cast grave doubt on the truth of this assertion. See *Cong. Globe*, 37th Cong., 2nd Sess., p. 1819.

34. New York *Times*, April 24, 1862. See also Boston *Post*, March 17, 25, April 1, 1862.

by a vote of 90 to 31.[35] The creation of the select committee did not entirely dishearten the proponents of confiscation legislation. As the representatives struggled to frame an acceptable measure, the Detroit *Daily Advertiser* hopefully asserted, "The impression seems to be gaining ground that a stringent confiscation and emancipation bill will be passed by the present Congress. . . . While it would be the most fatal blow that could be delt [*sic*] the rebels, it would afford incalculable relief to the loyal men of the nation."[36]

But the Congressional opponents of confiscation wasted no time in marshaling their forces. On Saturday afternoon, May 10, a self-styled "Conservative Caucus" was held in the hall of the House of Representatives. At that time the twenty-two Democrats, twenty Unionists, and one Republican (Kellogg of Illinois) present declared their opposition to confiscation and emancipation legislation and appointed a committee to recommend further action. Though to the modern reader the name might suggest a right-wing body, this group clearly spoke for the moderate bloc in Congress, for neither radicals nor extreme Peace Democrats (e.g., Vallandigham, May, and Wood) attended. The caucus included almost one quarter of the House membership (only three senators were present), and almost as many non-Republican members did not attend. This show of strength greatly encouraged the conservative Republicans, most of whom found it politically inexpedient to attend the caucus.[37]

35. *Cong. Globe,* 37th Cong., 2nd Sess., pp. 1815–1820. Four days later the Speaker announced the membership of the committee—Republicans Olin of New York, Eliot of Massachusetts, Beaman of Michigan, and Hutchins of Ohio, Unionist Mallory of Kentucky, and Democrat Cobb of New Jersey. But Olin, when he had introduced the motion to raise the committee, had declared that he did not wish to be a member. He now asked to be excused and his place was taken by Sedgwick of New York. Normally, the representative making a motion to raise a select committee was made chairman of that committee when raised. Olin's statement, therefore, was intended as a repudiation on his part of any desire for personal political profit in this matter. See *ibid.,* pp. 1846, 1861.

36. Detroit *Daily Advertiser,* May 6, 1862.

37. New York *Herald,* May 11, 1862; Washington *National Intelligencer,* May 10, 12, 1862; Boston *Post,* May 13, 1862; San Francisco *Daily Alta California,* June 10, 1862. The New York *Herald* (May 14, 1862) said that the caucus consisted of twenty-seven Unionists, thirteen Democrats, and two Republicans. My analysis of the identical lists of participants printed in the New York

Four days after the caucus meeting, Eliot reported two bills from the select committee—a confiscation bill (H.R. No. 471) and an emancipation bill (H.R. No. 472). The confiscation bill provided for the immediate seizure of the property of the Confederate leaders. Sixty days after the President should issue a warning proclamation, the property of all those who continued to participate in or support the rebellion would also be subject to confiscation. Though judicial proceedings were required, placing property owners on trial was not necessary, for proceedings in rem and under prize law were authorized. The emancipation bill was sufficiently broad in its scope to affect practically all slaveholders. The Second Session of the Congress was now some five and one-half months old and —it being an election year—few representatives desired to prolong the session. It was unanimously agreed, therefore, that beginning on May 20, the measures would be debated jointly, and on May 26 a final vote would be taken on both proposals.[38]

During the week set aside for the discussion of the bills, twenty Republicans and one Democrat (Noell of Missouri) made speeches favoring the measures, and four other Republicans received permission to print supporting remarks on the day the final vote was taken. Noell's defense of the bills was admittedly somewhat apologetic and was apparently confined to the confiscation bill, though he did not specifically condemn the emancipation proposal. Five Democrats, seven Unionists, and three Republicans (Thomas and Train of Massachusetts, and Eliakim P. Walton of Vermont) made speeches in opposition to the measures, and remarks in the same vein were printed by four other Democrats and Unionists. In addition, Spaulding of New York made a rather noncommittal speech, while Kerrigan of New York, in some printed remarks, supported the confiscation bill while opposing the emancipation measure.

Herald (May 11, 1862), Washington *National Intelligencer* (May 12, 1862), and Boston *Post* (May 13, 1862), however, convinces me that the party division in the caucus was as indicated above. The caucus committee concluded to take no further action except to appoint a committee to manage opposition on the floor if this became necessary. See New York *Herald,* May 14, 1862; Washington *National Intelligencer,* May 15, 1862.

38. *Cong. Globe,* 37th Cong., 2nd Sess., pp. 2128, 2232–2233. The committee members apparently believed that the chances of obtaining approval for the confiscation bill were considerably greater if the emancipation clauses were not attached to it.

All in all, thirty-seven speeches were made in the House during a five-day period. To accommodate the members, evening sessions were held, lasting until 11:45 on May 22 and until 9:20 on May 23. The unusual Saturday session was devoted almost entirely to these addresses (delivered for the most part to empty benches) and lasted until 9:15 that night.[39] It is doubtful that anyone's mind or vote was changed by these speeches, but the necessary "record" had been made.

From the first, little hope had apparently been entertained for amending the bills. Two amendments were introduced to the confiscation bill, but on May 26 these were defeated by large margins, and the measure, in its original form, was passed by a vote of 82 to 68. Two Virginia Unionists (Brown and Whaley) and one Democrat (Noell of Missouri) joined with seventy-nine Republicans in supporting the bill. Nine Republicans, however, were to be found in the opposition. The Massachusetts delegation in particular seems to have had difficulty in swallowing the measure, for five Republicans from that state voted nay.[40]

The emancipation bill did not fare so well. Four amendments were quickly beaten by large margins, but on the final vote the measure went down to defeat, 74 to 78. All of the affirmative votes were Republican, but not all of the Republican votes were affirmative. The nine members of the majority party who had opposed the confiscation bill were now joined by seven others, all from states having a common boundary with at least one slave state.[41]

The negative votes of these conservative or legalistic Republicans

39. *Ibid.*, pp. 2232–2246, 2265–2274, 2292–2305, 2323–2327, 2341, 2356, Appendix, 146–157, 162–227, 232–242, 259–268, 271–277; New York *Herald,* May 24, 1862. Democrat Robert H. Nugen of Ohio apparently felt it necessary to produce a speech for home consumption. But lacking either time or ability to prepare an address, he had printed under his name some remarks made a month earlier by his colleague William Allen. Cf. *Cong. Globe,* 37th Cong., 2nd Sess., Appendix, pp. 119, 123, 239–242.

40. *Cong. Globe,* 37th Cong., 2nd Sess., pp. 2360–2361. The five Massachusetts Republican dissenters were Dawes, Delano, Rice, Thomas, and Train. Diven of New York, Granger of Michigan, Horton of Ohio, and Nixon of New Jersey cast the other negative Republican votes.

41. *Ibid.*, pp. 2361–2363. For further discussion of the emancipation bill, see Chapter 3. The seven additional Republicans casting negative votes were Dunn, Mitchell, and Porter of Indiana, Kellogg of Illinois, Killinger of Pennsylvania, Stratton of New Jersey, and Trimble of Ohio.

naturally occasioned considerable opposition in their home states. "The course of our politicians in Congress . . . must from time to time pass in review," suggested one Massachusetts radical ominously to the governor of the Bay State. "You were doubtless in Mass. as much astounded at the vote of some of the Delegation as any here [in Washington]." *"Restoration,"* he later wrote disgustedly, "is the result to which this all tends."[42]

As has been noted, consideration of confiscation legislation had ceased in the Senate when the nature of the bill reported from the House select committee became known. To get the measure before the Senate, however, and to pass it in substantially the same form that it came from the House were two entirely different things. For there was no reason to presume that House passage of a bill would move the conservative and moderate senators to modify their views. The upper house took up the bill on June 23, and no sooner had it been read than Clark introduced, as a substitute, the measure reported from the Senate select committee.[43] Clark, speaking for a large bloc of moderate Republicans, had made his position crystal clear on June 20, when he had tried to get his colleagues to resume consideration of the Senate measure. When Sumner opposed this course and urged the consideration of the House bill instead, Clark stated bluntly, "I can vote for this [S. No. 310], and I cannot and will not vote for the House bill."[44]

Only four days (June 24, 25, 27, and 28) were devoted to this final Senate discussion of the confiscation measure. Saulsbury opened the debate with a lengthy and bitter attack on the bill, the Republican Party, and abolitionists. No other Democrat or Unionist took the floor, choosing rather to watch from the sidelines (probably with some glee) as the members of the majority party clashed in the arena.[45] During the debate, the senators addressed themselves more to the question of the powers of Congress than to the merits of the House bill or Clark's substitute. The

42. [Charles] Ingersoll to John A. Andrew, June 6, 12, 1862, John A. Andrew Papers, Massachusetts Historical Society.

43. *Cong. Globe,* 37th Cong., 2nd Sess., pp. 2878–2879. The select committees on confiscation in both houses had made their report on the same day, May 14, 1862.

44. *Ibid.,* pp. 2842–2843.

45. *Ibid.,* pp. 2896–2903, 2917–2933, 2959–2975, 2989–3006, Appendix, 303–307.

basis for this line of discussion was laid when, in the first speech in defense of the House bill, Howard of Michigan asserted that Congress had no constitutional power to order judicial proceedings against rebel property, but that through their control of the army they could bring the war power into play.[46] This stand evoked protesting speeches from Browning, Dixon, and Hale, who insisted that the "war power" could not bear on the southerners because, secession having been invalid, they were still citizens of the United States. Hale did, however, refer to Congress as the "supreme power."[47]

Irritated as they were by their inability to bend Lincoln to their will on the emancipation question, the radicals' inevitable next step was an assertion of congressional supremacy over the executive. Fittingly enough, "Bluff Ben" Wade led the attack. "Congress," he declared, "the legislative power sitting superior to him [the President] or any other magistrate in the nation, may regulate, modify, and direct whatever principles they please their chief commander shall act upon and execute."[48] Sumner, the haughty, polished leader of the New England abolitionists, was equally vehement, asserting that "he [the President] is only the instrument of Congress, under the Constitution of the United States."[49]

Lincoln's friend from Illinois, Senator Browning, vigorously dissented. Congress, he insisted, could raise, support, and disband armies, but here its power and authority ceased. "Congress can exercise no power relating to war or peace," he declared, "that is not expressly granted to it by the Constitution."[50]

Trumbull undertook to discuss the differences between the two bills and twitted the border-state senators for preferring Clark's substitute, a bill that authorized the President to arm slaves. He declared the substitute to be totally ineffective as a confiscation measure. His association with Lincoln in Illinois did not prevent Trumbull from condemning the President for appointing military governors without congressional approval. His stand elicited from Dixon the observation that "The Senator from Illinois has, at last, unmasked himself as an opponent of this

46. *Ibid.,* Appendix, pp. 303–307.
47. *Ibid.,* pp. 2917–2928.
48. *Ibid.,* p. 2930.
49. *Ibid.,* p. 2964.
50. *Ibid.,* pp. 2966, 2969–2970; quotation from p. 2966.

Administration." Trumbull denied this, though adhering to his views on the question of appointing military governors.[51]

On the final day of debate, as in Committee of the Whole, Wilkinson upheld the radical position in support of the House bill and singled out Browning for special castigation as being "sensitive when the interests of traitors are attacked." Cowan made the closing speech in support of Clark's substitute, favoring it because it would not alienate the loyal slave states.[52] Sumner then introduced an amendment admitting Negro testimony in all proceedings arising from the bill. This proposal was quickly defeated by a vote of 14 to 25.[53] The substitute was then adopted, 21 to 17. Voting in the affirmative were fifteen Republicans, three northern Democrats, and two Unionists and a Democrat from the border states. The opposition consisted of fifteen Republicans and two diehard opponents of any confiscation bill—Wilson of Missouri and Wright of Indiana. Six of the border-state senators were not present for the vote.[54] The measure, as amended, was now reported to the Senate.

In the Senate, Trumbull and Wade launched last-ditch attacks on the bill, which involved them in a controversy with Fessenden as to whether the measure, as it now stood, was "a true Republican bill." Trumbull insisted that the substitute would never have been adopted if only Republicans had been in the Senate.[55] The Senate, however, concurred in the amendment and then passed the bill by a vote of 28 to 13. Republicans cast twenty-seven of the twenty-eight affirmative votes, and this included thirteen of those who had opposed the substitute. The opposition consisted of seven border-state senators, one northern Unionist, two northern

51. *Ibid.,* pp. 2970–2973; quotation from p. 2973.

52. *Ibid.,* pp. 2990–2993; quotation from p. 2990.

53. *Ibid.,* p. 2995. The fourteen supporters of the amendment were Republicans Chandler of Michigan, Grimes of Iowa, Harlan of Iowa, Howard of Michigan, Howe of Wisconsin, King of New York, Lane of Kansas, Morrill of Maine, Pomeroy of Kansas, Sumner of Massachusetts, Trumbull of Illinois, Wade of Ohio, Wilkinson of Minnesota, and Wilmot of Pennsylvania.

54. *Ibid.,* p. 2996. Absent from the Senate were Bayard, Carlile, Kennedy, Latham, McDougall, Pearce, Powell, Saulsbury, Thomson, and Henry Wilson.

55. *Ibid.,* pp. 2998–3005. As a matter of fact, the Republicans in the Senate had split 15 to 15 on Clark's substitute. Trumbull's assertion, however, has one grain of truth in it. Had Henry Wilson been able to attend the Senate he would undoubtedly have opposed the substitute.

Democrats, and three Republicans—Browning of Illinois, who opposed the passage of any confiscation legislation, and Chandler and Howard of Michigan, who thought the bill too weak.[56]

On the same day that the measure passed the Senate, the conservatives in the lower house held a caucus to consolidate the opposition. The meeting adopted resolutions supporting the war and opposing confiscation and emancipation proposals. The influence of the gathering was somewhat weakened, however, by a relatively light attendance and the complete absence of any Republicans. This caucus was, in fact, much more heavily Democratic than that of the previous month.[57]

When the House took up the amended confiscation bill on July 3, 1862, Crisfield of Maryland moved to table the amendment. Since this action would have carried the bill into the congressional graveyard, the motion was decisively beaten. The House then voted overwhelmingly against concurring in the Senate amendment and sent the measure back to the Senate.[58] On July 8, Clark moved that the Senate insist on its amendment and call for a committee of conference. Sherman countered with a motion to recede from the Senate amendment. Only fourteen senators—mostly radical and advanced moderate Republicans—could be mustered in support of Sherman's motion, however, and the Senate then voted to call for a committee of conference.[59] The president pro tem appointed Clark, Harris, and Wright Senate members of this committee. None of these could be counted as supporters of a strong confiscation bill.[60] When, on the same day, this intelligence was communicated to the

56. *Ibid.*, p. 3006. The other affirmative vote was cast by Unionist Willey of Virginia.

57. Philadelphia *Inquirer*, June 28, 30, 1862; New York *Herald*, June 29, 1862. Some non-Democrats obviously thought that they detected a partisan purpose in the caucuses. See William P. Sheffield to Salmon P. Chase, July 9, 1862, Salmon P. Chase Papers, Historical Society of Pennsylvania.

58. *Cong. Globe*, 37th Cong., 2nd Sess., pp. 3106–3107.

59. *Ibid.*, p. 3166. The opposition to Clark's motion consisted of five Unionists, two Democrats, and three Republicans (James H. Lane, Trumbull, and Wilkinson). The Democrats and Unionists probably felt confident that Lincoln would veto the House bill.

60. *Ibid.* Wright's position at this juncture is difficult to determine. His votes on the measure when it was being considered in the Senate ten days earlier would seem to brand him as an opponent of any confiscation bill, but his votes on the

House, Eliot overrode the delaying tactics of Democratic representatives John S. Phelps of Missouri and William Allen of Ohio and quickly pushed through a motion agreeing to a committee of conference. The Speaker appointed Republicans Eliot of Massachusetts and Wilson of Iowa, and Democrat Corning of New York to this committee.[61]

The House radicals had, in the meantime, initiated a series of Republican caucuses which met on July 7, 8, 10, and 12. The primary purpose of these meetings, which only a few senators attended, was to prepare an address for use in the ensuing congressional campaign, but it seems highly probable that the gatherings were also designed to secure support for the House version of the confiscation bill. But once again the radicals found themselves in a minority. Even the final version of the campaign address was decidedly moderate in tone.[62]

Thus the conference committee was not harassed by radical pressures at odds with the predominant moderate temper of both houses. Under these circumstances, the committee took but a short time to reach a decision, and on July 11, Eliot reported its recommendations to the House. This report struck out two thirds of the Senate bill, leaving the sections dealing with confiscation as a punishment for treason and inciting an insurrection, the nonreturn of fugitives, the enlistment of Negro troops, and the colonization of freed slaves. The sections authorizing the seizure of rebel property were taken from the House bill but were generally somewhat weakened. Proceedings in rem were now required in all cases rather than permitted in a few instances, but proceedings under prize law were no longer authorized. The committee also inserted a new section emancipating the slaves of persons hereafter engaging in or aiding the rebellion. The proposed bill was, in short, a thoroughgoing compromise.[63]

Mallory of Kentucky and Cox of Ohio insisted that this was new

---

two roll calls on July 8 were identical with those of James H. Lane, Trumbull, and Wilkinson. He was apparently undergoing a change of heart and eventually supported the confiscation bill reported by the committee of conference.

61. *Ibid.*, pp. 3178, 3187–3188. Eliot and Wilson had supported the House confiscation bill while Corning had opposed it.

62. New York *Herald*, July 9, 10, 11, 13, 14, 1862; Philadelphia *Inquirer*, July 9, 11, 1862; Washington *National Intelligencer*, July 11, 14, 1862.

63. *Cong. Globe*, 37th Cong., 2nd Sess., pp. 3266–3267. Cf. *ibid.*, pp. 2878–2879.

legislation and that the committee of conference had thus exceeded its powers. On this point of order they tried to block consideration of the report, but they were overruled by the Speaker. A tabling motion was beaten down, and the report was adopted by a vote of 82 to 42. Four border-state Unionists joined seventy-eight Republicans in support of the measure. Negative votes were cast by forty Democrats and Unionists and Republicans Granger of Michigan and Thomas of Massachusetts.[64]

The Senate received the committee report on the following day, and McDougall, observing that there seemed to him to be a good deal of new legislation embodied in the report, moved that it lie on the table and be printed. Clark, who had reported the measure, strenuously resisted this. Saulsbury raised the same point of order that Mallory and Cox had raised in the House, and with identical results. The opponents of confiscation made no attempt to prevent Senate action on the report, however; McDougall's motion was soundly defeated, and the report was adopted by a vote of 27 to 12. The only non-Republican affirmative vote was cast by Wright; and two Republicans—Browning of Illinois and Cowan of Pennsylvania—joined with ten Democrats and Unionists in opposing the adoption of the report.[65]

The confiscation legislation that was finally passed was the result of repeated compromises, most of which were unsatisfactory to the radicals. Both the House and Senate bills were substantially weaker than many members desired, and the conference committee version was less stringent than the House bill. Indeed, many of the radicals declared the final measure to be utterly impracticable and regarded its passage as at least a partial defeat.[66]

There were others, however, who voiced grave constitutional objections to the bill. Browning, convinced that the measure was unconstitutional, was actively urging Lincoln to veto it.[67] He found the President sympa-

64. *Ibid.*, pp. 3266–3268. The four border-state supporters of the measure were Blair of Virginia, Casey of Kentucky, Fisher of Delaware, and Maynard of Tennessee.

65. *Ibid.*, pp. 3275–3276. One Republican affirmative vote (Howe of Wisconsin) and one Democratic negative vote (Stark of Oregon) were recorded later in the day by unanimous consent. See *ibid.*, pp. 3276, 3287.

66. New York *Herald*, July 14, 1862.

67. Browning, *op. cit.* (July 14, 1862), I, 588.

thetic to his viewpoint, and it was soon bruited about that a veto message was being prepared. Hearing these rumors, Fessenden, the Senate Republican leader, called on Lincoln to ascertain the nature of his objections.[68]

It developed that the President's major reservation involved a constitutional issue—the bill provided for the forfeiture of real estate beyond the lifetime of the offender and this, Lincoln contended, was forbidden by the letter and spirit of the Constitution. He also feared that injustice might result from the indiscriminate use of in rem proceedings. Fessenden characterized the President's position as "mad." "Well," he wrote sourly, "we have what we barginned [*sic*] for, a splitter of rails, and have no right to complain."[69]

In order to give Congress a chance to act on the measure if he should return it, Lincoln requested both houses to postpone their adjournment from July 16 to July 17. In response to a query from the president pro tem of the Senate as to the reason for this unusual request, Lincoln indicated that a veto was likely. Both houses agreed to the extension.[70]

Some legislators saw other constitutional objections to the bill. Among them was Representative Horace Maynard of Tennessee, who, shortly before adjournment on July 15, obtained a suspension of the rules and introduced a joint resolution (H.R. No. 110) declaring that the act was not intended to be retroactive in its effect. Maynard's action could hardly have been inspired by any knowledge of Lincoln's views, for the President specifically stated that he considered the act entirely prospective in nature. Furthermore, the possibility of a veto was never mentioned in the brief discussion which preceded the passage of the resolution.[71]

68. William P. Fessenden to Hamilton Fish, July 15, 1862, Hamilton Fish Papers, Library of Congress; White, *Trumbull,* p. 175; *Cong. Globe,* 37th Cong., 2nd Sess., pp. 3375–3376.

69. Abraham Lincoln, "Message of July 17, 1862," in Richardson, *Messages and Papers,* VI, 85–86; William P. Fessenden to Hamilton Fish, July 15, 1862, Hamilton Fish Papers, Library of Congress.

70. Abraham Lincoln to Solomon Foot, July 15, 1862, Abraham Lincoln to Galusha A. Grow, July 15, 1862, both in Nicolay and Hay, *Lincoln's Works,* VII, 279; Solomon Foot to Abraham Lincoln, July 15, 1862, Lincoln Papers, Library of Congress; Abraham Lincoln to Solomon Foot, July 15, 1862, in Gilbert A. Tracy (editor), *Uncollected Letters of Abraham Lincoln,* p. 209; *Cong. Globe,* 37th Cong., 2nd Sess., pp. 3352, 3366–3367.

71. *Cong. Globe,* 37th Cong., 2nd Sess., p. 3370.

When Maynard's resolution reached the floor of the Senate on the following day, Clark moved an amendment stating that the act should not be construed to authorize the forfeiture of real estate beyond the lifetime of the offender. Trumbull voiced strong opposition to this proposal, saying that a life interest in real estate amounted to nothing. Clark replied with a cryptic observation that "It may be sometimes desirable to secure as much as we can, if we cannot get all we wish." Sherman, thereupon, demanded to know by what authority such a statement was made. Clark replied evasively that "it may be that there may be objections to the bill as it now stands, somewhere, and it may be that an amendment like this will cure the difficulty and enable us to get over it." As Sherman continued to press for a direct answer, however, Clark admitted that the amendment was framed to overcome a known objection of the President.[72]

This admission drew the cork on the barely repressed irritation of the radical senators, and bitter condemnation of "executive interference" poured forth. Henry S. Lane opposed surrender to "the dictation of any President," and Wade said of the course advocated by Clark, "it is disgraceful; it is a total surrender of the dignity of this body; it is an unconstitutional submission." He added later that the adoption of the amendment would be "destructive of the independence of the Senate."[73] In vain did Clark insist that the President had no desire to interfere and Fessenden assert that he had sought out Lincoln and obtained his views solely as a matter of common sense. King and Trumbull joined the hue and cry as the Democrats sat back and watched the Senate Republicans hold a grand public laundry of their dirty linen. But in the end, only eight Republicans could be found to join with seven Democrats and Unionists in opposition to Clark's amendment, which was passed by a vote of 25 to 15. The resolution, as amended, was agreed to without a division.[74]

When the joint resolution was returned to the House, no question of presidential interference was raised. The amendment was concurred in by

72. *Ibid.,* pp. 3373–3374; quotations from p. 3374.

73. *Ibid.,* pp. 3374–3383; quotations from pp. 3374, 3375, 3382.

74. *Ibid.,* pp. 3374–3383. The eight Republicans who voted against the amendment were Grimes and Harlan of Iowa, King of New York, Lane of Indiana, Trumbull of Illinois, Wade of Ohio, Wilkinson of Minnesota, and Wilmot of Pennsylvania.

a vote of 83 to 21 and no one challenged the wisdom or desirability of approving the modification, though such dedicated radicals as Stevens and Bingham voted against concurrence.[75]

It may be that Lincoln was stung by the references made during the Senate debate to the desirability of fixing on the President the responsibility for the failure of the confiscation bill. In any event, when he informed the House that he had signed the bill and the accompanying joint resolution, he specifically stated that he would have withheld his approval of the measure if the explanatory resolution and not been passed. Lincoln also transmitted to the House a copy of the veto message which he had prepared prior to the passage of the resolution. This message provoked no comment though the radical element in the House received it with visible disapproval.[76]

Lincoln's stand, the Philadelphia *Inquirer* approvingly declared, was "a signal illustration of the sterling conservatism of the President." The extreme Republicans undoubtedly agreed with the assessment, though they would have chosen other adjectives.[77]

Though the radicals professed great dissatisfaction with this act, they made no attempt to push additional confiscation legislation through the Thirty-seventh Congress. The debates on the confiscation bill had revealed that the composition of the Congress made passage of a stronger measure extremely unlikely. While it is true that Lincoln's views on the restraining force of the Constitution were decidedly flexible and subject to considerable change, his determined stand on the modification of the confiscation bill held little promise for presidential approval of a more stringent measure.

Thus, the radicals, who with irritated reluctance had accepted what they had thought was half a loaf, found themselves actually in possession

75. *Ibid.,* p. 3400.

76. *Ibid.,* p. 3406; New York *Herald,* July 18, 1862; Abraham Lincoln, "Message of July 17, 1862," in Nicolay and Hay, *Lincoln's Works,* VII, 280–286. The message definitely embodied the President's personal views. The draft of the message is in his own hand. See Mss. Nos. 17154–17162, Lincoln Papers, Library of Congress. This document has been dated (in pencil) July 17, 1862, but was probably written on either the fifteenth or the sixteenth.

77. Philadelphia *Inquirer,* July 18, 1862.

of only a few crumbs; for the confiscation act, except for those sections freeing the slaves of rebels, was generally acknowledged to be ineffective and unworkable. Even this slight triumph was soon to be submerged by the Emancipation Proclamation. Their burning hope for a radical economic reconstruction of the South turned to ashes.

But the defeat of stringent confiscation legislation was not without present significance or future importance. All of these discussions made obvious the fact that an overwhelming majority of the Republicans made a wide distinction between property rights in slaves and other personal property rights: one was a moral issue; the other an economic and legal issue. Even the ultra-radical Wade asserted that his primary interest in confiscation legislation was to secure the emancipation of the slaves. "I care something for the confiscation of the property of the leading rebels;" he added, "but I do not wish to touch the property of the masses of the people."[78]

The extreme radicals, in their demand for widespread confiscation of real estate, seem to have been inspired more by the temporary motives of vindictiveness and a desire for easy revenue than by any basic principles —for overwhelmingly the Republicans shared with the Democrats and the Unionists the belief that private property was sacrosanct. Thus, for all except a very few Republicans at the radical and conservative extremes, the final bill probably represented a more acceptable compromise than many observers realized or than they themselves cared to admit openly. It struck vigorously and directly at slave property, and only moderately (and through judicial process) at other property interests. It is notable that in both houses not a single radical Republican voted against the conference committee report (the confiscation bill in its final form). It is also significant that the most violent of the radicals' speeches were concerned with the question of congressional supremacy, rather than with confiscation per se.

But what of the future? If the near hysteria of wartime could not produce a significant assault on the private property of enemies, what chance was there that, in calmer times, corporate property rights would be challenged? The decades following the Civil War gave the answer—

78. *Cong. Globe,* 37th Cong., 2nd Sess., p. 1895.

none. For if the concept of the "sanctity" of private property be accepted, effective control of predatory corporations becomes extremely difficult, if not absolutely impossible. Such control was unthinkable until corporate property rights became—like property rights in slaves—a moral issue. Here, too, then, even in apparent failure, the Thirty-seventh Congress contributed to the structure of modern America.

CHAPTER 5

Congress and Public Improvements: Public Lands

Perhaps the acts of the Thirty-seventh Congress had more lasting consequences in the field of disposal of the public domain and fostering of public improvements than in any other sphere of activity. Legislation in this area is so inextricably interwoven that a complete separation of public land acts from those dealing with public improvements is extremely difficult. To a number of legislators, some of the measures appeared to be mutually incompatible; in other cases, a considerable amount of log-rolling and vote-trading was in evidence. As a result of the very considerable differences of opinion within the ranks of the majority party—and in the entire Congress—a conglomerate mass of legislation emerged. Bearing not the vaguest relationship to a logical policy, it was, nevertheless, destined to have far-reaching effects on the American society and economy.

The Homestead Act

To the casual observer, it would seem that the election of 1860 made nothing more certain than the passage of a homestead bill. For fifteen years, agitation for such a measure had been growing. The House had repeatedly passed such legislation in the fifties, only to see it die in the Senate. This last legislative bastion fell in the summer of 1860, but President Buchanan vetoed the resulting measure. In the thirteenth plank of their Chicago platform, the Republicans had specifically demanded homestead legislation, a circumstance that was thought to have played no small part in their victory in the Northwest. With the Republicans in control of both the Senate and the House, and with a Republican president from the Northwest in the White House, surely immediate passage of homestead legislation should have presented no problem. In practice, it was not so simple.[1]

The Special Session of the Thirty-seventh Congress was only four days old when Republican Cyrus Aldrich of Minnesota introduced a homestead bill in the House. This measure was referred to the Committee on Agriculture, but because of the shortness of the session and the restrictions imposed by Holman's resolution, nothing more was heard of the bill during the summer.[2]

Early in the Second Session (December 4, 1861), Lovejoy of Illinois reported Aldrich's bill to the House and demanded the previous question on its passage. In the absence of Republican John F. Potter of Wisconsin, the chairman of the Committee on Public Lands, the ranking Democratic member of that committee, Vallandigham of Ohio, led the fight to prevent immediate action. The House seconded the previous question but refused (58 to 69) to order a vote on the main question. Potter had returned by this time, and he now castigated Lovejoy for bringing before the House in this manner an issue which he knew was being considered by the Committee on Public Lands and which fell within the special purview of that committee. The discussion which followed revealed that the committee was attempting to resolve the apparent conflict between homestead legislation and the anticipated grant of land bounties to veterans of the present war. It also developed that the agriculture committee had yet to hold its first meeting during this session and that Lovejoy had

1. Roy M. Robbins, *Our Landed Heritage: The Public Domain, 1776–1936,* p. 204; Winston, *op. cit.,* pp. 130–139; "1860—Republican Platform," in Cooper, *op. cit.,* Book II, 41–43.

2. *Cong. Globe,* 37th Cong., 1st Sess., pp. 23, *passim.* It would seem that a more natural reference for the homestead bill would have been to the Committee on Public Lands. One can only surmise that Aldrich hoped to reap some personal political capital by having the measure referred to the Committee on Agriculture, of which he was a member. From the viewpoint of practical operations, such reference was not a wise move. Among the nine members of this committee, only Chairman Lovejoy and Shanks, other than Aldrich, could be considered ardent champions of a homestead bill, while the Committee on Public Lands contained a majority of dedicated supporters of such legislation. For committee membership, see *ibid.,* pp. 21–22. Conclusions as to the attitudes of various members are drawn from subsequent votes and speeches. See *Cong. Globe,* 37th Cong., 2nd Sess., *passim.*

not been instructed (as he had asserted) to report the bill. On the motion of Potter, the measure was referred to the Committee on Public Lands.[3]

Potter's committee had not been idle, and on December 10, the Wisconsin representative reported a homestead measure to the House. The bill (H.R. No. 125) provided for the transfer of public lands to individual settlers upon the payment of a ten-dollar entry fee and occupancy of the property for five years. The size of the grant was set at 160 acres of land valued for pre-emption at $1.25 per acre, or 80 acres valued at $2.50 per acre. The recipient was required to be a citizen of the United States (or to have declared his intention of becoming a citizen), to be at least twenty-one years of age or the head of a family. The conflict between land bounties and homestead legislation was resolved by establishing cash bounties of $30 for men serving three months or longer. These bounties could not be assigned to third parties, nor could the bounties or the homesteads be attached for prior debts.[4]

When the House began consideration of the measure on December 18, the cash-bounty provision immediately drew fire from Holman of Indiana. He strongly favored a homestead bill, but thought the soldiers also entitled to land bounties. Republican William Vandever of Iowa, however, insisted that land bounties profited only speculators. Democrat Vallandigham and Republicans Julian of Indiana and Arnold of Illinois joined Potter and Lovejoy in urging immediate action on the bill. These men stressed the fact that the public lands were not now producing any revenue and insisted that the credit of the nation would be increased if these lands were occupied and developed. Other representatives, however, professed to doubt the wisdom of immediate passage. Covode of

3. *Cong. Globe,* 37th Cong., 2nd Sess., p. 14. It seems probable that Lovejoy was motivated primarily by a desire for personal political aggrandizement. The only other logical explanation for his course of action is that he feared that the Committee on Public Lands would support a land-bounty policy at the expense of homestead legislation. Considering the personnel of that committee, such action was, to say the least, unlikely. Senators, too, desired quick action, and on December 9 Harlan introduced a homestead bill in the upper house. See *ibid.,* p. 26.

4. *Ibid.,* pp. 39–40. The fifth section of the act of July 22, 1861, had provided for $100 bounties for men volunteering for two years or more. This act merely extended this provision to those who served for a shorter period of time. See *Cong. Globe,* 37th Cong., 1st Sess., Appendix, pp. 27–28.

Pennsylvania thought the measure should not go into effect until one year after the end of the war, and Edwards of New Hampshire feared that the bill would weaken public credit at a most inopportune time. Justin S. Morrill frankly said that he was opposed to any such legislation at this time and moved to postpone further consideration of the bill until the first Monday in February 1862. Samuel C. Fessenden and "Pig Iron" Kelley thought that the public lands might prove profitable at a later date, and Roscoe Conkling needed more time to consider the relative merits of a land-bounty program and a system of cash bounties. Crittenden flatly urged the abandonment of all agitation for a homestead act and all other legislation not directly related to the prosecution of the war.[5]

Potter expressed surprise at the apparent change of attitude on the part of many Republicans, and both he and Lovejoy declared, probably correctly, that the vote on the postponement motion would disclose the true friends of homestead legislation. For the political consequences of a direct vote against the homestead bill less than a year before a general election were too grave to contemplate, especially by members of a party that had made the necessity of such legislation one of its major platform planks. If the issue could be postponed, however, under the guise of the necessity for prosecuting the war, action on the measure might be avoided indefinitely. The postponement motion carried, 88 to 50.

The vote was almost entirely sectional and bore little relationship to party lines. Among the New England representatives, only Eliot of Massachusetts voted against postponement. In the middle states of New York, Pennsylvania, and New Jersey, all but one of the Democratic and two thirds of the Republican representatives favored postponing the bill. Unionist Whaley of Virginia cast the only border-state vote against the motion, and from the Middle West, only eight representatives (all Republican) favored postponement. All the far western representatives voted to postpone the measure. Statistically, the Democrats gave the homestead bill slightly better support than did the Republicans—41.4 percent of the Democrats opposed the delay, while only 39.6 percent of the majority party cast negative votes.[6]

5. *Cong. Globe,* 37th Cong., 2nd Sess., pp. 132–139.

6. *Ibid.,* pp. 136, 139–140. Observers attributed some of the eastern opposition to the immediate passage of a homestead act to the fear that this would endanger the chances of passing a land-grant college act. In particular, this

Occupied by the consideration of the legal tender bill, appropriation measures, and the Senate amendments to the legal tender proposal, the House did not consider the Homestead bill again until late in February. In the meantime, opponents of such legislation were making an oblique attack on the measure. Early in January, Wickliffe of Kentucky introduced a resolution directing the Committee of Ways and Means to report a bill pledging the proceeds from the sale of public lands for the payment of the national debt. At the insistence of Colfax, however, the resolution was changed to one of inquiry, rather than instruction. About six weeks later, Wickliffe tried to introduce such a bill. No previous notice having been given, however, a suspension of the rules was necessary, and this the House refused to order. Also during mid-February the Senate attached a similar provision to the legal tender bill, but the House rejected this amendment, primarily because many representatives viewed it as a threat to the passage of homestead legislation. The supporters of the homestead measure saw clearly that if the proceeds from the sale of public lands should be pledged to extinguishing the national debt, the opponents of homestead legislation would then contend that the elimination of this revenue would be an act of bad faith. It was already quite clear that many eastern Republicans were seeking an excuse to avoid action on the homestead issue.[7]

The House finally resumed consideration of the homestead bill on February 21, 1862. As the measure came before the House, Speaker Grow took an unprecedented step. For ten years, as a Free-Soil Democrat and a Republican, he had been fighting for homestead legislation on the floor of the House, and in 1859 he had introduced a bill practically identical to the present one. Grow now called Washburne of Illinois to the chair, came down to the floor, and spoke briefly in favor of the immediate passage of the bill. The effect of this dramatic break with tradition is difficult to determine, but it is perhaps significant that no Republican subsequently spoke against the measure or in any way delayed action on it.[8]

---

consideration was thought to have influenced Justin S. Morrill's action in moving to postpone the measure. See New York *Herald,* December 19, 1861.

7. *Cong. Globe,* 37th Cong., 2nd Sess., pp. 229, 773, 859, 889–891.

8. *Ibid.,* pp. 909–910; Robbins, *op. cit.,* p. 206; Benjamin H. Hibbard, *A History of the Public Land Policies,* p. 364; Fuller, *op. cit.,* pp. 149–157. There can be little doubt that Grow deliberately violated tradition to increase the

One week later, the House again took up the homestead bill. Democrats Holman and James A. Craven of Indiana lamented the absence of a land-bounty provision, and Windom of Minnesota made a speech replete with statistics (and pertinent omissions), designed to prove that a homestead policy would produce more revenue than land sales. Two minor amendments were then adopted, and Potter called the previous question on the passage of the bill. The measure received House approval by an overwhelming majority. Only sixteen representatives—seven Democrats and nine Unionists—voted against the bill.[9]

The Senate received the measure on March 3 and referred it to the Committee on Public Lands, headed by Harlan of Iowa. The other Republican members were Clark of New Hampshire and Pomeroy of Kansas. Democrats Rice of Minnesota, Johnson of Tennessee, and Nesmith of Oregon and Unionist Carlile of Virginia completed the committee membership. Johnson, of course, had been for many years an ardent champion of homestead legislation, but he left the Senate almost immediately to become military governor of Tennessee and was replaced on the committee by Unionist Wright of Pennsylvania. A majority of the committee probably favored the bill, but several members apparently questioned the wisdom of the cash-bounty provision. The committee retained control of the measure for three weeks, finally reporting it on March 25 with amendments which struck out the sections relating to cash bounties for soldiers.[10]

---

effectiveness of his plea for the homestead bill. When he came down to the floor of the House, Stevens tried to refer the measure to the Committee of the Whole, where the Speaker would have been free to participate in debate, but Grow brushed this suggestion aside. See *Cong. Globe,* 37th Cong., 2nd Sess., p. 909.

9. *Cong. Globe,* 37th Cong., 2nd Sess., pp. 1030–1035. Two negative votes (both Unionist) were later recorded by unanimous consent. See *ibid.,* p. 1042. It would seem to be impossible to determine the actual vote on the measure in the House. The *Globe* (p. 1035) records the vote as 107 to 16, but lists only 106 affirmative votes. The *House Journal* records the vote as 105 to 16, but lists 114 affirmative and 18 negative votes. See U.S. House of Representatives, *Journal of the House of Representatives of the United States: Being the Second Session of the Thirty-seventh Congress,* pp. 376–377. At least five affirmative votes were recorded by unanimous consent after the passage of the bill. See *Cong. Globe,* 37th Cong., 2nd Sess., p. 1042.

10. *Cong. Globe,* 37th Cong., 2nd Sess., pp. 9, 1036, 1037, 1260, 1347.

For another month, however, the Senate floor was occupied by matters thought to be more important or, at least, more urgent: slavery in the District of Columbia, federal encouragement of state emancipation, various appropriation bills, the confiscation bill, and attacks on the Committee on the Conduct of the War. Despairing of ever getting the measure before the Senate for regular consideration, Wade, on April 30, finally moved to take the bill up during the morning hour. He noted, however, that Harlan, chairman of the committee from which the measure had been reported, was absent, and the bill was postponed until his return. The bill was again taken up on May 2, and the amendments proposed by the Committee on Public Lands were quickly adopted without discussion and without a division. Carlile then spoke briefly in opposition to the measure. "I am," he declared frankly, "opposed at all times, and particularly at a time like the present, to disposing of the public domain of this country without adequate compensation." Pomeroy expressed a desire to speak on the subject, and at his request the measure was postponed to May 5.[11]

On that date, Pomeroy made a moderately long speech, constructed along standard lines, in support of the bill; but no other senator thought it necessary to enlighten his colleagues (or his constituents) as to his position on the measure. The next day, the Senate was obviously ready to dispose of the homestead bill. Carlile had earlier introduced an amendment striking out the entire bill and substituting a measure granting land bounties to the veterans of the present war. This substitute was defeated by a vote of 11 to 28 and the homestead bill was passed by a margin of almost five to one. Only four Democrats and three Unionists cast their votes against the measure.[12]

The House received the bill with the Senate amendments on the same day. For some reason, however, the measure was allowed to gather dust

11. *Ibid.*, pp. 1871, 1915–1916, *passim;* quotation from p. 1916.

12. *Ibid.*, pp. 1937–1940, 1951. The vote on the passage of the homestead bill was 33 to 7. The senators voting against the bill were Democrats Bayard and Saulsbury of Delaware, Stark of Oregon, and Powell of Kentucky and Unionists Carlile and Willey of Virginia and Davis of Kentucky. All of these except Bayard had voted for Carlile's amendment. Five other senators voted for the amendment but supported the bill after its defeat. These were Henderson, Kennedy, McDougall, Robert Wilson, and Wright.

on the speaker's table for the remainder of the week while the House debated the contested election of the delegate from Nebraska, the creation of Arizona Territory, and the prohibition of slavery in the territories. On May 12, Potter moved that the House take up the bill, nonconcur in the amendments, and call for a committee of conference. This course was followed, and the Speaker named Republicans Potter and Aldrich and Unionist Edwin H. Webster of Maryland as House members of the conference committee. On the same day, the Senate insisted on its amendments and agreed to a committee of conference. President pro tem Foot of Vermont appointed Senators Harlan, Clark, and Wright as Senate members of the committee. Three days later, the recommendations of this committee were reported to the two houses. The report amounted to a distinct Senate victory. The Senate amendments, by and large, were retained, though the committee of conference added a few more. The only important Senate change—striking out the cash-bounty provisions—was allowed to stand. Both houses agreed to the conference committee report without discussion and without a division, and the homestead bill was passed.[13]

Although there was at this time undoubtedly much latent opposition in Congress to homestead legislation, it was simply not politically feasible for this antagonism to take the form of direct votes against the measure. The paucity of opposition in the Senate is undoubtedly explained by the fact that the western states had proportionately greater representation in the upper house. In the final analysis, the position of the Republican Party in the Middle West was (as the elections of 1862 demonstrated) entirely too shaky to permit that party's political campaigners to go before the electorate without a homestead act on the statute books.

The Land-Grant College Act

Like the homestead act, an act to establish land-grant colleges had been passed by a previous Congress. Like the homestead act, it had been vetoed by Buchanan. Like the homestead act, it had attracted wide support and its passage by the Thirty-seventh Congress was confidently expected. Yet some congressmen considered these two proposals to be, to some extent,

13. *Ibid.,* pp. 1972, 2061, 2069, 2147–2148, 2158.

mutually antagonistic. Such legislation obviously could not be considered during the Special Session in the summer of 1861, but the Second Session of the Thirty-seventh Congress was only four days old when Justin S. Morrill gave notice of his intention to introduce a bill to grant public lands to such states as would establish colleges "for the benefit of agriculture and the mechanical arts." For five years Morrill had been urging the adoption of such a bill. His support in Congress had come primarily, but not exclusively, from the eastern states. It was Morrill's bill that had been passed by the Thirty-fifth Congress and vetoed by Buchanan. Morrill introduced his proposal on December 16, 1861, and it was referred to the Committee on Public Lands.[14]

This was a normal reference for the measure, but not a happy one. It languished in the committee for over five months, only to be reported at last with an adverse recommendation. This was not surprising, since representatives and senators from the western states had many misgivings about such legislation, and westerners dominated the Committee on Public Lands. The chairman, Potter of Wisconsin, was a bitter opponent of the bill and the same could be said of three other western Republicans on the committee, Julian of Indiana, Trimble of Ohio, and Kellogg of Michigan. Covode of Pennsylvania favored the measure, but Crisfield of Maryland could, at best, be counted on for only half-hearted support. Vandever of Iowa was absent on military duties during most of the middle portion of the session, but he too, undoubtedly, opposed the bill's passage. Neither Vallandigham of Ohio nor Woodruff of Connecticut, the other two members of the committee, ever committed themselves on the land-grant college act by voice or vote.[15]

14. *Cong. Globe,* 37th Cong., 2nd Sess., pp. 33, 99; Manuscript memoir by Justin S. Morrill, *ca.* 1874, quoted in Parker, *op. cit.,* pp. 262–271. Edmund J. James insists that Professor Jonathan B. Turner of Illinois College originated the land-grant college plan and urged it upon Morrill. William B. Parker, however, reduces James's arguments to a shambles (*op. cit.,* pp. 278–284). See Edmund J. James, *Origin of the Land Grant Act of 1862,* Vol. IV, No. 1 of *The University [of Illinois] Studies,* 20–32.

15. *Cong. Globe,* 37th Cong., 2nd Sess., p. 2432. For committee membership, see *Cong. Globe,* 37th Cong., 1st Sess., p. 22. Conclusions as to the attitudes of various members are drawn from subsequent votes and speeches. See *Cong. Globe,* 37th Cong., 2nd Sess., *passim.* Primarily, the westerners feared (correctly) that the states would dispose of their land warrants in large blocks to eastern buyers.

In the meantime, finding his bill blocked in committee with the strong probability that any report made would be an adverse one, Morrill cast about for another line of attack. The Vermonter, the second-ranking member of the Committee of Ways and Means, had been assigned the task of drafting the tax bills and shepherding them through the House. These duties left him no time to engage in a floor fight over the failure to report the land-grant college bill. Consequently, he handed Senator Wade of Ohio a copy of the measure and requested him to introduce it in the upper house. Wade gladly did this on May 5, 1862, more than three weeks before the House committee made its report. The measure was referred to the Committee on Public Lands.[16]

This committee, like its counterpart in the House, was dominated by westerners, but the members, individually, were not such rabid opponents of the measure. Harlan, the chairman, though from a western state, had been instructed by the Iowa legislature to vote for the land-grant college bill and so gave the measure his consistent backing. Firm support was given to the bill by Clark of New Hampshire, Carlile of Virginia, and (somewhat surprisingly) Rice of Minnesota. Wright of Indiana strongly opposed the measure and Pomeroy of Kansas and Nesmith of Oregon, though they supported the bill on the final vote, aided in obstructing its progress through the Senate and in hedging it about with restrictions. On May 16, Harlan reported the measure to the Senate with some unimportant minor amendments.[17]

Wade called the bill up for consideration three days later. The measure provided for the granting of public lands to any states which established at least one college "where the leading object shall be (without excluding other scientific and classical studies, and including military tactics) to teach such branches of learning as are related to agriculture and the mechanic arts." The grant would consist of thirty thousand acres of land (valued for pre-emption at $1.25 per acre) for each senator and repre-

Thus, huge tracts of land in the western ("public land") states would be turned over to speculators, and settlement would be inhibited.

16. Justin S. Morrill, Manuscript memoir, *ca.* 1874, quoted in Parker, *op. cit.,* pp. 262–271; *Cong. Globe,* 37th Cong., 2nd Sess., p. 1935.

17. *Cong. Globe,* 37th Cong., 2nd Sess., p. 2160. For committee membership, see *ibid.,* pp. 9, 1260. Conclusions as to the attitudes of various members are drawn from subsequent votes and speeches. See *ibid., passim.*

sentative from the state. The proceeds from the sale of this land had to be invested in safe bonds yielding at least five percent interest, and the income could not be used for the erection of buildings. The states were required to replace any money lost from the fund, and colleges had to be established within five years. The last section cautiously stipulated that no state could apply for a land grant while in rebellion against the government of the United States. The committee amendments were quickly adopted and, at the request of James H. Lane, the bill was temporarily laid aside.[18]

Lane's intentions quickly became clear when the Senate resumed consideration of the measure two days later. At that time, the Kansas senator introduced an amendment which would have permitted the states to take land only in the territories, and not in the "public land states." He declared that if the amendment was not adopted, the state of Kansas would be placed in the hands of absentee landlords. Wade vigorously resisted this amendment, however, saying he saw no reason for making such exceptions or for renouncing federal control of public land, wherever situated. Pomeroy, as might be expected, supported the view of his colleague and insisted that such an amendment was essential to the future prosperity of Kansas. At this point the special order for the day intervened.[19]

On the following day Wade again moved to take up the measure, and Lane immediately began an extended, though disorganized, speech on the evils of the bill. It would, he charged, block the construction of a Pacific railway, invalidate the homestead bill, turn all of Kansas over to absentee owners, and allow the southern states to settle their Negroes in that region. He was most vehemently opposed to this last possibility. "The people of Kansas," he declared, "are opposed to the settling of free negroes within our borders. Kansas desires, above all other things, that the white and the colored races may be separated, and widely separated."

18. *Ibid.*, p. 2187.

19. *Ibid.*, pp. 2248–2250. All discussion of the land-grant college bill, except on the last day of consideration, took place during the morning hour because of the continuation of the tax bill (H.R. No. 312) as a special order throughout the last of May and the first of June. This accounts for the consideration of the measure being so drawn out, for only a short time could be devoted to it during each day's session.

Wilkinson said that he was opposed to the bill also but saw no reason for this extended discussion on a mere motion to take up the bill for consideration. Wade pointed out that Lane's speech was quite obviously designed to delay and, if possible, prevent the consideration of the measure. This was undoubtedly Lane's purpose, and he succeeded admirably; for scarcely had the Senate voted by a narrow margin to take up the bill when the morning hour expired.[20]

When the Senate resumed consideration of the measure on May 24, Lane had modified his amendment to prohibit the location of more than one million acres of the land grants in any one state. Harlan then made a very moderate speech defending the proposal as a measure of justice to the eastern states, and denying that the effects of the bill on the "public land states" would be as calamitous as Lane alleged. The measure was then postponed to May 27, then to May 28. The Senate considered the bill briefly on the twenty-eighth and at greater length on the thirtieth. Wilkinson and Wright spoke in opposition to the measure, Lane again supported his amendment, and Wade announced that he would not oppose this modification.[21]

There followed a ten-day period during which the land-grant college bill was not mentioned, though Wade continued active in debate on other measures. The Senate, meanwhile, continued to consider the tax bill as a special order while devoting the morning hour to such miscellaneous bills as those establishing Arizona Territory, changing the form of jurors' oaths, prohibiting polygamy in the territories, and regulating the employment of convicts imprisoned in the District of Columbia penitentiary. In the House, Morrill, the author of the land-grant college measure, took advantage of a session of the Committee of the Whole on a totally unrelated topic to defend the proposal and urge its passage.[22]

The bill was again taken up in the Senate on June 10, and Wade was obviously determined to push it to a vote before adjournment. Lane's amendment was adopted without a division, and his colleague Pomeroy introduced another amendment even more restrictive in nature. Pomeroy's proposal would have prohibited the states from transferring to any

20. *Ibid.*, pp. 2275–2277; quotation from p. 2276.

21. *Ibid.*, pp. 2328–2329, 2366, 2394–2396, 2440–2443.

22. *Ibid.*, pp. 2451–2494, 2506–2526, 2537–2560, 2569–2587, 2595–2611, 2615–2620, Appendix, 256–259.

one person more than 640 acres of the land acquired under the terms of this measure. Wilkinson and Doolittle joined Pomeroy in support of this proposal, while Wade and Collamer opposed its adoption. Howe characterized the whole bill as totally worthless, saying, "You never will get a fund out of it in the State of New York or any other State that will keep a professor of agriculture from starving for one week." Pomeroy's amendment was adopted by a vote of 20 to 19, then reconsidered and defeated without a division. After some other amendments were received and acted upon, the bill was passed, 32 to 7. The opposition consisted of five Republicans, one Democrat (Saulsbury of Delaware), and one Unionist (Wright of Indiana). All of the Republicans who voted against the measure came from the "public land states:" Wisconsin Senators Doolittle and Howe, Iowa's Grimes, Lane of Kansas, and Wilkinson from Minnesota.[23]

The House received the bill on June 11, and on the following Tuesday (June 17), Justin S. Morrill called it up for consideration. Potter immediately moved that it be referred to the Committee on Public Lands, but Morrill urged the House to pass the measure at this time. Potter protested that it had never been before a House committee; Morrill replied that it had been before the country for five years. The House refused, by a vote of 31 to 83, to send the bill into committee. Potter now waged a last-ditch battle to delay the passage of the measure. He moved to postpone further consideration of the bill to the first Tuesday in January 1863. The Speaker ruled the motion out of order. He demanded the reading of the bill at length. The bill was read. He moved to adjourn, and the motion was defeated without a division. He moved to table the measure, and the motion was defeated without a division. He begged to be allowed to submit amendments to the bill. The Speaker replied that no debate was in order. Potter had delayed action on this measure for seven months, and Morrill and the bill's other supporters were in no mood to grant him any quarter. The land-grant college bill was passed by a vote of 91 to 25.[24]

The majority was composed of fifty-seven Republicans, fourteen Democrats, and twenty Unionists, while eight Democracts and one Unionist

23. *Ibid.*, pp. 2625–2634; quotation from p. 2626.
24. *Ibid.*, pp. 2663, 2769–2770.

joined with sixteen Republicans in opposing the bill. As might be expected, the measure received strong support in New England and the middle states. Only two Republicans (Frederick A. Conkling and Frank of New York) and two Democrats (Browne of Rhode Island and Ward of New York) cast negative votes. Absenteeism was high, however, with thirty-one eastern representatives not voting. From the border states, from Delaware on the Atlantic to Kentucky on the Mississippi, not a single negative voice was raised, and only three congressmen failed to vote.

In the Middle West, some unusual voting patterns emerged. Congressmen from this area opposed the bill by a vote of eighteen to twenty-one, but two thirds of these affirmative votes came from the Ohio delegation, which split twelve to three in favor of the measure. In view of the open western opposition to the bill, one of the amazing aspects of the vote was the large number of absentees from the Middle West. Twenty-one representatives, more than one third of the total membership from the area, failed to vote on the land-grant college act. Not a single representative from the states of California, Oregon, or Kansas voted on the measure.[25]

Thus, after six years of effort, the Morrill Land-Grant College Act came into existence. The total impact on national education and culture of the institutions formed under the terms of this act, if not as great as Morrill hoped, has been, at least, greater than Howe prophesied.

The Thirty-seventh Congress thus brought to a close two lengthy controversies involving public lands—the struggles for homestead and land-grant college legislation. There were those in the Republican Party who insisted that the existence of a rebellion made the enactment of such legislation unwise but, in essence, this should be recognized simply as the

25. *Ibid.*, p. 2770. The vote of 91 to 25 mentioned above is my "best guess" in the matter. The *Globe* (p. 2770) records the vote as 90 to 25, but lists 91 affirmative voters. The *House Journal* (p. 880) lists the vote as 89 to 25, but records 91 affirmative voters. It was later charged that midwestern support for the land-grant college bill had been obtained by a promise of support by New Englanders for the Illinois ship canal bill (see Chapter 6). This might account for the large number of absentees among the delegations from the midwestern states. The entire charge has an unlikely ring. With the solid backing of the representatives from New England and the middle and border states, the bill was assured of passage regardless of the position of the midwesterners. Still, there seems to be no other convincing explanation for the absence of the midwestern representatives. See *Cong. Globe,* 37th Cong., 2nd Sess., p. 3058.

re-emergence of the same sectional economic interests which had been antagonistic to the proposals for the past decade. Others genuinely considered the two measures mutually antagonistic. Some earnest supporters of the Land-Grant College Act feared that the passage of homestead legislation would create in the western states an opposition to further extensive federal grants (except to railroads). To a certain extent, these fears were realized, though some such antagonism probably existed prior to the passage of the Homestead Act. Ardent advocates of homestead legislation, on the other hand, feared that the removal from entry of such sizable tracts of land (to be located at the pleasure of the warrant holder), coupled with the grants to railways, would render unworkable and incongruous the land system of which the Homestead Act was the base. This, too, proved largely correct. Ultimately, party pledges, political realities, and the necessity for balancing benefits to eastern and western interests overcame this opposition.

But the Thirty-seventh Congress not only helped shape modern America by bringing earlier lines of development to a culmination. This body also made new approaches to public land utilization—especially in the field of internal improvements. Time would demonstrate that the distribution of federal bounty could foster interests other than population expansion and public education, and that settlers and states were not the only possible recipients of this bounty.

CHAPTER 6

Congress and Public Improvements: Transportation Legislation

The Pacific Railroad Act

Like the homestead bill and the land-grant college act, the proposal for government aid in constructing a transcontinental railway had been a subject of agitation for a considerable period of time. Like the homestead act, the Pacific railway measure had been specifically endorsed in the Republican Party platform of 1860, and in both Democratic platforms as well. Unlike the other two public land measures, however, no bill granting federal aid for the construction of a railroad to the Pacific had ever managed to clear both houses of Congress. In 1855 and in 1859 the Senate had passed bills providing for government aid in constructing three separate transcontinental railways simultaneously, but the House had refused to act on either measure. Late in 1860, the House had, in its turn, passed a bill granting federal aid to two railways. The Senate, however, adopted a number of amendments to the bill which the House rejected.[1]

Sectional jealousy and constitutional scruples ranked high among the considerations that had prevented Congress from passing a Pacific railway act before 1861. Secession, by removing most of the southern senators and representatives, had removed one of the most potent sources of sectional jealousy. And constitutional scruples rapidly disintegrated under the impact of continued demands for the passage of legislation, often novel in character and sweeping in scope, declared to be essential to the successful prosecution of the war.

Since the Pacific railroad bill was viewed as a military measure, the Holman resolution posed no barrier to its introduction and consideration

1. For political platforms, see Cooper, *op. cit.*, Book II, 41–44. For the legislative history of the Pacific railway bill prior to 1861, see Lewis H. Haney, *A Congressional History of Railways in the United States, 1850–1887*, Bulletin of the University of Wisconsin, No. 342, Economics and Political Science Series, Vol. VI, No. 1, 56–62.

during the Special Session of the Thirty-seventh Congress. Consequently, on July 8, 1861, Republican Samuel R. Curtis of Iowa introduced in the House the first Pacific railroad proposal of this Congress. Curtis moved that his bill be referred to a select committee of five. At the insistence of other representatives, this number was changed to nine, and Curtis's motion then prevailed. Four days later, the Speaker announced the committee personnel. Curtis, as was to be expected, was given the chairmanship. The other members of the committee were Republicans James H. Campbell of Pennsylvania, John B. Alley of Massachusetts, Francis P. Blair, Jr., of Missouri, Richard Franchot of New York, and Isaac N. Arnold of Illinois; Unionist Edwin H. Webster of Maryland; and Democrats Samuel S. Cox of Ohio and Andrew J. Thayer of Oregon.[2]

This committee underwent several changes. On July 29, 1861, Curtis submitted his resignation as a member of Congress to accept an appointment as a brigadier general. Campbell thus succeeded to the chairmanship of the committee, and Republican Aaron A. Sargent of California was later named to fill the vacancy. Thayer's election to the House had been contested, and on July 30, 1861, he was declared not entitled to his seat. His successor, Democrat George K. Shiel, was subsequently appointed to fill Thayer's position on the select committee. On March 4, 1862, shortly after the committee had made its first reports, Cox asked to be excused from further service. His request was granted, and Democrat William A. Hall of Missouri was named to replace him.[3]

Throughout the most important months of the committee's existence, then, the membership consisted of Campbell, Alley, Francis P. Blair, Jr., Cox, Webster, Franchot, Arnold, Sargent, and Shiel. With the exception of Cox, none of these men opposed the passage of a Pacific railway bill. The members from the Pacific states (Sargent and Shiel), as would be expected, were ardent champions of the measure. The two Republicans from the Middle West (Blair and Arnold) were residents of St. Louis and Chicago, cities which saw tremendous commercial possibilities in the completion of the transcontinental rail route. The sole New England member of the committee (Alley) was a manufacturer of shoes and leather, and was undoubtedly well aware of both California's position as a

2. *Cong. Globe,* 37th Cong., 1st Sess., pp. 23, 91–92.

3. *Ibid.,* pp. 357, 444; *Cong. Globe,* 37th Cong., 2nd Sess., pp. 19, 178, 1046, 1083, *passim.*

supplier of hides and the cost of ocean shipping. He was later connected with the Union Pacific. Franchot of New York was already engaged in railroad promotions and would eventually be associated with the Central Pacific. Webster made no statements regarding the measure, but supported the bill on the final vote. Campbell, whatever his personal views, as committee chairman gave the bill his consistent support.[4]

Quite similar steps were being taken in the Senate. On July 12, 1861, McDougall of California introduced a resolution declaring the construction of a Pacific railroad to be an imperative public necessity and announced that he would move its reference to a select committee. The Senate considered the resolution on July 16, and McDougall urged the establishment of a special committee to consider the measure while Congress was not in session. McDougall's proposal carried and, as expected, the Vice President named the Californian chairman of the committee. His colleagues were Pomeroy of Kansas, Clark of New Hampshire, Cowan of Pennsylvania, and Polk of Missouri (later replaced by Robert Wilson, also of Missouri). On May 7, 1862, the day following the passage of the Pacific railway bill by the House, and long after the committee had made its initial reports, James H. Lane of Kansas secured the enlargement of the body. The president pro tem named Lane, Wade of Ohio, Browning of Illinois, and Kennedy of Maryland as additional members. Later still, on May 28, while the Senate was considering the House bill, Harlan of Iowa was added to the committee.

Thus, both senators from Kansas and members of the upper house from California, Iowa, and Missouri—states directly and vitally interested in the Pacific railroad—made up half the membership of the select committee. Of the entire group, in fact, only Clark seemed to have any real misgivings about the measure, though not all were as enthusiastic as some of the bill's supporters might have wished. On the same day that the committee was first formed, Latham of California introduced a Pacific railway bill.[5]

Little more was heard of the proposal during this session except the introduction of bills in both houses authorizing a grant of public lands

4. *Cong. Globe,* 37th Cong., 2nd Sess., *passim; Bio. Dir.* (1928), pp. 637, 985–986.

5. *Cong. Globe,* 37th Cong., 1st Sess., pp. 83, 134–135, 154–155; *Cong. Globe,* 37th Cong., 2nd Sess., pp. 504, 1983, 2394, 2415, *passim.*

and government credit to the "Peoples' Pacific Railroad Company" to aid that company in constructing a transcontinental railway. This was a Maine corporation, organized by a "down-East" promoter, with headquarters in Boston. There seems to have been little prospect that aid would be granted to the company, but the proposal was never dropped as long as the Pacific railway issue was before Congress.[6]

When the Second Session of this Congress convened and weeks passed without any further action, the rumblings of discontent among the proponents of the Pacific railway measure grew louder. On January 31, 1862, Sargent took advantage of a session of the Committee of the Whole to made a speech urging immediate favorable action on the scheme. During the following week, Pomeroy, in the Senate, and Missouri Unionist James S. Rollins, in the House, introduced new Pacific railroad bills. Finally, on February 26, the Senate committee reported a bill which was ordered printed and immediately recommitted. The House committee took an identical course six days later. Campbell reported the measure (H.R. No. 364) to the House for action on March 14, and it was made a special order for March 25. On that date, Campbell, giving no reason but saying that he spoke for the select committee, moved that it be postponed until April 1. The bill was postponed.[7]

Still, the supporters of the measure were not dismayed. "The prospect of the passage of the Pacific Rail Road Bill is regarded as excellent," wrote Thomas Ewing, Jr., an official of the Leavenworth, Pawnee, and Western Railroad Company of Kansas, which was authorized to construct a portion of the line. "The Senate is nearly certain; but I can not get data satisfying me as to the House." Ewing, who was actively lobbying for the bill's passage, noted, however, that although he had not been able to canvass the lower house, "We have friends in all the Delegations, and from their reports the friends of it [the Pacific railroad bill] are sanguine of its passage in the next two weeks."[8]

6. Josiah Perham to John P. Hale, October 12, 1860, John P. Hale Papers, New Hampshire Historical Society; Francis E. Hyde, "Josiah Perham," *DAB,* XIV, 462–463; *Cong. Globe,* 37th Cong., 1st Sess., pp. 224, 253; *Cong. Globe,* 37th Cong., 2nd Sess., pp. 161, 169, 1710–1711. The measure was introduced by Washburne in the House and by Morrill in the Senate.

7. *Cong. Globe,* 37th Cong., 2nd Sess., pp. 599–603, 665, 1062, 1235, 1360.

8. Thomas Ewing, Jr., to Thomas Ewing, Sr., March 28, 1862, Thomas Ewing Papers, Library of Congress.

On the first of April, however, Stevens announced that he was ready for the House to begin considering the tax bill. In response to this very plain hint, the House postponed the Pacific railroad bill to April 8. The pace was even slower in the Senate. McDougall was finally able to report a bill (S. No. 260) on April 4, but was unable to get it made a special order.[9]

The lower house finally began consideration of the Pacific railroad bill on the eighth of April. Since the measure involved the appropriation of money, it was referred to the Committee of the Whole. The committee proposal provided for a grant of a considerable amount of public land and more than sixty million dollars in government bonds to aid in constructing a transcontinental railroad.

The bill contemplated two eastern branches which would join at some point not more than three hundred miles west of the Missouri River, to form the main line of the Pacific railroad. The northern branch would terminate on the western boundary of Iowa and would be constructed by a combination of four Iowa companies or any one of them. The southern branch would connect with Kansas City, Missouri, and would be constructed by two Missouri companies and a Kansas company. A new corporation would be organized to construct the line from the western boundary of Kansas to the Nevada border. Within the territory of Nevada, the construction would be undertaken by the Nevada Railroad Company; west of that territory, the Central Pacific Railroad Company of California would take over.

The first day's consideration of the measure was consumed by Campbell's explanation of the various provisions of the bill. The chairman of the select committee insisted that the interests of the government were carefully guarded and that the railway was a work of urgent military and political necessity.[10]

The House spent the greater part of the next day's session in Committee of the Whole listening to speeches by California Republicans Phelps and Sargent and "Pig Iron" Kelley of Pennsylvania in favor of the Pacific railroad bill. This marked the end of any action on the measure for over a week, for Lovejoy, a bitter enemy of the bill in its present form, managed

9. *Cong. Globe,* 37th Cong., 2nd Sess., pp. 619, 959, 1480, 1538.
10. *Ibid.,* pp. 1577–1580.

to get further discussion postponed. Still unperturbed, the bill's supporters predicted speedy and favorable action. "I think on the whole there is not much doubt of the passage of a bill through both branches this Session," Thomas Ewing, Jr., wrote his father on April 9. The committee continued work on the bill, even if the House did not, and some of the additional provisions that they now added were distasteful to the railroad officials concerned. Still, "it is the best we can get done in the House," remarked Ewing, while expressing the hope that the Senate would strike out the objectionable portions.[11]

Beginning on April 17, the lower house devoted two more days to consideration of the bill. Lovejoy of Illinois launched a bitter attack on the measure, claiming it was a log-rolling scheme put together by the railroad interests. Dunn of Indiana and some of the territorial delegates spoke in favor of the measure, and Edwards of New Hampshire gave it his modified support. Wilson of Iowa, though strongly in favor of the construction of a transcontinental railroad, insisted that the present bill discriminated against Iowa railroads. He claimed that it gave the Kansas and Missouri companies too much influence on the location of the main line. New England Republicans Frederick A. Pike of Maine and Justin S. Morrill of Vermont favored postponing consideration of the measure to the next session of Congress, but Kelley, "Frank" Blair, and Samuel C. Fessenden of Maine urged immediate action. Albert S. White of Indiana said he favored government aid for the construction of a Pacific railroad, but could not support this bill, while Sheffield of Rhode Island stated frankly that he had not read the measure carefully because he had no intention of voting for it. After these two days of discussion (with no action), further consideration was postponed to April 28.[12]

11. *Ibid.*, pp. 1590–1598; Thomas Ewing, Jr., to Thomas Ewing, Sr., April 9, 14, 1862, Thomas Ewing Papers, Library of Congress.

12. *Cong. Globe,* 37th Cong., 2nd Sess., pp. 1698–1711, 1726–1728. Some observers professed to see an extreme sectional division in the debates at this time. It is true that most of the opponents of immediate action were easterners, but there does not appear to have been a sufficient degree of solidarity to justify any charge of sectional politics. See New York *Herald,* April 18, 1862. The actions of Lovejoy must have been a disappointment to the proponents of the bill, for they earlier thought that they had attached him (and other abolitionists) to the measure by stressing the employment opportunities which such construction would offer for the "contrabands." See Thomas Ewing, Jr., to Thomas Ewing, Sr.,

Campbell announced on this date that the select committee had held an additional meeting during the past week and had adopted some of the suggestions made by various members. He reported these amendments and said that he would call them up shortly. The apparent lack of progress was most discouraging to some of the measure's supporters. W. A. Wallace, the Washington correspondent of the San Francisco *Daily Alta California,* wrote on April 30 that no Pacific railroad legislation would be enacted at this session. The measure would undoubtedly pass if it came to a vote, he explained, but the bill's opponents were determined to prevent this.[13]

Wallace was proved to be unduly pessimistic, however, for when Campbell called the measure up again, no major interruptions were allowed. Thus, on April 30, 1862, the House began its initial action on the bill. With painful slowness, a section providing for the organization of the Union Pacific Railroad Company was hammered out in the Committee of the Whole. Albert S. White pushed through an amendment which gave the federal government representation on both the board of commissioners which was to set up the company, and on the board of directors which would control the corporation after it was formed.

Much of the session on the thirtieth was spent in adding name after name to the list of incorporators. Repeated pleas by the chairman of the select committee failed to influence the members, nor did Windom's suggestion that attached to the measure should be "the appendix to the census report, which contains the names of the heads of families in the United States" bring the parade to a halt. Finally, the members apparently ran out of names, and the committee rose and reported no resolution on the bill.[14]

Discussion continued on the following day. In general, amendments

---

March 28, 1862, Thomas Ewing Papers, Library of Congress. At this juncture, however, the Maine-born Lovejoy gave nominal support to a substitute which he had introduced granting the construction rights for a Pacific railroad to the People's Pacific Railroad Company of Maine. He may, in fact, have been opposed to the passage of any Pacific railroad bill at this time.

13. *Cong. Globe,* 37th Cong., 2nd Sess., p. 1846; San Francisco *Daily Alta California,* May 27, 1862.

14. *Cong. Globe,* 37th Cong., 2nd Sess., pp. 1888–1892. The "Union Pacific amendment" came in part from the select committee, in part from Wilson, and in part from Stevens.

which would place additional restrictions on the companies were defeated. Lovejoy, Sheffield, and Holman were active in proposing such modifications. Despite some needling from other members, Stevens pushed through an amendment requiring the companies to use only American-made iron. The next day (May 2) was Friday, and Campbell yielded to Lovejoy's entreaties to permit the day to be spent in considering bills of a private character. The Pacific railroad measure, therefore, was postponed to May 5 and continued as a special order. Pennsylvania Republican Robert McKnight's suggestion that it be postponed to the next session was not well received. "I do not think," McKnight asserted, "the House is in any temper to pass that bill now." But the House quite obviously was inclined to pass "that bill" and this very inclination was undoubtedly what moved McKnight to urge a postponement.[15]

On Monday, it was obvious that the managers of the bill (Campbell of Pennsylvania and Sargent of California) intended that action on the measure be concluded before adjournment. The discussion was quite lengthy. The authorization for the Nevada Railroad Company to build a section of the road was struck out, and the entire central portion was placed in the hands of the Union Pacific Railroad Company. Two new branches were added, one eliminated, and a number of minor changes made.

Lovejoy, aided by Albert S. White, Justin S. Morrill, and William Kellogg of Illinois, continued to spearhead the opposition forces. Lovejoy expressed doubt that the railroad would ever be constructed under the terms of this act, and proposed an amendment declaring all work done on the line forfeited to the United States government if the entire road was not completed by January 1, 1876. Campbell replied that he and the entire select committee were convinced that the line would be built without any additional appropriation. "Well, sir," replied Lovejoy, "then the gentleman's credulity is immensely large, that is all." Campbell denied this but made no serious objection to Lovejoy's proposed amendment, which was adopted.[16]

Late in the day, the Committee of the Whole concluded its work and reported the bill to the House. Stevens then made a brief speech support-

15. *Ibid.*, pp. 1906–1913, 1928.
16. *Ibid.*, pp. 1943–1949; quotation from p. 1947.

ing the measure. His remarks, characteristically, contained many attacks and allusions which were at least unnecessary. The House concurred in the amendments and ordered the previous question on the measure. The bill was then postponed until two o'clock the following day. This would allow the measure to be printed, and it was agreed that the vote would then be taken without further discussion.[17]

The supporters of the bill were now confident of success. Thomas Ewing, Jr., predicted that the measure would pass the House by a majority of thirty votes and would encounter no difficulty in the Senate. The bill was not perfect, he admitted. He thought Lovejoy's amendment very bad, but believed that Congress would not enforce this provision if substantial progress had been made. Ewing also considered the land-grant clause "very defective as it now is," but this fact did not perturb him. "That we will have changed," he confidently declared, "so as to protect us from loss in case the squatters take the land next [to] the road as the location is being made."[18]

The bill was passed, 79 to 49, on May 6, 1862. Thirteen Democrats and ten Unionists joined with fifty-six Republicans in supporting the measure, while negative votes were cast by eighteen Republicans, twenty Democrats, and eleven Unionists. An analysis of the vote does not sustain the charge of sectional politics sometimes associated with House action on the Pacific railroad bill. Eastern congressmen did not oppose the measure with any degree of consistency. The New England delegation split eleven to nine in favor of the bill and in the middle states the margin was even greater—twenty-eight to twelve. Twenty-seven representatives from this area failed to answer the roll call. Congressmen from the long, thin chain of border states stretching from the Atlantic to the Mississippi voted ten to nine against the bill. As might be expected, not a single negative vote was cast from the states of California, Missouri, Iowa, Minnesota, and Michigan. The older midwestern states, however, divided on the measure. The Ohio delegation favored the bill by a twelve to six margin, but Indiana and Illinois representatives took the opposite view of the question by votes of seven to two and five to two respectively. As a result of the

17. *Ibid.*, pp. 1949–1950.

18. Thomas Ewing, Jr., to Thomas Ewing, Sr., May 6, 1862, Thomas Ewing Papers, Library of Congress.

large number of absentees, not a single vote was cast from the states of Oregon, Kansas, Wisconsin, and New Hampshire. Excluding pairs, twenty-seven Republicans, twelve Democrats, and two Unionists failed to answer when their names were called.[19]

When the Senate received the bill on the following day, it was referred to the Select Committee on the Pacific Railroad.[20] That committee, in close collaboration with interested railroad officials, drafted a number of amendments and reported the measure back to the Senate on May 12. At this time McDougall urged prompt action, pointing out that the two Missouri senators would have to return to their home state in a few days and that action was desired before they left. He announced that he would call the bill up on the following day and move that it be made a special order for one week later. The friends of the measure, he declared, had no desire to debate it, merely to vote on it.[21]

The bill was not destined to move as smoothly through the Senate as McDougall hoped. When, on May 13, the California senator attempted to have the measure made a special order for two days later, Fessenden, the Senate Republican leader, strongly resisted such assignment. He thought the measure too important to be rushed through the upper house and also announced that he intended to take up the tax bill on that day and press it continually until it was passed. Fessenden obviously did not approve of the railroad bill and denied that this Congress, or the Republicans in it, were pledged to pass such a measure. The Senate refused, by a vote of 17 to 19, to make the Pacific railroad bill a special order, and the measure was temporarily laid on the table.[22]

With the exception of a single Unionist from Kentucky (Davis), every senator who voted against making the Pacific railroad bill a special order

19. *Cong. Globe,* 37th Cong., 2nd Sess., p. 1971. Five of the Republicans and two of the Democrats who did not vote had been present immediately before the final vote was taken.

20. *Ibid.,* p. 1983. It was at this point that, on Lane's motion, four more members were added to this select committee.

21. *Ibid.,* pp. 2055, 2081–2082; Thomas Ewing, Jr., to Thomas Ewing, Sr., May 12, 1862, Thomas Ewing Papers, Library of Congress. Both Henderson and Robert Wilson retained their membership in the Missouri convention, which was, at this time, the governing body of the state, and it was thought that their presence would be necessary to make a quorum in that body.

22. *Cong. Globe,* 37th Cong., 2nd Sess., pp. 2081–2082.

was a Republican. Eight Republicans, however, joined with seven Democrats and two Unionists in supporting the motion. Sectional splits were much more obvious in the Senate than they had been in the House. Every senator from New England (except two absentees) cast a negative vote. The vote from the middle and border states was noteworthy primarily because of its scantiness. From the seven states running from Lake Champlain south to the Potomac and west to the Mississippi, only six votes (five of them affirmative) were cast. The senators from Kansas, Missouri, and the Pacific states (except for a single Democratic absentee from Oregon) cast the expected affirmative votes. Support from the rest of the midwestern states was not nearly so consistent, however. Only five senators from the seven states lying between Ohio on the east and Iowa and Minnesota on the west favored making the bill a special order, while eight opposed the motion.

If this vote can be taken as a test of active and dedicated support for the Pacific railroad bill, the Republicans certainly do not emerge as shining champions of the measure. Less than one third of the members of the majority party voting (roughly one fourth of all Republican senators) favored making the bill a special order. On the contrary, every Democratic vote cast (almost two thirds of all the Democratic senators) was in support of the motion. Even the Unionists made a better record than the Republicans. One third of all the Bell-Everett senators supported the motion.[23]

Thwarted in his attempt to get the bill made a special order, McDougall announced the next day that he would call the measure up during the morning hour on Tuesday, May 20, 1862. He gave this lengthy notice, he said, "trusting that Senators will examine the bill, so we can have action without discussion." There was about as much chance of the Senate's following McDougall's suggestion as there was of Charles Sumner's becoming a slave trader. On May 20, in the face of very considerable opposition from important Senate leaders like Fessenden and Henry Wilson, the upper house finally voted 23 to 16 to take up the measure. Every negative vote was Republican. Of the sixteen senators who opposed taking the bill up, ten came from New England states and two others came from middle states. From the entire northeastern area, only Sumner

23. *Ibid.*, p. 2082.

of Massachusetts, Harris of New York, and Cowan of Pennsylvania supported the motion. Harlan, the chairman of the Committee on Public Lands, indicated that his committee was not satisfied with some of the provisions of the bill and moved that it be referred to that body for consideration. McDougall resisted this proposal strenuously. The Senate took no immediate action on Harlan's motion, for the reading of the bill not only consumed the remainder of the morning hour, but was still in progress when the special order (the confiscation bill) intervened.[24]

Though McDougall continued to take an active part in the deliberations of the Senate, nothing more was heard of the Pacific railroad bill for some three weeks. But the select committee was busy, and when McDougall again called the measure to the Senate's attention on June 9, it was to arrange for the bill's reprinting with additional amendments. On this day and the next, the Californian again tried to get the measure made a special order but was balked by the strenuous opposition of Fessenden, Clark, and other party leaders. On the tenth, he yielded to these pressures only with the greatest reluctance. "It must be made a special order . . . ," he cried despairingly, "or it never will be considered by the Senate during the present session of Congress. . . . I have tried for thirty or forty days to get an opportunity to explain some preliminaries, but have not been able to get the floor. . . . No one has been able to say anything about the bill reported from this committee months ago."[25]

During the next week, McDougall pushed the bill almost constantly, but very little was actually accomplished. Some of the minor committee amendments were acted upon on June 11, and McDougall made a speech defending the measure and denying that it would, in the long run, be an item of any expense to the government. Later in the day, Doolittle of Wisconsin had a proposed amendment printed which would authorize the construction of a Northern Pacific railway on terms similar to those provided for in the present bill. McDougall said he personally favored such a road but urged that the present bill not be encumbered with provisions regarding additional routes. On the following day, Latham

24. *Ibid.*, pp. 2114, 2216–2217; quotation from p. 2114. The motion to take up the Pacific railroad bill was supported by all the Unionist senators, almost two thirds of the Democratic senators, and less than one third of the Republican senators.

25. *Ibid.*, pp. 2618, 2637–2638; quotation from p. 2638.

spoke in favor of the bill, and a few changes were made. Morrill began a rather disorganized speech opposing the measure; Doolittle interrupted to move that the Senate go into executive session. After some discussion, this motion carried by a vote of 20 to 18, and another day had passed without any appreciable progress on the Pacific railway bill.[26]

On June 14 and 16, McDougall again tried to proceed with the bill. The fourteenth, however, was a Saturday, and it is doubtful that there was a quorum present at any time. The day was spent in action on noncontroversial measures and in the careful avoidance of any roll-call vote. The Pacific railroad bill could scarcely be called noncontroversial. Wilson intimated as much and, on his motion, the Senate went into an executive session. By this time, the delaying tactics were so obvious that the New York *Times* editorially took McDougall to task for permitting them. The Californian should force the measure to a vote, declared the editors. A majority of the senators were pledged to pass a Pacific railroad bill and defeat, if it must come, should be in the form of an open vote, not the result of devious parliamentary maneuvering. The *Times'* criticisms of McDougall were not entirely deserved. Though the Californian was not notably effective, he was active in attempting to get the Pacific railroad bill through the upper house. It is easier to demand Senate action than to obtain it when important Senate leaders are cool to the proposition being advanced.[27]

McDougall managed to get the measure to the floor on the sixteenth, but he yielded to Hale to dispose of a resolution fixing the hour of the daily meeting. This seemingly routine measure was dragged out sufficiently to consume the remainder of the day, and again the Senate adjourned without further action on the Pacific railway bill.[28]

26. *Ibid.*, pp. 2653–2656, 2659, 2675–2680, Appendix, 307–308. An examination of Morrill's remarks on the twelfth leaves the distinct impression that he was "stalling." The executive session insisted on so strenuously by Doolittle, though a moderately long one, was devoted to routine action on appointments. See U.S. Senate, *Journal of the Executive Proceedings of the Senate,* XII, 342–346.

27. *Cong. Globe,* 37th Cong., 2nd Sess., pp. 2717–2722; New York *Times,* June 16, 1862.

28. *Cong. Globe,* 37th Cong., 2nd Sess., pp. 2732–2737. Trumbull and Fessenden consumed more time than any other senators in discussing the resolution changing the hour of the daily meeting. It is perhaps worthy of notice that

A great deal of progress was made on the seventeenth, however. Practically the entire session was spent in action (mostly favorable) on the amendments proposed by the select committee. The main controversy was occasioned by Harlan's proposal to relocate the eastern terminus of the Union Pacific in such a way as to make it more favorable to the Iowa railroads. The Senate select committee, after considerable skirmishing, had already made a modification in the route to accommodate Harlan, who had been added to the committee primarily to accord representation to Iowa interests. McDougall, obviously much irritated, took Harlan to task for agreeing to the compromise in committee and then trying to defeat it on the floor. After lengthy debate, Harlan's amendment was defeated by a vote of 18 to 21. Practically all of Harlan's support came from New England Republicans (who desired to embarrass the bill) and from senators from the upper midwestern states which would have benefited from the change. Before adjournment on the seventeenth, all of the committee amendments were acted upon and the bill was reported to the Senate.[29]

On the next day (June 18), another lengthy session was devoted to the Pacific railway bill. With the exception of several items on which separate votes were demanded, the amendments were quickly concurred in. One modification excepted (by Anthony of Rhode Island) would have struck out of the House bill the provision which specifically reserved to Congress the right to amend or repeal the act. The two California senators championed the amendment, but Clark of New Hampshire and Howard of Michigan opposed any change which would restrict the future power of Congress over the entire project. After considerable discussion, the Senate voted to nonconcur in the amendment. The effect of this action was to retain the

---

both of these senators had aided in delaying the Pacific railway bill on earlier occasions. In fact, the New York *Times* correspondent in Washington charged that the delay in disposing of the Pacific railway bill was the result of a covert opposition to the measure on the part of certain (unnamed) New England senators who favored another proposal. See New York *Times,* June 19, 1862. The reference to another proposal probably was aimed at the People's Pacific Railroad Company, a New England organization.

29. Thomas Ewing, Jr., to Thomas Ewing, Sr., May 28, June 7, 1862, Thomas Ewing Papers, Library of Congress; *Cong. Globe,* 37th Cong., 2nd Sess., pp. 2749–2762. There was obviously no quorum during most of the day's session.

provision specifically reserving to Congress the right to amend or repeal the act.[30]

Another major controversy resulted from Collamer's proposal to withhold from the companies a portion of the government bonds until the entire line from the Missouri River to the Sacramento River was completed. The Vermont senator proposed that the government retain fifty percent of the bonds due on either end of the line and twenty-five percent of those due on the center section. This was, naturally, strongly opposed by McDougall. Other friends of the road, especially Sherman and James H. Lane, directed their efforts toward reducing the percentage of the bonds to be withheld, evidently conceding that some provision of this nature was almost certain to be incorporated in the bill. Senators not notably friendly to the measure (e.g., Morrill) seconded their pleas, and even Collamer was apparently convinced of the inevitability of a reduction before an executive session brought the discussion to a close.[31]

On June 19, Collamer's amendment was modified to require the withholding of twenty-five percent of the bonds due for building the eastern and western extremities of the road and fifteen percent of the bonds due on the central portion. The proposal was then adopted. Most of the day's lengthy session was spent debating proposals to eliminate the eastern branches authorized by the bill. Clark led the fight to lop off these branches and several other Republican senators, notably Ten Eyck of New Jersey, Morrill of Maine, and Howe of Wisconsin supported him. But such pruning ran counter to the demands of powerful local interests, and a number of senators rushed to the defense of these lines. McDougall and Wade were undoubtedly inspired more by a fear that such cutting would lead to the defeat of the entire measure than by any devotion to individual lines. Most of the defenders of the branches, however, represented the states most directly concerned—Kansas (James H. Lane), Iowa (Grimes and Harlan), and Minnesota (Rice and Wilkinson).

When the Senate eliminated the Leavenworth branch, Clark turned his

30. *Cong. Globe,* 37th Cong., 2nd Sess., pp. 2776–2789. There were, of course, sometimes extensive discussions on minor points. A good example of this type of debate on the eighteenth would be the clash between St. Joseph, Missouri, interests and Atchison, Kansas, interests in determining the exact location of one of the branches. See *ibid.,* pp. 2776–2778.

31. *Ibid.,* pp. 2785–2789.

attention to the Sioux City line. He announced his intention to move to abolish each of the branches successively, starting with the least important, as long as the Senate would sustain him. The solons quickly brought this program to an end when they refused, by a vote of 16 to 23, to strike out the Sioux City branch. Doolittle then attempted to reverse this pruning process by proposing a number of additional sections authorizing a huge grant of land to aid the construction of a Northern Pacific railroad. McDougall insisted that such a provision would embarrass the bill, and the amendment was defeated, 15 to 23. After some additional discussion on various minor points, the Senate found itself without a quorum and consequently adjourned.[32]

On the following day, the final assault on the branch lines was made when Trumbull of Illinois moved to locate the eastern terminus of the line on the Missouri River rather than on the one-hundredth meridian. Such action would effectively destroy any real possibility of constructing profitable eastern branches. Several western senators—Harlan, Doolittle, and Pomeroy—immediately voiced strong opposition to this proposal. They admitted that the branches had been attached to the main line to protect and advance the interests of existing companies, but insisted that this was in accordance with established policy. Wade asserted that the branches alone would be of considerable value to the government whether the main line was ever completed or not. Trumbull's amendment was defeated by a vote of 18 to 35. A faint echo of the old tradition of public control of corporations clothed in the public interest was heard when Henderson introduced an amendment authorizing Congress to fix the passenger and freight rates on the road. The proposal was quickly rejected without a division. After acting upon a number of other minor amendments, the Senate finally reached a vote on the Pacific railroad bill. The measure was passed, 35 to 5. The opposition consisted of three Republicans (Howe of Wisconsin, King of New York, and Wilkinson of

32. *Ibid.,* pp. 2804–2818. It is possible that Clark's real objective was to defeat the entire measure. The sections authorizing the construction of the various branches represented a delicate balance struck among conflicting railroad interests in the western states. It was at least doubtful that the House would consent to pass the bill without providing for the construction of these branch lines. Throughout the entire debate, Clark had certainly given no indication of friendliness toward the measure.

Minnesota); one Democrat (Pearce of Maryland); and one Unionist (Wright of Indiana).[33]

The House received the amended measure on Monday, June 23, and returned it to the Select Committee on the Pacific Railroad. The committee wasted no time. On the following day, Campbell reported the bill back to the House with the recommendation that that body concur in the Senate amendments. The majority of the changes, he said, were "more in form than in substance," and the friends of the measure were willing to accept the additional strictures placed on the companies rather than run the risk of the bill's defeat. The House concurred in the Senate amendments by a majority of almost five to one. Among the Republicans, only Frederick A. Conkling of New York and Justin S. Morrill of Vermont cast votes against concurrence. Of the eighteen members of the majority party who had opposed the original bill, twelve voted to concur in the amendments and four were absent. The remaining negative votes were cast by fifteen Democrats and four Unionists. After years of disputation, the deed was done. "It appears to us," exulted the San Francisco *Daily Alta California,* "that there is abundant cause for joy and public rejoicing." And so it seemed to many.[34]

This action did not, to be sure, terminate the activities of the Thirty-seventh Congress in the field of Pacific railroad legislation. Early in the Third Session, McDougall introduced a bill amendatory to the Pacific railroad act—a measure intended to ease the restrictions on the railroad companies. Most of the changes were not of any great importance but were designed to make it easier to sell stock and acquire right of way, and to confirm certain corporate changes that had taken place. The fourth section of the bill, however, was by no means unimportant. In effect, it repealed the original bill's bond-retention provision. Though the Senate eliminated this proposal, McDougall did succeed in inserting another section which revised the bond-withholding provision in a manner advan-

33. *Ibid.,* pp. 2832–2840. Ten Eyck was excused from voting on the bill. He said he did not wish to vote against a Pacific railroad bill but he could not conscientiously support this measure. Henry S. Lane announced that he opposed the addition of the various branches and had done his best to get them eliminated, but he felt bound to support the bill as a measure of public necessity.

34. *Ibid.,* pp. 2879, 2905–2906; San Francisco *Daily Alta California,* June 28, 1862.

tageous to the companies. Another interesting proposition was advanced by one of the Kansas senators. During the debate on the bill, Pomeroy (probably with a view to utilizing the labor of "contrabands") attempted to insert an amendment authorizing the enlisting of railway workers by the companies under "a military organization" with the terms of enlistment to be enforced by the army. Many senators declared this to be equivalent to slavery, and Harlan vehemently asserted that if the road could not be built by free labor, it had better not be built at all. On the final vote, only McDougall and Pomeroy supported the amendment. Pomeroy also tried to insert a provision permitting the companies to purchase foreign iron if a sufficient quantity of American iron was not available at less than $60 a ton. This proposal was quickly defeated by a vote of 11 to 25.

After three days of debate, the Senate passed the bill on February 25, 1863. It was all wasted effort, for despite the frantic last-minute efforts of Campbell, the House was unable to act upon, or even consider, the measure before the expiration of the session.[35]

The Third Session of the Thirty-seventh Congress did pass one act, however, which bore directly on the construction of the transcontinental railway. The Pacific Railway Act had given the President the power to fix the gauge of the entire line, and on January 21, 1863, he issued an executive order establishing the gauge at five feet. It may be possible that from an engineering point of view this decision represented the highest wisdom, but from the economic and political viewpoint it was a sad mistake. Though many of the roads in the South and all of the roads in California were constructed on this gauge, most of the railroads in the states north of the Ohio (with the exception of Missouri) were built on a gauge of 4 feet, 8½ inches. Thus, the construction of the transcontinental railway on the wider gauge would necessitate either the regauging of most of the eastern lines or the unloading and reloading of the through freight shipped westward over those lines.[36]

35. *Cong. Globe,* 37th Cong., 3d Sess., pp. 171–172, 1179–1181, 1240–1248, 1277–1278, 1487–1488, 1542. It is worthy of note that every proposal made at this time was favorable to the companies, often at the expense of other economic interests, the government, and the nation as a whole.

36. Abraham Lincoln, "Executive Order of January 21, 1863," in Richardson, *op. cit.,* VI, 160. For a discussion of the gauges of the various lines, see *Cong.*

Three days after the issuance of the President's executive order, Harlan introduced a bill to establish the gauge of the Pacific railroad at 4 feet, 8½ inches. The Select Committee on the Pacific Railroad, to which the measure was referred, reported it back to the Senate on February 5. Though the bill encountered spirited opposition from the California senators, it was debated for short periods on only two days—February 14 and 18—and passed by a vote of 26 to 9. Six of the negative votes were cast by senators from the states of California, Oregon, Kansas, and Missouri. On March 2, the bill passed the House without discussion and without a division.[37]

This was the last piece of Pacific railway legislation considered by the Thirty-seventh Congress. One could hardly say that this Congress established the Pacific railroad, for several supplementary acts were passed before the companies finally began work on the line. But the Thirty-seventh Congress had opened the door of the treasury to these interests, and future events would demonstrate that the railroad corporations had no hesitancy in accepting the invitation. In the years that followed the Civil War, the railway interests of the country—and especially the Union Pacific Railroad, created by this act—sustained and encouraged by federal funds, mushroomed into one of the most powerful and ruthless lobbies that the republic had ever known. At first glance it may, in fact, seem strange that open lobbying was not more in evidence in 1862 than this

---

Globe, 37th Cong., 3d Sess., pp. 958–960. Lincoln requested opinions from the members of his cabinet as to the correct gauge for the Pacific railway, but there is some difference of opinion as to whether he called for these opinions before he issued the executive order fixing the guage or only after opposition to the five-foot guage had begun to develop. McDougall, speaking on the Senate floor, asserted (*Cong. Globe,* 37th Cong., 3d Sess., p. 959) that he consulted with the cabinet before issuing the order. Welles, on the other hand, noted (*Diary,* [January 24, 1862], I, 228–229) the President's request on January 24, three days after the order was issued. McDougall and Campbell (the chairmen of the Senate and House select committees) had recommended the five-foot guage to the President within a month after the passage of the original bill. See James A. McDougall and James H. Campbell to Abraham Lincoln, July 15, 1862, Lincoln Papers, Library of Congress.

37. *Cong. Globe,* 37th Cong., 3d Sess., pp. 492, 726, 958–960, 1046–1049, 1064, 1484. On January 30, 1863, Wilson introduced a similar bill in the House, but nothing more was ever heard of it. See *ibid.,* p. 626. Lincoln signed the bill on March 3. See *ibid.,* Appendix, p. 233.

account would indicate. Actually, this circumstance is easily explained. The railroads directly concerned were local companies. The Union Pacific did not yet exist, and the Central Pacific was a weak California corporation. The other roads involved were small Missouri, Iowa, and Kansas companies. These local interests could depend on the senators and representatives from their states to work actively in their behalf. One Kansas line did, in fact, have a vigorous lobbyist in the nation's capital—Thomas Ewing, Jr.—but most of the other railways apparently preferred to rely primarily on their congressional advocates. They could scarcely have been disappointed by the activity and accomplishments of such legislators as McDougall, Latham, Harlan, Sargent, James F. Wilson, and Francis P. Blair, Jr. It should also be noted that various New England members gave active support to the competing People's Pacific Railroad Company of Maine. Thus, it is clear that corporate influence on legislation was already much in evidence—only the form was different. The public may have demanded the passage of *a* Pacific railway act, but the railroad corporations had considerable influence on the framing of *the* Pacific Railway Act.

The passage of the Pacific Railroad Act, however, had a still more obvious result. It made possible the breaking of the Great Plains transportation barrier. It was highly unlikely that the first transcontinental railway would be financed by private capital. The size of the task and the area in which the construction would take place also made city, state, and territorial support unobtainable and, in any event, insufficient. This left only the federal government as a source of the needed funds, and in the absence of such legislation as that passed by the Thirty-seventh Congress, the delay in constructing the line might well have been so lengthy as to endanger national unity. In 1861–63, the talk of the secession of the west coast states did not seem fantastic. Nor could the economic development of the Great Plains proceed without access to the East by rail. The region seemed destined by nature to be an area of commercial agriculture. Such an economy can exist only if the agricultural commodities can be transported to market. In the last half of the nineteenth century only railroads could accomplish this task in the Great Plains area. Hence, the Thirty-seventh Congress initiated a sequence of events which made it feasible for one quarter of the continental United States to be occupied. It is certain that the federal government was defrauded; it is probable that the cost to the nation was exorbitant; but eventually this and other transcontinental lines were built. Ignoring the cries of the calamity-howlers who—for personal, political, or sectional reasons—desired the defeat or postponement of the Pacific Railroad Act, Congress had confidently seized its opportunity and made a sizable and important addition to the blueprint for modern America.

The Illinois Ship Canal Bill

In the public land legislation of the Thirty-seventh Congress, a balance had been struck between benefits to the eastern and western sections of the country. The Homestead Act was viewed as beneficial primarily to the western states, whose rapid growth it was expected to foster. The Land-Grant College Act, however, was thought to be especially advantageous to the eastern states, which, because of their greater population, would be entitled to the lion's share of the lands distributed.

The construction of the transcontinental railroad would obviously be of most direct value to the states west of the Mississippi. It was, perhaps, only natural that Congress should also be asked to pass internal improvement legislation which would be of more direct benefit to the Midwest and East. Such legislation was the ship canal bill. The opposition it met, however, was to develop along lines totally unlike those marked out by congressional action on the public land bills. Hostility to the ship canal bill was centered in the eastern area itself and sprang primarily from certain powerful vested interests in that region.

Early in the Second Session of the Thirty-seventh Congress, Arnold of Illinois introduced a resolution directing the House Committee on Roads and Canals to inquire into the expediency of enlarging the Illinois and Michigan Canal (connecting Lake Michigan and the Illinois River) "so as to open steam navigation between the Mississippi river and the lakes."[38] Though the resolution was adopted, there were no immediate or striking results. It is somewhat difficult to understand why the committee permit-

38. *Cong. Globe,* 37th Cong., 2nd Sess., p. 56. The date was December 11, 1861. Arnold was an attorney for the Illinois and Michigan Canal Company. See Isaac N. Arnold to Richard Yates, March 25, 1862, Richard Yates Papers, Illinois State Historical Library.

ted month after month to pass without reporting on this matter. The Commitee on Roads and Canals was certainly not overworked. It made only seven reports to the House during the entire Second Session. Furthermore, Arnold, as a member of the committee, was in a position to press for action on the resolution. On the basis of their subsequent votes and speeches, five of the nine members apparently favored the proposal. But the chairman, Mallory of Kentucky, was opposed to the project, and this may have been the reason for the delay. No report was forthcoming until April 28, 1862, and by that time the views of the Committee on Roads and Canals were no longer of any importance.[39]

On January 20, 1862, "Frank" Blair, chairman of the Committee on Military Affairs (one of the two busiest House committees), secured the passage of a resolution directing his committee to inquire into the expediency of constructing a ship canal from Chicago to the Illinois River. The military affairs committee was at least as friendly to the proposal as the Committee on Roads and Canals. In addition, its chairman was an ardent supporter of the project, for his home city St. Louis might be expected to profit greatly from such construction. One month later, the group submitted a thirteen-page report which advocated the construction of the canal for reasons of military necessity and commercial advantage. The report and the bill which accompanied it were ordered printed, and the bill was recommitted.[40]

The Committee on Military Affairs had made a rapid start, but many months would pass before any real action would be taken on the measure. For more than seven weeks, nothing was heard about the subject. Then, on April 14, Blair tried to report a ship canal bill (H.R. No. 288), but he was unable to obtain unanimous consent and the House refused to suspend the rules to permit the report to be made. Seven weeks later, Blair sandwiched the bill between two other proposals at the tail-end of a long day's session and secured its printing and recommittal. Finally, on

39. For committee membership, see *Cong. Globe,* 37th Cong., 1st Sess., p. 21. See also *Cong. Globe,* 37th Cong., 2nd Sess., pp. 1846, *passim.*

40. *Cong. Globe,* 37th Cong., 2nd Sess., pp. 400, 902–903; Committee on Military Affairs, U.S. House of Representatives, *Report* [*on a Ship Canal to Connect the Mississippi River and Lake Michigan*], Ho. Com. Repts., 37th Cong., 2nd Sess., No. 37, [1144].

June 13, 1862, the ship canal bill was reported to the House for action. It was referred to the Committee of the Whole, reported back to the house without action, and postponed to June 24.[41]

The bill endorsed by the military affairs committee provided for the construction by the federal government of a ship canal six feet deep and 160 feet wide, from Lake Michigan to the Mississippi River. Work would start when Illinois transferred the ownership of the Illinois and Michigan Canal to the federal government and the President approved a plan for the construction. The Secretary of War was to direct the building and operation of the canal, and when the tolls collected should have reimbursed the government for the costs incurred, the canal was to be returned to the state.[42]

On the twenty-fourth, Blair offered some additional amendments, and the bill was again postponed. The proposed modifications were quite significant. One of them limited expenditures on the Illinois canal to ten million dollars, and the other authorized the spending of more than three million dollars to enlarge the Erie and Oswego canals in New York.[43]

This latter amendment was particularly important. Many New Yorkers undoubtedly would have supported the ship canal bill in its original form, for the enlargement of the Illinois and Michigan Canal would benefit the Erie Canal by increasing the volume of lake commerce. The proposal to expend this large a sum in improving the Erie and Oswego canals, however, practically insured the support of the entire New York delegation.

The details of the Erie Canal amendment had apparently been common knowledge for some time, for throughout May and June the Phila-

41. *Cong. Globe,* 37th Cong., 2nd Sess., pp. 1659–1660, 2537, 2711, 2713–2714. The supporters of the measure had not been idle during this long interval, however. Not only had significant log-rolling amendments been drafted (and other voting commitments probably made), but an appeal for presidential support had been made. But Lincoln, despite the importance of the measure to Illinois, apparently did not actively press for the bill's passage. See Isaac N. Arnold to Abraham Lincoln, June 9, 1862, Lincoln Papers, Library of Congress; Philadelphia *Inquirer,* June 6, 21, 1862.

42. *Cong. Globe,* 37th Cong., 2nd Sess., p. 2711.

43. *Ibid.,* pp. 2906, 3023.

delphia *Inquirer* launched numerous attacks on the proposal. Referring to it as a "Great Scheme of Plunder," this journal charged that the measure was to be carried by the use of a corruption fund raised from New York sources and promises of votes for such disparate proposals as the New York–Washington Airline Railroad, the Lexington–Cumberland Gap Railroad, and the location of a navy yard on League Island in Pennsylvania. The *Inquirer* denied that the canal enlargement would benefit the nation as a whole and insisted that benefits would be narrowly sectional. "All other men," the editor sarcastically remarked, "to be sure, can see that it would vastly swell the internal business of New York City, at the cost, not only of all her sister cities near the seaboard, but of all the great intermediate towns—now halting points—between herself and the Mississippi. . . . But New Yorkers do not see this, or, seeing, disregard it! Their views are purely national. Oh, certainly!"[44]

Formal debate on the ship canal bill began in the House on June 30, 1862. The opening remarks were made by the representative who had reported the measure, Francis P. Blair, Jr. Presenting the bill as "the twin measure to that which has been passed by Congress for the construction of a Pacific Railroad," the Missouri congressman defended the proposal primarily on the grounds that it would permit the rapid transfer of naval vessels to the Great Lakes in the event of a war with Britain. This same argument was advanced in speeches by Republicans Arnold of Illinois, and Ely, Pomeroy, Olin, and Van Horn of New York, though Pomeroy and Van Horn also stressed commercial advantages.

After opposition speeches by Democrats James R. Morris and Clement L. Vallandigham of Ohio, Thaddeus Stevens launched a satirical attack on the bill by introducing an amendment authorizing an appropriation of one hundred million dollars for the canalizing of the Susquehanna River to its source and the construction of a canal from thence to Lake Erie. He asserted that the canal bill was a purely political measure designed to increase the re-election prospects of a number of representatives. His motion to postpone the bill until the following January was narrowly defeated (57–58), and Francis P. Blair, Jr., then called the previous

44. Philadelphia *Inquirer,* May 2, 8, 9, 13, 21, 29, June 6, 19, 21, 1862. The quotation is from the issue of June 19.

question on the measure. At this point the opponents of the bill entered and demanded the yeas and nays on a series of dilatory motions with the obvious intention of preventing a vote. This effort was successful, and the House finally adjourned without further action on the bill.[45]

On the following day, after some speaking and skirmishing, Blair renewed his call for the previous question. The opponents of the measure forced a roll-call vote on a procedural motion, and thus whipped a large number of absentees into the House. Holman of Indiana then moved to table the bill, and this motion was carried by a vote of 65 to 63. The majority was composed of thirty-five Republicans, eighteen Democrats, and twelve Unionists.[46]

The distinct sectional alignment of the vote revealed clearly the nature of the major groups opposing the bill's passage. As might be expected, the principal opposition came from other transportation interests—primarily the established railroad lines and the elements interested in the Ohio River trade. The Pennsylvania and the Baltimore and Ohio railroads, in particular, did not view the project with any great favor. The New Englanders split thirteen to eight in favor of tabling the bill. Except for New York City Republican F. A. Conkling, the entire New York delegation opposed the motion, a clear indication of the significance of the Erie Canal amendment. All of the representatives from Pennsylvania and New Jersey, on the other hand, voted to table the bill. The members from the border states split twelve to four in favor of the motion, and all of the members from the Pacific states opposed the tabling motion. Outside of Ohio and Indiana, only two affirmative votes were cast by representatives from the Midwest. The split in these two states directly reflected the opposition of Ohio River commercial interests to the canal project. Of the four Ohioans who opposed the motion, three represented districts bordering on Lake Erie. Only two members from Indiana cast negative votes—one from the Lake Michigan district and the other representing the district immediately south of the lake. Sheffield subsequently entered a

45. *Cong. Globe,* 37th Cong., 2nd Sess., pp. 3023–3034. The statement that Morris's speech was in opposition to the bill is an assumption based on the Ohio representative's subsequent votes. Morris failed to give a copy of his speech to the *Globe* reporters. See *ibid.,* p. li.

46. *Ibid.,* pp. 3055–3056, 3057.

motion to reconsider the vote tabling the bill and stated his intention to move the measure's postponement to the next session.[47]

On the following day (July 2), Sheffield called up his reconsideration motion, and Holman immediately moved to table it. This would have buried the bill beyond all practical hope of resurrection, but the House defeated Holman's motion, 56 to 71. Ten representatives from Ohio, Indiana, and New England, who had voted to table the bill on July 1, now voted against tabling the reconsideration motion.[48] By the use of delaying tactics, opponents of the bill, led by Holman, F. A. Conkling, and William Allen, managed to prevent final action on the motion; but the preliminary votes indicated that the supporters of reconsideration had a comfortable majority. Consequently, when the motion was taken up again on July 3, no further delay was attempted. The vote tabling the bill was reconsidered, and Holman then withdrew the tabling motion. The resurrected canal bill was postponed until December 18, 1862.[49]

Before the House again considered the canal bill, some changes took place in the personnel of the Committee on Military Affairs. "Frank" Blair resigned his seat in Congress to enter the army as a colonel in July 1862, and Unionist James S. Jackson of Kentucky, serving as a brigadier

47. *Ibid.,* p. 3056; New York *Herald,* July 2, 1862. In the course of later debate during the day, Potter intimated that a number of western representatives had supported the land-grant college act in order to obtain New England support for the ship canal bill. Washburne and Justin S. Morrill both denied that any understanding had existed, but Washburne did express his surprise that Morrill and other New Englanders had opposed the ship canal bill "after we of the West had generously came [*sic*] forward and voted for his measure." See *Cong. Globe,* 37th Cong., 2nd Sess., pp. 3058–3059.

48. *Cong. Globe,* 37th Cong., 2nd Sess., p. 3082. These ten representatives were Republicans Hutchins, Shellabarger, and Worcester of Ohio, Mitchell and Shanks of Indiana, Morrill and Walton of Vermont, Edwards of New Hampshire, and Loomis of Connecticut, and Unionist Sheffield of Rhode Island. The representatives from Ohio and Indiana all came from the northern sections of those states, and two of the Ohio congressmen (Hutchins and Worcester) represented districts which had an outlet on Lake Erie. Other alterations in the voting (including members absent on July 1 but voting on July 2, members voting on July 1 but absent on July 2, and members paired on July 1 but voting on July 2) slightly favored the opponents of the bill.

49. *Ibid.,* pp. 3082–3083, 3107.

general, was killed in the battle of Perryville on October 8, 1862. Jackson had seldom been seen in the Capitol, but Blair was a vigorous advocate of the canal scheme. The power of appointing replacements rested with the Speaker; Galusha Grow was a Pennsylvanian—and the Pennsylvania delegation spearheaded the opposition to the canal bill. Grow appointed his colleague McPherson to replace Blair; and Yeaman, Jackson's successor in the House, also replaced the deceased Kentuckian on the committee. Both men opposed the canal bill. Olin, however, had succeeded Blair as chairman; and thus, though five of the nine members now opposed the measure, the committee chairmanship continued in friendly hands.[50]

On the first day of the Third Session, Roscoe Conkling secured the passage of a resolution directing the House Committee on Naval Affairs to ascertain the most efficient method of placing armed vessels on the Great Lakes. The resolution specifically included the question of canal construction or enlargement within the scope of the committee's inquiries; but if Conkling thought thus to gain more ammunition for the supporters of the canal scheme, he was at the wrong arsenal. Of the eight members of the Committee on Naval Affairs, at least five (including Conkling's brother, F. A. Conkling) opposed the passage of the canal bill.[51]

More than a month passed before the naval committee made its report. This interval was marked by successive postponements of the canal measure on the floor and by vigorous behind-the-scenes efforts by lobbyists (especially from New York) to develop additional support for the

50. *Cong. Globe,* 37th Cong., 3d Sess., pp. 20, 1230; *Bio. Dir.* (1928), pp. 707, 1143. The *Biographical Directory* (p. 707) states that Jackson resigned on December 13, 1861, but this is undoubtedly incorrect. Though the Kentuckian was absent during most of the Second Session, his name continued to be called whenever a call of the House was ordered and he was present and participating in the business of the House in July of 1862. See *Cong. Globe,* 37th Cong., 2nd Sess., pp. 1045, 1227, 1314, 1340, 1483, 1614, 1910, 2560, 3186, 3333.

51. *Cong. Globe,* 37th Cong., 3d Sess., p. 2. For a list of committee members, see *Cong. Globe,* 37th Cong., 1st Sess., p. 22. Conclusions as to the attitudes of various members are drawn from their votes and speeches during the Second and Third Sessions of the Congress. The committee had originally had nine members, but Kentucky Unionist William H. Wadsworth had been excused from service on the committee in the spring of 1862, and this vacancy was apparently never filled. See *Cong. Globe,* 37th Cong., 2nd Sess., p. 2414.

proposal. The committee report on January 8 was, as might have been expected, an unfavorable one. On the following day, Henry Wilson introduced a similar bill in the Senate. The measure was referred to the Committee on Military Affairs, headed by Wilson, and reported back to the Senate on March 3. Wilson stated that the committee made no recommendation because of differences of opinion among the members, but that he, personally, favored the bill.[52]

By the time the Senate committee report was made, however, the issue was already settled in the House. The measure was brought before the House on January 16, but action on this day was limited to defeating Holman's tabling motion. Arnold, one of the bill's most ardent supporters, took advantage of a January 22 session of the Committee of the Whole to defend the measure, but it was not until almost two weeks later that the House gave the proposal any real attention.[53]

In the interim, the opposition press continued active. Though the Philadelphia *Inquirer* launched no attack like that of the previous spring, the Boston *Post* now entered the lists. This journal condemned the proposal because its "advantages are only imaginary" and because it was a part of a trend toward centralization of governmental functions which "is fast carrying us from a republic to a despotism." In a burst of candor, the editor added, "Another objection we urge is, that all these plans *leave out the New England States.*"[54]

On February 3, undisturbed by such opposition, Olin reported a new canal bill to the House. This version was essentially the same as the bill which would have resulted from the adoption of all of the committee amendments. There were several significant changes, however. The new measure provided for the federal government's permanent retention of the Illinois canal rather than its return to the state. This proposal also fixed the amount of federal aid at $13,346,824 for the Illinois project and $3,500,000 for the Erie canal enlargement. The states were required to furnish any additional money needed to complete the construction. The fifth section required that the tolls collected be paid into the federal

52. *Cong. Globe,* 37th Cong., 3d Sess., pp. 92, 236, 245, 1526; Frederick A. Conkling to Edwin D. Morgan, December 22, 1862, Edwin D. Morgan Papers, New York State Library.

53. *Cong. Globe,* 37th Cong., 3d Sess., pp. 294–302, 364–365, 463–465, 699.

54. Boston *Post,* January 22, 1863; italics in original.

treasury and "appropriated" therefrom for certain purposes. Holman contended that the bill thus made an appropriation and so must be referred to the Committee of the Whole. The Speaker sustained this point of order. Such reference would mean additional delay, so Olin secured the measure's recommittal to the military affairs committee instead.[55]

This recommittal did not mark a surrender, however, for on the following day, Olin again reported the bill to the House. The fifth section, meantime, had undergone some slight changes. There was no longer any mention of paying money into the treasury and the word "appropriated" did not appear. When Olin was asked if the committee had authorized him to report the measure in that form, he avoided answering until the bill had been read twice. By this time, McPherson of Pennsylvania had examined the bill and specifically declared that the committee had not authorized the reporting of this measure. Since the proposal had received its second reading, however, the Speaker ruled that the point of order came too late to prevent the reception and consideration of the bill. He also held that the measure, in its present form, did not make an appropriation and, therefore, did not have to be first considered in the Committee of the Whole. Another motion by Holman to table the bill was defeated, and the measure was postponed to February 6.[56]

The session of the sixth was consumed in almost continuous debate on the bill, with Republicans Olin and Dawes supporting the measure and Democrats Holman and Voorhees opposing it. Dawes and Voorhees, in particular, exchanged bitter words and were several times called to order by other members. Olin was once called to order by the Speaker, but during the latter part of the debate, Colfax occupied the chair temporarily and the discussion was allowed to range amazingly far afield without any check from that quarter. Writing at the end of this session, the Philadelphia *Inquirer*'s Washington correspondent predicted that the measure would pass the next day by a small margin despite the opposition of all the Democrats.[57]

55. *Cong. Globe,* 37th Cong., 3d Sess., pp. 699–701.

56. *Ibid.,* pp. 717–719. There can be little doubt that Olin reported the bill without the authorization of the Committee on Military Affairs.

57. *Ibid.,* pp. 766–772; Philadelphia *Inquirer,* February 7, 1863. Colfax was a supporter of the bill while Grow opposed it. It must also be said that Colfax had a less scrupulous regard for the duties and responsibilities of the Speaker than Grow had.

The following day was a Saturday, and the entire session was consumed in interminable and irritating, but not very informative, discussion of the canal bill. William Kellogg led off with a speech supporting the measure in which he charged that the opposition to the bill was inspired by the Pennsylvania Railroad. F. A. Conkling denied this, defended the report of the Committee on Naval Affairs, which Olin had previously attacked, and opposed the passage of the bill. Other opposition speeches were made by Trimble, Stevens, Porter, and Vallandigham. The latter two representatives insisted that the measure was nothing but an attempt to favor one commercial route over all others. Washburne closed the debate for the bill's supporters with a speech stressing the military and commercial advantages of the project. He then moved the previous question on the bill's passage. The proponents of the canal scheme made a determined effort to force the measure to a vote, but instead the House decided by a two-vote margin to adjourn.[58]

"The friends of the canal bill were sanguine of its passage by the House," gleefully reported the Philadelphia *Inquirer,* "but the vote to adjourn carried on Saturday evening, when the canal men wanted to get a vote on its passage, confident of success, indicated its defeat in the House." "The feeling of the Canal men is less hopeful than hitherto . . . ," added the Washington correspondent of the New York *Times.* "It is generally conceded now that the vote on the main question will be very close." Certainly the number of members in attendance on Monday would be much greater, and the chances of the bill's passage in a full House did indeed seem slim.[59]

The supporters of the measure were prepared to fight to the last ditch, however, and on Monday, February 9, after the main question was ordered, Olin made his closing remarks in favor of the bill's passage, stressing primarily the commercial advantages of the project. An amendment offered by Stevens, requiring the state of New York to transfer the Erie Canal to the federal government, was defeated by a single vote. The question then recurred on an amendment previously offered by Diven. This proposal authorized the payment of $3,500,000 to the state of New York and $13,347,000 to the state of Illinois, provided those states

58. *Cong. Globe,* 37th Cong., 3d Sess., pp. 806–816, Appendix, 106–108.

59. Philadelphia *Inquirer,* February 9, 1863; New York *Times,* February 9, 1863.

should, within three and five years respectively, make the enlargements in their canals outlined in the original bill. This substitute was adopted by a vote of 71 to 57, and the bill, as amended, was rejected by a vote of 60 to 72. Seven months of agitation had only produced a more decided majority against the measure than had been made evident in the vote on the motion to table the original bill the previous summer.[60]

"The Illinois Canal bill met its death in the House this morning," reported the Washington correspondent of the Philadelphia *Inquirer,*

> and its friends are enraged in consequence. All sorts of wrongs are charged by them upon other schemes which were to be *log-rolled* through by joint arrangements.
>
> The wrath of the canal men is principally directed towards the [New York–Washington] air line [railroad] party, who it is generally believed deliberately betrayed them, and threats not loud but deep, are offered by the Northern members, that they will be revenged by killing off the air line when it puts its head above water.

"Thus," added the editor approvingly, "a very pernicious measure, that would have subjected the Treasury to endless plunder and waste, has been put out of the way for the present, and we trust finally."[61]

But what had been the forces at work which put the "very pernicious measure . . . out of the way"? Like the tally of the previous summer, the final vote was decidedly sectional. Some shifts had taken place, however. The New England representatives, who had stood thirteen to eight against the bill in July, now voted sixteen to four for the measure. One quarter of the New York delegation, on the other hand, now cast negative votes. There were few other voting shifts, though the opposition was somewhat more solid in Ohio and the border states. There had been relatively little change in the total Republican vote. The members of this party had supported the bill by a vote of 46 to 35 in July; now the figure was 48 to 35. The major shifts came within the ranks of the two minority parties. In February, seventy-five percent of the Democrats and a slightly

60. *Cong. Globe,* 37th Cong., 3d Sess., pp. 826–831.

61. Philadelphia *Inquirer,* February 10, 1863. The Senate Committee on Military Affairs authorized an adverse report on the New York–Washington Air Line Railroad Bill two days later (February 11) but the connection between this action and the canal bill fight would seem to be extremely tenuous. See *ibid.,* February 12, 1863.

larger percentage of the Unionists voted against the bill. These men were canny politicians well aware of the political advantage that could be reaped from the partisan administration of a sixteen million dollar "slush fund." The outcome of the 1862 elections probably made them even more sensitive than usual to such possibilities, for in that year the Democrats won important victories in the states of New York and Illinois—the two states in which this money would have been expended. On the whole, however, it would seem that commercial rivalries played a larger part in the defeat of the ship canal bill than did political rivalries.[62]

Taking a backward look, it is obvious that these four major public-land and internal-improvement proposals—the Homestead Act, the Land-Grant College Act, the Pacific Railroad Act, and the Ship Canal Bill—form a pattern which illustrates the changing concept of Congress regarding the role of the national government in the life of the nation's citizens. The initial measure provided for the distribution of the public lands to individuals for settlement purposes. In the eyes of many, this was merely returning the land to its rightful owners. Though a great change in American public-land policy was thus effected, the Homestead Act was essentially the culmination of the agitation of an earlier era and was the logical end of the road marked by the mileposts of the relief acts of 1821–1832, the pre-emption acts of 1830–1841, and the graduation act of 1854. The Land-Grant College Act, though more novel in its character, was basically the application on a national scale of a principle long established on the state and local level—the use of public lands to foster public education. Since the states still administered the grants, the most significant shift here was the extent of the federal involvement.

The Pacific Railway Act was a more radical departure still. There were precedents for the granting of federal lands to aid the construction of railways, but in 1862 the national government undertook to distribute these lands directly to the railroad companies, rather than through the agency of the states. In a project the size of the transcontinental railroad, land grants alone were not thought to be sufficient, and large amounts of federal securities were made available to the companies on a loan basis. Through the government members of the Union Pacific board of direc-

62. *Cong. Globe,* 37th Cong., 3d Sess., pp. 830–831; New York *Herald,* February 10, 1863; *Tribune Almanac* (1863), pp. 51–52, 58–59; New York *Times,* February 9, 1863.

tors, the national government also became directly involved, in a minority role, in the construction and operation of the railway. In the case of the Illinois Ship Canal Bill, there was no thought of using public lands. The supporters of this measure asked for both federal money and federal construction; and had the bill passed, the government would have continued indefinitely as the sole operator of a major transportation work.

The pattern is clear. The concept of the disposal of public lands for the benefit of the entire population was superseded by a concept of the expenditure of federal funds for the benefit of a small but powerful group of individuals and corporations. The use of the states as agents was discarded. The federal bounty (both natural and fiscal) was to be distributed selectively and directly, rather than broadly and indirectly. In short, the Thirty-seventh Congress ushered in four decades of neo-Hamiltonianism: government for the benefit of the privileged few. The design was Hamiltonian, too, in another sense—for the agrarians were not numbered among the privileged. The Homestead Act was rendered unworkable by the removal of huge blocks of land from entry under the Land-Grant College Act and the Pacific Railroad Act. Subsequent grants further restricted the land available for homesteading. In the postwar era, public lands were handed over to private transportation interests, while legislation ostensibly designed to assist the farmers was notoriously ineffective.

In the construction of the edifice of modern America, however, one section of the 1861–63 blueprint was not followed. The Union Pacific was not hampered in its predatory operations by the government directors, but rather the corporation came to have great influence in the legislative halls. Other interests, desirous of demonstrating that they, too, were powerful, and hence deserving of preference, hastened to the feast. The federal government ceased to exert any considerable control over the utilization of its bounty. It is perhaps not without significance that the Thirty-seventh Congress defeated the ship canal bill with its provision for government ownership of public transportation.

There sometimes seems to be a fearful inevitability about the increasing corporate influence in the federal government in the ensuing years. The corruption of the Grant era almost appears to be a natural growth (rather than a cancer) on the body politic. It might be said that (except for a few judicious erasures) the Thirty-seventh Congress had drawn the blueprint for the Gilded Age.

CHAPTER 7

Congress and Taxation: Revenue Measures

The question of finances probably gave the Thirty-seventh Congress as much trouble as any other single issue. The financial problem divides itself roughly into three areas—currency, government borrowing, and taxation. Currency legislation is discussed elsewhere in this study. Government borrowing ultimately provided the overwhelming preponderance of the money used by the federal government in fighting the war. The reasons which moved the President, the Secretary of the Treasury, and the Congress to rely on the sale of interest-bearing government securities have been repeatedly listed and analyzed and certainly require no additional discussion.[1] Nor will the loans themselves be discussed here, for, aside from the gold interest clause and certain peculiarities in interest rates and redemption provisions, they were significant primarily because of their size. Not so taxation. Not only was the tax legislation of the Thirty-seventh Congress, in part, a tacit acknowledgment of changes which had already taken place in the American economy by 1861; it was also to be influential in the highest degree on the tax structure of the nation following the Civil War.

On July 5, 1861, the second day of the Special Session of the Thirty-seventh Congress, Secretary Chase made his report. He estimated the financial needs of the government for the fiscal year 1861–1862 at slightly less than $320,000,000. He proposed that one quarter of this amount should be raised by taxation. The Morrill Tariff, Chase said, should produce about $30,000,000 annually, and receipts from land sales should yield an additional $3,000,000. The Secretary proposed that the import duties on sugar be increased and that duties be placed on tea and coffee, currently on the free list. He estimated that these taxes would produce an additional $20,000,000 yearly. Another $7,000,000, Chase

1. E.g., Arthur C. Bining, *The Rise of American Economic Life,* p. 342.

thought, could be raised "from proposed duties on articles now exempt, and from changed duties on articles now either lightly burdened or so heavily taxed that the tax amounts to a prohibition." These estimates accounted for three quarters of the desired tax income and left $20,000,000 to be obtained either by direct taxation or by excise taxes or by a combination of both. The Secretary refused to make any recommendation as to how these funds should be procured, leaving this "to the superior wisdom of Congress."[2]

However inadequate these recommendations might appear in retrospect, many contemporary observers considered them to be sound. The House referred the report to the appropriate committees, and in the Senate it was ordered to lie on the table.[3]

Chase's report seemed to indicate that he favored eliminating some of the Morrill Tariff's protective features. This stand was not advanced enough for some of the representatives, however, and even before the reception of the Secretary's report, Vallandigham of Ohio had served notice that he would introduce a bill to revise the tariff. He did this on July 8. His proposal would have repealed the Morrill Tariff and reenacted the Tariff of 1857. As a matter of course, the measure was referred to the Committee of Ways and Means and (also as a matter of course) was never heard of again. "Thaddeus will take care of that," commented the Washington correspondent of the Philadelphia *Inquirer.*[4]

The *Inquirer*'s reference was, of course, to committee chairman Thaddeus Stevens, whose iron interests in his home state of Pennsylvania inclined him to be anything but hostile to the Morrill Tariff with its high duties on foreign iron. The second-ranking Republican member of the committee was the author of the Morrill Tariff, Justin S. Morrill of Vermont. Other members of the committee included the Boston banker William Appleton, the Albany ironmaster Erastus Corning, and Valentine B. Horton, who was financially interested in both coal mining and salt manufacturing. Two other Republican members, Elbridge G. Spauld-

2. *Cong. Globe,* 37th Cong., 1st Sess., p. 13; Salmon P. Chase, *Report of the Secretary of the Treasury, Sen. Exec. Docs.,* 37th Cong., 1st. Sess., No. 2 [1112].

3. *Cong. Globe,* 37th Cong., 1st Sess., pp. 11, 13; San Francisco *Daily Alta California,* July 27, 1861.

4. *Cong. Globe,* 37th Cong., 1st Sess., pp. 10, 23; Philadelphia *Inquirer,* July 10, 1861.

ing of New York and John L. N. Stratton of New Jersey, came from important manufacturing states. Only two members of the committee, Democrats John S. Phelps of Missouri and John A. McClernand of Illinois, could be counted on to support tariff reduction.[5]

The outspoken newspaper opposition in the industrial states to any reduction of import duties stiffened the resistance of the committee members. Pennsylvania papers were particularly bitter about Chase's proposal (included in a bill prepared by the Treasury Department) to reduce the rates on iron and steel. "They had better abandon all idea of raising money by a revision of the Tariff," declared the Philadelphia *Inquirer*, "and resort exclusively to popular loans, than to adopt the perilous policy developed in the proposed reduction of duties on iron."[6]

Under the stress of necessity and the Washington heat, rapid action was the rule during the short Special Session. On July 16, Stevens, from the Committee of Ways and Means, reported a bill (H.R. No. 54) to provide for increased revenue from imports. The measure was referred to the Committee of the Whole and made a special order for the following day. Vallandigham expressed the hope that a full discussion would be allowed, but Stevens made no commitment on this score.[7]

On July 17 the House, after limiting debate to one hour, proceeded to consider the tariff bill. The measure as reported from the Committee of Ways and Means made no change in the basic protective nature of the Morrill Tariff. The most important provisions laid duties on tea and coffee and many other less significant items previously on the free list and more than tripled the duties on sugar. Vallandigham moved an amendment repealing the Morrill Tariff and re-enacting the Tariff of 1857 with an additional ten percent levy on all duty-free articles except tea and coffee. The Ohio Democrat acknowledged that he had no hope that his amendment would be adopted, but desired "that the record shall remain right for *the hereafter*." He followed this statement with an attack on the original bill. Stevens and F. A. Conkling of New York spoke in defense of the measure, and a general discussion followed.

5. *Cong. Globe,* 37th Cong., 1st Sess., p. 21; *Bio. Dir.* (1928), pp. 646–647, 848–849, 1114; Richard N. Current, *Old Thad Stevens,* pp. 122–124.

6. Philadelphia *Inquirer,* July 10, 11, 12, 13, 15, 17, 1861; quotation from issue of July 11.

7. *Cong. Globe,* 37th Cong., 1st Sess., p. 152.

Several amendments were proposed, primarily directed toward striking out the duties on sugar, coffee, and tea. The Republican leadership seemed to be firmly in control, however, and the amendments were defeated; but as the day wore on, this control began to weaken, and finally an amendment introduced by Arnold of Illinois reducing the duty on coffee from five to three cents was adopted by a vote of 64 to 51. Stevens immediately leaped into the breach and moved that the committee rise. He then threatened to bring in a direct tax bill if the tariff rates should be reduced. On this note the House adjourned.[8]

The lines had tightened by the next day, and the Committee of the Whole rejected a similar reduction on tea. A number of other amendments were considered and most of them defeated. The committee did insert a provision placing a heavy tax on liquors but twice refused to reduce the rates on iron. When the bill was reported to the House, Stevens immediately presented a substitute practically identical with the bill as originally reported. Stevens now applied the party whip forcefully. "I want to try the naked question whether the Committee of Ways and Means can be sustained by the House," he declared, "because it depends altogether on that whether we will deem it worth while to proceed any further in attempting to raise revenue. . . . If the committee cannot be sustained in their action by the House, we may as well give the matter up." The application of the lash proved effective. Arnold publicly repudiated his earlier proposal, and Stevens's substitute was adopted by a vote of 82 to 48. The bill was then passed without a division.[9]

The majority was composed of seventy-four Republicans, five Democrats (four from New York and one from New Jersey), and three Unionists (Appleton of Massachusetts, Sheffield of Rhode Island, and Upton of Virginia). Making up the minority were twenty-six Democrats, thirteen Unionists, and nine Republicans. Six of these negative Republican votes came from the midwestern states, where that party was still deeply divided on the tariff issue. The other three were Buffington of Massachusetts and Edward H. Rollins of New Hampshire—both of whom were engaged in mercantile pursuits—and that perennially out-of-step representative, Van Wyck of New York. The division was along

8. *Ibid.*, pp. 171–176.
9. *Ibid.*, pp. 202–205.

both sectional and party lines. The New England representatives supported the substitute by a vote of 18 to 5, while those from the Middle West split evenly on the measure—22 to 22—with all of the affirmative votes being cast by Republicans. Only three negative votes were cast from New York and New Jersey, and only one affirmative vote from the border states. The Pennsylvania delegation divided exactly along party lines, with fourteen Republicans supporting the substitute and six Democrats opposing it.[10]

The bill was received in the Senate the next day and referred to the Committee on Finance. Here Senator Simmons of Rhode Island took control and drafted a substitute which he reported to the Senate on July 25. The Simmons substitute reduced the House-imposed duty on sugar but left those on tea, coffee, and spices essentially unchanged. Duties on most other imports, including those on the free list, were increased by ten percent. The Morrill rates would be retained for articles on which the duties already exceeded forty percent and for some insignificant items specifically listed. After an explanation, the bill was postponed until the following day.[11]

The Senate, as in Committee of the Whole, took up the bill on July 26. The amendment was considered section by section and was quickly approved with practically no discussion and only a few minor changes. Simmons then obtained another day's postponement to allow him to draft additional amendments.[12]

This maneuver was undoubtedly occasioned by the obvious difficulty which the additional revenue bill (H.R. No. 71) had encountered in the House. Stevens had reported this measure from the Committee of Ways and Means on July 23, and it was considered on the following day. The bill was designed to lay a direct tax of $30,000,000 on the states, and to institute a system of excise and license taxes. After a lengthy discussion on July 24, however, the House, despite Stevens's protests, recommitted the measure to the Committee of Ways and Means by a vote of 70 to 61.

10. *Ibid.*, p. 205; *Bio. Dir.* (1928), pp. 757, 1476. Forty-one members (almost one fourth of the House membership) failed to answer to their names on the roll call. Seventeen of these had been present earlier in the day, and nine had been in the House immediately before the vote was taken.

11. *Cong. Globe*, 37th Cong., 1st Sess., pp. 208, 253–255.

12. *Ibid.*, pp. 278–279.

The committee was instructed to consider the expediency of permitting state, rather than federal, officers to collect the taxes.

The motion to recommit was made by Roscoe Conkling and was supported by almost one third of the Republicans, more than ninety percent of the Democrats, and about seventy percent of the Unionists. The strongest opposition to the bill's recommittal came from New England, while the motion drew the support of almost all the border-state representatives. Congressmen from the Middle West supported recommittal by a margin of almost two to one, while those from New York, New Jersey, and Pennsylvania split about evenly on the issue.[13]

On the following day, Stevens reported that the committee had been unable to devise any constitutional method to carry into effect the instructions of the House. Consideration of the measure was then resumed, and two more days were spent in discussion. Though every proposed amendment was defeated, it was obvious that irritation with the bill was mounting. Wickliffe of Kentucky had already indicated his intention to move a postponement when debate on the measure was resumed on July 27. Shortly after the discussion was renewed, the Committee of the Whole voted 58 to 55 to strike the enacting clause from the bill and so reported it to the House. A lengthy and not very informative debate followed. Wickliffe moved that the measure be recommitted to the Committee of Ways and Means with instructions to report, no later than the eighteenth day of the next session, a bill providing for a revenue tariff and such other taxes as might be necessary. McClernand proposed that the postponement clause be omitted and the committee directed to report a bill reducing the direct tax to $20,000,000 and increasing the number of items on which excise and license taxes should be laid. This substitute was adopted by a vote of 73 to 33, with only four Republicans in opposition. Upon these terms, the bill was returned to the Committee of Ways and Means.[14]

While the House retreated from the brink of legislative action, demands outside of Congress for the passage of a tax bill were mounting. "The Northern people are not only ready and willing to be taxed," cried

13. *Ibid.*, pp. 229, 246–252.

14. *Ibid.*, pp. 268–274, 280–287, 299–308. The Republicans casting negative votes were John Covode of Pennsylvania and Anson P. Morrill, Frederick A. Pike, and Charles W. Walton of Maine.

the San Francisco *Daily Alta California,* "but they insist upon being taxed. . . . They will be taxed from the crown of their heads to the soles of their feet; taxed for all they hear and all they see, for everything movable and immovable under the whole canopy of Heaven, taxed for the very air they breathe" until the rebellion should be crushed.[15]

Simmons was willing to do his part. Before the House had taken final action on the measure (but after the Committee of the Whole had voted to strike the enacting clause from the original bill), he reported his amendment to the Senate. The session was growing old, and he dared not wait for the House action to raise the necessary additional revenue. Simmons's amendment laid a five percent tax on all income except that derived from government securities (taxed at 2½ percent) and that of United States citizens living abroad (taxed at 7½ percent). A system of assessors and collectors was provided and these officials were authorized to seize the property of anyone who should refuse to pay the tax and, if necessary, to imprison such persons.[16]

On the following Monday (July 29), the Senate, as in Committee of the Whole, gave its attention to these proposals. Simmons opened the discussion with a speech defending the bill generally and touching only briefly on the sections laying an income tax. In answer to a question by Clark of New Hampshire, the Rhode Island senator insisted that the tax would be levied on the net, rather than gross, income. He was decidedly opposed, however, to the insertion of the word "net" into the text of the measure, and the Senate, by a vote of 10 to 18, sustained him in this matter. The new sections were quickly approved, and the bill was reported to the Senate.

The discussion which followed concerned itself almost entirely with the tariff sections of the measure. Sumner of Massachusetts, chairman of the Committee on Foreign Relations, expressed grave doubts that the ten percent across-the-board increase would augment the revenue. He suggested, on the contrary, that the rates would be prohibitory and would probably cause a decrease in imports sufficient to diminish the revenue.

15. San Francisco *Daily Alta California,* August 6, 1861. The late date of this statement is explained by the fact that there was at this time no telegraphic communication with the west coast and there was, thus, generally a two- or three-week delay before news of congressional action reached California.

16. *Cong. Globe,* 37th Cong., 1st Sess., pp. 297, 314.

The higher rates, he added, were certain to cause dissatisfaction in Europe and thus complicate foreign relations. Simmons, a yarn manufacturer, had probably calculated even more closely than Sumner the protective aspects of the tariff increase. Both he and Fessenden replied to Sumner, but neither attempted to come to grips with the question of whether or not the tariff would produce additional revenue. Sumner's motion to strike the ten percent increase was decisively defeated, 7 to 29.[17]

It was only very late in the day, after the bill's supporters had beaten down all attempts to modify the measure, that the constitutionality of laying an income tax was first questioned by Rice. The replies of Fessenden and Collamer to Rice's inquiries were more notable for their evasions than for their explanations. The Minnesota senator's questions, brief as they were, stirred Saulsbury's constitutional conscience and perhaps that of other senators as well. In any event, repeated attempts failed to produce a quorum for a final vote and, after the Republicans had received a tongue-lashing from Fessenden, their senate leader, the Senate was forced to adjourn.[18]

Fessenden's fear of an adjournment was entirely justified. On Monday evening, the vote which had revealed the absence of a quorum had shown the Senate to be divided 27 to 7 in favor of the bill; but when the final vote was taken on the measure, about an hour after the opening of the next day's session, it passed by the very narrow margin of 22 to 18. Four Republicans who had supported the bill on the twenty-ninth now cast negative votes. Five other members of the majority party who had previously favored the measure were not present for the vote, though all were in the Senate later in the day. The majority consisted of twenty-one Republicans and one Democrat (McDougall of California), while negative votes were cast by five Republicans, eleven Democrats, and two Unionists. No New England senator voted against the bill, and no border-state senator voted for it. Only a single vote from the middle states was cast against the measure, but the middlewestern senators opposed the bill by a margin

17. *Ibid.*, pp. 313–321; *Bio. Dir.* (1950), pp. 1813–1814.

18. *Cong. Globe,* 37th Cong., 1st Sess., pp. 321–323. On this same day Stevens reported an amended revenue bill to the House in accordance with the instructions of that body. The measure was passed and sent to the Senate and referred to the Committee on Finance, but nothing more was ever heard of it. See *ibid.*, pp. 323–331, 336.

of eight to five, with five absentees. The Pacific coast senators split almost evenly on the measure, with two supporting it, one opposing it, and one not voting.[19]

The bill was now returned to the House and, on the motion of Stevens, that body immediately refused to concur in the Senate amendments and asked for a committee of conference. The Senate insisted on its amendments and the president pro tem appointed Simmons, Collamer, and Bright to meet with Representatives Stevens, Justin S. Morrill, and Corning to work out the differences between the two houses. The committee made its report on August 2, and on that same date the New York *Times* carried an account of the monthly meeting of the New York Chamber of Commerce. This body had adopted a resolution declaring that success in floating government loans "will depend upon the enactment by Congress, now in session, of revenue and internal tax bills adapted to the existing emergency."[20]

Had the conference committee produced a bill "adapted to the existing emergency?" It was difficult to tell. The measure reported was a somewhat weird combination of sections drawn from the original House bill, the Senate amendments to it, and the additional revenue bill passed by the House on July 29. In general, the tariff provisions were taken from the original measure. The ten percent across-the-board increase was eliminated, but additional duties were laid on liquors. The income tax provision was taken from the Senate amendment, but the rate was fixed at three percent rather than five. The measure reported by the conference committee also included the section from the House additional revenue bill laying a direct tax of $20,000,000.

In the Senate, the report led to considerable discussion, consisting largely of explanations by various senators of the votes they intended to give. The Senate then approved the report, 34 to 8. Bright of Indiana, Latham of California, five border-state Democrats, and one border-state

19. *Ibid.*, pp. 323, 335–336. The four Republicans who changed their votes were Grimes and Harlan of Iowa, Harris of New York, and Trumbull of Illinois. The five Republicans who supported the bill on the twenty-ninth, but absented themselves on the thirtieth were Bingham and Chandler of Michigan, Hale of New Hampshire, James H. Lane of Kansas, and Wade of Ohio. One Republican (Browning of Illinois) voted against the bill on both occasions.

20. *Ibid.*, pp. 343–344, 354, 395, 415; New York *Times*, August 2, 1861.

Unionist cast the negative votes. Four Democrats and one Unionist joined the Republicans in supporting the committee action.

In the House, Stevens allowed very little discussion before forcing the report to a vote. It was approved by a vote of 89 to 39. The opposition consisted of twenty-seven Democrats, ten Unionists, and two Michigan Republicans—Beaman and Trowbridge.[21]

When the Special Session of the Thirty-seventh Congress came to an end four days later, the taxation policy of Congress was already roughed out. Import duties had been increased, a direct tax had been imposed, and an income tax had been levied for the first time in American fiscal history. Excise and license taxes had not been enacted, but this was largely accidental. The additional revenue bill passed by the House on July 29 had included such taxes, but the committee of conference set these duties aside. Time was to show that during this summer session Congress had labored under a gross misapprehension regarding the fiscal needs of the nation. In extenuation, it should be added that this misapprehension was shared with practically everyone else in government circles, including the Secretary of the Treasury, upon whose recommendations Congress had relied heavily in determining taxation requirements.

The Second Session of the Thirty-seventh Congress convened on December 2, 1861, and the report of the Secretary of the Treasury was sent in one week later. It was already apparent to Chase that his previous estimates were grossly inaccurate. The Secretary reported that the revenue would fall short of his July figures by some thirty percent and that expenditures would exceed his earlier estimate by almost seventy percent. Even in the face of this situation, Chase could bring himself to make only some very hesitant steps in the direction of tax increases. He implied that he disliked the income tax but did not go so far as to recommend its repeal. He called for higher import duties on tea, coffee, and sugar; an increase in the direct tax; and the imposition of a few excise taxes.[22]

That the Secretary's proposals were woefully inadequate to deal with

21. *Cong. Globe,* 37th Cong., 1st Sess., pp. 395–400, 415–416. The conference committee fixed the tax on the income from federal securities at 1½ percent and that on the incomes of United States citizens residing abroad (if derived from domestic sources) at 5 percent.

22. Salmon P. Chase, *Report of the Secretary of the Treasury, Sen. Exec. Docs.,* 37th Cong., 2nd Sess., No. 2, [1121].

the existing financial crisis was obvious even to many contemporaries. "It has been, in our view," commented the Democratic Boston *Post* somewhat later, "the short-coming of Mr. Chase from the beginning, that his measures have not been sufficiently large, broad and confident. Prudence in financiering is excellent, but it must be real, not sham prudence. Real prudence obtains a *sufficiency of means,* and neither in his negotiations, his tax estimates, nor his preparations for the future, has the present Secretary of the Treasury been up to the times."[23]

Chase's proposals for tariff revisions were few and simple, and it was, consequently, relatively easy to frame a bill embodying them. On December 23, Justin S. Morrill, from the Committee of Ways and Means, asked leave to report a bill to revise the tariff (H.R. No. 176). Vallandigham naturally objected, but the rules were suspended and the measure received. Morrill explained that the bill laid additional duties of one-half cent per pound on sugar, five cents per pound on tea, one cent per pound on coffee, and one cent per gallon on molasses. He pointed out that this was strictly in accordance with the recommendations of the Secretary of the Treasury, and added that the committee would report a tariff bill covering other articles later in the session. Morrill expressed doubt that the measure would produce additional revenue, but thought that it would decrease importation of these items and thus reduce the flow of money out of the country.

Vallandigham made a short speech opposing this bill in particular, and high tariffs in general. He urged a complete revamping of the tariff laws so as to produce the greatest possible revenue and charged that the East was exploiting the Northwest. It is not probable that Vallandigham expected his words to have any great effect. They didn't. Under the pressure of the previous question, the House passed the bill by a vote of 77 to 29. There was very little crossing of party lines. In addition to sixty-five Republicans, the majority consisted of five Democrats from New York and New Jersey and seven Unionists from Maryland, Virginia, and Tennessee. Only four Republicans opposed the measure—Dunn and Porter of Indiana, Sloan of Wisconsin, and Aldrich of Minnesota.[24]

23. Boston *Post,* January 28, 1862.

24. *Cong. Globe,* 37th Cong., 2d Sess., pp. 169–170. The five Democrats casting affirmative votes were Haight, Odell, Steele, and Ward of New York and

There was no disposition in the Senate to delay the bill. The new sugar crop would soon be arriving, and the Committee on Finance had already unofficially considered the measure and given it unanimous support. When the Senate received the House bill, therefore, it was not referred to any committee but very shortly thereafter was taken up and passed without a division.[25]

With a bare minimum of debate, another upward revision of the tariff was thus hastily passed. It was, as a matter of fact, passed a bit too hastily. Some two weeks later, Stevens had to bring in a joint resolution to "explain" the law, so as to render goods in warehouses not subject to the increased duties. This action had been recommended by Secretary Chase and gave Vallandigham the opportunity to make some gratuitous comments on the folly of hasty legislation. Stevens declined the gambit, however, and the joint resolution was immediately passed by the House and, with only slightly more debate, by the Senate.[26]

It was almost six months, however, before anything more was heard of the broader tariff measure which Morrill had promised. After extensive consultation with agents of various special interests, the committee succeeded in drafting a bill which Stevens reported to the House on June 20, 1862, when it was made a special order for the following Wednesday.[27] The House devoted three days—the twenty-fifth and twenty-seventh of June and the first of July—to debate on the measure. Most of the time was consumed in discussing amendments proposed by the Committee of

---

Cobb of New Jersey. Unionists voting for the bill were Blair, Upton, and Whaley of Virginia; Calvert, Thomas, and Webster of Maryland; and Maynard of Tennessee.

25. *Ibid.,* pp. 161–162, 166, 168. The Senate was, in fact, engaged in debating relatively unimportant matters until the tariff bill arrived. An earlier motion to adjourn had been withdrawn at Fessenden's request to allow action on this bill before adjournment.

26. *Ibid.,* pp. 189, 198–199, 221–222, 240. There was no division in the House, but a roll-call vote in the Senate revealed a much closer division than might have been expected—23 to 15. Four Democrats joined nineteen Republicans in support of the resolution, while the opposition consisted of eight Republicans, five Democrats, and two Unionists. Seven of the negative Republican votes came from the Middle West.

27. *Ibid.,* p. 2845; Valentine B. Horton to Thomas Ewing, Sr., March 15, 1862, Thomas Ewing Papers, Library of Congress; Philadelphia *Inquirer,* June 11, 1862.

Ways and Means. The measure was well characterized by Ward of New York on the second day of debate. "This bill," he declared, "instead of being a bill to create a revenue, is to prohibit importation." Only Justin S. Morrill, who had the bill in charge, made any attempt to treat the measure as a revenue tariff, and even he stressed its protective aspects at least as much. After numerous amendments, none of them individually of any great importance, the House passed the bill without a division on July 1.[28]

The Senate Committee on Finance retained the measure for five days and reported it with numerous amendments on July 7. The upper house considered the tariff bill on July 8 in a session devoted almost entirely to action on the amendments reported by the finance committee. The general tendency of these amendments was to revise the schedules upward. It is extremely doubtful that a quorum was present during most of the day. After an attempt by Powell to abolish the banks fishery bounty (long a bone of contention between New England and the southwestern states) was beaten down by a vote of 12 to 24, the tariff bill, as amended, was passed without a division.[29]

The measure, now burdened with ninety-nine Senate amendments, was returned to the House. On the motion of Stevens, and without consideration, the lower house rejected these amendments and called for a committee of conference. This came as no surprise to the Senate, for Fessenden had frequently mentioned the probability of such action. The Senate agreed to the House request, and Senators Fessenden, Simmons, and Howard met with Representatives Stevens, Justin S. Morrill, and Washburne to work out a compromise.

28. *Cong. Globe,* 37th Cong., 2nd Sess., pp. 2936–2940, 2978–2986, 3050–3055. Despite the sizable increases, the rates were still not high enough to suit many manufacturers. Various committees descended on Washington to urge additional upward revision, especially during the period immediately before the House began consideration of the measure. In particular, it was charged that Pennsylvania interests had been sacrificed while the rates on New England products had been increased disproportionately. See Philadelphia *Inquirer,* June 23, 24, 30, 1862.

29. *Cong. Globe,* 37th Cong., 2nd Sess., pp. 3062, 3134, 3167–3177. Simmons seems to have had primary responsibility for drafting the amendments, though Fessenden controlled the bill in the Senate. See James F. Simmons to Mrs. James F. Simmons, July 6, 1862, James F. Simmons Papers, Rhode Island Historical Society.

The result was a recommendation that sixty of the Senate amendments be accepted by the House, that the Senate recede from twenty-one of its amendments, and that the House accept eighteen of the Senate amendments after some modification. The essential character of the measure remained unchanged. The report of the committee was accepted with practically no discussion by both houses on July 11, and the President signed the bill three days later. The Tariff of 1862 has been computed to have raised the average of all duties to thirty-seven percent and cut the free list in half.[30]

One major consideration repeatedly advanced to justify these higher tariff rates was that, without such increases, domestic industry would be unable to compete with foreign firms because of the taxes laid on American manufacturers by the recently enacted internal revenue bill. This was a sweeping measure which seemed to consider equality of tax burden as synonymous with universality of taxation. Hesitant though Chase's recommendations in this field were, congressmen faced the issue more squarely and were soon talking in terms of new revenue legislation designed to produce more than one hundred million dollars annually. House members began to feed their various pet tax bills into the legislative hopper early in 1862. By the middle of January, the Committee of Ways and Means had accumulated so many proposals that Justin S. Morrill, chairman of the subcommittee on taxation, questioned the advisability of printing any more.[31]

Citizens outside the halls of Congress were equally full of revenue schemes. During the month of January, issue after issue of the New York *Times* contained the latest of these proposals. The paper editorially advocated income and excise taxation fashioned after the British model, but its columns contained communications from its readers ardently espousing property taxes, sales taxes, dog taxes, stamp taxes, and dozens of other propositions.[32]

30. *Cong. Globe,* 37th Cong., 2nd Sess., pp. 3173, 3174, 3197, 3213, 3254–3255, 3268–3269; Sidney Ratner, *American Taxation, Its History as a Social Force in Democracy,* p. 78.

31. *Cong. Globe,* 37th Cong., 2nd Sess., pp. 228, 229, 230, 384.

32. New York *Times,* January 3, 8, 13, 1862. See also Philadelphia *Inquirer,* January 10, 1862; Boston *Post,* January 7, 1862; Detroit *Daily Advertiser,* February 12, 1862; Detroit *Free Press,* December 11, 1861.

It quickly became obvious that the drafting of an internal revenue bill was no task to be accomplished in a few sittings of a House committee. Weeks would undoubtedly be consumed in this chore alone; and no Congress, however responsive to its leadership, could be expected to enact such legislation without considerable discussion. In the meantime, some assurance had to be given to the government's creditors that Congress was more cognizant of financial realities than was the Secretary of the Treasury. Such assurance was suggested by the editors of the New York *Times* when they observed, "A simple resolution that Congress *will,* at an early day, . . . *impose all-sufficient taxes* to support the national credit, . . . would be sufficient, for the moment."[33]

On January 15, Corning of New York, a Democratic member of the Committee of Ways and Means, reported a joint resolution (H.R. No. 32) pledging the passage of tax legislation which would yield, together with tariff duties, at least $150,000,000. Vallandigham announced his support of the resolution but urged that it be debated at length. With this in view, he moved to postpone further consideration for one week. Horton of Ohio, also a member of the Committee of Ways and Means, pressed for immediate action but acknowledged the desirability of extended debate on the tax measure itself. At this point Bingham of Ohio obtained the floor and delivered a lengthy and contentious speech having little to do with finances but strongly favoring confiscation and emancipation legislation. Justin S. Morrill then arose and, in a rather irritated manner, reminded the members of the House of the subject under consideration and moved the previous question.

Despite the protests of several representatives who desired to reply to Bingham's tirade, the previous question was seconded, Vallandigham's postponement motion defeated, and the resolution passed by a vote of 134 to 5. The opponents of the resolution were all Democrats—Allen of Ohio, Robinson of Illinois, Shiel of Oregon, Voorhees of Indiana, and Wood of New York.[34]

The Senate wasted no time. Fessenden reported the resolution from the Committee on Finance two days later and explained that its passage was necessary to reassure the public and to preserve national credit. With

33. New York *Times,* January 13, 1862.

34. *Cong. Globe,* 37th Cong., 2nd Sess., pp. 344–349.

practically no discussion, the Senate gave its approval by a vote of 39 to 1. Powell cast the lone dissenting vote, asserting that the resolution amounted to a pledge to lay direct taxes in the amount of $120,000,000 on the American people. Since he did not approve of such a tax program, he declined to support the resolution.[35]

Thus the public was promised that something would be done about the deplorable state of public finances, and an illusion was created that something was being done. Both the promise and the illusion diminished the pressure on Congress and encouraged an air of optimism in the Capitol. "Public events seem to be taking a more cheerful appearance," wrote John W. Crisfield. "Money, which is the chief element in putting down the rebellion, I think can be obtained. The Country is very rich, and we have only wisely to tap its resources, and copious streams will flow."[36]

But though the passage of the joint resolution may have somewhat lessened the pressure on the House Committee of Ways and Means, the work of drafting a tax measure was strenuous enough under any circumstances. This unenviable task was given to an all-Republican subcommittee headed by Justin S. Morrill of Vermont and including Hooper of Massachusetts, Horton of Ohio, and Stratton of New Jersey. The main burden fell on Morrill, in part because Hooper (and, perhaps, Horton, as well) was also engaged in the maturing of the legal tender bill. During the days that followed, many rumors were heard regarding the progress which the subcommittee was making on the assignment. On February 5, it was asserted that the measure had been laid before the full committee, but this report was denied the following day.[37]

The subcommittee still had not made its report by the middle of the month, despite the urging of the press, and despite the fact that representatives of many economic interests were in Washington generously offering their valuable assistance to the committee members. The delicate

35. *Ibid.*, p. 376. Not voting on the resolution were four Democrats (Bayard and Saulsbury of Delaware, Bright of Indiana, and Pearce of Maryland), one Republican (Simmons of Rhode Island), and one Unionist (Willey of Virginia).

36. John W. Crisfield to Mrs. John W. Crisfield, January 27, 1862, Crisfield Papers, Maryland Historical Society.

37. New York *Herald*, January 18, 31, February 6, 7, 1862; Philadelphia *Inquirer*, February 11, 1862; Woodburn, *op. cit.*, pp. 250–251.

balancing of interests that was called for was best summed up by the New York *Times,* which, as the bill was reported, declared the drafting of the measure to be

a task of inconceivable magnitude. A thousand conflicting interests had to be consulted, local and sectional jealousies conciliated, the burdens distributed as equitably as possible between loyal and disloyal communities, and districts which depend upon agriculture and those which depend upon commerce, and the more or less wealthy classes of society. Indeed, merely to enumerate the shallows and quicksands which had to be kept in view, would overtask him who catalogues the stars.[38]

By early March, however, the committee work on the bill was completed, and on the third of that month it was reported to the House. Looking at the monumental measure, one newspaperman reported, "It covers two reams of paper, and is the longest bill ever introduced into Congress."[39]

The House began its consideration of the internal revenue bill on March 12. Justin S. Morrill, as spokesman for the Committee of Ways and Means, made the opening speech, outlining the nature of the taxes and the methods to be used to collect them. He acknowledged the desirability of authorizing the assumption of the federal taxes by the states but insisted that it was impossible to follow such a policy when excise, license, and income duties were involved. He estimated that the tax bill, as now framed, would produce almost $102,000,000 annually. Two hours of totally extraneous discussion followed, and Stevens then moved that further debate on the internal revenue bill be limited to five minutes. On this motion, Richardson demanded the yeas and nays, and (doubtless because no quorum was present) the House adjourned without further action.[40]

38. New York *Herald,* February 14, 1862; Philadelphia *Inquirer,* January 24, February 5, 17, 1862; New York *Times,* January 23, March 3, 1862. The quotation is from the *Times,* March 3, 1862.

39. *Cong. Globe,* 37th Cong., 2nd Sess., p. 1040; New York *Herald,* March 4, 1862. It was reported that Chase had finally sent a draft bill to the committee on March 1, but that the committee had refused to consider it because of the additional delay such consideration would entail. See Philadelphia *Inquirer,* March 5, 1862.

40. *Cong. Globe,* 37th Cong., 2nd Sess., pp. 1194–1205.

On the next day, when the question recurred on Stevens's proposal, the vote failed to produce a quorum. After a brief discussion, the House leader withdrew the motion but served notice that he would hold those members who debated the bill strictly to the question. When Richardson of Illinois attempted to discuss the policy of the government, Stevens quickly made it apparent that he had meant what he had said. After being repeatedly called to order for straying from the question, Richardson finally sat down, indicating that he intended to be as harsh on any Republicans who digressed as Stevens had been on him.

But on the bill itself there was still plenty to be said. For four weeks, the measure was considered almost daily and generally to the exclusion of any other major legislation. The first point of discussion was the collection system established by the bill. Despite Morrill's explanation, some representatives remained unconvinced that the taxes could not be collected by state officers. The controversy was so long and fruitless that the House eventually limited debate on the pending amendment to one minute. The amendment was withdrawn and the matter was temporarily dropped.[41]

The subject arose again during the next day's debate, when Eliot introduced an amendment which would have permitted the states to collect the taxes. After lengthy discussion, the amendment was defeated. Stevens had, in the meantime, moved that general debate on the bill be closed, and the remainder of the session was devoted to action on various minor amendments dealing with the assessors and collectors and their duties.[42]

When the internal revenue bill had been reported to the House, the Philadelphia *Inquirer* declared the measure to be imperfect because the committee had had no previous experience on which to draw. "Therefore," the editor concluded, "unless Congress is largely aided by the intelligent business men of the country, there will be a great risk that the best bill that body may be able to devise will be partial and oppressive in its operation."[43]

41. *Ibid.*, pp. 1217–1228. Roscoe Conkling, Shellabarger, and Pendleton led the fight for state collection of taxes while Richardson joined with a number of Republicans (led by Justin S. Morrill) in opposing the amendment.

42. *Ibid.*, pp. 1236–1245.

43. Philadelphia *Inquirer*, March 4, 1862.

The "intelligent business men" were apparently of the same opinion, for as early as the fourteenth, the New York *Herald* observed that "A legion of committees from various cities are here with axes to grind," and voiced the prediction that if the views of these gentlemen should prevail, there would be no tax laid on anything except whiskey. The ensuing weekend, and especially Sunday the sixteenth, was given over to lobbying. Delegations from the New York City Chamber of Commerce and the Boston and Philadelphia Boards of Trade were much in evidence. Drug interests were powerfully represented and were attempting to lower the tax on patent medicines. A delegation of New England industrialists insisted that the tax on manufactures was unwisely conceived and too high; they urged that the three percent tax on manufactured articles be replaced by a one percent general sales tax. The lobbyists persisted in their endeavors throughout the following weeks, as the House continued to discuss and perfect the bill. They concentrated their fire on the Committee of Ways and Means, and in some instances as many as fifty or sixty interested parties were milling about the door of the room occupied by this important committee.[44]

Despite these distractions, the debate on the internal revenue bill continued unabated, though generally before a very small House. The members of the Committee of Ways and Means, especially Morrill, evidenced a considerable willingness to accept minor alterations as long as the major provisions remained unchanged. Several of the sections showed evidence of having been carelessly, or at least hastily, drawn; and a good deal of constructive amendment took place in the Committee of the Whole. The discussion on the seventeenth, eighteenth, and nineteenth dealt primarily with the machinery of collection; and on the twentieth, the committee reached the sections laying taxes on whiskey, beer, and other alcoholic beverages. The proceedings on this day were considerably interlarded with laughter, with an almost excessive amount of merriment greeting Stevens's dissertation on the effects of lager beer.[45]

44. New York *Herald,* March 15, 17, 18, 19, 23, 1862; Philadelphia *Inquirer,* March 18, 1862; Elijah Ward to Erastus Corning, March 25, 27, 1862, P. H. Watson to Erastus Corning, April 3, 1862, all in Erastus Corning Papers, Albany Institute of History and Art. The quotation is from the *Herald,* March 15, 1862.

45. *Cong. Globe,* 37th Cong., 2nd Sess., pp. 1252–1259, 1273–1279, 1286–1296, 1303–1314; Philadelphia *Inquirer,* March 20, 1862.

Action on relatively minor amendments consumed two more days (March 21 and 26). Horton took an increasingly active role in the management of the bill during this period. On the twenty-seventh—the committee having reached the sections laying taxes on manufactures—the House leadership decided that some statement of the principles on which the bill had been framed should be made to the House. Hooper outlined the policy upon which the Committee of Ways and Means had acted in the drafting of the measure. Their aim, he said, was first to tax luxuries and then to tax manufactures; and further, they intended to tax manufactures at the level of consumption and not in any partially finished state. On the same day, however, the Committee of the Whole contravened those principles when it voted to place a tax on coal. A similar proposal to tax cotton was defeated by the close vote of 53 to 55. Four days later, however, a one-cent-per-pound tax on cotton was voted by the House.[46]

The twenty-eighth and thirty-first of March and the first and second of April were spent in the consideration of amendments relating to various specific taxes. Repeated attempts by various members to secure tax preference for items produced in their districts were rarely successful. On the first of April, Colfax of Indiana, who continuously occupied the chair while the internal revenue bill was in the Committee of the Whole, came down to the floor to lead the fight to eliminate the tax on newspaper and periodical advertising. Colfax was himself a newspaper owner and editor and so had considerable personal interest in the matter. His efforts proved unavailing, however, and the tax stood. Stevens and Horton jointly controlled the course of the measure in committee during this period, and much of the action on the bill was undoubtedly taken in the absence of a quorum. Roll calls and divisions were studiously avoided, and rumors were heard that many members, fearing political repercussions, were reluctant to act on the measure and were deliberately absenting themselves. It was, in fact, asserted in the press that "Mr. Stevens is obliged to crack the parliamentary whip vigorously over the team to keep them in the traces."[47]

46. *Cong. Globe,* 37th Cong., 2nd Sess., pp. 1322–1330, 1383–1390, 1403–1414, 1458–1459.

47. *Ibid.,* pp. 1432–1442, 1452–1464, 1480–1489, 1508–1514; *Bio. Dir.* (1928), p. 834; Schuyler Colfax to Charles Sumner, March 26, 1862, Charles Sumner Papers, Harvard University; New York *Herald,* April 2, 1862. The force of Colfax's opposition to the tax on advertising was probably considerably

On April 3, the committee took up the sections laying income and inheritance taxes. These sections imposed a tax of three percent on the incomes of all residents of the United States in excess of $600 per year. Incomes derived from domestic sources and paid to United States citizens residing abroad were taxed at five percent. Salaries and income from sources taxed elsewhere were exempted from taxation under this clause. Taxes ranging from three fourths of one percent to five percent, depending on the relationship of the heir to the deceased, were laid on inheritances. In a separate section, all government salaries over $600 were taxed at three percent, and government paymasters and disbursing officers were ordered to withhold this amount.

The major controversy of the day arose on the question of whether or not the term "income" meant "net income." Morrill and Stevens, speaking for the Committee of Ways and Means, asserted that it did, but both strenuously resisted any attempt to insert the word "net" in the text of the bill. Republicans Robert McKnight of Pennsylvania and Lovejoy of Illinois and Unionist Mallory of Kentucky led the fight to have the word inserted, and Lovejoy and Mallory went so far as to charge the committee members with misrepresentation. The Committee of the Whole finally voted, by a margin of 37 to 36, to insert the word "net." The number of members voting did not constitute a quorum, but this fact seems to have escaped the attention of all concerned. Stevens immediately served notice that he would oppose the amendment when it was reported to the House, and after some additional discussion the committee rose.[48]

On Friday, April 4, the committee worked its way through the last sections of the bill. "Frank" Blair's proposal to levy a tax of two dollars on each slave provoked extensive but not very enlightening discussion and was finally defeated by a vote of 47 to 62. After a few other amendments were received and acted upon, the committee rose and reported the bill to the House. Further action was then postponed until the following Monday, and the bill and the amendments were ordered printed.[49]

Throughout the entire lengthy period of discussion, the House leader-

---

diminished by the fact that Justin S. Morrill had in his possession a letter from Horace Greeley advocating such a levy. See Horace Greeley to Justin S. Morrill, March 18, 1862, Justin S. Morrill Papers, Cornell University.

48. *Cong. Globe,* 37th Cong., 2nd Sess., pp. 1527–1536.

49. *Ibid.,* pp. 1544–1550.

ship had kept the measure firmly in hand: though it had permitted minor amendments, no real opportunity had been offered to modify the basic principles on which the bill was framed.

On Monday, April 7, the House began its consideration of the amendments made by the Committee of the Whole. Since there were well over three hundred of these, the task was understandably somewhat tedious. As soon as the measure was before the House, Stevens moved the previous question. He allowed Francis P. Blair, Jr., to introduce a slave-tax amendment but adamantly refused to withdraw the motion again for any purpose. The previous question was seconded, and members were thus effectively barred from introducing any amendments which would have added new provisions to the bill.[50]

Appreciable portions of two days' sessions were now devoted to action on the amendments. Most were approved without objection, several were defeated, and a few were further modified. Stevens was successful in his attempt to strike out the provision defining taxable income as net income. On the eighth, the question was taken on Blair's slave-tax amendment, and it was defeated by a vote of 51 to 75. Voting in the affirmative were fifty Republicans and one Unionist (Clements of Tennessee), while the majority consisted of twenty-nine Republicans, twenty-eight Democrats, and eighteen Unionists. Stevens supported the proposal, but many ardent antislavery men apparently saw it as a recognition of slave property and consequently opposed it. The position of such Republicans as Bingham of Ohio, Hooper of Massachusetts, Julian of Indiana, Lovejoy of Illinois, and Potter of Wisconsin can scarcely be explained in any other way. Negative votes were also cast by a number of conservative Republicans—such as Benjamin F. Thomas of Massachusetts and Dunn of Indiana—who probably doubted the constitutionality of any such tax.[51]

Stevens then spoke briefly in support of the bill, declaring its passage to be an imperative necessity, and defending the principles on which it was drafted. He promised that compensatory tariff duties would be laid on items subjected to internal taxation and took a gratuitous slap at the Canadian Reciprocity Treaty. The House passed the measure by a vote of 125 to 14. In the minority were twelve Democrats, one Unionist (Wick-

50. *Ibid.*, p. 1564.
51. *Ibid.*, pp. 1564–1566, 1576.

liffe of Kentucky), and one Republican (James Buffington of Massachusetts).[52]

The Senate received the bill on April 10, 1862, and it was immediately referred to the Committee on Finance. A subcommittee of that body, composed of Simmons of Rhode Island, Pearce of Maryland, and Howe of Wisconsin, had already been informally considering the measure; but such consideration had not produced (nor would it produce) any unanimity of opinion on the whole question of internal taxation. Public opinion was even more divided. Even that normally reliable weather-vane organ, the New York *Times,* twirled madly in response to gusts from various quarters and during the month of April editorially advocated such widely divergent taxation schemes as the placing of a heavy excise tax on a few widely consumed articles and the laying of a sales tax on all goods and services.[53]

The committee retained the bill for almost a month and made many alterations in it. Indeed, Fessenden, the chairman of the committee, had to crack the whip strenuously in order to get the measure reported at all. He vigorously resisted attempts to discuss any other proposal before the House bill was perfected, though both McDougall and Simmons, the chairman of the internal revenue subcommittee, had drafted new bills. In the end, only Fessenden and one other member of the committee actually favored the measure, but a majority voted to report it to the Senate for action. The view of the Republican Senate leader is probably best expressed in his own words. On April 25 he wrote,

It will be another week, at least before I can report this infernal tax bill, and it will be a doubtful concern at best. There is no time to make a new one, and

52. *Ibid.,* pp. 1576–1577. The negative Democratic votes were cast by Allen, Cox, Pendleton, Vallandigham, and White of Ohio; Kerrigan of New York; Knapp and Richardson of Illinois; Law and Voorhees of Indiana; Norton of Missouri; and Shiel of Oregon. Democrat Browne of Rhode Island later recorded his vote against the bill, and Ward announced that he was authorized to say that Wood would have voted against the measure if he had been present. See *ibid.,* p. 1583.

53. *Ibid.,* pp. 1603, 2421; New York *Times,* April 9, 30, 1862. The Philadelphia *Inquirer* (April 4, 1862) asserted that the subcommittee consisted of Simmons, Pearce, and Dixon. On the floor of the Senate, however, Simmons said that the other two members of the group were Pearce and Howe, and specifically praised Howe's application to the task.

all we can do is to patch this. It will be odious, of course, and overwhelmed by all with curses, both loud and deep. I have made up my mind, however, to put it through in the best shape I can.[54]

It took a little longer than Fessenden had predicted to bring the bill out of committee, and it was not until May 6 that the Maine senator was able to report the measure to the Senate. McDougall immediately presented a substitute to be printed, and Simmons served notice that he intended to submit a number of important amendments at a later date. The bill as reported, Simmons informed the Senate, was not "the exact expression of a majority of the Committee on Finance."[55]

For some two weeks now the Senate apparently took no further interest in the internal revenue bill. The upper house, instead, considered an array of miscellaneous measures including bills to charter a street railway in Washington and to establish a Department of Agriculture; the Civil and Indian appropriation bills; a resolution of inquiry regarding the battle of Pittsburg Landing; and the confiscation bill. On May 21, obviously irritated by the delaying tactics employed by the radical senators to prevent a vote on the confiscation bill, Fessenden moved to take up the tax measure. The motion carried, 33 to 9. This vote dispelled the rumor that some radical senators would prevent the taking up of the internal revenue bill unless the President adopted their program in regard to the conduct of the war.[56]

The internal revenue bill was the major legislation before the Senate for more than two weeks. Every day (including two Saturday sessions) was devoted in large part to this business. Acting as in Committee of the Whole, the Senate spent the first day considering the collection methods embodied in the bill. This discussion was continued on May 22, when

54. William P. Fessenden to ? , April 25, 1862, quoted in Fessenden, *op. cit.,* I, 190; *Cong. Globe,* 37th Cong., 2nd Sess., pp. 2421–2422. Other members of the Committee on Finance not mentioned in the above paragraphs were Republicans Sherman of Ohio and Cowan of Pennsylvania. See *Cong. Globe,* 37th Cong., 2nd Sess., pp. 9, 736. There seems to be no real evidence to sustain the charge voiced by the Washington correspondent of the *Times* that the delay in reporting the tax bill was "doubtless dishonest, the object being, in all probability, to enable too hasty speculators and monopolists to get their 'loads' off." See New York *Times,* May 3, 1862.

55. *Cong. Globe,* 37th Cong., 2nd Sess., p. 1966.

56. *Ibid.,* pp. 2250–2254, *passim;* New York *Herald,* May 22, 1862.

liquor and license taxes were also taken up. On this day, Sherman attempted to obtain a reduction of the tax on whiskey, and Sumner tried to get the tax increased. Both failed. Friday was devoted to the consideration of license and manufacturing taxes. Considerable controversy arose over a finance committee proposal to strike out the one-cent tax on cotton. Grimes, Trumbull, Sherman, Howe, and Wilmot vigorously opposed the recommendation, and Fessenden, Cowan, and Clark defended it. So great was the agitation that the section was finally informally passed over.[57] The Saturday session of May 24 was spent in considering the sections laying various excise taxes. The Senate voted to strike out the taxes on carriages, watches, dogs, billiard tables, yachts, and pianos. The tax on insurance companies was changed from one of ten percent on premiums to one of three percent on gross receipts. Sumner, Dixon, and Simmons fought a losing battle to reduce this tax to one percent. The last of the committee amendments were dealt with on the following Monday, and several minor individual amendments (mostly by Fessenden) were disposed of. Courtesy and custom had dictated that senators withhold major amendments until this time. The bill was now open to such amendments.[58]

Considerable opposition to taxing agricultural products had existed from the beginning. On May 27 three senators from tobacco states—Henderson and Wilson of Missouri, and Powell of Kentucky—spearheaded a drive to reduce the tax on tobacco. Their efforts were unsuccessful, however, and the motion to reconsider the vote on that section of the bill was defeated, 17 to 25. The majority was composed of twenty-two Republicans, two Democrats (Rice of Minnesota and McDougall of California), and one Unionist (Wright of Indiana). Six Republicans, six Democrats, and five Unionists voted affirmatively. Ten of the affirmative votes were cast by the senators from the important tobacco-raising states of Kentucky, Virginia, Maryland, Missouri, and Ohio, and two more were cast by Republican senators from New York (Harris) and Connecticut (Dixon), each of these states having produced about six million pounds of tobacco in 1860.[59]

57. *Cong. Globe,* 37th Cong., 2nd Sess., pp. 2254–2262, 2278–2288, 2308–2321.

58. *Ibid.,* pp. 2329–2341, 2344–2356.

59. *Ibid.,* pp. 2367–2368.

Sectional economic interests also determined the outcome of another similar issue on the twenty-seventh, but in this case the agricultural commodity involved was cotton. When the Senate resumed consideration of the amendment striking the tax on raw cotton, such New England senators as Sumner and Wilson of Massachusetts, Simmons of Rhode Island, Clark of New Hampshire, and Fessenden of Maine energetically supported the elimination of the tax. Other Republicans—Chandler of Michigan, Howe of Wisconsin, and King of New York—failed to see any reason for discriminating among agricultural products. The amendment carried, however, by a vote of 20 to 16. In the majority were thirteen Republicans, four Democrats, and three Unionists, while fifteen Republicans and one Unionist (Wright of Indiana) cast negative votes. Of the thirteen affirmative Republican votes, ten came from New England, and nine of these senators had voted against reconsidering the tobacco tax.[60]

As the day's session came to an end, Henry Wilson precipitated an extensive discussion by moving to strike out the section laying a license tax on retail liquor dealers. Wilson, an ardent teetotaler, declared this trade to be evil and asserted that the United States should not sanction it. The debate continued until adjournment and into the next day's session as well. Fessenden argued that taxation did not imply approval, and this view was seconded by most of the senators. Wilson's amendment was defeated, 5 to 32.[61]

Debate on a slave-tax amendment proposed by Sumner, the arch-abolitionist, consumed the remainder of the session of the twenty-eighth and all of the session of the twenty-ninth. This amendment provoked varying reactions from the senators. Simmons supported the proposition but suggested that the tax be placed at five dollars rather than the ten-dollar figure Sumner had proposed—a suggestion Sumner adopted. Sherman opposed the amendment; King supported it; and Pomeroy, viewing the proposal as unconstitutional and an acknowledgment of the property status of slaves, declared himself unwilling to tax any interest which he was not disposed to protect. Howe bitterly denounced such views. "If this country ever is effectually and completely ruined," he declared, "I am

60. *Ibid.*, pp. 2368–2375.

61. *Ibid.*, pp. 2376–2378, 2396–2400. The five senators voting for Wilson's motion were Harris, Pomeroy, Wilmot, Henry Wilson, and Wright.

afraid it will be effected by its morality. It is embarrassing to be more virtuous and moral than the law allows." The expected constitutional objections voiced by border-state senators were seconded by a number of antislavery Republicans. The Senate reduced the tax to two dollars and then defeated Sumner's proposal, as amended, 14 to 22. All fourteen affirmative votes were cast by Republicans, but almost as many—twelve—joined with five Democrats and five Unionists to defeat the amendment.[62]

The sessions of May 30 and 31 were not very productive. On the thirtieth, Simmons and McDougall outlined their substitute measures. Simmons proposed to eliminate the taxes on manufactures and to rely primarily on income and excise taxes. McDougall espoused the plan advocated by the New York City Chamber of Commerce and the Philadelphia and Boston Boards of Trade, resting primarily on a general sales tax. Consideration of minor and technical points consumed the Saturday session of May 31, and it was obvious that, after the week's arduous labors, tempers were wearing thin. A controversy developed between Fessenden and Howe when the Senate Republican leader censured the Wisconsin senator (who was also a member of the Committee on Finance) for proposing modifications rejected by the finance committee. Fessenden was in turn condemned by Harris for his intransigence in regard to accepting amendments. The internal revenue bill, as now framed, he declared, would ruin the Republican Party. Fessenden's rejoinder was a slashing attack on senators who placed party above country and who feared to take the responsibility for actions necessary to sustain the government. It was a vitriolic speech. All in all, the week ended on a rather sour note. "I want to come home very much," fumed Senator Simmons, "but the Tax bill hangs on and I cannot come untill [*sic*] that is through with."[63]

62. *Ibid.,* pp. 2400–2408, 2419–2430; quotation from p. 2405. The twelve Republicans who voted against the tax on slaves were Browning of Illinois, Cowan of Pennsylvania, Dixon and Foster of Connecticut, Doolittle of Wisconsin, Hale of New Hampshire, Harris of New York, Lane of Indiana, Pomeroy of Kansas, Sherman of Ohio, Ten Eyck of New Jersey, and Wilson of Massachusetts.

63. *Ibid.,* pp. 2443–2451, 2454–2477, Appendix, 227–232; James F. Simmons to Mrs. James F. Simmons, June 1, 1862, James F. Simmons Papers, Rhode Island Historical Society. The New York *Herald* charged that the dilatory action

And "hang on" it did, but Monday was to prove more productive. The Senate acted upon a number of amendments, the most notable of which was one presented by Fessenden which converted the flat three percent income tax into a graduated levy ranging from three to seven-and-one-half percent. Only Zachariah Chandler, the Michigan millionaire, voiced any opposition to this proposal, and he expressed the opinion that such a tax would be an incentive to conceal income. The amendment was agreed to without a division. After some additional discussion, the bill was reported to the Senate.[64]

Now the action slowed down once again, the proposals already acted upon as in Committee of the Whole were trotted out again, and the same arguments were voiced. The liquor tax was again attacked as too high and too low, but no change was made. The committee amendment eliminating the tax on cotton was thoroughly rehashed on June 3 and 4. Of the cotton tax, Chandler said, "Every man who is in favor of letting the rebels go scot free, and in favor of the perpetuation of negro cotton-growing, of course will vote to strike this out. Every rebel will vote for it; every disunionist will vote for it; every traitor will vote for it; and I do not think any loyal man will vote to strike it out." This and other tirades may have had some effect. In any event, after almost two days of debate, the tax was reduced to one-half cent per pound, and the committee amendment striking it out was rejected.[65]

McDougall presented his long-awaited substitute on June 5, but it could command the support of only three senators—McDougall, Browning, and Pomeroy. Late on the same day, when many of the senators had departed, Sumner introduced an amendment taxing slaves at two dollars each. A bare quorum of the senate hastily adopted the proposal, without any discussion, by a vote of 19 to 16. The majority consisted of eighteen

on the internal revenue bill resulted from the determination of radical senators to prevent an adjournment and thus stay in Washington to "agitate the slavery question and dragoon the Executive." See New York *Herald,* May 31, 1862.

64. *Cong. Globe,* 37th Cong., 2nd Sess., pp. 2479–2494. The income tax, even in an ungraduated form, was already attracting considerable opposition from the wealthier classes. E.g., Hamilton Fish to William P. Fessenden, January 25, April 21, May 16, 1862, letterpress copies in Hamilton Fish Papers, Library of Congress. Fessenden apparently was not impressed by Fish's arguments.

65. *Cong. Globe,* 37th Cong., 2nd Sess., pp. 2508–2526, 2540–2560; quotation from p. 2523.

Republicans and one Democrat (Rice of Minnesota), while eight Republicans, four Democrats, and four Unionists cast negative votes. Of the thirteen senators absent, eleven undoubtedly would have cast negative votes. The passage of the amendment was made possible, however, by the affirmative votes of Pomeroy, who had previously opposed the proposition, and Rice, who would subsequently vote against it. An attempt to force the bill to a final vote collapsed when friends of Fessenden indicated that he desired to speak briefly on the measure but lacked the strength to proceed at this time. Fessenden himself refused to ask for a delay, saying that he could not conscientiously do so after having repeatedly urged speedy action on the bill. The Senate, however, adjourned.[66]

This adjournment gave the opponents of the slave-tax scheme the chance that they needed. On the next day (June 6), someone prevailed upon Anthony to enter a motion to reconsider the vote by which the amendment was accepted. After a lengthy discussion, the amendment was reconsidered and defeated, 17 to 23. This was the final road-block. Fessenden spoke in support of the measure, Simmons added a few words, and the vote was taken. The bill passed, 37 to 1. Only Powell resisted the pressure for unanimous support of the measure.[67]

Thus the internal revenue bill, with 315 Senate amendments, was returned to the House on Monday, June 9, and immediately referred to the Committee of Ways and Means. On June 12, Stevens asked unanimous consent to regard the amendments as nonconcurred in. Train objected, and Stevens then moved that the House nonconcur in the amendments and ask for a committee of conference. It was immediately apparent that there would be considerable opposition to such a course. Colfax pointed out the major shortcoming: the Senate amendments, if considered by the House, could be acted on individually. Some could be accepted, some rejected, and others modified. The report of a committee of conference, however, could not be in any way amended, but must be either accepted or rejected in its entirety. The House, Colfax insisted, should not delegate its legislative duties to a committee of conference.

Justin S. Morrill contended that Stevens's motion was designed merely as a timesaver, but Mallory and William Kellogg voiced additional

66. *Ibid.*, pp. 2572–2587.
67. *Ibid.*, pp. 2598–2611.

opposition. At this juncture, Stevens closed debate by calling the previous question, but announced that he would withdraw his motion if one third of the House should divide against it. When Wickliffe called for the yeas and nays, however, the House leader withdrew this pledge. The motion was carried by a vote of 80 to 58.[68]

The upper house insisted upon its amendments and agreed to a committee of conference. The Senate members of this committee were Fessenden, Harris, and Henderson. To represent the House, the Speaker appointed Stevens, Justin S. Morrill, and Holman. Even in committee, acting on the mass of amendments that the Senate had added to the bill was no brief task. They were, as Pennsylvania's Kelley observed, "numerous & important so that no well founded guess as to when it [the tax bill] will come up for action can be made."[69]

By the middle of the following week, it was rumored that the committee had acted on 295 of the amendments, but it was the first of the week following (June 23) before the report was brought back to the House and Senate. The House was to accept 253 of the Senate modifications, and the Senate was to recede from sixteen of its amendments. The other forty-six Senate additions were to be modified. Fessenden made the report in the upper house and patiently explained the committee recommendations to a rather unruly Senate. After about an hour's discussion of the various propositions, the Senate gave its approval to the work of the conference committee.[70]

In the House, Stevens presented the report, explained it briefly, and answered several dozen questions in the half-hour devoted to the matter. Lovejoy and William Kellogg urged that the report be printed, and Wickliffe pleaded, "Let us have, at least, the appearance of legislating upon the tax bill." Stevens, however, adamantly refused to give way and finally moved the previous question. The report was adopted by a vote of

68. *Ibid.,* pp. 2620, 2680–2682. Many members of the House undoubtedly wished to get back to their home districts as soon as possible in this campaign year. This consideration probably influenced a number of votes.

69. *Ibid.,* p. 2675; William D. Kelley to John M. Read I, June 12, 1862, John M. Read I Papers, Library Company of Philadelphia.

70. New York *Herald,* June 18, 1862; *Cong. Globe,* 37th Cong., 2nd Sess., pp. 2873–2877.

106 to 11. The eleven negative votes were cast by one Unionist and ten Democrats.[71]

The bill signed by the President on July 1, 1862, filled more than seventeen triple-column pages of exceedingly fine print. It contained 119 sections laying excise taxes, stamp taxes, manufacturing taxes (both specific and ad valorem), income taxes (the committee of conference retained the Senate principle of graduation, but made the maximum tax five percent), inheritance taxes, gross receipts taxes, and license taxes on practically every occupation, commodity, or service in the country.

The act also created the Internal Revenue Bureau in the Department of the Treasury, which resulted in the doubling of the departmental staff by March 1863. Both the bureau and the tax system that called it into existence were essentially new creations. On previous occasions (notably during the War of 1812) excise and stamp taxes had been levied, but many of the taxes imposed by the internal revenue bill of 1862 were, insofar as the federal government was concerned, novel. Certainly taxation on this scale had never before been attempted in the United States. With the passage of this act, the federal tax base was made almost synonymous with the existence of wealth or earning capacity in any form. Every citizen now had direct contact with, and felt the direct influence of, the federal government. A great centralizing force had been set in motion.[72]

The adoption of an income tax by Congress was an acknowledgment, either conscious or unconscious, of changes that had taken place in the American economy. Purely financial operations were playing an increasingly important role in American economic life, and a considerable portion of the nation's wealth now existed in the form of liquid and rapidly revolving capital which could be reached most adequately by a tax

71. *Cong. Globe,* 37th Cong., 2nd Sess., pp. 2890–2891; quotation from p. 2890. One Democrat, Browne of Rhode Island, later changed his vote on the bill from nay to yea, saying he had been under the impression that the direct tax had been repealed rather than suspended. See *ibid.,* p. 2903.

72. *Ibid.,* Appendix, pp. 364–381; George S. Boutwell, *Reminiscences of Sixty Years in Public Affairs,* I, 313; Harry E. Smith, *United States Federal Internal Tax History, From 1861 to 1871,* p. 1; Paul Studenski and Herman E. Krooss, *Financial History of the United States,* pp. 149–153.

on income. The heavy reliance on manufacturing taxes was an additional acknowledgment of national economic changes.

The revenue legislation of the Thirty-seventh Congress was also indicative of the future of federal taxation. True, the protective tariff was firmly fastened on the country, but so was excise taxation. Never again would tariff collections account for more than ninety percent of the federal revenue, as they did in 1861. The needs of the government had resulted in a drastic redrawing of the federal tax base. Never again would it be contracted to its prewar scope.

What had emerged was a tax structure that seemed ideally adapted to the "Gilded Age." One of the most equitable of the taxes laid by the Thirty-seventh Congress—the income tax—was one of the first to be repealed. What remained was a series of excises which were often evaded by unscrupulous manufacturers and distributors and which, in any event, could be easily and inconspicuously passed on to the unsuspecting consumer.

The tax structure had been shaped by, and remained responsive to, vested economic interests powerful enough to bring their views forcibly to the attention of legislators. The new tax structure was certainly more productive than the old, but whether it was significantly more equitable is doubtful. Equitable or not, the tax blueprint of the Thirty-seventh Congress (except for its experiment with income taxation) would be followed for the remainder of the century. Thus, in a burgeoning entrepreneurial economy, it was the politically mute consumer who shouldered the tax burden.

CHAPTER 8

Congress and the Currency: Reform and Stabilization

It could hardly be said that a national currency system existed in 1861. Only gold and silver were legal tender, though the federal government would also accept its own treasury notes in payment of taxes. These certificates circulated in a limited fashion and in varying amounts. Notes of eastern banks were often redeemable in specie, but this was rarely true of bank notes in other sections of the country. Such a situation was rife with weaknesses and difficulties at any time; under the impact of war economy it was probably predestined to collapse. Some congressmen were forced unwillingly to the conclusion that changes had to be made, while others welcomed the opportunity to make modifications that they had long advocated.

The Special Session of the Thirty-seventh Congress made no basic change in the currency of the United States. To be sure, the Secretary of the Treasury was authorized to issue $50,000,000 in treasury notes, but these were not made legal tender, though they were receivable for all government taxes except import duties. Throughout 1861, the economy of the country continued to operate primarily on the basis of gold coin and private and state bank paper. This unwieldy and unorganized currency situation was already showing obvious signs of strain, however, when Congress reconvened on December 2, 1861. Consequently, in his annual report, Secretary of the Treasury Chase presented to Congress two plans for establishing a regulated national currency.

One possibility envisioned by the Secretary of the Treasury was an increase in the number of treasury notes in circulation, coupled with a tax on bank notes, eventually resulting in a replacement of the bank notes by treasury notes. He pointed out, however, that this plan had many hazards, including the temptation to issue excessive amounts of treasury notes; the risk of currency depreciation; the transmission of regional economic crises throughout the entire currency system; and the possible inability of the government to redeem its notes in coin. These dangers, Chase thought, outweighed the probable benefits of the program, and he declared that he could not recommend that Congress follow this course in its future currency legislation. The second alternative involved the circulation of uniform bank notes through the medium of private and state banking associations. These banks would be required to hold quantities of United States bonds as security for the redemption of the notes. This plan, the Secretary maintained, would provide the most desirable form of circulating credit available.[1]

It was obvious from the first that Chase's recommendations aroused no great enthusiasm, either in Congress or in financial circles. The Secretary's ardent support of the national banking scheme made few immediate converts in Congress; and in any event the program he envisioned was too broad to permit rapid action. It was to be eight months, as a matter of fact, before the first piece of legislation looking toward the establishment of a national banking system was introduced in the House.[2]

All of Chase's warnings against continued issuance of treasury notes might well have been valid, but such issues undeniably did provide an immediate source of government funds. Probably this consideration, rather than any thought of revamping the currency of the country, moved Spaulding of New York, on December 30, to introduce a bill authorizing an additional issue of treasury notes. Some importance might be attached to the introduction of the measure, since Spaulding was a member of the powerful Committee of Ways and Means and chairman of the subcommittee on currency and loans.[3] On the same day, the entire currency situation had assumed a radically different complexion when the New York banks suspended specie payment despite the fact that some $25,000,000 in gold remained in their vaults. The suspension had been anticipated for some time, and in the major cities around the country—Boston, Philadelphia, Albany, Cleveland, and Pittsburgh—the specie-paying banks quickly followed suit.[4]

1. Salmon P. Chase, "Report of the Secretary of the Treasury," *Cong. Globe,* 37th Cong., 2nd Sess., Appendix, pp. 25–26.

2. *Cong. Globe,* 37th Cong., 2nd Sess., p. 3258.

3. *Ibid.,* p. 181; Woodburn, *op. cit.,* p. 251.

4. New York *Herald,* December 31, 1861; New York *Times,* December 30, 31, 1861.

It might be noted that the continued issuance of treasury notes, accompanied by the government's refusal to relax the subtreasury system, greatly irritated the bankers in general. Some blamed the suspension on government policy and congressional legislation, or the absence thereof. "It is idle to disguise the fact that Congress is rapidly losing the confidence of the people of this country," declared the editor of the Philadelphia *Inquirer*. He berated the legislators for wasting time in the discussion of emancipation and confiscation schemes and allowing the military and financial needs of the nation to remain unsatisfied. "It is, therefore," he concluded, "Congress that is responsible for the suspension, and for the prospect of baseless paper inflation which is before us."[5]

At first some observers believed that the "suspension of specie payments by the Banks will favor the adoption of Secretary Chase's scheme of finance," because it would relieve the government of the "odium of substituting a paper for a hard money circulation, all circulation being paper now." This did not prove to be the case. In fact, the bank suspensions immediately increased the support for a financial program about which Chase had expressed grave misgivings—reliance on treasury notes. It is interesting to note that Spaulding, who was overwhelmingly more influential than any other single congressman in shaping the currency legislation of this session, apparently abandoned Chase's national banking plan only after the decision to suspend specie payment was made.[6]

During the period between December 23, 1861, and January 6, 1862, when most of the members of Congress had left Washington for their homes, the Committee of Ways and Means remained hard at work in the capital city. "I came here in November," Spaulding wrote some six weeks later, "and have not left my post for a single hour since that time." The press kept the nation well informed of the committee's actions; there was, consequently, little surprise when, on January 7, the second full day's session of the new year, Spaulding reported back to the House a bill to

5. Philadelphia *Inquirer*, January 1, 1862; Studenski and Krooss, *op. cit.*, p. 143. Don C. Barrett supports the viewpoint of the bankers in this matter. See *Greenbacks and the Resumption of Specie Payments, 1862–1879*, pp. 7–15.

6. New York *Times*, January 1, 1862; Elbridge G. Spaulding to Erastus Corning, December 24, 1861, Erastus Corning Papers, Albany Institute of History and Art.

authorize the issuance of an additional $100,000,000 in legal tender treasury notes. On the following day, Richardson of Illinois introduced a resolution directing the Committee on the Judiciary to inquire into the power of Congress to make such notes legal tender. The resolution was passed without discussion and without a division.[7]

Despite the pressing need for funds to carry on the war, the House took no further action on the treasury note bill for two weeks. The explanation for this delay is to be found in occurrences outside the Capitol. During the second and third weeks in January, representatives of the banking and commercial interests of New York, Boston, and Philadelphia flocked to the capital. Their initial plan seems to have been to bypass Chase and appeal to the House Committee of Ways and Means. Such a course offered the bankers little prospect of success, for the committee members were even less favorably inclined toward the financiers' proposals than was Chase. The resulting series of meetings involved Chase, the bank and mercantile representatives, the House Committee of Ways and Means, and the Senate Committee on Finance.

A program which the bank representatives reluctantly approved was hammered out in these conferences. It was agreed that the banks in the three metropolises would receive the outstanding treasury notes at par and make every effort to sustain their credit. In return, the government was to use interest-bearing bonds rather than non–interest-bearing treasury notes to discharge its obligations. Congress would be urged to enact a national banking act. These actions, it was hoped, would render it unnecessary to make the treasury notes legal tender—a forlorn hope, as it turned out.[8]

It quickly became apparent, however, that during the final stages of the

7. Elbridge G. Spaulding to Thurlow Weed, February 9, 1862, Thurlow Weed Papers, University of Rochester; New York *Herald,* January 1, 1862; New York *Times,* December 31, 1861, January 5, 1862; *Cong. Globe,* 37th Cong., 2nd Sess., pp. 218, 229. The House was forced to solve the question of constitutionality on its own initiative, however, for no report from the Committee on the Judiciary was forthcoming during the time the issue was before the House.

8. New York *Herald,* January 11, 12, 16, 1862; Washington *National Intelligencer,* January 14, 1862; New York *Times,* January 13, 14, 1862; Philadelphia *Inquirer,* January 13, 15, 16, 1862; David Donald (editor), *Inside Lincoln's Cabinet,* pp. 58–64; S. A. Mercer to Salmon P. Chase, January 6, 1862, Salmon P. Chase Papers, Library of Congress.

negotiations, the opinions of the congressional leaders had not been given adequate consideration. On Friday, January 17, and over the weekend that followed, there was increasing evidence of congressional dissatisfaction with the agreement, and one observer reported, "There seems no probability, whatever, of its adoption."

The actions of the nation's bankers extricated Chase and the congressional leaders from this embarrassing situation. On January 20, Chase was informed by telegraph that the banks of Boston had refused to honor the agreement. Financial institutions in New York and Philadelphia soon followed suit; and it was now common knowledge that Congress, the Secretary, and the financiers were straining in three different directions regarding the determination of the nation's fiscal policy.[9]

So far as Congress was concerned, the period of waiting was at an end. On January 22, 1862, Spaulding reported a revised legal tender bill, and the measure was made a special order for January 28. Since the agreement with the bankers had been rejected, Chase felt constrained to give his reluctant support to the legal tender proposal. It is probable that he was also influenced by the increasing support for the plan in the northern press and among private citizens. On January 23, the New York *Times* commented on "the unanimity with which it [the treasury note scheme] is received in this commercial city," and three days later declared,

> There is no thought of leaving this Currency [treasury notes], without the [legal tender] stamp referred to, to the tender mercies of such of our self-important and selfishly inclined bank leaders who have already given evidence of what they might do with it, by what they have done with the plain United States Notes already in circulation at their own counters and through their own Clearing-house. The Secretary now thoroughly understands not only the bearing of this opposition—partial it is known to be, as not one out of ten of the bank officers in New-York participate in its factious spirit—but the true drift of the popular feeling and preference on the subject.[10]

9. Donald, *op. cit.,* p. 64; New York *Herald,* January 23, 1862; New York *Times,* January 18, 20, 1862; Philadelphia *Inquirer,* January 18, 1862; William Owner Diary, Vol. I, January 20, 1862, Library of Congress. The quotation is from the *Times,* January 20, 1862.

10. *Cong. Globe,* 37th Cong., 2nd Sess., p. 435; New York *Times,* January 23, 26, 1862; New York *Herald,* January 24, 1862; Boston *Post,* January 21, 1862;

This measure (H.R. No. 240) was largely the work of Spaulding and was reported from the Committee of Ways and Means by the narrowest of margins. One member of the committee, John S. Phelps of Missouri, was absent on military duties throughout this period. This left eight committee members to declare themselves on the legal tender question. Spaulding and Republican Samuel Hooper of Massachusetts strongly favored the measure from the beginning, and Stevens, though originally inclined to doubt the bill's constitutionality, eventually gave it his support. Justin S. Morrill of Vermont, Horton of Ohio, and Corning of New York voiced strong and unwavering opposition. Maynard of Tennessee did not engage in the committee discussion but favored the bill. Stratton of New Jersey also avoided discussion but indicated that he did not support the measure. He agreed, however, to vote for the bill to be reported to the House.[11]

The opening gun in the currency battle was fired even before the legal tender bill emerged from committee. On January 23, Republican John B. Alley of Massachusetts made a lengthy speech supporting a three-pronged economic program consisting of a $150,000,000 tax bill, a $100,000,000 legal tender bill, and a national banking bill. Alley supported the treasury note bill on grounds of necessity and urged that the notes be issued in denominations of ten dollars and upwards. One observer characterized the speech as "the most valuable yet made on the currency question, and expresses the principles that will prevail in Congress."[12]

The House, in Committee of the Whole, took up the legal tender bill on January 28 and devoted a large portion of the next ten days to considering it. Before debate on the proposal was closed, nine representatives made speeches opposing the measure, and ten speeches supporting it were delivered. The supporters of the legal tender bill (all of whom were Republicans) harped on the necessity for raising money to carry on the

---

Silas M. Stilwell to Samuel Shaw, January 18, 1862, Salmon P. Chase Papers, Library of Congress. The *Post* had, in fact, advocated making the treasury notes legal tender as early as January 7, 1862.

11. Elbridge G. Spaulding, *A Resource of War—The Credit of the Government Made Immediately Available. History of the Legal Tender Paper Money Issued During the Great Rebellion,* pp. 13, 15; *Cong. Globe,* 37th Cong., 2nd Sess., p. 2065; Woodburn, *op. cit.,* p. 252; Barrett, *op. cit.,* p. 27.

12. *Cong. Globe,* 37th Cong., 2nd Sess., pp. 457–460; New York *Times,* January 25, 1862.

war, declared that Congress had the right to make anything legal tender, and praised the measure as an integral part of the over-all economic program. The bill's opponents—four Republicans, two Democrats, and three Unionists—were supported and encouraged by a small but active bank lobby, and concentrated their fire on the legal tender provision, which they declared to be unconstitutional, inflationary, and dishonest. They also bitterly condemned the Committee of Ways and Means for not presenting a tax bill first. Nor were they impressed by the plea of necessity, which Roscoe Conkling characterized as "that market price of principle at which every virtue has been sold for six thousand years." But Chase, now completely converted to the necessity of legal tender notes, came to the aid of the measure's supporters and sent in a letter urging immediate passage of the bill with the legal tender clause intact.[13]

During the course of debate, both Vallandigham and Roscoe Conkling had presented substitutes. Neither of these proposals contained a legal tender provision. On February 5, the day before the vote on the bill was to be taken, representatives opposing legal tender held a bipartisan caucus in an attempt to strengthen their position. On the following day, in accordance with an agreement reached at the caucus, Vallandigham and Conkling withdrew their substitutes to permit Horton to introduce a proposal drafted by Justin S. Morrill and supported by one half of the Committee of Ways and Means (Morrill, Horton, Corning, and Stratton). This substitute provided for the issuance of interest-bearing, non–legal-tender notes.[14]

Considerable maneuvering occurred at this point because of Stevens's

13. *Ibid.,* pp. 522–527, 549–552, 614–618, 629–642, 655–665, 679–689, Appendix, 42–51, quotation from p. 633; New York *Times,* January 30, 1862; Salmon P. Chase to Thaddeus Stevens, January 29, 1862, copy in Justin S. Morrill Papers, Cornell University. Speaking against the legal tender bill were Republicans Morrill of Vermont, Riddle of Ohio, Roscoe Conkling of New York, and Thomas of Massachusetts, Democrats Pendleton and Vallandigham of Ohio, and Unionists Sheffield of Rhode Island, Wright of Pennsylvania, and Crisfield of Maryland. Prominent among the bill's supporters were Hooper and Alley of Massachusetts, Bingham and Blake of Ohio, Campbell and Stevens of Pennsylvania, Kellogg of Illinois, Edwards of New Hampshire, Pike of Maine, and Spaulding of New York.

14. *Cong. Globe,* 37th Cong., 2nd Sess., pp. 114–115, 692–693; Barrett, *op. cit.,* pp. 52–53; New York *Times,* February 6, 1862; Philadelphia *Inquirer,* February 5, 1862.

apparent intention to prevent a direct vote on Horton's amendment. A vote was eventually obtained on the proposal, however, and it was defeated, 55 to 95. Stevens offered an amendment that was then adopted without a division. This amendment was essentially the same as the bill originally reported from the Committee of Ways and Means. The bill as amended was then passed, 93 to 59. This vote revealed some crossing of party lines, though the majority of the measure's supporters were Republicans, while Democrats and Unionists constituted the core of the opposition. Six Democrats and eight Unionists joined with seventy-nine Republicans to form the majority. Nineteen Republicans, however, cast negative votes. New England and the middle states gave the bill a sizable majority in the East, though the Rhode Island, Vermont, and New Jersey delegations solidly opposed it. The measure received almost unanimous support in Delaware, Virginia, Tennessee, and Missouri, but only a single vote from Kentucky and Maryland. In the Middle West, the Ohio and Indiana delegations split thirteen to seven and six to five, respectively, in favor of the bill; the Illinois representatives voted four to two against it. The representatives from the new northwestern states of Michigan, Minnesota, Wisconsin, and Iowa gave solid support to the measure, while the lone Kansas vote went to the opposition. The two California representatives favored the legal tender bill, and the single Oregon legislator opposed it. It is evident that many and diverse influences were at work on the various congressmen.[15] There would seem to be little validity in the New York *Herald*'s allegations that the abolitionist element in the Republican Party made a concerted attempt to block the treasury note bill until their program should be accepted.[16]

So, on February 7, 1862, the Senate received the measure and referred it to the Committee on Finance. On the following day, at the other end

15. *Cong. Globe,* 37th Cong., 2nd Sess., pp. 689–695; Elbridge G. Spaulding to Thurlow Weed, February 9, 1862, Thurlow Weed Papers, University of Rochester. One negative and two affirmative votes were later recorded by unanimous consent. See *Cong. Globe,* 37th Cong., 2nd Sess., pp. 707, 736. It is interesting to note, in connection with the affirmative votes cast by the California representatives, that one year later the San Francisco *Daily Alta California* (February 18, 1863) was advocating that California be exempted from the operation of the Legal Tender Act.

16. New York *Herald,* February 8, 9, 1862.

of Pennsylvania Avenue, Secretary Chase penned a personal note to the chairman of the committee, urging that the legal tender clause be left unchanged.[17] There was additional evidence in the form of resolutions, editorials, and letters that the abhorrence of legal tender notes voiced by the representatives of the New York, Philadelphia, and Boston bankers was not shared by all of the financial men of the country.[18] Even so, all available pressure might well be needed to get the bill through the Senate with the legal tender clause intact.

The first, and perhaps most formidable, hurdle was the Committee on Finance. Here Howe of Wisconsin, Sherman of Ohio, and McDougall of California supported the bill with varying degrees of enthusiasm, while Collamer of Vermont and Pearce of Maryland opposed the bill's passage with the legal tender clause attached. This placed the issue squarely in the hands of the chairman, William Pitt Fessenden of Maine. Burdened with leadership as well as legislative responsibilities, acutely conscious of the government's financial distress but convinced that the legal tender scheme was basically dishonest, Fessenden was in an agonizing position. "This legal tender clause is opposed to all my views of right and expediency," he declared.

It shocks all my notions of political, moral, and national honor. I am beset with letters and telegrams, and told on every hand that not to yield is death to credit; that without it we shall be utterly bankrupt and cannot carry on the war. I do not believe it, and yet ought I to set up my own judgment as a

17. *Cong. Globe,* 37th Cong., 2nd Sess., p. 697; Salmon P. Chase to William P. Fessenden, February 8, 1862, Senate Files, Thirty-seventh Congress, Miscellaneous Papers of the Committee on Finance (Sen. 37A–E4), National Archives.

18. E.g., "Resolutions of the Chamber of Commerce of the State of New York," February 6, 1862, in *Cong. Globe,* 37th Cong., 2nd Sess., p. 736; James Mitchell to Elihu B. Washburne, January 18, 1862, Elihu B. Washburne Papers, Library of Congress; A. B. Ely to William P. Fessenden, February 19, 1862, William P. Fessenden Papers, Library of Congress; George Opdyke to Salmon P. Chase, January 28, February 8, 1862, Salmon P. Chase Papers, Library of Congress; Philadelphia *Inquirer,* February 7, 11, 1862. There were some observers who damned all factions with a fine, impartial fervor. "The City Capitalists as represented by the Banks are opposed by the Country," declared one such critic. "Neither Mr. Chase[,] Banks or Com[.] of Ways & Means appears to be up to the occasion." See C. A. Stetson to Thurlow Weed, January 29, 1862, Thurlow Weed Papers, University of Rochester.

standard of action? This thing has tormented me day and night for weeks; the thing is wrong in itself, but to leave the government without resources at such a crisis is not to be thought of. Would that some kind spirit would only lift the curtain and tell me what I ought to do.[19]

Necessity ruled. The bill was reported back to the Senate with amendments on February 10, and the next day Fessenden served notice in no uncertain terms that the bill would be taken up on February 12 and disposed of at that time, if possible.[20]

On the announced day, Fessenden, putting the best face on the matter that he could, grimly brought the measure before the Senate. In his opening statement, Fessenden declared that the bill should be passed with the legal tender clause intact if necessary to support the government. It was quickly obvious that he did not think that such necessity existed, however, for the Senate leader condemned the provision as destructive of financial confidence, an admission of bankruptcy, and a stain on the national honor. Despite these personal misgivings, Fessenden in his official capacity pressed for the bill's passage as vigorously as its most ardent champion might wish.[21]

Collamer followed Fessenden's speech with an attack on the legal tender provision, and the Senate, as in Committee of the Whole, then proceeded to consider the measure for amendment. Though interrupted by frequent speeches on the merits of the bill and various amendments, the Senate made rapid progress. Some of the amendments were minor, but others were designed to alter the measure in important particulars.

On the recommendation of the finance committee, the Committee of

19. Quoted in Fessenden, *op. cit.,* I, 194. For the views of the various members of the committee, see *Cong. Globe,* 37th Cong., 2nd Sess., pp. 763–771, 789–791, 803–804, Appendix, 51–56, 58–60.

20. *Cong. Globe,* 37th Cong., 2nd Sess., pp. 719, 739–740.

21. *Ibid.,* pp. 763–766, 771, 772. Opposing, as he did, one of the basic elements of the measure, it is difficult to see why Fessenden persisted in retaining the bill under his control on the floor of the Senate. He could quite easily have placed it in charge of some other member of the Committee on Finance (e.g., Sherman) as he was later to do with the national banking bill. Sherman certainly had no reservations regarding the legal tender clause. "My remedy for paper money," he was later to write to his brother, "is, by taxation, to destroy the banks and confine the issue to Government paper." See John Sherman to William T. Sherman, November 16, 1862, in Thorndike, *op. cit.,* p. 168.

the Whole approved amendments which made all interest on United States bonds payable in gold; authorized the Secretary of the Treasury to sell bonds at market (not par) value for coin; set up a sinking fund for retiring the federal debt (including all proceeds from tariff duties, land sales, and sales of confiscated rebel property); and authorized the issuance of bonds redeemable in five years and payable in twenty years, rather than straight twenty-year bonds as provided for in the original bill. But a committee amendment authorizing the Secretary of the Treasury to receive the notes on deposit and pay interest on such deposits was defeated. Fessenden did not call for a division at this time but announced that he would renew the amendment in the Senate and demand the yeas and nays. Proceedings were finally brought to a halt by the lack of a quorum, but only late in the day, after action on the committee amendments had been completed.[22]

Consideration of the legal tender bill was resumed on February 13, immediately after the morning hour, and Collamer introduced an amendment striking the legal tender clause. This was the basic point of difference on the measure, and considerable debate followed. The legal tender provision was defended by Sherman, Doolittle, Howard, McDougall, and Sumner, and attacked by Cowan, Bayard, and Willey. The amendment was then defeated by a narrow margin—17 to 22. Eight Republicans joined nine Democrats and Unionists in support of the amendment, while seventeen Republicans, three Democrats, and two Unionists cast negative votes. The vote, to a considerable extent, was more sectional than political. The senators from the states east of the Alleghenies and north of the Mason-Dixon line split almost evenly on the issue, giving a slight majority in favor of the amendment. South of the line, however, only one

22. *Cong. Globe,* 37th Cong., 2nd Sess., pp. 767–775. It was obvious throughout most of the day's proceedings that no quorum was present. Every effort was made to avoid a division which would demonstrate this deficiency officially. Sherman indicated that the bill could be passed this day without a division if the legal tender clause was left intact. Fessenden, however, refused to agree to this proposal, and said that in the absence of Collamer he would himself move to strike the legal tender provision. The Washington correspondent of the Philadelphia *Inquirer* declared on February 11 that so great was the opposition to the legal tender clause in the Senate that it would be impossible to pass the bill unless the gold interest amendment was adopted. Chase, he added, had agreed to this change in order to save the bill. See *Inquirer,* February 12, 1862.

negative vote was cast. Only three senators from west of the Alleghenies voted to strike the legal tender clause.[23]

After the bill was reported to the Senate and the modifications approved, Fessenden renewed his amendment establishing a deposit system. This proposition stirred up considerable debate but was finally passed by a vote of 21 to 18. Again, party lines seemed to mean little—eleven Republicans were in the minority. The vote was even more pronouncedly sectional than that on the legal tender issue. Senators from the New England and middle states cast only two votes against the proposal, and only three affirmative votes were cast by senators from the midwestern states.[24]

Both the legal tender and the deposit provisions were of vital interest to creditors, and the sectional vote clearly reflected this interest. The traditional view of the creditor was that nothing but gold and silver should be made legal tender. Though the eastern senators were defeated on this issue, they did manage to salvage something for their moneyed constituents, for the deposit system provided for a safe and certain return, for those who possessed surplus capital.

With the passage of the deposit-system amendment, the measure had cleared the last Senate hurdle. After a few more comments by senators who desired to explain their votes, the bill was passed, 30 to 7.[25]

"Allow me to congratulate you on the passage by the Senate of the Treasury Note Bill, legal tender and all," Mayor George Opdyke of New York wrote exuberantly to Secretary Chase. "I feel quite sure . . . that the 'specie interest' clause . . . will prove to be a mischievous error. But no matter. The main point is gained in securing the legal tender clause. Without it we should have had financial chaos."[26]

But the time for rejoicing had not yet arrived. The measure was returned to the House on Friday, February 14, and placed in the hands of the Committee of Ways and Means.[27] A weekend now intervened—a

23. *Cong. Globe,* 37th Cong., 2nd Sess., pp. 787–800.

24. *Ibid.,* p. 802.

25. *Ibid.,* pp. 802–804. The senators voting against the measure were Collamer, Cowan, Kennedy, King, Pearce, Powell, and Saulsbury.

26. George Opdyke to Salmon P. Chase, February 14, 1862, Salmon P. Chase Papers, Library of Congress.

27. *Cong. Globe,* 37th Cong., 2nd Sess., pp. 827–828.

weekend that saw the capture of Fort Donelson by Federal forces under the command of U. S. Grant. The news of this victory was announced in the House during the morning hour on Monday, and a waning of enthusiasm for the treasury note bill was immediately apparent. Some representatives insisted that the war would be over in sixty days and that the necessity for the issuance of legal tender notes, therefore, no longer existed. Others thought that the plan would be equally beneficial in peacetime.

The bank lobbyists now redoubled their efforts. "The pressure for striking it [the legal tender clause] out is great," reported a New York *Times* correspondent. "A Committee waited upon the Secretary of the Treasury to-day, urging him to address to Congress a letter against that feature of the bill." Editorially, the *Times* sternly opposed any such action, and thus adhered to its position as announced a month previously, when the editors had declared legal tender notes to be "a valuable auxiliary to the operations of the Treasury in time of War, and a most convenient Currency to the People at all times."[28]

It was not only the legal tender clause, however, that endangered the passage of the measure. While one element of the House membership was prepared to renew the attack on this portion of the bill, other representatives were no less violently opposed to some of the Senate amendments—notably those providing for the payment of bond interest in gold and permitting the sale of bonds at market, rather than par, value. In consequence of this divergence of views, the Committee of Ways and Means was evenly divided on the question of approving the measure in its present form. Stevens reported the bill back to the House on February 18, urging the members to give it their earnest consideration. The Senate amendments, he said, "are very important, and, in my judgment, very pernicious." No attempt was made to consider the measure this day, however, for the House adjourned thirty minutes after convening, ostensibly to pay honor to the gallant dead. It may be true, however, as one newspaper correspondent intimated, that many members were more immediately concerned with painful memories of the previous night's celebrations than they were with the memory of those who fell in battle.

28. *Ibid.*, p. 850; New York *Herald*, February 18, 1862; New York *Times*, January 16, February 19, 1862.

Some observers asserted that a session on the treasury note bill on the eighteenth would have resulted in a complete deadlock with the Senate and a probable loss of the bill.[29]

The Committee of the Whole took up the legal tender bill on February 19, and it was obvious that the members were in a state of at least partial rebellion against the House leadership. Spaulding, the author of the original measure, opened the attack on the Senate amendments which, he declared, would render the bill "incongruous and tend to defeat its great object, namely, to prevent all forcing of the Government to sell its bonds in the market to the highest bidder for coin." Dunn of Indiana also spoke against the amendments, and Unionist Calvert of Maryland, Republicans Justin S. Morrill of Vermont, Pomeroy of New York, and Democrat James E. English of Connecticut made supporting speeches. Diven appealed for the defeat of the entire measure.[30]

The Committee of the Whole followed the recommendations of the Committee of Ways and Means regarding most of the Senate amendments. These recommendations included the rejection of the amendment authorizing the sale of bonds at market value for coin and—after additional modification—approval of the section establishing a deposit system. When the all-important coin-interest amendment was reached, however, the representatives took the bit in their collective teeth, and despite a committee recommendation to the contrary, concurred in the Senate amendment. After considerable debate, the Committee of the Whole also rejected the sinking-fund amendment. Late in the day, the measure was reported to the House. Stevens immediately introduced and called the previous question on an amendment which would effectively kill the legal tender clause. The previous question was seconded, and the House adjourned.[31]

The next day, Stevens and Hooper made bitter attacks on the Senate amendments in general and on the gold-interest clause in particular. This

29. *Cong. Globe,* 37th Cong., 2nd Sess., p. 874; New York *Herald,* February 19, 1862; Philadelphia *Inquirer,* February 18, 1862. The Senate, apparently not feeling the necessity for honoring the gallant dead, held a full session on the eighteenth. See *Cong. Globe,* 37th Cong., 2nd Sess., pp. 859–873.

30. *Cong. Globe,* 37th Cong., 2nd Sess., pp. 881–888; quotation from p. 882.

31. *Ibid.,* pp. 888–891. The *Globe* shows no Committee of Ways and Means recommendation on the sinking-fund amendment. See *ibid.,* p. 889.

provision, Stevens charged, was designed to benefit the few at the expense of the many. With one exception the House followed the committee recommendations on the various amendments. When the coin-interest clause was reached, Stevens's anti–legal-tender amendment was defeated by a vote of 67 to 72, and the Senate amendment was concurred in, 88 to 56. Though most of the Republicans followed in the train of their House leader, thirty-nine broke ranks and voted for the gold-interest provision. Only two Democrats and four Unionists joined the majority of the Republicans in opposing this amendment. The Republican Party was not yet the dedicated servant of the bondholders that it was later to become. Even in the states where the largest numbers of bonds had been sold, most Republican representatives opposed the coin-interest provision. The Massachusetts Republicans split evenly on the issue, but representatives of the majority party from New York voted two to one against the amendment; and in the Pennsylvania delegation, the margin was three to one.[32]

In only one case did the House members reject the recommendations of the Committee of the Whole: by a vote of 72 to 66, they approved the Senate amendment authorizing the Secretary of the Treasury to sell bonds at market value for coin. Hooper interruped the consideration of the next-to-last major amendment to declare that he was disgusted with the bill as it now stood. He moved to table the pending amendment. This would have carried the bill with it and would have thus defeated the measure. Only twenty-one votes (fifteen of them Republican) could be mustered in favor of the motion, however; and the bill, with the action of the House thereon, was returned to the Senate.[33]

The next step was obviously the formation of a committee of conference on the measure. From the Senate, the Vice President appointed Fessenden of Maine, Sherman of Ohio, and Carlile of Virginia, while Speaker Grow named Stevens of Pennsylvania, Horton of Ohio, and Sedgwick of New York. Of this number, only Stevens and Sherman had worked actively to get a legal tender bill through Congress. Horton had sponsored a competing measure in the House, and Sedgwick had supported the substitute; both Horton and Sedgwick had been among the

32. *Ibid.*, pp. 899–902. Among states with five or more Republican representatives, only Ohio produced a Republican majority for the gold-interest provision.

33. *Ibid.*, p. 902. The Republicans split 36 to 53 against the bond-sale amendment.

Republicans who had refused to follow Stevens's leadership when the House was taking action on the Senate amendments. Fessenden had opposed the legal tender clause in the Senate and had only reluctantly supported the measure in its final form. Carlile had neither spoken nor voted on the bill.[34]

The action of the House had left the views of the two legislative bodies quite close together. The committee of conference, consequently, had little trouble in adopting a report, which was submitted to the two houses on February 24. The report eliminated several minor points of difference and proposed a compromise on the sinking-fund issue. The fund would be retained, but only the receipts from import duties (which had to be paid in gold) would be set aside for this purpose. The Senate adopted this report without a division, and the House vote was favorable by a wide margin—97 to 22.[35]

Thus, under the lash of necessity, the Thirty-seventh Congress reluctantly passed one of its most important pieces of legislation. But were the "greenbacks" necessary? Don C. Barrett insists that they were not. They never accounted for more than one seventh of the funds used to carry on the war, he declares, nor were they the means by which the immediate financial crisis was solved. The major fiscal faults of the government, it seems to Barrett, were (1) the failure to market bonds in England in the fall of 1861; (2) the failure to adopt adquate tax measures; and (3) the failure to relax the subtreasury system.[36] But one may admit the accuracy of these facts and the justice of these strictures and still not agree with Barrett's conclusion; for the Barrett analysis completely ignores the most important aspect of the whole legal tender situation—the "greenbacks" as

34. *Ibid.,* pp. 898–899, 909.

35. *Ibid.,* pp. 929, 938–939. The major objection to the sinking-fund clause voiced in the House was to the inclusion of the proceeds from land sales. It was feared by some representatives that this pledge would be used to prevent the passage of a homestead bill. See *ibid.,* pp. 889–891.

36. Barrett, *op. cit.,* pp. 25–57. Certainly some contemporary observers thought (whether correctly or not) that the "greenbacks" were necessary to sustain government finances. "My opinion is," wrote Samuel Hooper late in 1862, "that we could not have gone through this past year without the government notes." See Samuel Hooper to John A. Andrew, December 27, 1862, John A. Andrew Papers, Massachusetts Historical Society.

currency. With specie payment suspended, there was no such thing as a national currency in general circulation. The specie supply of the country was, in any event, insufficient to meet the currency needs of an expanding economy into which the government alone was pouring an additional $1,000,000,000 a year. To leave that economy dependent on a motley array of irredeemable, often counterfeited, frequently worthless bank paper was not only to invite, but to insure, disaster.

Already the United States stood on the threshold of a new financial era —credit, not coin, was the important consideration. Actually, the major fault of Congress and the government lay not in going too far, but in not going far enough. Had the government called in all gold and given in exchange "greenbacks" or bonds, made gold sales a government monopoly, and refused to sell gold except upon proof of legitimate international trade or manufacturing requirements, many of the economic disorders of the period might well have been avoided.

In the struggle for the passage of the treasury note bill with the legal tender provision attached, the Thirty-seventh Congress had apparently lost sight of the major currency reform recommendation of the Secretary of the Treasury. This was, perhaps, not surprising, for public reaction to Chase's national banking proposal had been mixed since he first voiced his support of the measure in his report of December 9, 1861.

The editor of the Boston *Post,* while declining to enter into a detailed discussion of the plan, stressed the damage that would be done to the states, for if United States securities should constitute the only acceptable basis for bank note issue, the market for state bonds would be dried up. "The present time," he concluded, "is not favorable to such a modification of the currency." The San Francisco *Daily Alta California,* on the other hand, had unstinted praise for the measure and insisted that both the nation and the banks would benefit. "One of the most happy effects of the war, . . ." this journal declared enthusiastically, "will be the establishment of a uniform paper currency issued on principles of undoubted correctness, throughout the Republic." Most Eastern bankers, however, were opposed to the scheme, and close observers were soon predicting its failure. This opinion certainly seemed valid, for despite Chase's ardent support of the proposal, no progress was made during the 1861–1862 congressional session beyond the introduction of a fifty-page bill by

Hooper one week before final adjournment and its reference to the Committee of Ways and Means.[37]

Chase's late and reluctant conversion on the legal tender issue had in no way dampened his enthusiasm for the establishment of a national banking system. In his report to the Third Session of this Congress, on December 4, 1862, he chided the legislators for having ignored his previous recommendations, and in strong terms renewed his plea for a national banking act. This, Chase thought, should be coupled with a tax on bank note circulation and would have most beneficial effects on the economy of the country and the fiscal operations of the government.[38]

Congress, however, and particularly the House of Representatives, remained cool to the Secretary's scheme. It was not until late in the day's session on January 7, 1863—more than a month after Congress had reconvened—that Hooper again introduced a bill designed to accomplish the aims outlined by Chase. The bill was referred to the Committee of Ways and Means, but this committee wasted little time on the measure, perhaps because it had, in fact, had the proposal under consideration for quite some time. Indeed, on the day before the introduction of Hooper's bill, the committee had rejected Chase's plea to attach the national bank legislation to the bond bills. Consideration of the measure had not brought the committee to an acceptance of Chase's views, however. Less than twenty-four hours after the bill had been introduced, it was reported to the House with the recommendation that it not pass. Further consideration of the measure was postponed to January 16.[39]

37. Boston *Post,* January 6, 1862; San Francisco *Daily Alta California,* January 9, March 16, 1862; Wesley C. Mitchell, *A History of the Greenbacks,* p. 37; Edwin D. Morgan to Thurlow Weed, January 27, 1862, Thurlow Weed Papers, University of Rochester; Philadelphia *Inquirer,* July 12, 1862; *Cong. Globe,* 37th Cong., 2nd Sess., p. 3258.

38. Salmon P. Chase, *Report of the Secretary of the Treasury, Sen. Exec. Docs.,* 37th Cong., 3d Sess., No. 1, [1149].

39. *Cong. Globe,* 37th Cong., 3d Sess., pp. 226, 235–236, 237; New York *Times,* December 15, 1862, January 7, 1863; Henry D. Cooke to Jay Cooke, January 3, 7, 1863, Jay Cooke Papers, Historical Society of Pennsylvania. In the interim, Moorhead introduced another bill designed to accomplish the same purpose, but it remained buried in the Committee of Ways and Means. See *Cong. Globe,* 37th Cong., 3d Sess., p. 402.

On that date Chase had just returned from a week-long trip to the financial centers of the North, where he had (with some success) been attempting to garner support for his proposal. Fearing an unfavorable vote in the House, the Secretary prevailed upon the members of the Committee of Ways and Means to delay action for another week. When the lower house again reached the measure, on February 3, it was postponed for an additional week.[40]

There could be little doubt that support in the country at large for the national banking scheme was increasing. The Philadelphia *Inquirer* declared that the proposal "should, and it must, meet with the heartiest acceptance of all men not interested in the business of dealing in money as a commodity. . . . Against such a reform as this it is idle to set up the interests of the system to be reformed." In financial circles, the editor of this journal insisted, the plan was opposed only by western banks which made great profits from uncontrolled note issue. Actually, support came from the interior, as well. "The people of the West," declared the Detroit *Advertiser and Tribune,* "having had an agreeable experience of 'greenbacks' this year, will go heartily and almost unanimously for Mr. Chase's plan."[41]

Thus supported, the Secretary of the Treasury grew increasingly hostile to additional issues of treasury notes and enlisted the aid of the President in his battle for a national banking system. In a special message to Congress on January 17, Lincoln announced that he had signed a bill passed by Congress authorizing an additional issue of $100,000,000 in treasury notes but regretted that such action was necessary. He strongly urged the passage of measures taxing bank circulation and establishing a national banking system.

The Senate referred the message to the Committee on Finance, but it was not ordered printed—a departure from the usual practice with presidential communications. In the House, Washburne attempted to have the message considered by a select joint committee of five representatives and

40. *Cong. Globe,* 37th Cong., 3d Sess., p. 697; Philadelphia *Inquirer,* January 17, 1863; Welles, *op. cit.* (January 16, 1863), I, 223–224.

41. Philadelphia *Inquirer,* December 13, 17, 1862; Detroit *Advertiser and Tribune,* December 13, 1862; Henry D. Cooke to Jay Cooke, January 24, 1863, Jay Cooke Papers, Historical Society of Pennsylvania.

four senators. It was obvious from the first that this proposal had little chance of success, and after a floor battle which carried over into the next day's session, Washburne withdrew his motion. His sole purpose, he said, was to get a fair hearing for the national banking scheme, and it was well known that the Committee of Ways and Means opposed such legislation. The message was referred to the Committee of Ways and Means and ordered printed.[42]

Washburne was undoubtedly right in his analysis of the situation. Another week passed, another bill was introduced and referred to the Committee of Ways and Means, and still neither that committee nor the House took any action. Conferences between the Secretary of the Treasury and members of the Senate and House committees proved unproductive. This deadlock had been foreseen by Henry D. Cooke, brother and Washington agent of financier Jay Cooke. Early in January, Henry wrote his brother that the decisive body in framing financial legislation would be the Senate finance committee with Fessenden and Sherman as its ruling members. Cooke was on intimate terms with Sherman and worked actively to indoctrinate Fessenden with the "proper" ideas regarding the bank bill. Abandoning hope for House-initiated action and pressured by his friend Henry Cooke, Sherman, on January 24, agreed to sponsor the measure. Two days later, he introduced a national banking bill in the Senate. It was referred to the Committee on Finance. One week later, Sherman reported the measure back to the Senate and announced that he would call it up on February 4. On that date, it was further postponed until Monday, February 9, to enable the other committees to get their business transacted during the remainder of the week. Sherman indicated, however, that the Committee on Finance intended to pre-empt the following week.[43]

Everything was ready. Fessenden, pressed by Sherman and Chase, had finally agreed that the national banking act should be the first measure taken up during the week allotted to the Committee on Finance. From the

42. Philadelphia *Inquirer,* January 19, 1863; *Cong. Globe,* 37th Cong., 3d Sess., pp. 381, 392–393, 402; Abraham Lincoln, "Message of January 17, 1863," Richardson, *op. cit.,* VI, 149–150.

43. *Cong. Globe,* 37th Cong., 3d Sess., pp. 505, 666, 703; Philadelphia *Inquirer,* February 2, 1863; Henry D. Cooke to Jay Cooke, January 3, 24, 1863, Jay Cooke Papers, Historical Society of Pennsylvania.

other end of the avenue, Chase cheered the bill's supporters on and aided in the drafting of amendments.[44]

Sherman, the sponsor of the bill, brought the measure before the Senate on Monday afternoon. From this moment until the Senate reached a final vote on the measure, Sherman countenanced no interruption and little delay. It should be noted, in all fairness, that there was no evidence of any disposition on the part of the opponents of the bill to prevent the Senate from coming to a conclusion on the measure. Sherman made the major speech in support of the bill, while the primary opposition effort was an address by Collamer. Chandler of Michigan, Wilson of Massachusetts, and Doolittle of Wisconsin also spoke in favor of the bill; and Howard of Michigan, Carlile of Virginia, and Davis and Powell of Kentucky seconded Collamer's disapproval. The Senate engaged in intensive debate on the measure for three days.

The opposition displayed its greatest strength in its attempts to attach specie clauses to the bill. Powell and Howard introduced amendments requiring the banks to retain specie reserves equal to one fourth of their circulation, requiring thirty percent of the capital stock to be paid for in specie, and requiring the redemption of the bank notes in specie one year after the end of the war. The first two amendments were defeated by votes of 14 to 22 and 19 to 21, and the last lost by virtue of a tie vote, 18 to 18. From these debates, the measure emerged unchanged in any major particular. Briefly, the bill authorized the establishment of national banks whose circulation would be secured by holdings of United States securities.[45]

Late on the third day of debate, the Senate, at the suggestion of Powell, agreed to adjourn and take a vote without further discussion at one o'clock on the following day, February 12. A close division was expected. The supporters of the measure claimed a majority of two, while the opponents were equally confident of a four-vote advantage. The bill's defenders proved the better prophets (or negotiators). The vote was 23

44. John Sherman to Salmon P. Chase, February 7, 1863, Salmon P. Chase Papers, Historical Society of Pennsylvania; Salmon P. Chase to John Sherman, February 9, 1863, John Sherman Papers, Library of Congress.

45. *Cong. Globe,* 37th Cong., 3d Sess., pp. 820–826, 840–852, 869–882; John Sherman to William T. Sherman, March 20, 1863, in Thorndike, *op. cit.,* pp. 194–196.

to 21. Only one Democrat and one Unionist (both from Oregon) voted in the affirmative. Seven Republicans, however, opposed the measure, and among these were some of the most influential members of the majority party in the Senate—Collamer of Vermont, oldest member of the Senate, chairman of the important Committee on the Post Office and Post Roads, and second-ranking Republican on the finance committee; Foot of Vermont, president pro tem of the Senate; King of New York, chairman of the Republican National Committee in 1860; and Trumbull of Illinois, chairman of the powerful Committee on the Judiciary. The finance committee membership split four to three against the bill, and one can only wonder by what process of legerdemain Sherman had been able to get the measure reported to the Senate.[46]

The narrow margin had, in fact, been obtained only by the application of the most stringent political pressures. Howard of Michigan had spoken against the bill on the previous day but now voted for it. He later asserted that he had supported the proposal with the greatest reluctance and only because he considered it an administration measure. Howe of Wisconsin was thought to have been antagonistic to the measure until the day of the final vote. Henry S. Lane of Indiana was known to oppose the bill, but though present later in the day, he did not vote on the measure. And Sherman arranged a special conference between Anthony of Rhode Island and Secretary Chase, which resulted in still another last-minute conversion to the cause. The midwestern Republicans supported the bill almost solidly, while the members of the majority party from the New England and middle states split eleven to five in its favor. By whatever means, the victory was won, and the bill was sent to the reluctant House.[47]

46. *Cong. Globe,* 37th Cong., 3d Sess., pp. 882, 896–897; Philadelphia *Inquirer,* February 12, 1863. Sherman (*op. cit.,* I, 293) says that the bill was favorably reported, but the *Globe* does not indicate any committee recommendation. See *Cong. Globe,* 37th Cong., 3d Sess., p. 666. The other Republicans opposing the measure were Cowan of Pennsylvania, Dixon of Connecticut, and Grimes of Iowa.

47. *Cong. Globe,* 37th Cong., 3d Sess., p. 897; Welles, *op. cit.* (February 17, 1863), I, 237–238; New York *Herald,* February 13, 1863; Sherman, *op. cit.,* I, 299; DeWitt C. Clarke to Frederick W. Seward, [February 12, 1863], William H. Seward Papers, University of Rochester. There is some evidence that the conversion of Anthony also secured the vote of his colleague, Arnold. See Sherman, *loc. cit.* Hale and Bayard, both of whom would probably have opposed the bill, were also absent when the vote was taken.

When the House received the bill that same day, Stevens moved that it be referred to the Committee of Ways and Means. Thomas of Massachusetts objected, however, and the measure remained on the Speaker's table. Thomas was an opponent of the bill, and his action was probably designed to delay and, if possible, prevent action on the bill. If so, it was not successful. One week later, on February 19, the measure was taken from the table. Hooper immediately took it in charge and moved its reference to the Committee of Ways and Means. He never intended, however, that this course should actually be pursued. His purpose was to use this opportunity to debate the measure and then to withdraw the motion and put the bill on its passage.[48]

The major supporting speech was made by Spaulding, who stressed the long-range value of the plan and assured the representatives that it would have no immediate drastic effect. Fenton of New York also favored the bill, while Harrison of Ohio opposed it. On the following day, Republican Stephen Baker of New York and Democrat Warren P. Noble of Ohio opposed the measure, Alley of Massachusetts supported it, and Noell of Missouri recommended committing it to the Committee on the Judiciary for an inquiry into the question of constitutionality. Noell said he was not now prepared either to support or to oppose the bill.

At this point, Hooper threw consternation into the ranks of the opponents of the measure by withdrawing his motion and demanding the previous question on the bill's passage. Roscoe Conkling and others had earlier asked Hooper what course the leadership proposed that the bill should take through the House and at what point amendments would be permitted. Hooper had referred the gentlemen to Stevens for an answer, and the House Republican leader had replied, "It is proposed, I believe, by the friends of this bill to allow whatever discussion is desired . . . and . . . to withdraw the motion to commit and allow gentlemen to offer such amendments as they desire." Having received this assurance, the opponents of the bill made no factious opposition to its consideration, nor did they attempt to force the measure itself to be brought before the House. Should Hooper's motion prevail, at no time during the debate would the bill itself have been subject to amendment before the House. Hooper's course in the matter was, therefore, bitterly condemned by Roscoe Conkling. Hooper made no defense of his actions; and Stevens

48. *Cong. Globe,* 37th Cong., 3d Sess., pp. 914, 916, 1113–1114.

merely said that, had he called the previous question himself, he would withdraw it to receive amendments.[49]

The previous question was narrowly seconded by a vote of 71 to 67, and the main question was ordered by an even narrower margin—75 to 73. Despite his statements in favor of permitting amendments, Stevens voted to order the main question. Even so, the strategy of the Republican leadership could have been balked had not four opponents of the bill and two representatives who were not present for the vote on the measure joined with the bill's supporters in ordering the main question. Conkling and Sheffield fought a brief delaying action, but it proved to no avail—the national banking bill was passed, 78 to 64.

This majority, which came as a surprise to many observers, had been achieved only by stringent pressures. Not only had the House leadership been active in the fight, but the President's aid had been enlisted and Secretaries Chase and Usher were energetically canvassing for votes on the floor of the House on the day of the bill's passage. Nineteen Republicans joined thirty-three Democrats and twelve Unionists in opposition to the measure. The majority was composed of sixty-seven Republicans, two Democrats, and nine Unionists. Though the earlier prediction that all New England and middle-state representatives would oppose the bill did not prove correct, the Republican opposition to the measure was definitely centered in New York, New Jersey, and New England. Only four negative votes were cast by Republican representatives from states west of the Alleghenies.[50]

49. *Ibid.*, pp. 1113–1119, 1141–1147. It would seem to be impossible to absolve Stevens and Hooper of the charge of double-dealing on the management of this measure. Hooper's refusal to make a direct statement regarding his personal intentions, Stevens's careful phrasing of his answer to Conkling, and the subsequent actions of both men lead one to the inescapable conclusion that the Republican leadership of the House never intended to permit any amendments to be submitted. Though Stevens was not at this time the dictator of the House that he was later to become, it is inconceivable that Hooper should have proceeded as he did without the approval and support of Stevens. It should be remembered that at this time (February 20, 1863) the Thirty-seventh Congress had less than two weeks of "life" remaining, and extensive debate or amendment in the House would have gravely endangered the passage of the bill.

50. *Ibid.*, pp. 1147–1148; New York *Herald,* February 12, 1863; Philadelphia *Inquirer,* February 6, 21, 1863; Salmon P. Chase to Abraham Lincoln,

It is not easy to account for this near-solid opposition of the eastern Republicans to the National Banking Act—at least not in simple terms. The banks of the eastern states were, in general, already under close state supervision; thus the bill's note-issue restrictions would not distress the eastern bankers and would greatly simplify exchange and clearinghouse operations. In the West, on the other hand, such restrictions would greatly diminish the immense profits that the largely unregulated banks were deriving from unrestrained (and unsecured) note issue. It would seem, then, that the banking interests of the East would have been less violent in their opposition to the measure than those in the West. As has been noted, however, it was western Republicans who favored the bill (in both the House and the Senate) and easterners who opposed it. One can only suggest that all banking interests were antagonistic to the measure and that the Republican division in Congress resulted primarily from a different degree of responsiveness on the part of the representatives to the demands of the bankers. In the East, the bankers were powerful and organized, and congressmen found it wise to listen sympathetically to their views. In the West, the bankers spoke with less force and less unity, while agricultural, industrial, and transportation interests were more important and more vocal. From the viewpoint of these latter interests, the National Banking Act had many attractive features.[51]

Thus, within a period of less than four weeks, Congress passed legislation designed to reconstruct completely the financial operations of the

---

February 19, 1863, Lincoln Papers, Library of Congress. It was charged that the Democratic opposition to the measure sprang from a desire to have the issue dealt with by the Thirty-eighth Congress. It was thought at this time that there would be no Republican House majority in that Congress. See J. Fred Meyer to Salmon P. Chase, February 16, 1863, Salmon P. Chase Papers, Library of Congress.

51. It might also be speculated that the eastern bankers (formerly largely Whig) were now overwhelmingly Republican while many of the western bankers retained Democratic leanings dating from the Jackson Period. This statement is not intended to suggest that the Republican Party was basically of Whig origin. An additional anticipated result of the National Banking Act which might please western interests and (perhaps) distress eastern bankers was a possible reduction in the sale of drafts on eastern banks for settling domestic accounts. And, finally, the eastern banks would undoubtedly find it necessary (or at least desirable) to dispose of some of their state bonds and purchase federal bonds. Under present market conditions this might prove difficult and unprofitable.

nation. Though the act did increase the market for government bonds, it is hardly accurate to classify it as a war measure. No one familiar with the situation thought that any major change would take place within two years, and few people expected the war to last that long. Basically, it was an act designed to accomplish, on a permanent basis, what the issuance of legal tender treasury notes had already accomplished on a supposedly temporary basis—the creation of a national currency.

At first glance, it would seem that the currency changes of the period 1861–63 were merely the byproduct of the frantic search for revenue. A careful examination of the circumstances, however, makes it clear that this was hardly the case. It is true that the suspension of specie payments by the major banks (in effect, a declaration of their unwillingness to support the government's financial policy), coupled with a critical shortage of funds, gave primary impetus to the introduction of the legal tender bill. But it is also quite clear that many persons, in and out of Congress, were equally impressed by the currency aspects of the measure. The consideration and passage of the National Banking Act presents the situation even more clearly. The measure could be expected to stimulate the government bond market, but its congressional supporters addressed themselves almost entirely to the advantages of the uniform, well-secured national currency which the act would provide. It is clear, then, that the members of the Thirty-seventh Congress were thoroughly aware of the currency changes which they were effecting and were, indeed, often primarily motivated by a desire to reform the currency of the nation.

The decades that followed repeatedly demonstrated the advantages of the new currency system. This is not to say that there were not obvious and serious weaknesses in the nation's fiscal organization during the postwar period; but there can be little doubt that the nation benefited from the structure of the currency formulated by the Thirty-seventh Congress.

CHAPTER 9

Toward Congressional Dominance: Direct Assault

One of the most significant federal legislative developments of the period 1861–1863 was the continuing attempt by congressional leaders to establish the dominance of Congress over the executive and judicial branches of the government. By the end of the last session of the Thirty-seventh Congress, this position had by no means been achieved, but the pressures to that end were unmistakable. The most immediate and obvious point of attack was the presidency of the United States.

In some respects, Lincoln was remarkably vulnerable to such pressures. The first president of a new party in which congressional leadership had already been established; a compromise candidate; a minority president; without executive experience; having run behind the state tickets in more than half the nonslaveholding states; out of sympathy with such influential party leaders as Stevens, Wade, Henry Wilson, Sumner, and Bingham—it would appear that he lacked the necessary weapons in his political arsenal to repel the congressional advance. This appearance was, at least in part, deceptive. Stubborn determination, shrewd political maneuvering, adroit use of popular pressures, and occasionally sheer luck enabled Lincoln to resist congressional encroachment in many instances. There can be little doubt, however, that at other times he carelessly, apathetically, or grudgingly allowed presidential prerogatives to be pared away by the congressional leadership.[1]

Few presidents have ever been subjected to more brutal abuse, not only from political opponents, but from supposed party friends as well. The sources and nature of this criticism constantly shifted. In the summer of 1861, the expressions of disfavor came primarily from the most extreme

1. For election returns, see *Tribune Almanac* (1860), pp. 61, 62; *ibid.* (1861), pp. 39–63; *ibid.* (1862), p. 62.

peace Democrats—men like Polk and Johnson of Missouri; Breckinridge, Powell, and Burnett of Kentucky; Saulsbury and Bayard of Delaware; and May of Maryland. Men of somewhat less-advanced views, such as Bright of Indiana, Vallandigham of Ohio, and Wood of New York occasionally joined the hue and cry.[2]

By late 1861, however, Lincoln's conservative course in regard to emancipation and his refusal to purge the army of Democratic generals had commended the policy of the administration to most Democrats and Unionists and to many conservative Republicans. Consequently, during the last months of 1861 and the first two thirds of 1862, much of the criticism of the President emanated from the more radical members of his own party. Joshua F. Speed summed the situation up quite accurately when he wrote,

> I am fully persuaded that there is mischief brewing here; a large and powerful party of the ultra men is being formed to make war upon the President and upon his conservative policy. They have led off under the lead of Trumbull who had never been a true friend to Mr. Lincoln, and who is stung & mortified at not being consulted about the ground to be taken in the message. . . .
>
> This organization must be headed. There is plenty of material in Congress with which to accomplish it. What they need is concert of action between the firm Southern men in Congress; the Northern democrats and the conservative Republicans under some active and competent leader.[3]

In their public assaults upon the President, the radicals minced no words. For example, in January 1862, on the floor of the House, Riddle of Ohio complained of Lincoln, "He coldly and timidly seats himself on the narrowest letter of the Constitution, and hesitatingly applies its feeblest and shortest instrumentalities to events bearing upon slavery."[4]

2. *Cong. Globe,* 37th Cong., 1st Sess., *passim.* There can be little doubt that at least some of these men were acting in concert in launching their attacks on Lincoln. The Philadelphia *Inquirer,* for instance, mentions a "caucus" of Vallandigham, Burnett, Breckinridge, and Wood shortly before one of Vallandigham's set speeches in opposition to administration policy. See Philadelphia *Inquirer,* July 12, 1861. The speech was delivered on July 10.

3. Joshua F. Speed to Joseph Holt, December 8, 1861, and November 28, 1861, Joseph Holt Papers, Library of Congress.

4. *Cong. Globe,* 37th Cong., 2nd Sess., p. 499. This statement was in reply to Menzies, who had just said of the President, "With the exception of some

Early in the following July, despite the imminence of the congressional elections, the Republican leader of the House bitterly declared, "I believe him [Lincoln] to be too easy and amiable, and to be misled by the malign influence of Kentucky counselors. . . . There are powers behind the throne greater than the throne itself as well in this country as elsewhere." This was a clear and spiteful attack on Mrs. Lincoln, for Stevens specifically stated that he did not refer to the Kentucky delegation in Congress.[5]

In private, the radicals were often even less restrained. "The symptoms give no promise of good," gloomily wrote Stevens in September of 1862.

> The removal of Hunter & Butler, and the continued refusal to receive negro soldiers convince me that the Administration are preparing the people to receive an ignominious surrender to the South. It is plain that nothing approaching the present policy will subdue the rebels. Whether we shall find *any body* with a sufficient grasp of mind, and sufficient moral courage, to treat this as a radical revolution and remodel our institutions, I doubt.[6]

Criticism from this quarter reached its height in the summer of 1862. Years later, George S. Boutwell was to recall that Chase in the cabinet and Sumner in the Senate headed a "formidable knot" of people in Washington who were bitterly critical of Lincoln's unwillingness to commit himself to a policy of emancipation. The recollections of Congressman George W. Julian of Indiana confirm this view. "No one at a distance," he declared,

> could have formed any adequate conception of the hostility of Republican members [of Congress] toward Mr. Lincoln at the final adjournment [of the Second Session of the Thirty-seventh Congress], while it was the belief of many that our last session of Congress had been held in Washington. Mr. Wade said the country was going to hell, and that the scenes witnessed in the French Revolution were nothing in comparison with what we should see here.[7]

This situation underwent a rapid change with the issuance of Lincoln's

---

unfortunate appointments, I do not believe that Andrew Jackson, or any other man, would have done better than Abraham Lincoln has done since he came into power." See *ibid.*, p. 496.

5. *Ibid.*, p. 3125.

6. Thaddeus Stevens to [Simon Stevens], September 5, 1862, Thaddeus Stevens Papers, Library of Congress.

7. Boutwell, *op. cit.*, I, 308; Julian, *op. cit.*, p. 220.

preliminary emancipation proclamation on September 22, 1862. The President's erstwhile Democratic and Unionist defenders became his bitter critics, while the radicals in his own party largely silenced their public outcries against him. The Chief Executive's second annual message, to be sure, was not well received by the radicals. His continued support of colonization and voluntary, compensated, gradual emancipation struck no answering chord in the breasts of such men as Stevens, Wade, and Sumner.[8] Even so, the radical leadership was notably less critical of the President during the final session of the Thirty-seventh Congress.

Of course, there was still some Republican opposition. Representative Conway of Kansas, for instance, declared the Chief Executive to be "a hindrance and a calamity," because he lacked "any belief in the superiority of northern civilization, or its right to rule this continent."[9] But the public assaults on the President by members of the majority party were few.

The Republicans' private utterances, however, reflected something less than unqualified satisfaction with Lincoln's position. About the middle of February 1863, Dawes of Massachusetts wrote angrily, "The President is an imbecile and should be sent to the school for feeble minded youth, or he is a bad man. I doubt more on that point than I used to."[10] Dawes was not alone. Riddle later recalled that by March 1863, there were only two members of the House "capable of being heard, who openly and everywhere defended him [Lincoln]—Mr. Arnold of Illinois and one of the Ohio delegation [Shellabarger?]."[11]

As far as many Democrats and Unionists were concerned, the truce had ended with the issuance of the preliminary Emancipation Proclamation. At the Willard Hotel, Democratic Representative Kerrigan of New York openly denounced Lincoln as a traitor and was saved from mob violence by the timely intervention of a policeman.[12] A few weeks later Saulsbury

8. Abraham Lincoln, "Second Annual Message," in Richardson, *op. cit.,* VI, 126–143; New York *Herald,* December 2, 1862.

9. *Cong. Globe,* 37th Cong., 3d Sess., Appendix, pp. 62–72; quotation from p. 64.

10. Henry L. Dawes to Mrs. Henry L. Dawes, February 12, 1863, Henry L. Dawes Papers, Library of Congress.

11. Riddle, *op. cit.,* p. 255.

12. New York *Herald,* December 18, 1862.

threw all decorum to the winds and characterized Lincoln as "a weak and imbecile man; the weakest man that I ever knew in a high place; for I have seen him and conversed with him, and I say here, in my place in the Senate of the United States, that I never did see or converse with so weak and imbecile a man as Abraham Lincoln, President of the United States."[13] The senator from Delaware was admittedly drunk at the time; he was shortly removed from the hall after threatening the sergeant-at-arms with a pistol. But there can be little doubt that he was expressing a resentment toward the President that many members of Congress shared.[14]

At the same time, that old Jacksonian, Amos Kendall, was penning an equally gloomy, though much more temperate, assessment of the political situation. "It appears to me," he wrote, "that our public affairs are from day to day becoming more alarming. . . . It is evident that the President has surrendered himself entirely to the rabid abolitionists and that the Republican Party is about to be reorganized upon that narrow platform. A desperate effort will be made and desperate means used by them to retain power." He deprecated extremism of the Saulsbury stripe, however, and advocated loyal, vigorous, political opposition using the Democratic Party as an instrument. Kendall and other conservatives obviously believed that the electorate would not sustain the radicals if the issues were clearly presented.[15]

Criticism might annoy and perhaps influence the President, but only impeachment proceedings could remove him. For many reasons, both practical and political, such action was neither possible nor desirable. Nor could Congress remain continuously in session in order to influence executive policy. If the radicals were to succeed, they must devise some method to control (or at least influence) the executive while Congress was not in session. The most obvious and apparently most vulnerable point of congressional assault in the battle for control of the federal government was the cabinet. If Congress could appreciably extend its

13. *Cong. Globe,* 37th Cong., 3d Sess., p. 549.

14. *Ibid.,* pp. 550, 552, 558–559, 584; New York *Herald,* January 28, 31, 1863.

15. Amos Kendall to John D. Caton, January 27, 1863, John D. Caton Papers, Library of Congress; Hiram Ketchum to Reverdy Johnson, March 7, 1863, Reverdy Johnson Papers, Library of Congress.

control over the President's advisers and, at the same time, render Lincoln more dependent on their counsel, a sizable step in the direction of congressional dominance would have been taken.

The personnel of the cabinet made it peculiarly vulnerable to attack. Its members represented practically all factions of a party that was remarkable for its diversity and lack of solidarity. Three of the secretaries —Bates, Seward, and Chase—had been major contenders for the presidential nomination, and the latter two frequently appeared to view their powers as equivalent to those of a Prime Minister. The later addition of Stanton (a born conspirator) did nothing for the internal solidarity of the cabinet. Any attempt to force a reconstruction of the cabinet and a greater dependence of the President on such a reconstructed cabinet was almost certain to be strongly, if clandestinely, supported by one or more of the secretaries.[16]

There seems to have been little open opposition to the President's advisory council during the early months of the war. By the time the Second Session of the Thirty-seventh Congress convened, however, the determination of the radicals to gain control of the cabinet was obvious to many people. "There is a strong feeling growing up in opposition to all the Cabinet except Chase," wrote one observer in the fall of 1861. "Trumbull, Grimes, Doolittle, Wilson, Sherman and others will be ready for strong measures if some decisive advantages over the rebels are not obtained before the meeting of Congress. Cameron is especially odious though hardly more so than Seward." In late 1861 and early 1862, there were numerous attempts to remove from office or damage the influence of Seward, Chase, Welles, Cameron, Bates, and Smith.[17] Only Cameron, Welles, and Seward were the objects of serious efforts, however.

In mid-December 1861, the House Special Committee on Government Contracts made a report that contained enough revelations of fraudulent

16. William E. Smith's assertion that the cabinet was divided into two groups —a Blair-Bates-Welles faction and a Seward-Chase-Stanton faction—must be regarded as a gross oversimplification of the actual situation. Blair, Bates, and Welles, indeed, might generally be found in considerable harmony, but the holders of the three most important offices in the cabinet often worked at cross purposes. See Smith, *op. cit.,* II, 2.

17. T. H. Bridge to John M. Read I, October 28, 1861, John M. Read I Papers, Library Company of Philadelphia. See also Bates, *op. cit.* (December 10, 1861, February 2, 3, 1862), pp. 211, 227–228.

operations and errors in judgment to render decidedly unsteady the positions of Cameron and (to a lesser extent) Welles. The committee's reports on the Hall Carbine affair and on the activities of Justus McKinstry and Alexander Cummins (which involved fraudulent and collusive purchases of supplies in St. Louis and New York) left little doubt that the operations of the War Department had been marked by a great deal of fraud and raised the suspicion that the Secretary himself might well be involved. Welles was condemned for his use of a private commission agent to secure vessels. Some of the radicals hoped that these revelations would be the levers by which Cameron and Welles could be pried from the cabinet.[18]

Against Cameron, Congress had other grievances. A number of resolutions had been passed calling on the Secretary of War for information. To several of these, Cameron failed to reply or replied in a manner totally unresponsive to the resolutions. This cavalier attitude irritated many congressmen, radical and conservative alike. Furthermore, the Pennsylvania political boss had attempted to force the Senate to speed up the confirmation of military appointments by letting it be known that he would not consider any recommendations to fill other positions until the nominations before the Senate were acted upon. Lincoln had never cared for Cameron and had only reluctantly named him to the cabinet. A head-on clash with the President occurred when Cameron, in a frantic attempt to curry favor with the radicals, surreptitiously inserted in his December 1861 report a section advocating the enlisting and arming of ex-slaves. The document was recalled and the offending section removed, but the episode apparently convinced Lincoln that Cameron must go. It might be added that some of the other secretaries—whether for moral or political reasons—were assuredly not opposed to Cameron's ouster.[19]

18. U.S. House of Representatives, Special Committee on Government Contracts, [*Partial*] *Report, Ho. Com. Repts.,* 37th Cong., 2nd Sess., No. 2, [1142, 1143]. This report was ordered printed on December 17, 1861, and was probably actually printed during that month, though the official publication date is 1862.

19. *Cong. Globe,* 37th Cong., 2nd Sess., pp. 6, 99, 110, 189–198, 271, 274, 288; James G. Randall, *The Civil War and Reconstruction,* p. 227; H. D. Maxwell to John M. Read I, March 25, 1861, John M. Read I Papers, Library Company of Philadelphia; J. P. Sanderson to Simon Cameron, August 20, 1861, Simon Cameron Papers, Library of Congress; Nicolay and Hay, *Lincoln,* V, 125–128.

Under these circumstances there should have been less surprise than there was when Cameron (despite earlier promises of support in high places) was eased out of the War Department and nominated to be Minister to Russia in mid-January 1862. His successor in office, Edwin M. Stanton, was confirmed with only two dissenting votes (Republicans Grimes of Iowa and Pomeroy of Kansas), but Cameron's nomination as Minister to Russia met with greater opposition. Fourteen senators (including six Republicans) opposed confirmation.[20] Because of the complicating factors involved, however, the removal of Cameron could not be viewed purely, or even primarily, as a cabinet change accomplished by congressional pressure. Such pressure, to be sure, played a part, but Lincoln was probably just as anxious to get rid of Cameron as the Congress was.

Welles's position was by no means as insecure as that of Cameron. No actual fraud was charged; indeed, he would seem to have been more guilty of stupidity than criminality. Welles's employment of his brother-in-law George D. Morgan as a navy agent had enabled Morgan to earn commissions amounting to more than $95,000 in little more than four months. He had apparently rendered valuable services to the government, but many congressmen thought them not *that* valuable. Moreover, Welles had the confidence and support of the President to an extent never enjoyed by Cameron; and most important, the operations of the navy had been much more successful than had those of the army.

Even so, attempts were made in Congress to censure the Secretary of the Navy. Early in January 1862, Hale reported from the Senate Committee on Naval Affairs a House bill appropriating money for the construction of twenty ironclad gunboats. The naval committee proposed an amendment requiring the money to be expended under the direction of

20. Thurlow Weed to Simon Cameron, July 26, [1861], William P. Fessenden to Simon Cameron, August 28, 1861, James Dixon to Simon Cameron, September 4, 1861, all in Simon Cameron Papers, Library of Congress; Abraham Lincoln to Simon Cameron, January 11, 1862 (two letters), Lincoln Papers, Library of Congress; Bates, *op. cit.* (January 13, 1862), p. 226; Senate of the United States, *Journal of the Executive Proceedings of the Senate,* XI, 76–87. The six Republicans opposing Cameron's confirmation were Foster of Connecticut, Grimes and Harlan of Iowa, Hale of New Hampshire, Trumbull of Illinois, and Wilkinson of Minnesota.

the President, rather than the Secretary of the Navy. Hale admitted that the modification would have no practical effect but said that it was intended to express the dissatisfaction of Congress with the actions of the Secretary. After two days of debate, the bill was laid aside when the Senate passed a resolution calling for all facts relating to the employment of George D. Morgan. The amendment was later withdrawn.[21]

On the basis of Welles's reply, the naval affairs committee reported a resolution declaring that the employment of an agent on a commission basis was unwise and not to be tolerated in any branch of the public service. The upper house debated this resolution on the first two Fridays in February and then tabled it by a vote of 31 to 5.[22]

One other attempt to censure Welles was made in mid-February, when the House attached to a naval appropriations bill a proviso that no person employed to procure vessels should receive more than five thousand dollars annually. In the Senate, however, this entire section of the bill was eliminated. Welles (though still the object of some intrigues) thus escaped congressional censure, and in any event it could hardly be said that his position in the cabinet was at any time endangered. Certainly the Secretary himself was not perturbed. "The attacks on me are a matter of course," he wrote his son in January 1862, "and do not give me great anoyance [*sic*]."[23]

The movement against Chase was a very minor one indeed. It grew out of charges that the cost of printing treasury notes was excessive and that fraud and the use of dummy companies had been involved in the award of the contract. In January 1862 the House passed a civil appropriations bill which dealt, in part, with the expenses of printing and circulating the treasury notes. Dawes of Massachusetts, an influential member of the Special Committee on Government Contracts, introduced an amendment

21. *Cong. Globe,* 37th Cong., 2nd Sess., pp. 219–221, 245–249, 619.

22. *Ibid.,* pp. 488, 698–703, 817–821. The five Senators who opposed tabling the resolution were Republicans Hale of New Hampshire, Harlan of Iowa, Sherman of Ohio, and Wilkinson of Minnesota and Unionist Robert Wilson of Missouri.

23. *Ibid.,* pp. 813–814, 1393; San Francisco *Daily Alta California,* May 27, 1862; Petition asking for Welles's removal, [April 1862], Gideon Welles to "My Dear Son" [Edgar T. Welles?], January 16, 1862, both in Gideon Welles Papers, Library of Congress.

which would have prevented Chase from making any additional payments on the treasury note printing contract. Dawes and Holman of Indiana made strong attacks on this contract, and Baker of New York added a general indictment of Chase's administration of the Treasury Department. The Secretary and the contract were defended briefly by Stevens and extensively by Republican Charles B. Sedgwick of New York. After three days of debate, the amendment was adopted by a vote of 91 to 43.

The proposal was supported by a majority of all parties in the House. The Republicans split, 48 to 35; the Democrats, 31 to 3; and the Unionists, 12 to 5. This should not be viewed as a radical attempt to gain influence in the cabinet, however, for most of the extremist members of the House (e.g., Bingham, Colfax, Lovejoy, and Stevens) voted against the amendment, and Chase was generally viewed as the most radical of Lincoln's advisers. In the end, the House action amounted to nothing, for the proviso was struck out in the Senate after Pearce of Maryland, the ranking Democratic member of the Committee on Finance, made a short but heavily documented speech refuting the charges against Chase.[24]

But at every opportunity, the radicals returned to their prime target in the cabinet—Seward. The radicals' opposition to Seward did not stem primarily from any dissatisfaction with his administration of the State Department, but rather from his conservative (some radicals would even say timorous) views on constitutional questions and his supposed Svengali-like influence over the Chief Executive. That Abraham Lincoln was exceedingly ill-cast in the role of Trilby should have been much more obvious than it apparently was.

Both the misconception of Seward's role and the determination to remove him persisted. More than a month before the Second Session of Congress convened, "Bluff Ben" Wade was writing bitterly to his wife that "Old Abe is a fool, but is under the entire control of Gov. Seward who is by nature a coward."[25] Some three months later, Attorney General Bates noted in his diary that "Out of doors, there is a formidable clique

24. *Cong. Globe,* 37th Cong., 2nd Sess., pp. 231–238, 274–285, 294–305, 703–705.

25. Benjamin F. Wade to Mrs. Benjamin F. Wade, October 25, 1861, Benjamin F. Wade Papers, Library of Congress.

organized against Mr. Seward, who, fearing his adroitness, work very privily against him." Senator Harris of New York and Secretary of War Stanton were mentioned as possible successors.[26]

Throughout 1862 the radicals attributed to Seward's malign influence Lincoln's reluctance to make emancipation a major aim of the war; his continued espousal of compensated, voluntary, gradual emancipation; his insistence on the modification of the confiscation act; and all of his other conservative attitudes and actions. As early as September 11, Governor Edwin D. Morgan of New York predicted an immediate "re-organization of the Cabinet & with it, that of the Army," and implied that Seward's removal would be an important part of this reorganization. But the weeks passed, and no such change occurred. That arch-radical, Thaddeus Stevens, agreed that Seward's removal would be "a great blessing," but expressed doubt that it could be accomplished. "But Fessenden," he added, taking cognizance of a widespread rumor, "is not the man for his successor. He has too much of the vile ingredient, called Conservatism. . . . Bancroft would be better. But no one will succeed."[27]

Stevens probably underestimated the extent of the growing dissatisfaction with the Secretary of State. His prediction, in the long run, proved correct; but late in 1862, the Senate Republicans launched an attack on Seward that came dangerously close to forcing him out of the cabinet. "*A profound Secret,*" wrote Zachariah Chandler to his wife on December 18, 1862, "The Senate has in Caucus commenced a warfare upon Gen. Seward & thinks he will have to leave the Cabinet before it is over."[28]

Warfare it was—and in earnest. On December 16, Senator Anthony of Rhode Island, chairman of the Senate Republican caucus, called a meeting at the request of Senator Clark of New Hampshire. When the Republican senators (except Hale and Sherman) had gathered in the reception room, the chairman asked the purpose of the meeting. Clark replied that he had requested the meeting because asked to do so by several senators, but that he had no knowledge of their intentions. Some

26. Bates, *op. cit.* (February 2, 3, 1862), pp. 227–228.

27. Edwin D. Morgan to Israel Washburn, September 11, 1862, Israel Washburn Papers, Library of Congress; Thaddeus Stevens to [Simon Stevens], November 17, 1862, Thaddeus Stevens Papers, Library of Congress.

28. Zachariah Chandler to Mrs. Zachariah Chandler, December 18, 1862, Zachariah Chandler Papers, Library of Congress.

delay followed this rather unlikely statement, and then Trumbull of Illinois and Wilkinson of Minnesota launched attacks on Seward, charging him with being opposed to a vigorous prosecution of the war. Foster of Connecticut and Grimes of Iowa concurred in these views, and Wade of Ohio asserted that Seward's removal should be demanded. Grimes then introduced a resolution declaring that the caucus had no confidence in the Secretary of State. Collamer of Vermont suggested that the real trouble lay in Lincoln's failure to consult the cabinet on policy matters. Fessenden of Maine, Field of New Jersey, and some others supported Grimes's resolution with varying degrees of enthusiasm, but Dixon and Howe indicated that they were unwilling to act on the basis of mere rumor. Doolittle of Wisconsin, King of New York, Cowan of Pennsylvania, and Browning of Illinois favored the raising of a committee to investigate the charges against Seward and to consult with the President. It was "a pretty full expression of feeling," wrote Foster to Hamilton Fish that night. "The result . . . will be a new Cabinet unless I am greatly mistaken." But though apparently no one defended the Secretary of State, the qualifications and reservations of the more conservative members of the caucus blunted the impetus of the radical attack. Fewer than half of the senators were willing to support Grimes's resolution in its original form. By a vote of 16 to 13, the caucus was adjourned until the following day.[29]

On the seventeenth, the caucus heard Senator Harris of Seward's home

29. Browning, *op. cit.* (December 16, 1862), I, 596–598; Manuscript account by William P. Fessenden, quoted in its entirety in Fessenden, *op. cit.*, I, 231–252, hereafter cited as "Fessenden Manuscript," see especially pp. 231–236; Lafayette S. Foster to Hamilton Fish, December 16, 1862, Hamilton Fish Papers, Library of Congress; Philadelphia *Inquirer,* December 20, 22, 1862. There seem to have been thirteen senators in favor of the immediate adoption of the Grimes resolution, eleven opposed to its adoption at any time, and five who were unready to take action. We can be fairly sure that Chandler, Foster, Field, Grimes, Trumbull, Wade, Wilson, and Wilkinson favored the resolution and that Browning, Cowan, Dixon, Doolittle, Harris, Howe, and King opposed it. It seems probable that Fessenden, Harlan, Pomeroy, Sumner, and Wilmot favored the proposal and that Anthony, Clark, Collamer, and Howard were opposed. If this analysis is correct (no record of the voting has been located), Foot, Henry S. Lane, James H. Lane, Morrill, and Ten Eyck would appear to have been unwilling to take immediate action. Other sources (e.g., San Francisco *Daily Alta California,* December 22, 1862) agree that there were twenty-nine senators present.

state read a resolution declaring "that in the judgment of the Republican members of the Senate, the public confidence in the present administration would be increased by a reconstruction of the Cabinet." Harris's sponsorship of this resolution and the subsequent support given to it (in modified form) by the moderates and conservatives was probably based on the belief that its adoption would lead to the resignation of the entire cabinet. This would leave Lincoln free to effect a complete reorganization of the executive branch of the government. In the choice of new advisors, the moderates undoubtedly believed that the President would be influenced by the recent congressional elections, in which the radicals had fared badly.[30]

Fessenden, Wade, and some other senators supported the resolution, but Doolittle and King indicated that they still preferred that a committee confer with the President. Sherman of Ohio shrewdly observed that the resolution might be construed as a call for a complete reorganization of the cabinet, which no one (according to Sherman) desired, and asserted that the real difficulty, in any event, was Lincoln, not the cabinet. Trumbull, on the other hand, expressed confidence in the President, but not in his advisers. Sumner then proposed "that a committee be appointed to wait upon the President in behalf of the Senators here present and urge upon him changes in conduct and in the Cabinet which shall give the administration unity and vigor." Fessenden, after consultation with Clark and Sherman, moved to amend Harris's resolution by striking out the words "by a reconstruction of the Cabinet," and inserting the phrase "by a change and partial reconstruction of the Cabinet," thus obviating Sherman's objection. Harris accepted this amendment, and Grimes accepted the new resolution in lieu of the one which he had introduced on the previous day. Sumner's proposal was attached as an additional section, and the entire resolution was adopted 28–0. Foot and Ten Eyck, though absent, were understood to favor the resolution. Preston King, a close personal and political friend of Seward, was present but did not vote.[31]

To head the committee entrusted with this delicate task, the caucus

30. Browning, *op. cit.* (December 17, 1862), I, 598–599; "Fessenden Manuscript," quoted in Fessenden, *op. cit.*, I, 236; Philadelphia *Inquirer*, December 20, 1862.

31. Browning, *loc. cit.;* "Fessenden Manuscript," quoted in Fessenden, *op. cit.*, I, 236–238.

selected Jacob Collamer of Vermont who, as a Whig representative, had served with Lincoln in Congress fifteen years before. The other members were Wade of Ohio, Grimes of Iowa, Fessenden of Maine, Trumbull of Illinois, Sumner of Massachusetts, Harris of New York, Pomeroy of Kansas, and Howard of Michigan. This committee accurately represented the varying shades of opinion regarding Seward among the Republican senators. It also contained some of the most influential men in the Senate and the chairmen of some half-dozen important committees. Collamer wrote to Lincoln the next day (December 18), and the President agreed to receive the committee at seven o'clock that evening.[32]

In the meantime, oblivious of the standing injunction of secrecy regarding caucus activities, King had gone directly from the Capitol to Seward and had informed him of the caucus actions. Seward immediately prepared his resignation, as did his son Frederick, who was Assistant Secretary of State. Frederick Seward and Senator King were then dispatched to the White House, and by shortly after six o'clock that evening (December 17), Lincoln had in his hands the resignations of the two top officials of the State Department.[33]

32. "Fessenden Manuscript," quoted in Fessenden, *op. cit.,* I, 238; Jacob Collamer to Abraham Lincoln, December 18, 1862, Lincoln Papers, Library of Congress; Lafayette S. Foster to Hamilton Fish, December 19, 1862, Hamilton Fish Papers, Library of Congress. The Philadelphia *Inquirer* (December 20, 1862) declared the committee to consist of six radicals and three antiradicals. Collamer, Harris, and Howard were undoubtedly considered to be the antiradicals. The same journal later (December 22, 1862) asserted that the committee had originally consisted of only seven senators and that Harris and Howard had been added later. There is no mention of this latter point by Fessenden, Foster, or Browning.

33. Bates, *op. cit.* (December 19, 1862), p. 269; "Fessenden Manuscript," quoted in Fessenden, *op. cit.,* I, 251; Gideon Welles, *Diary of Gideon Welles,* edited by Edgar T. Welles (December 19, 1862), I, 194; William H. Seward to Abraham Lincoln, December 16, 1862, Frederick W. Seward to Abraham Lincoln, December 16, 1862, both in Lincoln Papers, Library of Congress. The letters of resignation are dated December 16, but Welles says they were received by the President at about 6:00 P.M. on the seventeenth. The discrepancy probably results from an error in dating. It is entirely possible, however, that on the evening of the sixteenth King informed Seward of the caucus actions of that date and that the resignations were prepared at that time. It might be noted that King was not the only senator to violate the secrecy injunction regarding caucus activities. See Lafayette S. Foster to Hamilton Fish, December 16, 1862, Hamilton Fish Papers, Library of Congress.

Immediately after the adjournment of the Senate on December 18, Collamer informed the other committee members of the appointment with Lincoln that evening. He suggested that the views of the committee should be presented in writing, and to this the other senators assented. He then produced a draft which, after some minor modifications, was adopted. This document stated that the Republican senators had unanimously come to the conclusion that:

> 1st. The only course of sustaining this government and restoring and preserving national existence, and perpetuating the national integrity, is by a vigorous and successful prosecution of the war. . . .
>
> 2nd. The theory of our government, and the early and uniform political construction thereof is, that the President should be aided by a Cabinet council, agreeing with him in political principles and general policy, and that all important public measures and appointments should be the result of their combined wisdom and deliberation. This . . . we and the public believe does not now exist, and therefore such selections and changes in its members should be made as will secure to the country unity of purpose and action. . . .
>
> 3rd. The Cabinet should be exclusively composed of statesmen who are the cordial, resolute, unwavering supporters of the principles and purposes first above stated.

The statement further implied that changes should be made in the military commands as well.[34]

The committee met with Lincoln that night at the White House. Collamer read the paper which had been drafted and said that he had nothing to add. Wade expressed considerable dissatisfaction over the lack of military successes and about the recent political reverses in the Midwest. Grimes and Howard indicated a general want of confidence in Seward, and Fessenden asserted that the Secretary of State was not in harmony with the rest of the cabinet. Sumner based his opposition to the Secretary on his diplomatic correspondence, which he thought unwise and impolitic. Trumbull, Harris, and Pomeroy apparently took no part in the discussion. After some three hours spent in this fashion, Lincoln re-

34. "Fessenden Manuscript," quoted in Fessenden, *op. cit.,* I, 238–240.

quested the senators to meet with him on the following night to discuss the matter further. The committee agreed to this proposition.[35]

On the following morning, the President informed the cabinet (Seward being absent) of what had transpired and indicated his great distress concerning the situation. After emphasizing that he did not desire the resignations of the other secretaries, Lincoln suggested that the cabinet join him in meeting with the senatorial committee at 7:30 that night for a full discussion of the matter. In spite of Chase's vehement protests, this was agreed to; thus Lincoln, with keen insight into both politics and humanity, had set the stage for an inescapable showdown.[36]

The cabinet (minus Seward) and the committee (with the exception of Wade, who was absent on business for the Committee on the Conduct of the War) gathered in the White House on the evening of December 19. The members of the committee were apparently surprised at the presence of the cabinet. Of all those present, however, Chase was probably the most perturbed, for implicit in the statement presented by the committee and explicit in the senators' conversations with Lincoln on the eighteenth was the assumption that the cabinet was badly divided. Men intimately associated with both the executive and legislative branches of

35. *Ibid.*, I, 240–243; Bates, *op. cit.* (December 19, 1862), pp. 268–270; Nicolay and Hay, *Lincoln,* VI, 264–265; Lafayette S. Foster to Hamilton Fish, December 19, 1862, Hamilton Fish Papers, Library of Congress. Word of Seward's resignation had already reached the senators before they met with the President. Nicolay and Hay state that this interview took place on the morning of the nineteenth, while Fessenden gives the time as the evening of the eighteenth. Fessenden's version is much the more probable of the two. A special cabinet meeting was held at 10:30 on the morning of the nineteenth, and all authorities agree that the discussion between Lincoln and the committee was a lengthy one (Fessenden says three hours). The interview would have had to take place at an unbelievably early hour to have permitted Lincoln even to attend the cabinet meeting, let alone dispatch the necessary notes to assemble the secretaries. Foster (though not present) also supports the December 18 date, saying, "The Pres't. met our Senate Committee last eveg." It might also be noted that Collamer had written Lincoln on December 18 requesting "an interview with the President, at as early an hour, after six o'clock this evening, as may suit his convenience." See Jacob Collamer to Abraham Lincoln, December 18, 1862, Lincoln Papers, Library of Congress.

36. Bates, *op. cit.* (December 19, 1862), p. 269; Welles, *op. cit.* (December 19, 1862), I, 194–196.

the government shared a belief amounting to certainty that Chase had fostered and sustained this impression. Gideon Welles and Thomas Ewing were both convinced that statements made by the Secretary of the Treasury to his senatorial intimates had sparked the caucus action, and Orville H. Browning asserted (without contradiction) in a Republican senatorial caucus three days later that Chase had told senators who were members of the committee that Seward "exercised a back stair and malign influence upon the President, and thwarted all the measures of the Cabinet." Chase had certainly complained to Horace Greeley some three months earlier that there was little cabinet consultation on war policy. "I have," he lamented, "tried very hard to have it otherwise—unavailingly." But would the Ohio radical speak so in the presence of his cabinet colleagues? He would not. Embarrassed, flustered, and somewhat angry, he joined with the rest of the presidential advisers in declaring that no divisions existed within the cabinet. In short, from the radical point of view, he "betrayed the party & saved Seward," as the waspish Adam Gurowski declared.[37]

The senators, too, found it expedient to take a considerably milder tone. Fessenden and Trumbull urged the necessity of cabinet consultation on all important matters, but Blair and Bates vigorously championed the indivisible executive power and responsibility of the presidency. After an extended discussion, the President asked the senators to state their views on Seward's withdrawal. Collamer refused to go beyond the original committee statement. Trumbull, Sumner, and Grimes (especially the latter) were decidedly in favor of such a cabinet change, and Pomeroy said that he had reluctantly come to the same conclusion. Harris expressed mild opposition to the withdrawal of his fellow New Yorker; and both

37. Nicolay and Hay, *Lincoln,* VI, 256–266; "Fessenden Manuscript," quoted in Fessenden, *op. cit.,* I, 243–244; Welles, *op. cit.* (December 19, 20, 1862), I, 195–204; Browning, *op. cit.* (December 19, 22, 1862), I, 602–603; Bates, *op. cit.* (December 19, 1862), pp. 268–270; Philadelphia *Inquirer,* December 22, 1862; Salmon P. Chase to Horace Greeley, September 7, 1862, Horace Greeley Papers, New York Public Library; Adam Gurowski to John A. Andrew, December 27, 1862, John A. Andrew Papers, Massachusetts Historical Society. Welles thought that Stanton and Caleb Smith were also guilty of attacking Seward in their conversations with various senators. The Secretary of the Navy had noted an intense rivalry between Seward and Chase as early as the previous September. See Welles, *op. cit.* (September 16, 1862), I, 131–139.

Fessenden and Howard, inhibited by the presence of the cabinet, said that this was no place to discuss their opinions on this subject. The unhappy Chase seized on this hint with great relief and immediately suggested that the cabinet withdraw. So, at midnight, the cabinet left the White House —with Chase, one rather suspects, several lengths in the lead. The senators lingered for another hour. Fessenden informed Lincoln that he would advise the acceptance of Seward's resignation and that he would not have advised his initial appointment, had he been consulted. At one o'clock on the morning of the twentieth, the senators and the President parted.[38]

Though the confrontation had weakened the senatorial attack, the problem was by no means solved; nor should it be thought that the radicals would have been satisfied with the withdrawal of Seward. Notice had already been served that a shuffling of military commanders would be expected; and there could be little doubt that if Seward left the cabinet as a result of congressional pressures, Bates, Blair, and Welles would soon follow. Nor should the insistence of Fessenden and Trumbull on the necessity for cabinet consultation be overlooked. If the majority party in Congress (or, for that matter, in either house of Congress) should gain the power to dictate cabinet appointments, and if the President should consider himself bound by the opinions of a cabinet so constructed, a parliamentary form of government, for all practical purposes, would be established. There was, in short, far more at stake than merely the question of who should be the Secretary of State. Gideon Welles struck at the root of the matter when he wrote in his diary that "A Senatorial combination to dictate to the President in regard to his political family . . . cannot be permitted to succeed, even if the person to whom they object were as obnoxious as they represent." The action of the radical senators was, in fact, as the New York *Times* was later to say, "directly at war with the independence of the Executive and the stability of the Government."[39]

38. "Fessenden Manuscript," quoted in Fessenden, *op. cit.,* I, 243–248; Welles, *op. cit.* (December 20, 1862), I, 196–198; Bates, *op. cit.* (December 19, 1862), pp. 269–270.

39. Welles, *op. cit.* (December 20, 1862), I, 198–199; New York *Times,* December 21, 23, 1862; Philadelphia *Inquirer,* December 22, 1862; Lyman Trumbull to W. C. Flagg, January 21, 1862, Lyman Trumbull Papers, Illinois

On the morning of the twentieth, however, it appeared that the Senate radicals had achieved a considerable measure of success. Seward's resignation was thought to be irrevocable, and Washington was rife with rumors of a mass resignation of presidential advisers. Lincoln had been sent a number of slates for the new cabinet which most observers now seemed to think inevitable, and newspapers across the country were busily preparing to engage in the fascinating game of matching men and positions. More conservative Republicans urged Lincoln to hold fast to Seward, but even if the Secretary of State could be persuaded to resume his duties, how could the President spike the political guns of the senatorial cabal? "The explosion in the cabinet is astounding," commented George Bancroft. "No one knows what to expect, & hardly what to wish. . . . All are in a ferment & await the clearing up of the fog."[40]

On this very day, however, Lincoln's shrewd maneuvering bore fruit. The entire situation was becoming extremely embarrassing to Chase. He doubtless knew that several of his colleagues believed him responsible for the attack on Seward. After the meeting on the nineteenth, many senators

---

State Historical Library. Welles understood Fessenden to urge that the actions of the administration be determined by cabinet decisions, with the President having only one vote. Fessenden, however, says that he merely urged consultation, with the President not being bound by the decision of the cabinet. The statements of Bates, though of an indefinite nature, would seem to give slightly more support to the Fessenden version. Cf. "Fessenden Manuscript," quoted in Fessenden, *op. cit.,* I, 245; Welles, *op. cit.* (December 20, 1862), I, 197; Bates, *op. cit.* (December 19, 1862), p. 270.

40. Nicolay and Hay, *Lincoln,* VI, 267; Undated and unsigned paper containing proposals for cabinet (Ms. No. 20658), Thomas T. Davis to Abraham Lincoln, December 20, 1862, both in Lincoln Papers, Library of Congress; Boston *Post,* December 22, 1862; Philadelphia *Inquirer,* December 22, 1862; George Bancroft to [Alexander Bliss], December 21, 1862, Bancroft-Bliss Papers, Library of Congress. Some mention should be made of the slowness of the nation's press to pick up the story of the cabinet crisis. Seward's resignation was rumored in Washington on December 17 and was certainly known to persons outside the government by December 19. Substantial newspaper coverage, however, did not begin until December 22, by which time the crisis was resolved. This delay was occasioned by the refusal of the telegraphic censor to permit accounts of the cabinet upheaval to be dispatched from Washington. See "Fessenden Manuscript," quoted in Fessenden, *op. cit.,* I, 243; Browning, *op. cit.* (December 19, 1862), I, 602; Henry D. Cooke to Jay Cooke, December 19, 1862, Jay Cooke Papers, Historical Society of Pennsylvania; Philadelphia *Inquirer,* December 22, 1862.

were certain to consider him a spineless coward and a liar. Exactly what Chase really intended is difficult to determine; but on that Saturday morning, the Secretary of the Treasury—at the White House at Lincoln's request—informed the President that he had prepared a letter of resignation. He obviously meant to say more, but Lincoln interrupted to ask where it was. Chase replied that he had brought it with him and held it in his hand. The President stepped forward and whisked the paper from the secretary's reluctant fingers. His problem was solved. Treating both resignations as though they sprang from the same cause, Lincoln addressed a single letter to the two secretaries jointly and sent a copy to each. He alluded to both resignations, declared his unwillingness to accept either, and asked each man to resume his duties.[41]

Seward, following the President's lead, drafted a letter to be signed jointly by the two secretaries, agreeing to Lincoln's request. But either Chase refused to sign, or Seward, on further consideration, decided not to submit the paper to him, for on December 21 Seward informed the President independently that "I have cheerfully resumed the functions of this Department in obedience to your command." Chase's reply, on the other hand, was notable for neither brevity nor simplicity. On December 20, he wrote Lincoln a three-page letter explaining why he thought both resignations should be accepted. He did not immediately dispatch this communication, however, and Seward's return to the State Department cut the ground from under him. On the following Monday (December 22), Chase sent the President a note enclosing his letter of December 20. He had not, he said, much changed the opinions expressed therein, but he would resume his duties as Secretary of the Treasury. Thus, Lincoln's shrewdness and imagination had prevented a gross extension of congressional powers at the expense of the executive.[42]

"The trouble is all over for the present," John G. Nicolay was able to

41. Bates, *op. cit.* (December 20, 1862), pp. 270–271; Welles, *op. cit.* (December 20, 1862), I, 201; Nicolay and Hay, *Lincoln,* VI, 267–268; Abraham Lincoln to Salmon P. Chase and William H. Seward, December 20, 1862, Lincoln Papers, Library of Congress.

42. William H. Seward and Salmon P. Chase to Abraham Lincoln (draft letter), [December 20, 1862?], William H. Seward Papers, University of Rochester; William H. Seward to Abraham Lincoln, December 21, 1862, Salmon P. Chase to Abraham Lincoln, December 20, 22, 1862, all in Lincoln Papers, Library of Congress; Nicolay and Hay, *Lincoln,* VI, 268–271.

write on December 23. "The President determined that he would retain both Mr. Seward and Mr. Chase, meddlesome outsiders to the contrary notwithstanding. I think the Cabinet and the government is much stronger than it was before the shaking up it received." Attorney-General Bates, however, thought that the attempt by the Senate radicals had not been entirely unsuccessful. He was convinced that Seward thereafter supported radical measures much more readily and that a lasting impression had been made on Stanton.[43]

Statements of support for the President's actions came from various sections of the country. "The holding of a caucus to dragoon Mr. Lincoln would have set a very bad precedent if it had been successful," observed the pro-Republican San Francisco *Daily Alta California.* "It is gratifying to know that the Executive had the firmness to resist it." The Democratic Boston *Post* was more biting, declaring, "The self-constituted War Committee of New York, or the spectacled dames of Music Hall, have just as good a right to appoint a committee, and demand an audience with the President, to question his wisdom, and make suggestions as to his conduct of his executive affairs [as have the Republican senators]." There were, however, other journals which thought that the President should "surround himself with strong men, and . . . act in pursuance of his own best light, combined with their most careful and mature council."[44]

Irritated and dissatisfied though the Senate radicals might be, so thoroughly had the ground been cut from under them that they apparently abandoned hope of any further assault on the executive for the time being. Some observers expected the cabinet to dissolve over the question of the issuance of the final Emancipation Proclamation, but this event passed without incident and on January 14, 1863, a brief paragraph in the New York *Herald* announced that the Republican senatorial caucus had endorsed the cabinet. The situation was summed up three days later by the Senate Republican leader, when he wrote to William Cullen Bryant, "The Repub. Senators have taken no action since that, the result

43. John G. Nicolay to Therena [Bates], December 23, 1862, John G. Nicolay Papers, Library of Congress; Bates, *op. cit.* (December 20, 1862), p. 271. Bates probably made this comment on December 30, the date of the next diary entry.

44. San Francisco *Daily Alta California,* December 24, 1862; Boston *Post,* December 25, 1862; Detroit *Advertiser and Tribune,* December 23, 1862. The *Advertiser and Tribune* editorial was probably written before news of the resolution of the crisis was received.

of which you have seen. Our belief is that an unsuccessful movement would only be productive of evil, by giving colour to the idea that we were in antagonism with the Prest. and thus weakening confidence in a government none too strong." Fessenden added that he still thought a cabinet reorganization desirable and believed that political pressure from New York would accomplish more than further action by the Republican senators.[45]

The truce was by no means universal, however; during late January and early February, there were numerous reports of statements by, and gatherings of, various politicians indicating an unwillingness to consider the issue closed. A special House caucus of radical Republicans (to which the more conservative members of the majority party were not invited) was called, and it was understood that the purpose of the gathering was to force a radical reconstruction of the cabinet. But if an almost unanimous caucus of Senate Republicans had failed to achieve this aim, what could fewer than half of the House Republicans hope to accomplish?

There were, to be sure, some senators who had not given up hope of gaining at least partial ascendency over the executive. Lincoln's adroitness had convinced many in the upper house that such a program was impracticable, but there were others who were "constantly caucusing at the National and at Willard's," and whose intemperate statements left no doubt as to their desires. On February 10, 1863, the ultra-radical Zachariah Chandler unburdened himself to his wife:

> Seward I am afraid is a traitor to his Country. I believe *Sincerely* that he is today plotting for the dismemberment of the Government. I believe he would prefer to see England or France intervene rather than see the Rebellion crushed by force of Arms. We shall make one more effort upon Seward in the Senate I think. Unless we get rid of him I fear we Shall loose [*sic*] the Govt. . . . The Cabinet is weak and Lincoln weaker.[46]

45. Edward Everett to Robert Bonner, December 29, 1862, Edward Everett Papers, Library of Congress; New York *Herald,* January 14, 1863; William P. Fessenden to William C. Bryant, January 17, 1863, Bryant-Godwin Papers, New York Public Library.

46. New York *Herald,* January 18, 19, 25, 1863; Washington *National Intelligencer,* January 20, 1863; Zachariah Chandler to Mrs. Zachariah Chandler, February 10, 1863, Zachariah Chandler Papers, Library of Congress; James W. White to Simon Cameron, January 11, 1863, Simon Cameron Papers, Library of Congress.

The public utterances of this group were scarcely more restrained. The day after Chandler penned his indictment of the Secretary of State, the Washington correspondent of the New York *Herald* pointedly observed that "Some of the republican members of Congress daily make use of remarks in public places derogatory to the President and Cabinet, such as would subject newspaper editors and other parties not M. C.'s to imprisonment in the Old Capitol." But in the end, no new radical offensive was launched.[47]

There were probably several reasons why the direct attack on the executive failed. Decades of participation in Illinois politics had made Lincoln relatively insensitive to verbal assaults. The campaign of vilification in the 1860 election and in the pre-inaugural period further toughened his emotional calluses. Furthermore, he was a past master at side-stepping direct attacks. His ability to turn aside a thrust with a crude (but often shrewd) witticism is one of the most widely recognized elements of Lincoln's personality. Finally, it must not be forgotten that Lincoln was a professional politician. However inadequate his understanding of economic, social, or military issues might be, his assessment of the political situation was generally both strategically and tactically sound. Furthermore, the executive branch, because of its inherent power and unity, was (and is) the element of government least vulnerable to direct attack. Conversely, the congressional radicals were weakened by internal divisions, multiple leadership, and inertial resistance to the major governmental alteration which they desired. The radicals lost the battle to Lincoln for precisely the same reasons that Burnside was defeated at Fredericksburg—which defeat helped spark the radical assault on Seward. The radicals advanced under inadequately unified leadership, across unfavorable terrain, against a position of superior strength held by a more able commander.

But a final question must be raised: was the radical assault completely unsuccessful? Bates thought not, and certainly Stanton drew ever closer to the radicals. Even this qualified defeat had been partially neutralized, for there were means of acquiring influence over the executive other than direct assault. The radical leadership had quickly found (or forged) and employed levers useful for an indirect exertion of Congressional power.

47. New York *Herald,* February 12, 1863.

CHAPTER 10

Toward Congressional Dominance: Flank Attacks

Though a frontal assault on the executive by Congress proved largely ineffective, the radicals were quick to grasp other instrumentalities available to the legislative branch of the government. One of the most serviceable of these was the investigating committee. Though Congress was not able to demand a voice in the executive administration of the nation, time was to show that it was easier to assume such a role than to demand it. Investigating committees proved admirable vehicles for such slow insinuations of authority. The most powerful, most arrogant, and most famous of these committees was the Committee on the Conduct of the War.

This body owed its existence to a resolution introduced in the Senate by Chandler on December 5, 1861. The Michigan senator proposed the raising of a select committee of three to inquire into the Union defeats at Bull Run and Edward's Ferry (Ball's Bluff). James H. Lane of Kansas attempted to extend the scope of the investigations to include the two Missouri battles of Wilson's Creek and Lexington. After some discussion, Grimes of Iowa suggested the creation of a joint committee of two senators and three representatives to make a general inquiry into all military disasters. At this point, Fessenden, the Senate Republican leader, probably calculating the nature of the political stakes involved, arranged to have the matter postponed.[1]

When the question was again considered on the ninth, it was obvious that many senators had come to realize the potential power of such a body. Chandler, ostensibly, was at first recalcitrant, opposing Grimes's proposal because it made the scope of the committee activities too broad. It was doubtless this very aspect that endeared the scheme to many

1. *Cong. Globe,* 37th Cong., 2nd Sess., pp. 16–17.

senators. Nor should Chandler's protestations necessarily be taken at face value, for he was both a dedicated radical and also well aware of the power wielded by legislators acting in concert. During the previous fall, he, in combination with Trumbull of Illinois, Wade of Ohio, Wilkinson of Minnesota, and Pomeroy of Kansas, had made a foray against the administration with apparent success. Chandler's proposal was modified to provide for a joint committee composed of three senators and four representatives "to inquire into the conduct of the present war." The resolution then passed by a vote of 33 to 3, with Democrats Latham of California and Rice of Minnesota and Unionist Carlile of Virginia casting negative votes.[2]

On the following day, the House concurred in the Senate action without debate, without a division, and probably without any general understanding of the matter. To the committee the Vice President named Republicans Wade of Ohio and Chandler of Michigan—both dedicated radicals—and Democrat Andrew Johnson of Tennessee. The Speaker of the House appointed Republicans Daniel W. Gooch of Massachusetts, Covode of Pennsylvania, and Julian of Indiana—radicals all—and Democrat Moses F. Odell of New York. Both Johnson and Odell were advanced "War Democrats."[3]

The House members were appointed on December 19, 1861. On the following day, the committee met in the room of the Senate Committee on Territories, and elected Senator Wade chairman. The first joint investigating committee in American congressional history had embarked on a memorable career. The events of this career have been thoroughly narrated and analyzed by Professor T. Harry Williams in his book *Lincoln and the Radicals* and certainly require no further elaboration here. The committee was extremely active, meeting almost daily for some four

2. *Ibid.,* pp. 29–32; Zachariah Chandler to Henry W. Lord, November 16, 1861, Robert M. Zug Papers, Burton Historical Collections, Detroit Public Library.

3. *Cong. Globe,* 37th Cong., 2nd Sess., pp. 40, 110, 146. Chandler made the motion authorizing the Vice President to appoint the members of the committee from the Senate and announced at the time that he did not wish to be the chairman of the committee. On March 11, 1862, Wright of Indiana replaced Johnson on the committee. Johnson had left the Senate to become military governor of Tennessee. See *ibid.,* p. 1165.

months after its organization and quite frequently thereafter. Attendance was generally good, with Covode being the member most frequently absent. The minority members—Odell, Johnson, and later Wright—were occasionally absent. The chairman was the most energetic of the group in the interrogation of witnesses, but all members participated quite actively. Gooch generally took the lead in Wade's absence.[4]

The committee's activities were certain to give rise to controversy, for its avowed purposes and its membership made it clear that the body was constituted as a pressure group. It was most unlikely that it would make any significant contribution to the framing of legitimate legislation since the area of the group's operations lay outside the scope of congressional competence. During this same session of Congress, both the aims and the methods of this committee were subjected to biting criticism.

On February 14, 1862, the venerable Kentucky Unionist, Charles A. Wickliffe, condemned the very existence of the body as an attempt on the part of Congress to interfere with the legitimate functions of the executive. "If you embarrass the Executive with your joint committees, your resolutions, your propositions to make Territories of the States," he declared, "this war will not end in my time or yours."[5]

Some two months later, taking as the immediate issue the arrest and imprisonment of Brigadier-General Charles P. Stone, Senator McDougall of California found himself involved in a controversy with Wade which eventually led him to denounce the activities of the committee. McDougall declared that the committee ignored the constitution, law, and justice, held secret sessions, and relied on *ex parte* testimony. In fact, he delivered a lengthy analogy comparing the activities of the committee to the methods employed by the Inquisition and specifically likening Wade to Torquemada. Wade's violent replies attacking McDougall were designed to sustain the committee, but they contained statements that constituted implicit admissions of the truth of McDougall's charges. For instance, he

4. U. S. Congress, Joint Committee on the Conduct of the War, *Report of the Joint Committee on the Conduct of the War, Sen. Com. Repts.,* 37th Cong., 3d Sess., No. 108, Pt. 1, [1152]; New York *Herald,* January 10, 1862; Marshall E. Dimock, *Congressional Investigating Committees,* Vol. XLII, No. 1 of *Johns Hopkins University Studies in Historical and Political Science,* 111; Telford Taylor, *Grand Inquest,* p. 34; Williams, *op. cit.,* especially pp. 53–170.

5. *Cong. Globe,* 37th Cong., 2nd Sess., p. 838.

said, in General Stone's case, the committee was in possession of information which constituted a "probable cause for arrest" and implied that the general's continued imprisonment without trial resulted from an inability to obtain "technical evidence." "That man is not quite honest," he vehemently asserted, "who thus argues constitutional questions in this Senate, and invokes the Constitution in behalf of every man precisely as he would in times of peace. . . . The ordinary course of the common law and of the Constitution cannot be followed."[6]

Attacks on the Committee on the Conduct of the War, and particularly on Wade and Chandler, continued during the last session of the Thirty-seventh Congress—especially after the contents of their four volumes of testimony and reports became generally known. The reports, which were generally brief, were partisan but not violent. The testimony, more clearly than the reports, revealed the intransigence of the committee members.[7]

6. *Ibid.*, pp. 1662–1669, 1678–1680, 1732–1742; quotation from p. 1736. General Stone, a resident of California, had been accused of responsibility for the Union defeat at Ball's Bluff and apparently was suspected of treason as well. He had been arrested in February 1862 and, at the time of McDougall's speech, had been held for more than two months without trial and without charges being presented against him. See Charles F. Stone to [Benjamin F. Wade], May 3, 1862, copy in James G. Blaine Papers, Library of Congress. Which senator began the controversy must remain a moot question. McDougall's initial speech contains no references to the Committee on the Conduct of the War, but Wade immediately launched a violent attack upon the California senator and later charged that he had attacked the committee in his speech but had struck out all references to that body before the speech was published. McDougall did not specifically deny this charge, but he was not in the Senate when it was made and possibly was not apprised of it.

7. George C. Bates to James F. Joy, January 18, 1863, James F. Joy Papers, Burton Historical Collections, Detroit Public Library; Timothy O. Howe to Grace T. Howe, February 13, 1863, Timothy O. Howe Papers, State Historical Society of Wisconsin; U. S. Congress, Joint Committee on the Conduct of the War, *Partial Report of the Committee on the Conduct of the War, Sen. Com. Repts.*, 37th Cong., 3d Sess., No. 71, [1151]; U. S. Congress, Joint Committee on the Conduct of the War, *Report of the Joint Committee on the Conduct of the War, Sen. Com. Repts.*, 37th Cong., 3d Sess., No. 108, 3 pts., [1152, 1153, 1154]. The partial report of the committee [1151] concerns the battle of Fredericksburg and was ordered printed on December 23, 1862. The three parts of the full report are subtitled *Army of the Potomac* [1152], *Bull Run—Ball's Bluff* [1153], and *Western Department, or Missouri—Miscellaneous* [1154]. These last three vol-

The real impact of the committee, however, was made, not through its reports, but through its undoubted influence on military and political decisions. Is it too much to suggest that McClellan's occasionally timorous and erratic behavior and his eventual dismissal stemmed in part from the unrelenting campaign waged against him by the committee? Can one totally ignore the influence of the committee on the elevation to high command of Wade's favorites—Hooker, Pope, and Burnside—before calling on Meade, Grant, and William T. Sherman, who were distrusted by the chairman? These were executive decisions, to be sure, but there can be little doubt that the legislative branch of the government, through the influence of this powerful committee, was gradually and almost surreptitiously arrogating to itself an increasing share of the national executive power.[8]

Though none was so powerful as the Committee on the Conduct of the War, other congressional bodies contributed, wittingly or unwittingly, to the usurpation of executive power by Congress. For instance, many of the charges of fraud leveled against various cabinet members were based on revelations of the House Select Committee on Government Contracts. This committee was raised at the insistence of Republican Charles H. Van Wyck of New York. His resolution, calling for a committee of five, was passed without a division on July 8, 1861. Two days later, Fenton, probably desiring a place on the committee which he feared would be denied him, secured the passage of a motion increasing the membership to seven. On July 12, 1861, when the Speaker of the House announced the personnel of the body, Van Wyck, in accordance with congressional protocol, was named chairman. Other members of the group were Republicans Washburne of Illinois, Fenton of New York, and Dawes of Massachusetts; Democrats Holman of Indiana and William G. Steele of New Jersey; and Unionist Jackson of Kentucky. Holman, though only in his

---

umes are dated April 6, 1863, the committee having been given the power to sit during the recess of Congress by a concurrent resolution passed by the House and the Senate on March 2, 1863.

8. Benjamin F. Wade to Abraham Lincoln, February 14, April 2, 1862, both in Lincoln Papers, Library of Congress; Adam Gurowski to Zachariah Chandler, March 8, 12, 1862, both in Zachariah Chandler Papers, Library of Congress; Bates, *op. cit.* (April 22, 1862), p. 253; James G. Randall, *Lincoln, the President,* II, 242*n;* Williams, *op. cit.,* pp. 53–170.

second term, had already established his reputation as a conscientious, eagle-eyed defender of the public treasury; and Dawes was a man of monolithic integrity. Washburne and Fenton, while somewhat more amenable to party pressures, both possessed a fair share of political courage and stamina. Steele was an unknown quantity and essentially remained so, while Jackson, because of the press of his military duties, seldom attended the committee sessions. The weakest element in the committee was probably its chairman—not because he was either a corruptionist or an unbending anti-administration man, for Van Wyck was neither of these—but because of his emotional approach, his erratic and occasionally vindictive behavior, and his necessary absence on military duty.[9]

When the committee was less than a week old, the membership asked the House to pass a resolution extending the scope of investigations to include all government contracts, past and future. The resolution also gave the committee leave to sit during the adjournment of Congress and at any place they deemed necessary, authorized the employment of a clerk, and permitted the Speaker to issue subpoenas for the use of the committee during recesses of Congress. After a brief but bitter struggle, the resolution was passed by a vote of 81 to 42.[10]

The committee was quite active during the period between the First and Second Sessions of the Thirty-seventh Congress, and moderately active during the Second Session and just before and during the Third Session. Attendance on the part of five of the members was fairly good, but Van Wyck and Jackson were rarely present. Despite Van Wyck's nonattendance and general lack of information concerning the cases investigated by the committee, he persisted in attempting to exercise the powers of chairman. The situation became untenable, and the members finally removed him as chairman and substituted Washburne in his stead. The first and only major report of the committee was ordered printed on

9. *Cong. Globe,* 37th Cong., 1st Sess., pp. 23, 56, 91. The opinions and conclusions expressed regarding the members of the committee are based on the total activities of the representatives throughout this Congress and at other periods of their lives.

10. *Ibid.,* pp. 168–170. The original resolution had empowered the committee to investigate only contracts already negotiated and only those which had been negotiated in violation of certain laws or administrative policies. See *ibid.,* p. 23.

December 17, 1861, and conclusively demonstrated that the members had not, as the New York *Herald* charged, "been on a sort of summer and fall pleasure excursion over the country, producing little or nothing of value."[11]

This document dealt primarily with the *Cataline* affair, and the activities of J. M. McKinstry, Alexander Cummings, George D. Morgan, Captain E. M. Davis, General John C. Frémont, and Simon Stevens. The report strongly condemned a number of important government officials, but it played no favorites. However much the radicals might welcome revelations implicating Secretary of War Cameron and Secretary of the Navy Welles, they were somewhat less than delighted when the committee pried into the activities of some of their own friends and connections. Simon Stevens was the protégé of Thaddeus Stevens; E. M. Davis was the brother of Republican Representative William M. Davis of Pennsylvania; and, after the issuance of his emancipation order, John C. Frémont was the blood-brother of all radicals. Although the findings of the committee were frequently used as clubs to attack conservative cabinet members, the committee itself does not seem to have used its power to influence the executive branch of the government to do anything except wipe out fraud in government contracts.[12]

The radicals, disturbed by this all-too-equitable distribution of condemnation, were by no means as friendly toward the House Special Committee on Government Contracts as they were toward the Joint Committee on the Conduct of the War. During the first four months of 1862, the galleries of the lower house echoed back charges and countercharges—at-

11. Committee on Government Contracts, *Partial Report,* [1142, 1143]; *Cong. Globe,* 37th Cong., 3d Sess., pp. 1549–1551; New York *Herald,* December 2, 1861.

12. Committee on Government Contracts, *Partial Report,* [1142, 1143]; William M. Davis to Elihu B. Washburne, January 20, 1862, E. M. Davis to Committee on Government Contracts, April 9, 1862, both in Elihu B. Washburne Papers, Library of Congress. The *Cataline* was an inferior vessel chartered by the government at an excessive fee through the instrumentality of Cummings; Morgan had collected enormous commissions on government ship charters; Cummings, McKinstry, and Davis were accused of fraud in purchasing military supplies; and Frémont and Stevens were implicated in the Hall Carbine affair—an involved operation in which the government repurchased (after quite inexpensive modification) arms which it had only recently disposed of as obsolete.

tacks on, and defenses of, the House committee. Dawes and Stevens crossed swords briefly on January 8, to the discomfort of the House leader; two days later, a major exchange began. On January 10, the civil appropriations bill being under consideration, Stevens yielded the floor to Sedgwick on the understanding that the New Yorker would call the previous question at the conclusion of his remarks. Sedgwick then proceeded to make the committee's criticism of the treasury note printing contract and its attempt to prevent further payment under that contract the point of departure for a vigorous assault on the Commitee on Government Contracts. The House, however, refused to sustain his (and Stevens's) attempt to cut off a reply by moving the previous question.[13]

On the following Monday (the next day on which the House met), Dawes rose to defend the activities of the committee. His speech was a chronicle of fraud—replete with details, dates, and figures—fit to curl the hair of the most hardened boodler. It was an address which, in the words of one observer, "riveted the attention of the House," but it drew no applause from the radicals or the ultra-partisan Republicans in general. In fact, a few days later, Dawes wrote, "I am in terribly hot water. My speech has aroused the ire of the powers that be, and there is the awfulest hubbub you ever saw. Even Gen. Wilson is down on it, and there is a determination to crush me out."[14]

In February and March, occasional attacks were made on the Committee on Government Contracts as the accused persons and their congressional supporters attempted to prevent the passage of censure resolutions. It was not until April, however, that the real showdown came. On the twenty-first of that month, when the committee was meeting in New York, Thaddeus Stevens launched a bitter assault. He centered his attack on the sections of the committee report dealing with John C. Frémont. These sections also implicated the House leader's former law student, Simon Stevens. Referring to the document under attack as "that *ex parte* report," Stevens expressed doubt that the committee "had an honest

13. *Cong. Globe,* 37th Cong., 2nd Sess., pp. 236–238, 283–285; Henry L. Dawes to Mrs. Henry L. Dawes, January 24, 1862, Henry L. Dawes Papers, Library of Congress.

14. *Cong. Globe,* 37th Cong., 2nd Sess., pp. 298–300; Philadelphia *Inquirer,* January 14, 1862; Henry L. Dawes to Mrs. Henry L. Dawes, January 17, 1862, Henry L. Dawes Papers, Library of Congress.

purpose to know the truth." "If it were proper," he continued, "I would move to discharge this scandal-hunting committee from any further proceedings, for I believe in my conscience that they have committed more frauds than they have detected. They are spending the country's money and scandalizing the country's best men."[15]

These attacks, and especially Stevens's, made a decided impression on the House, and it appeared that the discharge of the committee was a distinct possibility. On April 25, therefore, Dawes of Massachusetts, perhaps the ablest of the Republican members of the committee, rose to reply. His rebuttal was vigorous, but not vicious. Dawes noted that the most violent attacks had been made when none of the members was present and charged a systematic attempt, inspired by former Secretary of War Cameron and led by Stevens and Kelley of Pennsylvania, to bring the committee into disrepute and accomplish its dissolution. In a speech packed with solid facts and sound arguments, he slashed the charges against the committee to ribbons. He clearly demonstrated that, stripped of their verbiage, the attacks on the committee were based solely on two minor errors in the report, one made by the printer and one by the committee. "Pig Iron" Kelley, renowned for his stentorian voice, renewed the assault, addressing himself to the charges against Alexander Cummings. His thrusts were violent, but in the face of constant interruptions by Dawes and William G. Steele, they were totally ineffectual.[16]

15. James H. Campbell to Simon Cameron, February 17, 1862, Alexander Cummings to Simon Cameron, May 1, 1862, both in Simon Cameron Papers, Library of Congress; Charles B. Sedgwick to George D. Morgan, April 14, 1862, Charles B. Sedgwick to Gideon Welles, undated, both in Gideon Welles Papers, Library of Congress; *Cong. Globe,* 37th Cong., 2nd Sess., pp. 710–711, 1062–1071, 1752–1753. Benjamin F. Thomas pointed out to Stevens that no members of the committee were present, but the Pennsylvanian refused to be deterred by that fact. The quotations are from the *Globe,* pp. 1752–1753. Dawes asserted in a private letter that Simon Stevens was the nephew of Thaddeus Stevens. See Henry L. Dawes to Mrs. Henry L. Dawes, January 24, 1862, Henry L. Dawes Papers, Library of Congress. Stevens, however, said on the floor of the House that despite the name the man in question was in no way related to him. See *Cong. Globe,* 37th Cong., 2nd Sess., p. 1851.

16. Henry L. Dawes to Mrs. Henry L. Dawes, April 25, 1862, Henry L. Dawes Papers, Library of Congress; *Cong. Globe,* 37th Cong., 2nd Sess., pp. 1835–1842.

The controversy continued on the twenty-eighth and twenty-ninth. Stevens again took the offensive, but it was a different matter when the members of the committee were present. Though he constantly shifted his point of attack, the House leader found his every thrust parried and turned back upon himself. He fell back upon sarcasm, personalities, and irrelevancies, and finally gave it up as a bad job. Roscoe Conkling added his voice to that of Stevens, while Washburne and Holman and, to a lesser extent, Dawes and Fenton entered the lists for the committee. It was obvious that the committee had won even before April 30, but on that date the House delivered the coup de grace. Stevens's motion to table the entire question was defeated by a vote of 17 to 107, and with one exception, the censorious resolutions of the House Committee on Government Contracts were adopted by large majorities. Dawes's observations regarding the political fate awaiting those who appeared to ignore or condone corruption had apparently struck home.[17]

17. *Cong. Globe,* 37th Cong., 2nd Sess., pp. 1848–1853, 1862–1871, 1886–1888, Appendix, 130–137. The split within the committee continued to widen as Van Wyck, feuding with Hiram Barney, Collector of New York Port, demanded an investigation of federal officials in New York City. In the spring of 1862, he went on a solo excursion to New York and took a great deal of testimony in a highly irregular manner, until the committee ordered him to desist. His charges, however, forced the committee to investigate the New York situation in the fall of 1862 and the winter of 1862–1863. The committee, on March 3, 1863, submitted a report stating that they found no evidence to sustain any charge of fraud against the federal officers in New York. Van Wyck filed a minority report which no other member of the committee had ever seen. This report mysteriously disappeared (to be found several days later under a table in the office of the Clerk of the House), but not before the clerk of the committee had seen it. It contained a violent attack on the other members of the committee (with the notable exception of Holman) charging them with bowing to political pressures and whitewashing the situation in New York. Washburne carried the matter to the floor of the House and aired the whole situation. The resulting controversy was undoubtedly damaging to the prestige of both Van Wyck and the committee. See *Cong. Globe,* 37th Cong., 3d Sess., pp. 1546, 1549–1551; U. S. House of Representatives, Select Committee on Government Contracts, *Final Report, Ho. Com. Repts.,* 37th Cong., 3d Sess., No. 49, [1173]; U. S. House of Representatives, Select Committee on Government Contracts, *Views of the Minority, Ho. Com. Repts.,* 37th Cong., 3d Sess., No. 50, [1173]; Hiram Barney to Elihu B. Washburne, March 27, 1862, Elihu B. Washburne Papers, Library of Congress; New York *Herald,* March 7, 1863.

The House Select Committee on Government Contracts never emerged as a pressure group like the Joint Committee on the Conduct of the War for several reasons. The area of operations of the House committee, though broad, was at least confined to the general field of government contracts. The committee did not possess what amounted to a writ of assistance empowering its membership to enter at any time into any and all activities of the government. Another factor was the attitude of the House committee members. From the first, they seem to have viewed their task as one of legitimate legislative investigation—that is, investigation which would result in the presentation of bills and resolutions designed to prevent frauds and correct abuses. A number of such bills and resolutions were, in fact, introduced and many were passed. By no means the least important aspect of the situation was the membership of the committee. These men were not advanced radicals. Though they differed with Lincoln on various points, most were in general agreement with his policies. They had no desire to substitute Wade or Stevens for Lincoln as the chief maker of government policy.

Yet, the House Select Committee on Government Contracts made its contribution to the movement toward congressional dominance. The radicals fashioned the disclosures of the committee into weapons for striking at various executive officers. To preserve their position, these officers found it necessary to make greater or lesser concessions to the demands of the radicals. Also, the legitimate investigative activities of the committee inevitably, if unintentionally, fostered among executive officers and employees a feeling of responsibility to Congress as well as to their administrative superiors. Thus, the Committee on Government Contracts, while operating with the utmost integrity and with no discernible political motivation, was involuntarily but unquestionably influential in forwarding congressional dominance.

To a limited extent, Congress also interfered with judicial officers. In March 1863, a bill was passed abolishing the federal circuit court in the District of Columbia and establishing in its place a supreme court of the District of Columbia with slightly enlarged powers. The effect (and the main purpose) of this act was to legislate out of office the incumbent circuit judges. During the First Session of the Thirty-seventh Congress, the House passed a bill which would have erected new judicial circuits in Missouri and Kentucky, apparently for the purpose of removing certain judges from office. But the matter was dropped when the bill failed to pass the Senate. Senator Hale launched a third assault in December 1861, when he introduced a resolution directing the Committee on the Judiciary to inquire into the expediency and propriety of abolishing the present Supreme Court of the United States and establishing a new one. The Senate passed this resolution, but the Committee on the Judiciary gave it short shrift. Ten days later, the committee members asked to be discharged from further consideration of the resolution, implying that they saw no means of accomplishing this.[18] All in all, it might be said that the Thirty-seventh Congress displayed a willingness and an occasional ability to dominate the judicial branch of the federal government, but with a few exceptions, had no incentive to do so.

There were some congressmen, of course, who, however much they might disagree with presidential policies and actions, utterly rejected any thought of a congressional assumption of executive powers and functions. Dawes was such a man. In the spring of 1862, in reply to a letter from his wife questioning the wisdom of his unpopular votes against the confiscation and emancipation bills, he explained his view of the constitutional questions involved.

> You ask "is not the whole aspect of things changed by the war itself." Certainly, my Dear, but not the power of Congress. We have no power except what is written in that instrument [the Constitution]. We are bound hand and foot by it. Not so, the President. The same instrument *Commands* him to put down this rebellion and it commands us to furnish him with the men and means. Just where our power ends his begins. He is Commander-in-Chief. Can march the army to the gulph [*sic*]. Can liberate every slave, and seize every dollar of rebel property, *if he is a mind to.* But it is because he *wont* that we are called upon to do what we *cant.*[19]

But such congressional leaders as Wade, Sumner, Sherman, Trumbull, and Stevens did not share Dawes's views. On January 28, 1862, debate in the Senate touched for a moment on the question of congressional versus presidential powers, and the radical leaders eagerly leaped into the breach. "The representatives of the people," declared Wade, "clothed

18. *Cong. Globe,* 37th Cong., 1st Sess., pp. 228–229, 421–426; 2nd Sess., pp. 8, 26–28, 37, 155; 3d Sess., pp. 1537–1539.

19. Henry L. Dawes to Mrs. Henry L. Dawes, May 28, 1862, Henry L. Dawes Papers, Library of Congress.

with all power, have a right to say precisely upon what principles that war shall be conducted from the beginning to the end." The junior senator from Ohio was equally as vehement as his senior colleague. "The President has no other duty to perform except simply to carry out the powers conferred on him by Congress," asserted Sherman. Trumbull of Illinois agreed. "Congress can disband the Army tomorrow," he said, "or we can say the President shall raise so many troops of one kind and so many of another. We govern the whole thing. . . . Congress may declare that its armies shall be armed with wooden swords."[20] Five months later, the Senate debates on the confiscation bill produced equally strong assertions of congressional superiority.[21]

There can, then, be no doubt that many in the ranks of the majority party in Congress desired the establishment of the legislative branch as the dominant force in the federal governmental structure. They made no secret of their aims and worked earnestly and sometimes effectively to achieve them. By March of 1863, they had made some progress in the direction of congressional dominance. That criticism of the President by the congressional leaders of his own party caused some modification in his policies is possible. That the assault on Seward had made cabinet members more amenable to congressional pressures and influences is probable. That congressional investigating committees—notably the Joint Committee on the Conduct of the War—exerted great influence in the administration of the government is undeniable. That congressional dominance of the federal government had not been achieved should be emphasized, but the purpose was unmistakable. Some weapons had been tried and found ineffectual; some had been found effective. Line by line, the blueprint was being drawn.

It was a blueprint that was to be followed with considerable consistency for the remainder of the century. Congressional influence on executive affairs gradually expanded during the remaining years of Lincoln's administration. Though the radical-inspired Chase-for-President movement collapsed, this bloc was successful in forcing Montgomery Blair out of the cabinet shortly before the 1864 election. During the early reconstruction years, President Andrew Johnson found himself hedged about

20. *Cong. Globe,* 37th Cong., 2nd Sess., pp. 513, 515, 517.

21. *Ibid.,* pp. 2930, 2964.

with so many legislative restrictions as to reduce him to the status of a figurehead in several areas of executive responsibility. The judicial branch was subjected to legislative manipulation, and the courts themselves were denied jurisdiction in certain fields. The attempt to remove the Chief Executive from office failed by virtue of a single senatorial vote. Congress (especially the Senate) was able to retain much of this influence during the Grant era; and with the partial exception of Grover Cleveland, no president before Theodore Roosevelt was able to break this grip. In short, the post–Civil War political scene was dominated by Congress. The radicals of 1861–1863 sketched the broad outlines, and their congressional successors filled in the details of the blueprint and erected the political structure of modern America.

CHAPTER II

The Blueprint for Modern America

In March of 1863, looking back on the laws passed by the Thirty-seventh Congress, Senator John Sherman of Ohio was moved to predict that they "will be a monument of evil or of good. They cover such vast sums, delegate and regulate such vast powers, and are so far-reaching in their effects, that generations will be affected well or ill by them."[1] Sherman's analysis was undoubtedly correct. Though many aspects of the operations of the Congress have not been discussed, it cannot be denied that the enactments of this Congress were numerous and significant. Foundations—social, economic, and political—had been laid for the construction of a new America.

The Thirty-seventh Congress had been active in drafting the blueprint for a new social order. In the emancipation of the slaves, Congress had played an important (perhaps decisive) role. By legislation slavery had been abolished in the territories and in the District of Columbia. By legislation the army had been prevented from protecting slavery in the states. By legislative action West Virginia had been compelled to adopt a program of gradual emancipation. Legislative enactments and urgings were slowly converting the army into a more active antislavery force. In part by legislative pressures, the Emancipation Proclamation had been wrung from a reluctant executive.

Also influential in determining the Negro's future was Congress' refusal to act vigorously to foster colonization. On this issue, congressmen made only the token concessions imperatively demanded by political expediency and avoided serious consideration of any proposal involving massive action. It is probable that economic rather than humanitarian

1. John Sherman to William T. Sherman, March 20, 1863, in Thorndike, *op. cit.*, p. 194.

motives were decisive in this instance, for many antislavery Republicans repeatedly voiced an aversion to Negroes and not infrequently declared that the abolition of slavery in the South would reverse the movement of Negroes to the North by removing the reasons for their leaving their "natural home." Many legislators undoubtedly realized that the nation could ill afford to lose some four million laborers. More specifically, the easterners wanted a continuing and bountiful supply of cheap cotton, and the midwesterners wanted an increasing southern market for their agricultural surpluses. Manufacturers and merchants in every city from Boston to St. Louis knew that, slave or free, men and women must have clothing for their bodies and shoes for their feet. The Thirty-seventh Congress was neither willing nor able, any more than were Americans of the late nineteenth or of the twentieth century, to describe in detail the position of the Negro in the United States; but a few bold and significant strokes had been laid on the national blueprint—the Negro would be legally free, American, and, it was hoped, southern.

Another piece of legislation with social implications was the Morrill Land-Grant College Act. This measure furnished public-land bait which lured greedy but unthinking state legislatures into establishing or adopting institutions of higher learning to which they later gave, in too many instances, reluctant and niggardly support. But in some cases the support was adequate, or even generous, and the commitment to quality university education real and lasting. Some of the greatest and most productive universities in the nation grew from these embryonic institutions. They touched and transformed a whole stratum of society which had little or no contact with the private (and largely religious) colleges and universities of the day. Though sometimes in the forefront of professional and advanced academic studies, these institutions were generally responsive (often too much so) to the popular mood. They were, therefore, often made centers of technological training on a far-too-elementary level. Acting through many institutions and in diverse ways, the Morrill Land-Grant College Act had considerable influence on the social fabric and educational practice of the nation. If these influences were mixed, so too were the motives and expectations of those who voted for the measure.

Although the Thirty-seventh Congress enacted legislation of great social significance, it cannot truly be said that it was a body with any deep social consciousness. Repeatedly, the membership demonstrated that its concern with slavery was based on narrowly moral, economic, and political—not humanitarian—considerations. Furthermore, the Congress was almost totally blind to the growing problems of the laboring class, although the inequities and social disintegration inherent in the new industrial society were already at least faintly visible to observers with any humanitarian consciousness. In December 1861, Lincoln devoted several paragraphs of his annual message to condemning

> the effort to place *capital* on an equal footing with, if not above, *labor* in the structure of government. . . . Now there is no such . . . thing as a free man being fixed for life in the condition of a hired laborer. . . . Labor is prior to and independent of capital. Capital is only the fruit of labor, and could never have existed if labor had not first existed. Labor is the superior of capital, and deserves much the higher consideration.[2]

The Congress, however, remained unimpressed. In the House, this portion of the President's message was not even referred to a committee. When this "oversight" was called to the attention of Thaddeus Stevens, the leader of the House majority replied, "There is no appropriate committee on metaphysics in the House." In a rare display of bipartisanship, Vallandigham commented, "I presume it will go then to the Committee on Unfinished Business."[3] And unfinished business it remained for the rest of the century. Here, too, a blueprint for modern America was emerging. Legislation modified the American social fabric on numerous occasions, but social considerations were not always the dominant influences in the drafting of such legislation.

In the area of economic development, too, the accomplishments of the Thirty-seventh Congress were influential. The Pacific Railroad Act initiated a series of legislative, financial, and engineering actions which resulted in the linking of the West by rail to the rest of the nation. Thus, economic ties matched and strengthened political bonds. Equally important, it now became possible to live and carry on commercial agriculture in the Great Plains region. The consequent opening of the Treasury doors to greedy corporate interests was to prove extremely significant. The nation and the states had constructed and operated transportation facili-

2. Abraham Lincoln, "First Annual Message," in Richardson, *op. cit.,* VI, 57.

3. *Cong. Globe,* 37th Cong., 2nd Sess., p. 20.

ties before. The states had previously made gifts (sometimes of federally granted lands) to private transportation corporations, but the defeat of the Illinois Ship Canal Bill served notice that Congress would not permit a return to the earlier practice of national construction and operation of transportation works. It is probably true that the canal measure failed to pass primarily because of its strictly sectional appeal and the opposition of other and more powerful commercial interests; but it is likely that an aversion to direct federal involvement in such activities contributed to its defeat.

In the case of the transcontinental railway, both land and money, in the form of loans, were distributed directly to private companies by the federal government. Throughout the remainder of the nineteenth century (and beyond), corporate interests—apparently insatiable—returned again and again to demand direct and indirect federal subsidies. To insure preferential treatment and noninterference, national legislative and executive officers were corrupted and representative government made a mockery. The Pacific Railroad Act had been framed in accordance with corporate demands, and it is perhaps not too much to suggest that the corruption of the Grant era was sparked by (but not confined to) the activities of those companies and individuals connected with the Pacific railway scheme.

The new tax structure, too, favored the more powerful economic interests. The protective tariff, for example, constituted an indirect subsidy to the manufacturers, financed by the consumers. Indeed, practically all of the new taxes were eventually paid by the consumer, for the various license, excise, and manufacturing levies, when not evaded, were easily transferred to the customers of the firms paying them. The income tax, to be sure, was designed to tap the growing reservoir of liquid capital and thus to bear more heavily on the wealthier segment of the population; but the tax on income proved the least-lasting element in the tax structure erected by the Thirty-seventh Congress.

The tax changes also had a political implication, for even with the later elimination of the income tax, a great centralizing force had been set in motion. Practically every citizen hereafter had direct contact with the federal government, and the nation, for the first time, had a permanent national internal tax system. This change in the tax structure had led to the establishment of the Bureau of Internal Revenue and a consequent doubling in size of the Treasury staff. Never again would either the federal tax base or the number of employees in the Treasury Department be contracted to the pre–Civil War level.

Perhaps no economic legislation of the Thirty-seventh Congress had greater or more lasting impact than those acts which dealt with the nation's currency. The Legal Tender Act created a truly national currency of significant proportions for the first time—that is, currency issued directly by the federal government which was a legal tender for all debts, public and private, throughout the nation. This was the situation that some congressmen—e.g., Stevens (immediately) and Pendleton (later)—desired to maintain permanently. But the pressures from the dominant financial interests made a partial retreat from this position necessary. There was, however, to be no return to the currency morass of the pre–Civil War era. The earlier, uncontrolled currency issues were undoubtedly profitable to the western wildcat bankers and, perhaps, even indirectly profitable to the eastern financial houses by giving them a practical monopoly on fiscal respectability. But commercial and industrial interests exploiting a national market needed a reliable national currency structure. Hence, the National Banking Act—designed to nationalize the currency permanently—was passed. The act accomplished its purpose, for although currency control was much less centralized than it would have been if greenback issue had been continued and expanded, the uniform value and appearance of the national bank notes (coupled with a subsequent tax on all other note issues) eliminated all competing currency. The bankers themselves quickly came to accept the new system, for note issue continued to be profitable, though the profits were reduced to some extent, and many exchange and clearing house difficulties were eliminated. Industrial and commercial interests rejoiced, and with good reason, for it seems at least doubtful that the nationalizing of business (operated primarily on credit) could have proceeded as rapidly as it did in the absence of a nationalized, credit-based currency.

Both the economic and the social effects of the Homestead Act were more psychological than real. The act fostered the illusion that the United States was a nation of sturdy, independent yeoman farmers, while in actuality the nation was rushing headlong toward its urban, industrial destiny. It was blandly assumed that the nation was making a significant economic concession to actual settlers, but the land available for homesteading in the post–Civil War period was distinctly limited in amount and value. In short, it was possible to utilize the provisions of the Homestead Act to acquire a plot of land that was, as a rule, too dry to farm by conventional methods; too small to run cattle on; too large to irrigate (even if water was available); and too remote from the rail lines to have adequate market access. It was not generally possible to acquire a "family farm." The era of the yeoman farmer had passed. The agricultural future belonged to the commercial farmer, and the nation's future belonged to the industrial classes. But the illusion of a sturdy yeomanry was politically and socially significant, for the American image remained rural long after the average American had become urban or, at the very least, nonagricultural. It was to this image that the Thirty-seventh Congress paid homage, and it was to this image that political leaders continued to pay homage for more than half a century.

The refusal of the Congress to enact sweeping confiscation legislation was also pregnant with meaning. Not even an enmity engendered by a civil war and battened on casualty reports could move the members of the Thirty-seventh Congress to authorize the widespread forfeiture of nonslave property rights. In the decades that followed, the "sanctity" of private property became an element of the American creed. Encouraged (or compelled) by politically potent corporate interests to consider private property sacrosanct, political leaders on the state level renounced earlier, well-established rights to control the use of physical property and franchises. The legal powers of the states were also reduced by the Fourteenth Amendment and the judicial interpretations thereof. The nation made few moves to regulate the activities of the corporations which it had removed from state control and which were, in any event, too large and powerful to be dealt with by the states. The Interstate Commerce Commission Act and the Sherman Antitrust Act were primarily designed to quiet agitation, not to initiate effective control.

Behind the fortifications of private property sanctity, increasingly powerful corporations remained entrenched until there occurred a revolution in the concepts of economic morality not unlike that of the 1850s. As the members of the Thirty-seventh Congress had drawn a distinction between slave and nonslave property, so the men of a later generation were eventually to consider corporate property as different from personal property. As the slave power was a moral issue, so corporate power became a moral issue. Then, and only then, did individuals and corporations come to be as answerable to the state for the use they made of their property as they had been under old English common law and earlier American statute law: for the Thirty-seventh Congress, even when acting negatively, had acted with effect.

In the political field, this Congress exerted obvious influences. It has often been asserted that the Civil War changed the American governmental concept from one of federalism to one of nationalism. In accomplishing this change, the Thirty-seventh Congress played a considerable role. Giant steps were taken toward the destruction of the slave system and the consequent removal of the most potent sectionalizing force in American life. The construction of the Pacific railroad bound the West to the East and also contributed to the nationalization of the American transportation system. The new tax structure had a centralizing effect, and a national currency had been created. Finally, the passage of numerous pieces of sweeping legislation of novel character accustomed the American people (or, at least, the numerically and politically dominant northern population) to thinking of problems in national terms and looking to Congress and the President for solutions. In 1863, the nationalizing of America was incomplete, but some of the most significant steps toward that goal had been taken.

Moreover, the unmistakable movement toward congressional dominance of the national government had important implications. The reconstruction period is readily recognizable as a time of congressional supremacy. In a broader sense, few would deny that the entire third of a century between 1865 and 1900 was, with few exceptions, pre-eminently an era of congressional—and particularly senatorial—dominance of the nation's political life. Eventually the urban, industrial society of the post–Civil War era produced moral and social problems which generated an irresistible demand for reform. The Congress proved itself unable or unwilling to assume a role of active leadership in this reform movement, and power and primacy slipped from its grasp to be seized again by the executive. But so long as a caretaker role was acceptable to the American electorate, Congress retained its dominance. In this, as in other areas of activity, wittingly or unwittingly, the Thirty-seventh Congress was participating in the drafting of a blueprint for the development of a new America. The strokes were sometimes broad and bold and sometimes faint and timid, sometimes considered and sometimes haphazard, sometimes affirmative and sometimes negative; but with an awesome inevitability, the blueprint slowly emerged.

Whether or not the blueprint was a desirable one was a question which evoked a variety of responses—responses, indeed, as varied as the opinions regarding the worth and ability of the Congress itself. "This Thirty-Seventh Congress . . . inaugurated and directed a new evolution in the onward progress of mankind," cried Adam Gurowski. "It is an historic body," declared a midwestern newspaper, "and has done its duty ably and fearlessly." Others disagreed. A Pennsylvania representative asserted that the Thirty-seventh Congress "contrasts poorly" with its predecessors; and John W. Crisfield spoke of the "imbecility" and "littleness of public men." A "congregation of incompetents," cried the Philadelphia *Inquirer.* "They may be very eminent as slang-wangers at county court meetings, but they have thus far shown themselves to be without the intellect to realize the true condition of the country, and utterly without the legislative ability to provide for it if they did." The nation, this journal later asserted, "is much the gainer in the fact that there are no longer any Congressional proceedings to record."[4]

A more restrained judgment (and a plea) came from one who had been intimately associated with the work of the Congress but had opposed a number of its most important measures. After it was all over, after the gavel had rapped for the last time and the Capitol echoed emptily in the midst of the swarming city, Fessenden, the Republican Senate leader, wearily surveyed the record:

> With all the labor and anxiety it has cost me, I am gratified to reflect that we have accomplished much. With all its faults and errors, this has been a great and self-sacrificing Congress. If the rebellion should be crushed, Congress will have crushed it. We have assumed terrible responsibilities, placed powers in the hands of the government possessed by none other on earth short of a despotism, borne contumely and reproach, taken the sins of others upon

4. Adam Gurowski, *Diary, November, 1862–October, 1863* (March 4, 1863), pp. 162–163; Detroit *Advertiser and Tribune,* March 6, 1863; Charles J. Biddle to Lewis S. Coryell, April 21, 1862, Lewis S. Coryell Papers, Historical Society of Pennsylvania; John W. Crisfield to Mrs. Mary H. Crisfield, January 22, 1863, Crisfield Papers, Maryland Historical Society; Philadelphia *Inquirer,* January 6, 1862, March 6, 1863.

ourselves and forborne deserved punishment of flagrant offenses for the public good, and suffered abuse for our forbearance. Well, future times will comprehend our motives and all we have done and suffered.[5]

One can but hope that Fessenden's expectation of eventual comprehension and understanding has been, at least in part, fulfilled.

5. William P. Fessenden to ?, March 1863, quoted in Fessenden, *op. cit.*, I, 254.

APPENDIX A

The Senate

This list is confined to those persons who actually served in the Senate of the United States in the Thirty-seventh Congress.

Anthony, Henry B.	Rep.	R. I.
Arnold, Samuel G.	Rep.	R. I.
Baker, Edward D.	Rep.	Ore.
Bayard, James A.	Dem.	Del.
Bingham, Kinsley S.	Rep.	Mich.
Bragg, Thomas	Dem.	N. Car.
Breckinridge, John C.	Dem.	Ky.
Bright, Jesse D.	Dem.	Ind.
Browning, Orville H.	Rep.	Ill.
Carlile, John S.	Un.	Va.
Chandler, Zachariah	Rep.	Mich.
Clark, Daniel	Rep.	N. Hamp.
Clingman, Thomas L.	Dem.	N. Car.
Collamer, Jacob	Rep.	Vt.
Cowan, Edgar	Rep.	Pa.
Davis, Garrett	Un.	Ky.
Dixon, James	Rep.	Conn.
Doolittle, James R.	Rep.	Wisc.
Douglas, Stephen A.	Dem.	Ill.
Fessenden, William P.	Rep.	Me.
Field, Richard S.	Rep.	N. Jer.
Foot, Solomon	Rep.	Vt.
Foster, Lafayette S.	Rep.	Conn.
Grimes, James W.	Rep.	Iowa
Hale, John P.	Rep.	N. Hamp.
Harding, Benjamin F.	Un.	Ore.
Harlan, James	Rep.	Iowa
Harris, Ira	Rep.	N. Y.
Hemphill, John	Dem.	Tex.
Henderson, John B.	Dem.	Mo.

Hicks, Thomas H.	Un.	Md.
Howard, Jacob M.	Rep.	Mich.
Howe, Timothy O.	Rep.	Wisc.
Hunter, Robert M. T.	Dem.	Va.
Johnson, Andrew	Dem.	Tenn.
Johnson, Waldo P.	Dem.	Mo.
Kennedy, Anthony	Un.	Md.
King, Preston	Rep.	N. Y.
Lane, Henry S.	Rep.	Ind.
Lane, James H.	Rep.	Kans.
Latham, Milton S.	Dem.	Calif.
McDougall, James A.	Dem.	Calif.
Mason, James M.	Dem.	Va.
Mitchel, Charles B.	Dem.	Ark.
Morrill, Lot M.	Rep.	Me.
Nesmith, James W.	Dem.	Ore.
Pearce, James A.	Dem.	Md.
Polk, Trusten	Dem.	Mo.
Pomeroy, Samuel C.	Rep.	Kans.
Powell, Lazarus W.	Dem.	Ky.
Rice, Henry M.	Dem.	Minn.
Richardson, William A.	Dem.	Ill.
Saulsbury, Willard	Dem.	Del.
Sebastian, William K.	Dem.	Ark.
Sherman, John	Rep.	Ohio
Simmons, James F.	Rep.	R. I.
Stark, Benjamin	Dem.	Ore.
Sumner, Charles	Rep.	Mass.
Ten Eyck, John C.	Rep.	N. Jer.
Thomson, John R.	Dem.	N. Jer.
Trumbull, Lyman	Rep.	Ill.
Turpie, David	Dem.	Ind.
Wade, Benjamin F.	Rep.	Ohio
Wall, James W.	Dem.	N. Jer.
Wigfall, Louis T.	Dem.	Tex.
Wilkinson, Morton S.	Rep.	Minn.
Willey, Waitman T.	Un.	Va.
Wilmot, David	Rep.	Pa.
Wilson, Henry	Rep.	Mass.
Wilson, Robert	Un.	Mo.
Wright, Joseph A.	Un.	Ind.

APPENDIX B

The House of Representatives

This list is confined to those persons who actually served in the House of Representatives of the United States in the Thirty-seventh Congress.

Aldrich, Cyrus	Rep.	Minn.
Allen, William	Dem.	Ohio
Allen, William J.	Dem.	Ill.
Alley, John B.	Rep.	Mass.
Ancona, Sydenham E.	Dem.	Pa.
Appleton, William	Un.	Mass.
Arnold, Isaac N.	Rep.	Ill.
Ashley, James M.	Rep.	Ohio
Babbitt, Elijah	Rep.	Pa.
Bailey, Goldsmith F.	Rep.	Mass.
Bailey, Joseph	Dem.	Pa.
Baker, Stephen	Rep.	N. Y.
Baxter, Portus	Rep.	Vt.
Beaman, Fernando C.	Rep.	Mich.
Biddle, Charles J.	Dem.	Pa.
Bingham, John A.	Rep.	Ohio
Blair, Francis P., Jr.	Rep.	Mo.
Blair, Jacob B.	Un.	Va.
Blair, Samuel S.	Rep.	Pa.
Blake, Harrison G. O.	Rep.	Ohio
Bridges, George W.	Un.	Tenn.
Brown, William G.	Un.	Va.
Browne, George H.	Dem.	R. I.
Buffington, James	Rep.	Mass.
Burnett, Henry C.	Dem.	Ky.
Burnham, Alfred A.	Rep.	Conn.
Calvert, Charles B.	Un.	Md.
Campbell, James H.	Rep.	Pa.
Carlile, John S.	Un.	Va.
Casey, Samuel L.	Un.	Ky.
Chamberlain, Jacob P.	Rep.	N. Y.

Clark, Ambrose W.	Rep.	N. Y.
Clark, John B.	Dem.	Mo.
Clements, Andrew J.	Un.	Tenn.
Cobb, George T.	Dem.	N. Jer.
Colfax, Schuyler	Rep.	Ind.
Conkling, Frederick A.	Rep.	N. Y.
Conkling, Roscoe	Rep.	N. Y.
Conway, Martin F.	Rep.	Kans.
Cooper, Thomas B.	Dem.	Pa.
Corning, Erastus	Dem.	N. Y.
Covode, John	Rep.	Pa.
Cox, Samuel S.	Dem.	Ohio
Cravens, James A.	Dem.	Ind.
Crisfield, John W.	Un.	Md.
Crittenden, John J.	Un.	Ky.
Curtis, Samuel R.	Rep.	Iowa
Cutler, William P.	Rep.	Ohio
Davis, William M.	Rep.	Pa.
Dawes, Henry L.	Rep.	Mass.
Delano, Charles	Rep.	Mass.
Delaplaine, Isaac C.	Dem.	N. Y.
Diven, Alexander S.	Rep.	N. Y.
Duell, Robert H.	Rep.	N. Y.
Dunlap, George W.	Un.	Ky.
Dunn, William M.	Rep.	Ind.
Edgerton, Sidney	Rep.	Ohio
Edwards, Thomas M.	Rep.	N. Hamp.
Eliot, Thomas D.	Rep.	Mass.
Ely, Alfred	Rep.	N. Y.
English, James E.	Dem.	Conn.
Fenton, Reuben E.	Rep.	N. Y.
Fessenden, Samuel C.	Rep.	Me.
Fessenden, Thomas A. D.	Rep.	Me.
Fisher, George P.	Un.	Del.
Flanders, Benjamin F.	Un.	La.
Fouke, Philip B.	Dem.	Ill.
Franchot, Richard	Rep.	N. Y.
Frank, Augustus	Rep.	N. Y.
Gooch, Daniel W.	Rep.	Mass.
Goodwin, John N.	Rep.	Me.

Granger, Bradley F.	Rep.	Mich.
Grider, Henry	Un.	Ky.
Grow, Galusha A.	Rep.	Pa.
Gurley, John A.	Rep.	Ohio
Hahn, Michael	Un.	La.
Haight, Edward	Dem.	N. Y.
Hale, James T.	Rep.	Pa.
Hall, William A.	Dem.	Mo.
Hanchett, Luther	Rep.	Wisc.
Harding, Aaron	Dem.	Ky.
Harrison, Richard A.	Un.	Ohio
Hickman, John	Rep.	Pa.
Holman, William S.	Dem.	Ind.
Hooper, Samuel	Rep.	Mass.
Horton, Valentine B.	Rep.	Ohio
Hutchins, John	Rep.	Ohio
Jackson, James S.	Un.	Ky.
Johnson, Philip	Dem.	Pa.
Julian, George W.	Rep.	Ind.
Kelley, William D.	Rep.	Pa.
Kellogg, Francis W.	Rep.	Mich.
Kellogg, William	Rep.	Ill.
Kerrigan, James E.	Dem.	N. Y.
Killinger, John W.	Rep.	Pa.
Knapp, Anthony L.	Dem.	Ill.
Lansing, William E.	Rep.	N. Y.
Law, John	Dem.	Ind.
Lazear, Jesse	Dem.	Pa.
Leary, Cornelius L. L.	Un.	Md.
Lehman, William E.	Dem.	Pa.
Logan, John A.	Dem.	Ill.
Loomis, Dwight	Rep.	Conn.
Lovejoy, Owen	Rep.	Ill.
Low, Frederick F.	Rep.	Calif.
McClernand, John A.	Dem.	Ill.
McIndoe, Walter D.	Rep.	Wisc.
McKean, James B.	Rep.	N. Y.
McKnight, Robert	Rep.	Pa.
McPherson, Edward	Rep.	Pa.
Mallory, Robert	Un.	Ky.

Marston, Gilman	Rep.	N. Hamp.
May, Henry	Dem.	Md.
Maynard, Horace	Un.	Tenn.
Menzies, John W.	Un.	Ky.
Mitchell, William	Rep.	Ind.
Moorhead, James K.	Rep.	Pa.
Morrill, Anson P.	Rep.	Me.
Morrill, Justin S.	Rep.	Vt.
Morris, James R.	Dem.	Ohio
Nixon, John T.	Rep.	N. Jer.
Noble, Warren P.	Dem.	Ohio
Noell, John W.	Dem.	Mo.
Norton, Elijah H.	Dem.	Mo.
Nugen, Robert H.	Dem.	Ohio
Odell, Moses F.	Dem.	N. Y.
Olin, Abram B.	Rep.	N. Y.
Patton, John	Rep.	Pa.
Pendleton, George H.	Dem.	Ohio
Perry, Nehemiah	Dem.	N. Jer.
Phelps, John S.	Dem.	Mo.
Phelps, Timothy G.	Rep.	Calif.
Pike, Frederick A.	Rep.	Me.
Pomeroy, Theobald M.	Rep.	N. Y.
Porter, Albert G.	Rep.	Ind.
Potter, John F.	Rep.	Wisc.
Price, Thomas L.	Dem.	Mo.
Reid, John W.	Dem.	Mo.
Rice, Alexander H.	Rep.	Mass.
Rice, John H.	Rep.	Me.
Richardson, William A.	Dem.	Ill.
Riddle, Albert G.	Rep.	Ohio
Robinson, James C.	Dem.	Ill.
Rollins, Edward H.	Rep.	N. Hamp.
Rollins, James S.	Un.	Mo.
Sargent, Aaron A.	Rep.	Calif.
Sedgwick, Charles B.	Rep.	N. Y.
Segar, Joseph E.	Un.	Va.
Shanks, John P. C.	Rep.	Ind.
Sheffield, William P.	Un.	R. I.
Shellabarger, Samuel	Rep.	Ohio

Sherman, Socrates N.	Rep.	N. Y.
Shiel, George K.	Dem.	Ore.
Sloan, Andrew S.	Rep.	Wisc.
Smith, Edward H.	Dem.	N. Y.
Spaulding, Elbridge G.	Rep.	N. Y.
Steele, John B.	Dem.	N. Y.
Steele, William G.	Dem.	N. Jer.
Stevens, Thaddeus	Rep.	Pa.
Stiles, John D.	Dem.	Pa.
Stratton, John L. N.	Rep.	N. Jer.
Thayer, Andrew J.	Dem.	Ore.
Thomas, Benjamin F.	Rep.	Mass.
Thomas, Francis	Un.	Md.
Train, Charles R.	Rep.	Mass.
Trimble, Carey A.	Rep.	Ohio
Trowbridge, Rowland E.	Rep.	Mich.
Upton, Charles H.	Un.	Va.
Vallandigham, Clement L.	Dem.	Ohio
Vandever, William	Rep.	Iowa
Van Horn, Burt	Rep.	N. Y.
Van Valkenburgh, Robert B.	Rep.	N. Y.
Van Wyck, Charles H.	Rep.	N. Y.
Verree, John P.	Rep.	Pa.
Vibbard, Chauncey	Dem.	N. Y.
Voorhees, Daniel W.	Dem.	Ind.
Wadsworth, William H.	Un.	Ky.
Walker, Amasa	Rep.	Mass.
Wall, William	Rep.	N. Y.
Wallace, John W.	Rep.	Pa.
Walton, Charles W.	Rep.	Me.
Walton, Eliakim P.	Rep.	Vt.
Ward, Elijah	Dem.	N. Y.
Washburne, Elihu B.	Rep.	Ill.
Webster, Edwin H.	Un.	Md.
Whaley, Kellian V. R.	Un.	Va.
Wheeler, William A.	Rep.	N. Y.
White, Albert S.	Rep.	Ind.
White, Chilton A.	Dem.	Ohio
Wickliffe, Charles A.	Un.	Ky.
Wilson, James F.	Rep.	Iowa

Windom, William	Rep.	Minn.
Wood, Benjamin	Dem.	N. Y.
Woodruff, George C.	Dem.	Conn.
Worcester, Samuel C.	Rep.	Ohio
Wright, Hendrick B.	Un.	Pa.
Yeaman, George H.	Un.	Ky.

Bibliography

Manuscripts

Aldine Collection, Maryland Historical Society, Baltimore, Maryland.

John A. Andrew Papers, Massachusetts Historical Society, Boston, Massachusetts.

Anti-Slavery Letters, Boston Public Library, Boston, Massachusetts.

Baldwin Papers, Historical Manuscripts Division, Yale University Library, New Haven, Connecticut.

George Bancroft–Alexander Bliss Papers, Manuscripts Division, Library of Congress, Washington, D.C.

Bayard Papers, Maryland Historical Society, Baltimore, Maryland.

Samuel J. Bayard Papers, Department of Rare Books and Special Collections, Princeton University Library, Princeton, New Jersey.

Thomas F. Bayard Papers, Manuscripts Division, Library of Congress, Washington, D.C.

Beecher Papers, Historical Manuscripts Division, Yale University Library, New Haven, Connecticut.

Jeremiah S. Black Papers, Manuscripts Division, Library of Congress, Washington, D.C.

James G. Blaine Papers, Manuscripts Division, Library of Congress, Washington, D.C.

Blair Family Papers, Manuscripts Division, Library of Congress, Washington, D.C.

Blair-Lee Papers, Department of Rare Books and Special Collections, Princeton University Library, Princeton, New Jersey.

Blair and Rives Papers, Manuscripts Division, Library of Congress, Washington, D.C.

Bradford Papers, Maryland Historical Society, Baltimore, Maryland.

Breckinridge Family Papers, Manuscripts Division, Library of Congress, Washington, D.C.

Orville H. Browning Papers, Illinois State Historical Library, Springfield, Illinois.

Brush Family Papers, Historical Manuscripts Division, Yale University Library, New Haven, Connecticut.

Bryant-Godwin Papers, Manuscripts Division, New York Public Library, New York, New York.

James Buchanan Papers, Historical Society of Pennsylvania, Philadelphia, Pennsylvania.

James Buchanan Papers, Manuscripts Division, Library of Congress, Washington, D.C.

James Buchanan Papers, New York Historical Society, New York, New York.

Buchanan-Johnson Papers, Manuscripts Division, Library of Congress, Washington, D.C.

Simon Cameron Papers, Manuscripts Division, Library of Congress, Washington, D.C.

Henry C. Carey Papers, Historical Society of Pennsylvania, Philadelphia, Pennsylvania.

Andrew Carnegie Papers, Manuscripts Division, Library of Congress, Washington, D.C.

Robert Carter Papers, Houghton Library, Harvard University, Cambridge, Massachusetts.

John D. Caton Papers, Manuscripts Division, Library of Congress, Washington, D.C.

William E. Chandler Papers, New Hampshire Historical Society, Concord, New Hampshire.

Zachariah Chandler Papers, Manuscripts Division, Library of Congress, Washington, D.C.

Salmon P. Chase Papers, Historical Society of Pennsylvania, Philadelphia, Pennsylvania.

Salmon P. Chase Papers, Manuscripts Division, Library of Congress, Washington, D.C.

Salmon P. Chase Papers, New Hampshire Historical Society, Concord, New Hampshire.

Salmon P. Chase Papers, Manuscripts Division, New York Public Library, New York, New York.

William W. Clapp Papers, Houghton Library, Harvard University, Cambridge, Massachusetts.

Schuyler Colfax Papers, Manuscripts Division, Library of Congress, Washington, D.C.

Roscoe Conkling Papers, Manuscripts Division, Library of Congress, Washington, D.C.

Jay Cooke Papers, Historical Society of Pennsylvania, Philadelphia, Pennsylvania.

Andre de Coppet Collection, Department of Rare Books and Special Collections, Princeton University Library, Princeton, New Jersey.

W. W. Corcoran Papers, Manuscripts Division, Library of Congress, Washington, D.C.

Erastus Corning Papers, Albany Institute of History and Art, Albany, New York.

Coryell Papers, Historical Society of Pennsylvania, Philadelphia, Pennsylvania.

Marshall Cousins Papers, State Historical Society of Wisconsin, Madison, Wisconsin.

Samuel S. Cox Papers, Special Collections, John Hay Library, Brown University, Providence, Rhode Island.

John A. J. Creswell Papers, Manuscripts Division, Library of Congress, Washington, D.C.

Crisfield Papers, Maryland Historical Society, Baltimore, Maryland.

John J. Crittenden Papers, Manuscripts Division, Library of Congress, Washington, D.C.

Caleb Cushing Papers, Manuscripts Division, Library of Congress, Washington, D.C.

Cushing Family Papers, Massachusetts Historical Society, Boston, Massachusetts.

Richard H. Dana Papers, Massachusetts Historical Society, Boston, Massachusetts.

Henry L. Dawes Papers, Manuscripts Division, Library of Congress, Washington, D.C.

William L. Dayton Papers, Department of Rare Books and Special Collections, Princeton University Library, Princeton, New Jersey.

James R. Doolittle Papers, Manuscripts Division, Library of Congress, Washington, D.C.

James R. Doolittle Papers, Manuscripts Division, New York Public Library, New York, New York.

James R. Doolittle Papers, State Historical Society of Wisconsin, Madison, Wisconsin.

Dormitzer Papers, New Jersey Historical Society, Newark, New Jersey.

Dorsey Papers, Maryland Historical Society, Baltimore, Maryland.

James M. Edmunds Papers, Michigan Historical Collections, University of Michigan Library, Ann Arbor, Michigan.

William M. Evarts Papers, Manuscripts Division, Library of Congress, Washington, D.C.

Edward Everett Papers, Manuscripts Division, Library of Congress, Washington, D.C.

Edward Everett Papers, Massachusetts Historical Society, Boston, Massachusetts.

Thomas Ewing Papers, Manuscripts Division, Library of Congress, Washington, D.C.

Reuben E. Fenton Papers, Department of Rare Books, Cornell University Library, Ithaca, New York.

William P. Fessenden Papers, Manuscripts Division, Library of Congress, Washington, D.C.

Hamilton Fish Papers, Manuscripts Division, Library of Congress, Washington, D.C.

George P. Fisher Papers, Manuscripts Division, Library of Congress, Washington, D.C.

S. G. Flagg Papers, Historical Manuscripts Division, Yale University Library, New Haven, Connecticut.

George G. Fogg Papers, New Hampshire Historical Society, Concord, New Hampshire.

Peter Force Papers, Manuscripts Division, Library of Congress, Washington, D.C.

James A. Garfield Papers, Manuscripts Division, Library of Congress, Washington, D.C.

John H. George Papers, New Hampshire Historical Society, Concord, New Hampshire.

Joshua R. Giddings–George W. Julian Correspondence, Manuscripts Division, Library of Congress, Washington, D.C.

Joseph Gilmore Papers, New Hampshire Historical Society, Concord, New Hampshire.

Charles T. Gorham Papers, Michigan Historical Collections, University of Michigan Library, Ann Arbor, Michigan.

Horace Greeley Papers, New York Historical Society, New York, New York.

Horace Greeley Papers, Manuscripts Division, New York Public Library, New York, New York.

Adam de Gurowski Papers, Manuscripts Division, Library of Congress, Washington, D.C.

John P. Hale Papers, New Hampshire Historical Society, Concord, New Hampshire.

John Harding Papers, Filson Club, Louisville, Kentucky.

William H. Harris Papers, Manuscripts Division, New York Public Library, New York, New York.

Ozias M. Hatch Papers, Illinois State Historical Library, Springfield, Illinois.

Thomas H. Hicks Papers, Maryland Historical Society, Baltimore, Maryland.

Joseph Holt Papers, Manuscripts Division, Library of Congress, Washington, D.C.

Jacob M. Howard Papers, Burton Historical Collection, Detroit Public Library, Detroit, Michigan.

Timothy O. Howe Papers, State Historical Society of Wisconsin, Madison, Wisconsin.

Thomas A. Jenckes Papers, Manuscripts Division, Library of Congress, Washington, D.C.

Andrew Johnson Papers, Manuscripts Division, Library of Congress, Washington, D.C.

Reverdy Johnson Papers, Manuscripts Division, Library of Congress, Washington, D.C.

James F. Joy Papers, Burton Historical Collection, Detroit Public Library, Detroit, Michigan.

Kernan Family Papers, Collection of Regional History, Cornell University Library, Ithaca, New York.

Horatio King Papers, Manuscripts Division, Library of Congress, Washington, D.C.

Preston King Papers, Manuscripts Division, New York Public Library, New York, New York.

Charles Lanman Papers, Manuscripts Division, Library of Congress, Washington, D.C.

Lincoln Papers, Manuscripts Division, Library of Congress, Washington, D.C.

John A. Logan Papers, Manuscripts Division, Library of Congress, Washington, D.C.

James Lovering Papers, New Hampshire Historical Society, Concord, New Hampshire.

Manton Marble Papers, Manuscripts Division, Library of Congress, Washington, D.C.

Gilman Marston Papers, New Hampshire Historical Society, Concord, New Hampshire.

James M. Mason Papers, Manuscripts Division, Library of Congress, Washington, D.C.

Brantz Mayer Papers, Maryland Historical Society, Baltimore, Maryland.

John A. McClernand Papers, Illinois State Historical Library, Springfield, Illinois.

Hugh McCulloch Papers, Manuscripts Division, Library of Congress, Washington, D.C.

Edward McPherson Papers, Manuscripts Division, Library of Congress, Washington, D.C.

Edwin D. Morgan Papers, New York Historical Society, New York, New York.

Edwin D. Morgan Papers, Manuscripts and History Section, New York State Library, Albany, New York.

Justin S. Morrill Papers, Collection of Regional History, Cornell University Library, Ithaca, New York.

Justin S. Morrill Papers, Manuscripts Division, Library of Congress, Washington, D.C.

New Jersey Letters Collection, Special Collections, Rutgers University Library, New Brunswick, New Jersey.

John G. Nicolay Papers, Manuscripts Division, Library of Congress, Washington, D.C.

William Owner Diary, Manuscripts Division, Library of Congress, Washington, D.C.

George W. Patterson Papers, Manuscripts Division, University of Rochester Library, Rochester, New York.

Pearce Papers, Maryland Historical Society, Baltimore, Maryland.

Nehemiah Perry Papers, Special Collections, Rutgers University Library, New Brunswick, New Jersey.

E. L. Pierce Papers, Houghton Library, Harvard University, Cambridge, Massachusetts.

Franklin Pierce Papers, Manuscripts Division, Library of Congress, Washington, D.C.

Franklin Pierce Papers, New Hampshire Historical Society, Concord, New Hampshire.

James S. Pike Papers, Manuscripts Division, Library of Congress, Washington, D.C.

John F. Potter Papers, State Historical Society of Wisconsin, Madison, Wisconsin.

Henry J. Raymond Papers, Manuscripts Division, New York Public Library, New York, New York.

John M. Read I Papers, Library Company of Philadelphia, Philadelphia, Pennsylvania.

Senate Files, National Archives, Washington, D.C.

William H. Seward Papers, Manuscripts Division, University of Rochester Library, Rochester, New York.

Horatio Seymour Papers, Manuscripts Division, New York Public Library, New York, New York.

John Sherman Papers, Manuscripts Division, Library of Congress, Washington, D.C.

James F. Simmons Papers, Manuscripts Division, Library of Congress, Washington, D.C.

James F. Simmons Papers, Rhode Island Historical Society, Providence, Rhode Island.

Edwin M. Stanton Papers, Manuscripts Division, Library of Congress, Washington, D.C.

Statesmen Collection, New Jersey Historical Society, Newark, New Jersey.

Thaddeus Stevens Papers, Lancaster County Historical Society, Lancaster, Pennsylvania.

Thaddeus Stevens Papers, Manuscripts Division, Library of Congress, Washington, D.C.

Charles Sumner Papers, Houghton Library, Harvard University, Cambridge, Massachusetts.

Samuel J. Tilden Papers, Manuscripts Division, New York Public Library, New York, New York.

Lyman Trumbull Papers, Illinois State Historical Library, Springfield, Illinois.

Lyman Trumbull Papers, Manuscripts Division, Library of Congress, Washington, D.C.

Amos Tuck Papers, New Hampshire Historical Society, Concord, New Hampshire.

John C. Underwood Papers, Manuscripts Division, Library of Congress, Washington, D.C.

Benjamin F. Wade Papers, Manuscripts Division, Library of Congress, Washington, D.C.

Robert J. Walker Papers, Manuscripts Division, Library of Congress, Washington, D.C.

Marcus W. Ward Papers, New Jersey Historical Society, Newark, New Jersey.

Israel Washburn Papers, Manuscripts Division, Library of Congress, Washington, D.C.

Elihu B. Washburne Papers, Manuscripts Division, Library of Congress, Washington, D.C.

Thurlow Weed Papers, Manuscripts Division, Library of Congress, Washington, D.C.

Thurlow Weed Papers, Manuscripts Division, University of Rochester Library, Rochester, New York.

Gideon Welles Papers, Manuscripts Division, Library of Congress, Washington, D.C.

Gideon Welles Papers, Manuscripts Division, New York Public Library, New York, New York.

David A. Wells Papers, Manuscripts Division, Library of Congress, Washington, D.C.

Andrew D. White Papers, Collection of Regional History, Cornell University Library, Ithaca, New York.

Henry Wilson Papers, Manuscripts Division, Library of Congress, Washington, D.C.

William H. Withington Papers, Michigan Historical Collections, University of Michigan Library, Ann Arbor, Michigan.

Woolsey Papers, Historical Manuscripts Division, Yale University Library, New Haven, Connecticut.

Richard Yates Papers, Illinois State Historical Library, Springfield, Illinois.

Robert M. Zug Papers, Burton Historical Collection, Detroit Public Library, Detroit, Michigan.

Contemporary Newspapers and Periodicals

The Atlantic Monthly

Boston *Post*

Congressional Globe and Appendix

Detroit *Advertiser and Tribune*

Detroit *Daily Advertiser*

Detroit *Free Press*

Harper's New Monthly Magazine

New York *Herald*

New York *Times*

The North American Review

Philadelphia *Inquirer*

San Francisco *Daily Alta California*

Washington (D.C.) *Daily National Intelligencer*

Wilkes' Spirit of the Times

Government Publications

All documents originated by the Thirty-seventh Congress have been examined. Only those having direct bearing on the material contained in this study are listed here. Arrangement is by author and serial number.

Chase, Salmon P. *Report of the Secretary of the Treasury.* Senate Executive Document 2; 37th Congress, 1st Session. Serial 1112. Washington, D.C.: Government Printing Office, 1861.

———. *Report of the Secretary of the Treasury.* Senate Executive Document 2; 37th Congress, 2nd Session. Serial 1121. Washington, D.C.: Government Printing Office, 1861.

———. *Letter from the Secretary of the Treasury, in Relation to the Issue of an Additional Amount of United States Treasury Notes.* House Miscellaneous Document 81; 37th Congress, 2nd Session. Serial 1141. Washington, D.C.: Government Printing Office, 1862.

———. *Report of the Secretary of the Treasury.* Senate Executive Document 1; 37th Congress, 3d Session. Serial 1149. Washington, D.C.: Government Printing Office, 1863.

Constitutional Convention of West Virginia. *Memorial of the Commissioners Appointed by the Convention of West Virginia Praying for the Admission of that State into the Union.* Senate Miscellaneous Document 99; 37th Congress, 2nd Session. Serial 1124. Washington, D.C.: Government Printing Office, 1862.

Lincoln, Abraham. *Message of the President of the United States to the Two Houses of Congress at the Commencement of the First Session of the Thirty-seventh Congress.* Senate Executive Document 1; 37th Congress, 1st Session. Serial 1112. Washington, D.C.: Government Printing Office, 1861.

———. *Message of the President of the United States to the Two Houses of Congress at the Commencement of the Second Session of the Thirty-seventh Congress.* Senate Executive Document 1; 37th Congress, 2nd Session. Serial 1117. Washington, D.C.: Government Printing Office, 1861.

———. *Message of the President of the United States, Informing Congress that He Had Approved and Signed the Act Entitled "An Act for the Release of Certain Persons Held to Service or Labor in the District of Columbia," and Recommending an Amendatory Act.* Senate Executive Document 42; 37th Congress, 2nd Session. Serial 1122. Washington, D.C.: Government Printing Office, 1862.

———. *Message of the President of the United States, in Relation to a Resolution Passed by the House of Representatives Censuring Hon. Simon Cameron, Late Secretary of War.* Senate Executive Document 50; 37th Congress, 2nd Session. Serial 1122. Washington, D.C.: Government Printing Office, 1862.

———. *Message of the President of the United States, Transmitting a Draft of a Bill to Compensate Any State which May Abolish Slavery within Its Limits, and Recommending Its Passage.* Senate Executive Document 68; 37th Congress, 2nd Session. Serial 1123. Washington, D.C.: Government Printing Office, 1862.

———. *Message of the President of the United States Informing Congress that He Had Approved the Bill "To Suppress Insurrection, Punish Treason and Rebellion, to Seize and Confiscate the Property of Rebels, and for Other Purposes," and the Joint Resolution Explanatory of Said Act.* Senate Executive Document 70; 37th Congress, 2nd Session. Serial 1123. Washington, D.C.: Government Printing Office, 1862.

———. *Message from the President of the United States, in Relation to Co-operating with Any State for the Gradual Abolishment of Slavery.* House Executive Document 69; 37th Congress, 2nd Session. Serial 1131. Washington, D.C.: Government Printing Office, 1862.

———. *Message of the President of the United States to the Two Houses of Congress at the Commencement of the Third Session of the Thirty-seventh Congress.* House Executive Document 1; 37th Congress, 3d Session. Serial 1156, 1157, 1158, 1159. Washington, D.C.: Government Printing Office, 1862.

Postmaster of the House of Representatives. *Congressional Directory,* [*Thirty-seventh Congress, Second Session*]. Washington: Postmaster of the House of Representatives, 1861.

———. *Congressional Directory,* [*Thirty-seventh Congress, Third Session*]. Washington: Postmaster of the House of Representatives, 1863.

Stanton, Edwin M. *Letter from the Secretary of War, in Answer to a Resolution of the House of Representatives of the 5th Instant, in Relation to Any Interest of Members of Congress in Government Contracts.* House Executive Document 151; 37th Congress, 2nd Session. Serial 1138. Washington, D.C.: Government Printing Office, 1862.

U. S. Congress, Joint Committee on the Conduct of the War. *Partial Report.* Senate Committee Report 71; 37th Congress, 3d Session. Serial 1151. Washington, D.C.: Government Printing Office, 1863.

———. *Report.* Senate Committee Report 108; 37th Congress, 3d Session. Serial 1152, 1153, 1154. Washington, D.C.: Government Printing Office, 1863.

U. S. House of Representatives. *Journal of the House of Representatives of the United States, being the First Session of the Thirty-seventh Congress.* 37th Congress, 1st Session. Serial 1113. Washington, D.C.: Government Printing Office, 1861.

———. *List of Members of the House of Representatives.* House Miscellaneous Document 1; 37th Congress, 1st Session. Serial 1115. Washington, D.C.: Government Printing Office, 1861.

———. *Standing Committees of the House of Representatives.* House Miscellaneous Document 2; 37th Congress, 1st Session. Serial 1115. Washington, D.C.: Government Printing Office, 1861.

———. *Journal of the House of Representatives of the United States, being the Second Session of the Thirty-seventh Congress.* 37th Congress, 2nd Session. Serial 1126. Washington, D.C.: Government Printing Office, 1862.

———. *Standing Committees of the House of Representatives of the United States, Thirty-seventh Congress, Second Session.* House Miscellaneous Document 11; 37th Congress, 2nd Session. Serial 1141. Washington, D.C.: Government Printing Office, 1861.

———. *Journal of the House of Representatives of the United States, being the Third Session of the Thirty-seventh Congress.* 37th Congress, 3d Session. Serial 1155. Washington, D.C.: Government Printing Office, 1863.

———. *Standing Committees of the House of Representatives of the United States, Thirty-seventh Congress, Third Session.* House Miscellaneous Document 4; 37th Congress, 3d Session. Serial 1171. Washington, D.C.: Government Printing Office, 1862.

U. S. House of Representatives, Committee for the District of Columbia. *Minority Report* [*on Emancipation in the District of Columbia*]. House Committee Report 58; 37th Congress, 2nd Session. Serial 1144. Washington, D.C.: Government Printing Office, 1862.

U. S. House of Representatives, Committee on Military Affairs. *Report* [*on a Mississippi River–Lake Michigan Ship Canal*]. House Committee Report 37; 37th Congress, 2nd Session. Serial 1144. Washington, D.C.: Government Printing Office, 1862.

U. S. House of Representatives, Select Committee on Compensated Emancipation. *Report.* House Committee Report 148; 37th Congress, 2nd Session. Serial 1145. Washington, D.C.: Government Printing Office, 1862.

U. S. House of Representatives, Select Committee on Confiscation and Emancipation. *The Views of the Minority.* House Committee Report 120; 37th Congress, 2nd Session. Serial 1145. Washington, D.C.: Government Printing Office, 1862.

U. S. House of Representatives, Select Committee on Government Contracts. *Report.* House Committee Report 2; 37th Congress, 2nd Session. Serial 1142, 1143. Washington, D.C.: Government Printing Office, 1862.

———. *Final Report.* House Committee Report 49; 37th Congress, 3d Session. Serial 1173. Washington, D.C.: Government Printing Office, 1863.

———. *The Views of the Minority.* House Committee Report 50; 37th Congress, 3d Session. Serial 1173. Washington, D.C.: Government Printing Office, 1863.

U. S. Senate. *Journal of the Senate of the United States of America, being the First Session of the Thirty-seventh Congress.* 37th Congress, 1st Session. Serial 1111. Washington, D.C.: Government Printing Office, 1861.

———. *List of Committees of the Senate of the United States for the First Session of the Thirty-seventh Congress.* Senate Miscellaneous Document 1; 37th Congress, 1st Session. Serial 1112. Washington, D.C.: Government Printing Office, 1861.

———. *Journal of the Senate of the United States of America, being the Second Session of the Thirty-seventh Congress.* 37th Congress, 2nd Session. Serial 1116. Washington, D.C.: Government Printing Office, 1861.

———. *List of Committees of the Senate of the United States for the Second Session of the Thirty-seventh Congress.* Senate Miscellaneous Document 1; 37th Congress, 2nd Session. Serial 1124. Washington, D.C.: Government Printing Office, 1861.

———. *Journal of the Senate of the United States of America, being the Third Session of the Thirty-seventh Congress.* 37th Congress, 3d Session. Serial 1148. Washington, D.C.: Government Printing Office, 1863.

———. *List of Committees of the Senate of the United States for the Third Session of the Thirty-seventh Congress.* Senate Miscellaneous Document 1; 37th Congress, 3d Session. Serial 1150. Washington, D.C.: Government Printing Office, 1862.

———. *Journal of the Executive Proceedings of the Senate.* Vols. XI, XII, and XIII. Washington, D.C.: Government Printing Office, 1887.

U. S. Senate, Committee on the Judiciary. *Report* [*on a Resolution for the Expulsion of James F. Simmons*]. Senate Committee Report 69; 37th Congress, 2nd Session. Serial 1125. Washington, D.C.: Government Printing Office, 1862.

Welles, Gideon. *Letter of the Secretary of the Navy in Answer to a Resolution of the Senate of the 9th Instant, Relative to the Employment of George D. Morgan to Purchase Vessels for the Government.* Senate Executive Document 15; 37th Congress, 2nd Session. Serial 1121. Washington, D.C.: Government Printing Office, 1862.

Books and Articles

Alexander, DeAlva S. *History and Procedure of the House of Representatives.* Boston: Houghton Mifflin Company, 1916.

———. *A Political History of the State of New York.* 3 vols. New York: Henry Holt and Company, 1906–1909.

Ambler, Charles H. "The Cleavage between Eastern and Western Virginia," *American Historical Review,* XV, No. 4 (July 1910), 762–780.

———. (editor). *Correspondence of R. M. T. Hunter, 1826–76.* Vol. II of American Historical Association, *Annual Report* [*for 1916*]. Washington: Government Printing Office, 1918.

———. *West Virginia: Stories and Biographies.* New York: Rand, McNally and Company, 1937.

Angle, Paul M. (editor). *New Letters and Papers of Lincoln.* Boston: Houghton Mifflin Company, 1930.

Arnold, Isaac N. *The History of Abraham Lincoln, and the Overthrow of Slavery.* Chicago: Clarke and Company, 1866.

Baltz, John D. *Hon. Edward D. Baker.* Lancaster, Pa.: Inquirer Printing Company, 1888.

Bancroft, Frederic (editor). *Speeches, Correspondence and Political Papers of Carl Schurz.* 6 vols. New York: G. P. Putnam's Sons, 1913.

Bancroft, Hubert H. *History of California.* 7 vols. Vols. XVII–XXIV of *Works of Hubert Howe Bancroft.* San Francisco: The History Company, 1884–1890.

———. *History of Oregon.* 2 vols. Vols. XXIX and XXX of *Works of Hubert Howe Bancroft.* San Francisco: The History Company, 1886–1888.

Barnes, Thurlow W. *Memoir of Thurlow Weed.* Boston: Houghton Mifflin Company, 1884.

Barrett, Don C. *Greenbacks and Resumption of Specie Payments, 1862–1879.* Cambridge: Harvard University Press, 1931.

Bassett, T. D. Seymour. "Nature's Nobleman: Justin Morrill, a Victorian Politician," *Vermont History,* XXX, No. 1 (January 1962), 3–13.

Bates, Edward. *The Diary of Edward Bates, 1859–1866.* Edited by Howard K. Beale. Vol. IV of American Historical Association, *Annual Report* [*for 1930*]. Washington: Government Printing Office, 1933.

Bates, Ernest S. *The Story of Congress, 1789–1935.* New York: Harper and Brothers, 1936.

Beale, Howard K. "Is the Printed Diary of Gideon Welles Reliable?", *American Historical Review,* XXX, No. 3 (April 1925), 547–552.

Bicknell, Thomas W. *The History of the State of Rhode Island and Providence Plantations.* 5 vols. New York: The American Historical Society, 1920.

Binkley, Wilfred E. *President and Congress.* New York: Alfred A. Knopf, 1947.

Biographical Directory of the American Congress, 1774–1927. Washington: Government Printing Office, 1928.

Biographical Encyclopedia of Maine of the Nineteenth Century. Boston: Metropolitan Publishing and Engraving Company, 1885.

A Biographical History of Eminent and Self-Made Men of the State of Indiana. 2 vols. Cincinnati: Western Biographical Publishing Company, 1880.

Blackiston, Harry S. "Lincoln's Emancipation Plan," *Journal of Negro History,* VII, No. 3 (July 1922), 257–277.

Blaine, James G. *Twenty Years of Congress, 1861–1881.* 2 vols. Norwich, Conn.: Henry Hill Publishing Company, 1884–1886.

Blanchard, Charles. *The Progressive Men of the Commonwealth of Pennsylvania.* Logansport, Ind.: A. W. Bowen and Company, 1900.

Bogardus, Frank S. "Daniel W. Voorhees," *Indiana Magazine of History,* XXVII, No. 2 (June 1931), 91–103.

Boutwell, George S. *Reminiscences of Sixty Years in Public Affairs.* 2 vols. New York: McClure, Phillips and Company, 1902.

Brigham, Johnson. *James Harlan.* Iowa City: State Historical Society of Iowa, 1913.

Brockett, Linus P. *Men of Our Day.* Philadelphia: Ziegler and McCurdy, 1872.

Brodie, Fawn M. *Thaddeus Stevens: Scourge of the South.* New York: W. W. Norton and Company, 1959.

Brooks, Noah. *Washington in Lincoln's Time.* New York: The Century Company, 1896.

Brown, George R. *The Leadership of Congress.* Indianapolis: Bobbs-Merrill Company, 1922.

Browning, Orville H. *The Diary of Orville Hickman Browning.* 2 vols. Edited by Theodore C. Pease and James G. Randall. Vol. XX of *Collections of the Illinois State Historical Society.* Springfield: Illinois State Historical Library, 1925.

Brummer, Sidney D. *Political History of New York State during the Period of the Civil War.* Vol. XXXIX, No. 2 of [*Columbia University*] *Studies in History, Economics and Public Law.* New York: Longmans, Green and Company, 1911.

Bryan, Wilhelmus B. *A History of the National Capital.* 2 vols. New York: The Macmillan Company, 1914–1916.

Buchman, Russell. "James A. McDougall: A Forgotten Senator," *Quarterly of California Historical Society,* XV, No. 3 (September 1936), 199–212.

Buell, Walter. "Zachariah Chandler," *Magazine of Western History,* IV, No. 2 (June 1886), 271–278; No. 3 (July 1886), 338–352; No. 4 (August 1886), 432–444.

Burdette, Franklin L. *Filibustering in the Senate.* Princeton: Princeton University Press, 1940.

Burpee, Charles W. *The Story of Connecticut.* 4 vols. New York: The American Historical Company, 1939.

Burton, Theodore E. *John Sherman.* Boston: Houghton, Mifflin and Company, 1906.

Butterfield, C. W. "Edgar Cowan," *Magazine of Western History,* V, No. 1 (November 1886), 144–156.

Cain, Marvin R. "Lincoln's Views on Slavery and the Negro: A Suggestion," *Historian,* XXVI, No. 4 (August 1964), 502–520.

Caldwell, Martha B. "Pomeroy's 'Ross Letter': Genuine or Forgery?", *Kansas State Historical Quarterly,* XIII, No. 7 (August 1945), 463–472.

Carman, Harry J. and Reinhard H. Luthin. *Lincoln and the Patronage.* New York: Columbia University Press, 1943.

Chase, Salmon P. *Diary and Correspondence of Salmon P. Chase.* Vol. II of American Historical Association, *Annual Report* [*for 1902*]. Washington: Government Printing Office, 1903.

Chidsey, Donald B. *The Gentleman from New York: A Life of Roscoe Conkling.* New Haven, Conn.: Yale University Press, 1935.

Clark, Charles B. "Politics in Maryland During the Civil War," *Maryland Historical Magazine,* XXXVI, No. 3 (September 1941), 239–262; No. 4 (December 1941), 381–393; XXXVII, No. 2 (June 1942), 171–192; No. 4 (December 1942), 378–399; XXXVIII, No. 3 (September 1943), 230–260; XXXIX, No. 2 (June 1944), 149–161; No. 4 (December 1944), 315–331; XL, No. 3 (September 1945), 233–241; No. 4 (December 1945), 295–309; XLI, No. 2 (June 1946), 132–158.

Clark, Dan E. *History of Senatorial Elections in Iowa.* Iowa City: The Clio Press, 1912.

Clark, Olynthus B. *The Politics of Iowa during the Civil War and Reconstruction.* Iowa City: The Clio Press, 1911.

Clarke, Grace J. "George W. Julian: Some Impressions," *Indiana Magazine of History,* II, No. 2 (June 1906), 57–69.

Cole, Arthur C. *The Era of the Civil War, 1848–1870.* Vol. III of *The*

Centennial History of Illinois. Edited by C. W. Alford. Springfield: Illinois Centennial Commission, 1919.

———. *The Irrespressible Conflict.* New York: The Macmillan Company, 1934.

———. "President Lincoln and the Illinois Radical Republicans," *Mississippi Valley Historical Review,* IV, No. 4 (March 1918), 417–436.

Coleman, Ann M. B. *Life of John J. Crittenden.* 2 vols. Philadelphia: J. B. Lippincott and Company, 1871.

Conkling, Alfred R. *The Life and Letters of Roscoe Conkling, Orator, Statesman, Advocate.* New York: Charles L. Webster and Company, 1889.

Connelley, William E. *James Henry Lane.* Topeka, Kans.: Crane and Company, 1899.

Constitution of the United States of America with the Amendments thereto: to which are added Jefferson's Manual of Parliamentary Practice, the Standing Rules and Orders for Conducting Business in the House of Representatives and Senate of the United States and Barclay's Digest. Washington: Government Printing Office, 1867.

Cooper, Thomas V. and Hector T. Fenton (editors). *American Politics.* Boston: B. A. Fowler and Company, 1888.

Coulter, E. Merton. *The Civil War and Readjustment in Kentucky.* Chapel Hill: The University of North Carolina Press, 1926.

Cox, Samuel S. *Union—Disunion—Reunion: Three Decades of Federal Legislation.* Providence, R.I.: J. A. and R. A. Reid, 1888.

Crenshaw, Ollinger. "The Knights of the Golden Circle," *American Historical Review,* XLVII, No. 1 (October 1941), 23–50.

Crockett, Walter H. *Vermont, The Green Mountain State.* 5 vols. New York: The Century History Company, 1921.

Current, Richard N. "Love, Hate, and Thaddeus Stevens," *Pennsylvania History,* XIV, No. 4 (October 1947), 259–272.

———. *Old Thad Stevens.* Madison: University of Wisconsin Press, 1942.

Curry, Leonard P. "Congressional Democrats: 1861–1863," *Civil War History,* XII, No. 3 (September 1966), 213–299.

Curry, Richard O. "A Reappraisal of Statehood Politics in West Virginia," *Journal of Southern History,* XXVIII, No. 4 (November 1962), 403–421.

Curtis, Francis. *The Republican Party.* 2 vols. New York: G. P. Putnam's Sons, 1904.

Dana, Charles A. *Recollections of the Civil War.* New York: D. Appleton and Company, 1899.

Davis, Stanton L. *Pennsylvania Politics, 1860–1863.* Cleveland: The Bookstore, Western Reserve University, 1935.

Dawson, George F. *Life and Services of General John A. Logan.* Chicago: Belford, Clarke and Company, 1887.

Dennett, Tyler (editor). *Lincoln and the Civil War in the Diaries and Letters of John Hay.* New York: Dodd, Mead and Company, 1939.

Dewey, Davis R. *Financial History of the United States.* 12th ed. New York: Longmans, Green and Company, 1939.

Diary of a Public Man. New Brunswick, N.J.: Rutgers University Press, 1946.

Dicey, Edward. *Six Months in the Federal States.* London: Macmillan and Company, 1863.

Dickinson, John R. (editor). *Speeches, Correspondence, etc., of the Late Daniel S. Dickinson of New York.* New York: G. P. Putnam and Sons, 1867.

Dimock, Marshall E. *Congressional Investigating Committees.* Vol. XLVII, No. 1 of *Johns Hopkins University Studies in Historical and Political Science.* Baltimore: The Johns Hopkins Press, 1929.

Dodd, William E. "The Fight for the Northwest, 1860," *American Historical Review,* XVI, No. 4 (July 1911), 774–778.

Donald, David (editor). *Inside Lincoln's Cabinet. The Civil War Diaries of Salmon P. Chase.* New York: Longmans, Green and Company, 1954.

Dubois, James T. and Gertrude S. Matthews. *Galusha A. Grow, Father of the Homestead Law.* Boston: Houghton, Mifflin Company, 1917.

Ellison, Joseph. *California and the Nation, 1850–1869.* Vol. XVI of *University of California Publications in History.* Berkeley: University of California Press, 1927.

Farnham, Wallace D. "The Pacific Railroad Act of 1862," *Nebraska History,* XLIII, No. 3 (September 1962), 141–167.

Fenton, William D. "Edward Dickinson Baker," *Quarterly of the Oregon Historical Society,* IX, No. 1 (March 1908), 1–23.

Fesler, Mayo. "Secret Political Societies in the North during the Civil War," *Indiana Magazine of History,* XIV, No. 3 (September 1918), 183–286.

Fessenden, Francis. *Life and Public Services of William Pitt Fessenden.* 2 vols. Boston: Houghton, Mifflin and Company, 1907.

Fischer, LeRoy H. "Adam Gurowski Discovers a Cabinet Secretary," *Lincoln Herald,* LXVI, No. 1 (Spring 1964), 3–13.

Fish, Carl R. "Conscription in the Civil War," *American Historical Review,* XXI, No. 1 (October 1915), 100–103.

———. "Lincoln and the Patronage," *American Historical Review,* VIII, No. 1 (October 1902), 53–69.

Fite, Emerson D. *Social and Industrial Conditions in the North during the Civil War.* New York: The Macmillan Company, 1910.

———. *The Presidential Campaign of 1860.* New York: The Macmillan Company, 1911.

Flick, Alexander C. (editor). *History of the State of New York.* 10 vols. New York: Columbia University Press, 1933–1937.

Follett, Mary P. *The Speaker of the House of Representatives.* New York: Longmans, Green and Company, 1902.

Ford, Worthington C. (editor). *A Cycle of Adams Letters, 1861–1865.* 2 vols. Boston: Houghton, Mifflin Company, 1920.

Forney, John W. *Anecdotes of Public Men.* New York: Harper and Brothers, 1874.

Fowell, William W. *A History of Minnesota.* 4 vols. St. Paul: Minnesota Historical Society, 1921–1930.

Fuller, Hubert B. *The Speakers of the House.* Boston: Little, Brown and Company, 1909.

Gallaher, Ruth A. "Samuel Ryan Curtis," *Iowa Journal of History and Politics,* XXV, No. 3 (July 1927), 331–358.

Galloway, George B. "Development of the Committee System in the House of Representatives," *American Historical Review,* LXV, No. 1 (October 1959), 17–30.

Gates, Paul W. "The Homestead Law in an Incongruous Land System," *American Historical Review,* XLI, No. 4 (July 1936), 652–681.

———. "Western Opposition to the Agricultural College Act," *Indiana Magazine of History,* XXXVII, No. 2 (June 1941), 103–136.

Glasson, William H. *Federal Military Pensions in the United States.* New York: Oxford University Press, American Branch, 1918.

———. *History of Military Pension Legislation in the United States.* Vol. XII, No. 3 of [*Columbia University*] *Studies in History, Economics and Public Law.* New York: Columbia University Press, 1900.

Going, Charles B. *David Wilmot, Free-Soiler.* New York: D. Appleton and Company, 1924.

Gray, Wood. *The Hidden Civil War.* New York: The Viking Press, 1942.

Greeley, Horace. *Recollections of a Busy Life.* New York: J. B. Ford and Company, 1868.

Grinnell, Josiah B. *Men and Events of Forty Years.* Boston: D. Lothrop Company, 1891.

Grissom, Daniel M. "Personal Recollections of Distinguished Missourians:

James S. Rollins," *Missouri Historical Review,* XVIII, No. 4 (July 1924), 546–552.

Grouert, Theodore G. "Senator Henry S. Lane," *Register of the Kentucky Historical Society,* XXXV, No. 112 (July 1937), 260–264.

Gurowski, Adam. *Diary, March 4, 1861–November 2, 1862.* Boston: Lee and Shepard, 1862.

———. *Diary, November, 1862–October, 1863.* New York: Carleton, 1864.

Halstead, Murat. *Caucuses of 1860: A History of the National Political Conventions of the Current Presidential Campaign.* Columbus, Ohio: Follett, Foster and Company, 1860.

Hamlin, Charles E. *The Life and Times of Hannibal Hamlin.* Cambridge, Mass.: Riverside Press, 1899.

Hammond, Bray. "The North's Empty Purse, 1861–1862," *American Historical Review,* LXVII, No. 1 (October 1961), 1–18.

Haney, Lewis H. *A Congressional History of Railways in the United States, 1850–1887. Bulletin of the University of Wisconsin,* No. 342, *Economics and Political Science Series,* Vol. VI, No. 1. Madison: University of Wisconsin Press, 1910.

Harbison, Wilfred A. "Lincoln and Indiana Republicans, 1861–1862," *Indiana Magazine of History,* XXXIII, No. 3 (September 1937), 277–303.

Harding, Samuel B. "Missouri Party Struggles in the Civil War Period," American Historical Association, *Annual Report* (1900), I, 85–103.

Harris, Wilmer C. *Public Life of Zachariah Chandler, 1851–1875.* Lansing: Michigan Historical Commission, 1917.

Hart, Albert B. *Commonwealth History of Massachusetts.* 5 vols. New York: The States History Company, 1927–1930.

Hatch, Louis C. *Maine: A History.* 5 vols. New York: The American Historical Society, 1919.

Haynes, George H. *Charles Sumner.* Philadelphia: George W. Jacobs and Company, 1909.

———. *The Senate of the United States.* 2 vols. Boston: Houghton, Mifflin Company, 1938.

Heck, Frank H. "John C. Breckinridge in the Crisis of 1860–1861," *Journal of Southern History,* XXI, No. 3 (August 1955), 316–346.

Hesseltine, William B. "Abraham Lincoln and the Politicians," *Civil War History,* VI, No. 1 (March 1960), 43–55.

Hibbard, Benjamin H. *A History of the Public Land Policies.* New York: The Macmillan Company, 1924.

Hoar, George F. *Autobiography of Seventy Years.* 2 vols. New York: C. Scribner's Sons, 1906.

Hofstadter, Richard. "The Tariff Issue and the Civil War," *American Historical Review,* XLIV, No. 1 (October 1938), 50–55.

Hollister, Ovando J. *Life of Schuyler Colfax.* New York: Funk and Wagnalls, 1886.

Hosmer, James K. *The Appeal to Arms, 1861–1863.* New York: Harper and Brothers, 1907.

Howland, Louis. *Stephen A. Douglas.* New York: C. Scribner's Sons, 1920.

Hubbart, Henry C. *The Older Middle West, 1840–1880.* New York: D. Appleton-Century Company, 1936.

Hunt, Gaillard. *Israel, Elihu, and Cadwallader Washburn.* New York: The Macmillan Company, 1925.

Hutchins, John. "Reminiscences of the Thirty-Sixth and Thirty-Seventh Congresses," *Magazine of Western History,* XIV, No. 3 (July 1891), 309–317; No. 4 (August 1891), 439–448; No. 5 (September 1891), 537–547.

Isely, Jeter A. *Horace Greeley and the Republican Party, 1853–1861.* Princeton: Princeton University Press, 1947.

James, Edmund J. *Origin of the Land Grant Act of 1862.* Vol. IV, No. 1 of *The University [of Illinois] Studies.* Urbana-Champaign: University Press, 1910.

Jellison, Charles A. *Fessenden of Maine: Civil War Senator.* Syracuse: Syracuse University Press, 1962.

Johannsen, Robert W. *Frontier Politics and the Sectional Conflict.* Seattle: University of Washington Press, 1955.

———. "Spectators of Disunion: The Pacific Northwest and the Civil War," *Pacific Northwest Quarterly,* XLIV, No. 3 (July 1953), 106–114.

Johnson, Allan. *Stephen A. Douglas: A Study in American Politics.* New York: The Macmillan Company, 1908.

Johnson, Allan and Dumas Malone (editors). *Dictionary of American Biography.* 20 vols. plus index plus 2 supplementary vols. New York: Charles Scribner's Sons, 1928–1940.

Jordon, Henry D. "Daniel Wolsey Voorhees," *Mississippi Valley Historical Review,* VI, No. 4 (March 1920), 532–555.

Julian, George W. *Political Recollections, 1840 to 1872.* Chicago: Janson, McClurg and Company, 1884.

Kendall, Amos. *Autobiography of Amos Kendall.* Edited by William Stickney. New York: Peter Force, 1949.

Kennedy, Elijah R. *The Contest for California in 1861: How Colonel E. D. Baker Saved the Pacific States to the Union.* Boston: Houghton, Mifflin Company, 1912.

Kentucky, General Assembly of. *Biographical Sketch of the Hon. Lazarus W. Powell.* Frankfort: The Kentucky Yeoman Office, 1868.

Kerr, Winfield S. *John Sherman, His Life and Public Services.* 2 vols. Boston: Sherman, French and Company, 1908.

Kirwan, Albert D. *John J. Crittenden: The Struggle for the Union.* Lexington: University of Kentucky Press, 1962.

Klement, Frank L. *The Copperheads in the Middle West.* Chicago: University of Chicago Press, 1960.

———. "Midwestern Opposition to Lincoln's Emancipation Policy," *Journal of Negro History,* XLIX, No. 3 (July 1964), 169–183.

Knapp, Charles M. *New Jersey Politics during the Period of the Civil War and Reconstruction.* Geneva, N.Y.: W. F. Humphrey, 1924.

Korngold, Ralph. *Thaddeus Stevens, A Being Darkly Wise and Rudely Great.* New York: Harcourt, Brace and Company, 1955.

Krug, Mark M. "The Republican Party and the Emancipation Proclamation," *Journal of Negro History,* XLVIII, No. 2 (April 1963), 98–114.

Lane, Jarlath R. *A Political History of Connecticut During the Civil War.* Washington: Catholic University of America Press, 1941.

Lanman, Charles. *Biographical Annals of the Civil Government of the United States.* New York: J. M. Morrison, 1887.

Laugel, Auguste. *The United States during the War.* London: H. Bailliere, 1866.

Laughlin, Scera B. "Missouri Politics during the Civil War," *Missouri Historical Review,* XXIII, No. 3 (April 1929), 400–426; No. 4 (July 1929), 583–618; XXIV, No. 1 (October 1929), 87–113; No. 2 (January 1930), 261–284.

Lee, Francis B. *New Jersey as a Colony and as a State.* 4 vols. New York: The Publishing Society of New Jersey, 1903.

Linden, Glenn M. " 'Radicals' and Economic Policies: The House of Representatives, 1861–1873," *Civil War History,* XIII, No. 1 (March 1967), 51–65.

———. " 'Radicals' and Economic Policies: The Senate, 1861–1873," *Journal of Southern History,* XXXII, No. 2 (May 1966), 189–199.

Lindsey, David. *"Sunset" Cox, Irrepressible Democrat.* Detroit: Wayne State University Press, 1959.

Luthin, Reinhard H. "Abraham Lincoln and the Tariff," *American Historical Review,* XLIX, No. 4 (July 1944), 609–629.

Magdol, Edward. *Owen Lovejoy: Abolitionist in Congress.* New Brunswick: Rutgers University Press, 1967.

Mallam, William D. "Lincoln and the Conservatives," *Journal of Southern History,* XXVIII, No. 1 (February 1962), 31–45.

Manchester, D. W. "Banks and Bankers of Buffalo: Hon. Elbridge Gerry Spaulding," *Magazine of Western History,* V, No. 6 (April 1887), 795–802.

Marshall, Jessie A. (editor). *Private and Official Correspondence of Gen. Benjamin F. Butler during the Period of the Civil War.* 5 vols. Norwood, Mass.: The Plimpton Press, 1917.

Mason, Virginia. *The Public Life and Diplomatic Correspondence of James M. Mason.* Roanoke, Va.: The Stone Printing and Manufacturing Company, 1903.

McClure, Alexander K. *Abraham Lincoln and Men of War-Times.* Philadelphia: The Times Publishing Company, 1892.

———. *Colonel Alexander K. McClure's Recollections of Half a Century.* Salem, Mass.: The Salem Press Company, 1902.

McCowan, Ada C. *The Congressional Conference Committee.* New York: N. P., 1927.

McCulloch, Hugh. *Men and Measures of Half a Century.* New York: Charles Scribner's Sons, 1889.

McCutcheon, Otis E. "Recollections of Zachariah Chandler," *Michigan History Magazine,* V, No. 1–2 (January–April 1921), 140–149.

McDougal, Henry G. "A Decade of Missouri Politics—1860 to 1870: From a Republican Viewpoint," *Missouri Historical Review,* III, No. 2 (January 1909), 126–153.

McGuire, James K. (editor). *The Democratic Party of the State of New York.* 3 vols. New York: United States History Company, 1905.

McKee, Thomas H. *The National Platforms of all Political Parties . . . From 1789 to 1896.* Washington: The Statistical Publishing Company, 1896.

McMaster, John B. *A History of the People of the United States during Lincoln's Administration.* New York: D. Appleton and Company, 1927.

McPherson, Edward. *The Political History of the United States during the Great Rebellion.* Washington: Philip and Solomons, 1865.

Mearns, David C. (editor). *The Lincoln Papers.* 2 vols. to date. Garden City, N.Y.: Doubleday and Company, 1948.

Meredith, Roy. *Mr. Lincoln's Contemporaries.* New York: Charles Scribner's Sons, 1951.

Miller, Thomas C. *West Virginia and Its People.* 3 vols. New York: Lewis Historical Publishing Company, 1913.

Milton, George F. *Conflict, The American Civil War.* New York: Coward-McCann, Incorporated, 1941.

———. *The Eve of Conflict: Stephen A. Douglas and the Needless War.* Boston: Houghton, Mifflin Company, 1934.

Mitchell, Wesley C. *A History of the Greenbacks, with Special Reference to the Economic Consequences of Their Issue, 1862–65.* Chicago: University of Chicago Press, 1903.

Moore, Frederick W. "Representation in the National Congress from the Seceding States, 1861–1865," *American Historical Review,* II, No. 2 (January 1897), 279–293; No. 3 (April 1897), 461–471.

Moore, John B. (editor). *The Works of James Buchanan.* 12 vols. Philadelphia: J. B. Lippincott Company, 1908–1911.

Moore, Joseph W. *The American Congress.* New York: Harper and Brothers, 1895.

Morrow, Curtis H. *Politico-Military Secret Societies of the Northwest, 1860–1865.* Worcester, Mass.: N. P., 1929.

Mowry, Duane. "Interesting Letter of Hon. John Bell, of Tennessee, to the Hon. James R. Doolittle, of Wisconsin," *American Historical Magazine,* IX, No. 3 (July 1904), 274–276.

The National Cyclopedia of American Biography. 41 vols. New York: J. T. White Company, 1897–1956.

Nettels, Curtis. "Andrew Johnson and the South," *South Atlantic Quarterly,* XXV, No. 1 (January 1926), 55–64.

Neu, Irene D. *Erastus Corning: Merchant and Financier, 1794–1872.* Ithaca: Cornell University Press, 1960.

Nevins, Allan. *The War For The Union.* Vols. I and II. New York: Charles Scribner's Sons, 1959, 1960.

Nichols, Roy F. *The Disruption of American Democracy.* New York: The Macmillan Company, 1948.

Nicolay, John G. and John Hay. *Abraham Lincoln: A History.* 10 vols. New York: The Century Company, 1914.

Nicolay, John G. and John Hay (editors). *Complete Works of Abraham Lincoln.* 12 vols. New York: Francis D. Tandy Company, 1905.

Parker, William B. *The Life and Public Services of Justin Smith Morrill.* Boston: Houghton, Mifflin Company, 1924.

Pierce, Edward L. *Memoir and Letters of Charles Sumner.* 4 vols. Boston: Roberts Brothers, 1877–1893.

Pierson, William W. Jr. "The Committee on the Conduct of the War," *American Historical Review,* XXIII, No. 3 (April 1918), 550–576.

Pillsbury, Hobart. *New Hampshire.* 7 vols. New York: The Lewis Historical Publishing Company, 1927.

Poore, Benjamin P. *Perley's Reminiscences of Sixty Years in the National Metropolis.* 2 vols. Philadelphia: Hubbard Brothers, 1886.

Porter, George H. *Ohio Politics during the Civil War Period.* Vol. XL, No. 2

of [*Columbia University*] *Studies in History, Economics and Public Law.* New York: Longmans, Green and Company, 1911.

Potter, David M. *Lincoln and His Party in the Secession Crisis.* New Haven: Yale University Press, 1942.

Prentis, Noble L. *Kansas Miscellanies.* Topeka: Kansas Publishing House, 1889.

Randall, James G. "Captured and Abandoned Property during the Civil War," *American Historical Review,* XIX, No. 1 (October 1913), 65–79.

———. *The Civil War and Reconstruction.* New York: D. C. Heath and Company, 1953.

———. *The Confiscation of Property during the Civil War.* Indianapolis: Mutual Printing and Lithographing Company, 1913.

———. *Constitutional Problems Under Lincoln.* Urbana: University of Illinois Press, 1951.

———. *Lincoln, The President.* 4 vols. New York: Dodd, Mead and Company, 1945–1955.

———. "Some Legal Aspects of the Confiscation Acts of the Civil War," *American Historical Review,* XVIII, No. 1 (October 1912), 79–96.

Ratner, Sidney. *American Taxation, Its History as a Social Force in Democracy.* New York: W. W. Norton and Company, 1942.

Reed, Henry C. *Delaware: A History of the First State.* 3 vols. New York: Lewis Historical Publishing Company, 1947.

———. "Lincoln's Compensated Emancipation Plan and Its Relation to Delaware," *Delaware Notes,* 7th Series (1931), 27–78.

Reid, Whitlaw. *Ohio in the War.* 2 vols. Cincinnati: Moore, Wilstach and Baldwin, 1868.

"Reminiscences of Stephan A. Douglas," *Atlantic Monthly,* VIII, No. 44 (August 1861), 205–213.

Rhodes, James F. *A History of the United States from the Compromise of 1850 to the Final Restoration of Home Rule at the South in 1877.* 7 vols. New York: The Macmillan Company, 1904–1906.

Richardson, James D. (editor). *A Compilation of the Messages and Papers of the Presidents.* 10 vols. plus 1 supplementary vol. Washington: Government Printing Office, 1896–1903.

Riddle, Albert G. "Benjamin Franklin Wade," *Magazine of Western History,* II, No. 1 (May 1885), 1–18; No. 3 (July 1885), 222–237; III, No. 2 (December 1885), 112–123; No. 3 (January 1886), 235–245; No. 5 (March 1886), 471–484; No. 6 (April 1886), 590–600; IV, No. 3 (July 1886), 299–313.

———. *Life of Benjamin F. Wade.* Cleveland: William W. Williams, 1886.

———. *Recollections of War Times.* New York: G. P. Putnam's Sons, 1895.

Robbins, Roy M. *Our Landed Heritage, The Public Domain, 1776–1936.* Princeton: Princeton University Press, 1942.

Roberts, A. Sellew. "The Federal Government and Confederate Cotton," *American Historical Review,* XXXII, No. 2 (January 1927), 262–275.

Robertson, James R. "Sectionalism in Kentucky from 1855 to 1865," *Mississippi Valley Historical Review,* IV, No. 1 (June 1917), 49–63.

Robinson, Edgar E. (editor). "Day Journal of Milton S. Latham," *Quarterly of the California Historical Society,* XI, No. 1 (March 1932), 3–28.

Robinson, William S. *"Warrington" Pen-portraits: A Collection of Personal and Political Reminiscences from 1848 to 1876.* Boston: Mrs. W. S. Robinson, 1877.

Roseboom, Eugene H. *The Civil War Era, 1850–1873.* Vol. IV of *The History of the State of Ohio.* Edited by Carl F. Wittke. Columbus: Ohio State Archaeological and Historical Society, 1944.

Russel, Robert R. *Improvement of Communication with the Pacific Coast as an Issue in American Politics, 1783–1864.* Cedar Rapids, Iowa: The Torch Press, 1948.

Russell, William H. *My Diary North and South.* Boston: T. O. H. P. Burnham, 1863.

Russell, William H. "Timothy O. Howe, Stalwart Republican," *Wisconsin Magazine of History,* XXXV, No. 2 (Winter 1951), 90–99.

Ryan, Daniel J. "Lincoln and Ohio," *Ohio Archaeological and Historical Publications,* XXXII (1923), 7–281.

Sala, George A. H. *My Diary in America in the Midst of War.* 2 vols. London: Tinsley Brothers, 1865.

Sampson, Francis A. "Hon. John Brooks Henderson," *Missouri Historical Review,* VII, No. 4 (July 1913), 237–241.

Sanborn, John B. "Some Political Aspects of Homestead Legislation," *American Historical Review,* VI, No. 1 (October 1900), 19–37.

Schafer, Joseph (editor). *Intimate Letters of Carl Schurz, 1841–1869.* Madison: State Historical Society of Wisconsin, 1928.

———. "Who Elected Lincoln?," *American Historical Review,* XLVII, No. 1 (October 1941), 51–63.

Scharf, John T. *History of Maryland from the Earliest Period to the Present Day.* 3 vols. Baltimore: John B. Piet, 1879.

Schouler, William. *A History of Massachusetts in the Civil War.* 2 vols. Boston: E. P. Dutton and Company, 1868–1871.

Schuckers, J. W. *The Life and Public Services of Salmon Portland Chase.* New York: D. Appleton and Company, 1874.

Schurz, Carl. *The Reminiscences of Carl Schurz.* 3 vols. New York: Doubleday, Page and Company, 1909.

Scott, Harvey W. *History of the Oregon Country.* 6 vols. Cambridge: The Riverside Press, 1924.

Seilhamer, George O. *Leslie's History of the Republican Party.* 2 vols. New York: The L. S. Williams Publishing Company, n.d.

Sellers, James L. "An Interpretation of Civil War Finance," *American Historical Review,* XXX, No. 2 (January 1925), 282–297.

———. "James R. Doolittle," *Wisconsin Magazine of History,* XVII, No. 2 (December 1933), 168–178; No. 3 (March 1934), 277–306; No. 4 (June 1934), 393–401; XVIII, No. 1 (September 1934), 20–41; No. 2 (December 1934), 178–187.

Seward, Frederick W. *Reminiscences of a War-Time Statesman and Diplomat, 1830–1915.* New York: G. P. Putnam's Sons, 1916.

Shannon, Fred A. "The Federal Government and the Negro Soldier, 1861–1865," *Journal of Negro History,* XI, No. 4 (October 1926), 563–583.

———. "The Homestead Act and the Labor Surplus," *American Historical Review,* XLI, No. 4 (July 1936), 637–651.

Sharkey, Robert P. *Money, Class, and Party.* Baltimore: Johns Hopkins Press, 1959.

Sharp, Walter R. "Henry S. Lane and the Formation of the Republican Party in Indiana," *Mississippi Valley Historical Review,* VII, No. 2 (September 1920), 93–112.

Shaw, William Lawrence. "McDougall of California," *California Historical Society Quarterly,* XLIII, No. 2 (June 1964), 119–134.

Sherman, John. *Recollections of Forty Years in the House, Senate and Cabinet.* 2 vols. New York: The Werner Company, 1895.

Shortridge, Wilson P. "Kentucky Neutrality in 1861," *Mississippi Valley Historical Review,* IX, No. 4 (March 1923), 283–301.

Shover, Kenneth B. "Maverick at Bay: Ben Wade's Senate Re-election Campaign, 1862–1863," *Civil War History,* XII, No. 1 (March 1966), 23–42.

Simon, John Y. "The Politics of the Morrill Act," *Agricultural History,* XXXVII, No. 2 (April 1963), 103–111.

Smith, Donnal V. *Chase and Civil War Politics.* Vol. II of *Ohio Historical Collections.* Columbus, Ohio: The F. J. Heer Printing Company, 1931.

Smith, Harry E. *The United States Federal Internal Tax History from 1861 to 1871.* Cambridge: The Riverside Press, 1914.

Smith, Joseph P. (editor). *History of the Republican Party in Ohio.* 2 vols. Chicago: The Lewis Publishing Company, 1898.

Smith, William E. *The Francis Preston Blair Family in Politics.* 2 vols. New York: The Macmillan Company, 1933.

Spaulding, Elbridge G. *A Resource of War—The Credit of the Government Made Immediately Available. History of the Legal Tender Paper Money Issued During the Great Rebellion.* Buffalo, N.Y.: The Express Printing Company, 1869.

Speed, Thomas. *The Union Cause in Kentucky, 1860–1865.* New York: G. P. Putnam's Sons, 1907.

Spring, Leverett W. "The Career of a Kansas Politician," *American Historical Review,* IV, No. 1 (October 1898), 80–104.

Stampp, Kenneth M. *Indiana Politics During the Civil War.* Vol. XXXI of *Indiana Historical Collections.* Indianapolis: Indiana Historical Bureau, 1949.

Stealey, O. O. *Twenty Years in the Press Gallery.* New York: Publishers Printing Company, 1906.

Steiner, Bernard C. "James Alfred Pearce," *Maryland Historical Magazine,* XVI, No. 4 (December 1921), 319–339; XVII, No. 1 (March 1922), 33–47; No. 2 (June 1922), 177–190; No. 3 (September 1922), 269–283; No. 4 (December 1922), 348–363; XVII, No. 1 (March 1923), 38–52; No. 2 (June 1923), 134–150; No. 3 (September 1923), 257–273; No. 4 (December 1923), 341–357; XIX, No. 1 (March 1924), 13–29; No. 2 (June 1924), 162–179.

Stephenson, George M. *The Political History of the Public Lands from 1840 to 1862.* Boston: Richard G. Badger, 1917.

Stephenson, Wendell H. *The Political Career of General James H. Lane.* Vol. III of *Publications of the Kansas State Historical Society.* Topeka: Kansas State Printing Plant, 1930.

Stevens, Walter B. *Centennial History of Missouri.* 4 vols. St. Louis: The S. J. Clarke Publishing Company, 1921.

Streeter, Floyd B. *Political Parties in Michigan, 1837–1860.* Lansing: Michigan Historical Commission, 1918.

Strong, George T. *The Diary of George Templeton Strong, 1835–1875.* 4 vols. Edited by Allan Nevins and Milton H. Thomas. New York: The Macmillan Company, 1952.

Stryker, Lloyd P. *Andrew Johnson: A Study in Courage.* New York: The Macmillan Company, 1929.

Studenski, Paul and Herman E. Krooss. *Financial History of the United States.* New York: McGraw-Hill Book Company, 1952.

Taylor, Grace N. "The Blair Family in the Civil War," *Register of the Kentucky Historical Society,* XXXVII, No. 125 (October 1940), 280–294; XXXIX, No. 126 (January 1941), 47–57; No. 127 (April 1941), 138–156.

Taylor, Telford. *Grand Inquest.* New York: Simon and Schuster, 1955.

Thayer, William R. *The Life and Letters of John Hay.* 2 vols. Boston: Houghton, Mifflin Company, 1915.

Thomas, Benjamin P. and Harold M. Hyman. *Stanton: The Life and Times of Lincoln's Secretary of War.* New York: Alfred A. Knopf, 1962.

Thompson, Alexander M. *A Political History of Wisconsin.* Milwaukee: C. N. Caspar Company, 1902.

Thompson, Robert M. and Richard Wainright (editors). *Confidential Correspondence of Gustavus Vasa Fox.* 2 vols. New York: The Naval History Society, 1918–1919.

Thorndike, Rachel S. (editor). *The Sherman Letters.* New York: C. Scribner's Sons, 1894.

Tracy, Gilbert A. (editor). *Uncollected Letters of Abraham Lincoln.* Boston: Houghton, Mifflin Company, 1917.

Trefousse, Hans L. *Benjamin Franklin Wade: Radical Republican from Ohio.* New York: Twayne Publishers, Inc., 1963.

———. "The Joint Committee on the Conduct of the War: A Reassessment," *Civil War History,* X, No. 1 (March 1964), 5–19.

The Tribune Almanac for 1861. New York: The Tribune Association.

The Tribune Almanac for 1862. New York: The Tribune Association.

The Tribune Almanac for 1863. New York: The Tribune Association.

The Tribune Almanac for 1864. New York: The Tribune Association.

"Trumbull Correspondence," *Mississippi Valley Historical Review,* I, No. 1 (June 1914), 101–108.

Utley, Henry M. and Byron M. Cutcheon. *Michigan as a Province, Territory and State, the Twenty-Sixth Member of the Federal Union.* 4 vols. New York: The Publishing Society of Michigan, 1906.

Vallandingham, Clement L. *The Record of Hon. C. L. Vallandigham on Abolition, the Union and the Civil War.* Columbus, Ohio: J. Walter and Company, 1863.

Vallandigham, James L. *A Life of Clement L. Vallandigham.* Baltimore: Turnbull Brothers, 1872.

Van Fossan, W. H. "Clement L. Vallandigham," *Ohio Archaeological and Historical Publications,* XXIII (1914), 256–267.

Voegeli, Jacque. "The Northwest and the Race Issue, 1861–1862," *Mississippi Valley Historical Review,* L, No. 2 (September 1963), 235–251.

Ware, Edith E. *Political Opinion in Massachusetts during the Civil War and Reconstruction.* Vol. LXXIV, No. 2 of [*Columbia University*] *Studies in History, Economics and Public Law.* New York: Columbia University Press, 1916.

"Washington City," *Atlantic Monthly,* VII, No. 39 (January 1861), 1–8.

Wasson, R. Gordon. *The Hall Carbine Affair: A Study in Contemporary Folklore.* New York: Pandick Press, 1948.

Weed, Thurlow. *Autobiography of Thurlow Weed.* Edited by Harriet A. Weed. Boston: Houghton, Mifflin Company, 1883.

Weeden, William B. *War Government, Federal and State, in Massachusetts, New York, Pennsylvania and Indiana, 1861–1865.* Boston: Houghton, Mifflin and Company, 1906.

Welles, Gideon. *Diary of Gideon Welles.* 3 vols. Edited by Edgar T. Welles. Boston: Houghton, Mifflin Company, 1911.

Wesley, Charles H. "Lincoln's Plan for Colonizing the Emancipated Negroes," *Journal of Negro History,* IV, No. 1 (January 1919), 17–21.

White, Horace. *The Life of Lyman Trumbull.* Boston: Houghton, Mifflin Company, 1913.

Willey, William P. *An Inside View of the Formation of the State of West Virginia.* Wheeling, W. Va.: The News Publishing Company, 1901.

Williams, George H. "Political History of Oregon from 1853 to 1865," *Quarterly of the Oregon Historical Society,* II, No. 1 (March 1901), 1–35.

Williams, Lucille S. "John Cabell Breckinridge," *Register of the Kentucky Historical Society,* XXXII, No. 101 (October 1934), 301–319; XXXIII, No. 102 (January 1935), 13–28.

Williams, T. Harry. "The Attack upon West Point during the Civil War," *Mississippi Valley Historical Review,* XXV, No. 4 (March 1939), 491–504.

———. "The Committee on the Conduct of the War," *Journal of the American Military History Institute,* III, No. 3 (Fall 1939), 139–156.

———. *Lincoln and the Radicals.* Madison: University of Wisconsin Press, 1941.

Wilson, Henry. *History of the Rise and Fall of the Slave Power in America.* 3 vols. Boston: James R. Osgood and Company, 1872–1877.

Wilson, James G. and John Fiske (editors). *Appleton's Cyclopedia of American Biography.* 6 vols. New York: D. Appleton and Company, 1888.

Winston, Robert W. *Andrew Johnson, Plebeian and Patriot.* New York: Henry Holt and Company, 1928.

Woodburn, James A. "Attitude of Thaddeus Stevens toward the Conduct of the Civil War," *American Historical Review,* XII, No. 3 (April 1907), 567–583.

———. *The Life of Thaddeus Stevens: A Study in American Political History.* Indianapolis: The Bobbs-Merrill Company, 1913.

Wright, Louise W. *A Southern Girl in '61.* New York: Doubleday, Page and Company, 1905.

Zachariah Chandler: An Outline Sketch of His Life and Public Services. Detroit: The Post and Tribune Company, 1880.

Zacharias, Donald W. "John J. Crittenden Crusades for the Union and Neutrality in Kentucky," *Filson Club History Quarterly,* XXXVIII, No. 3 (July 1964), 193–205.

Zimmerman, Charles. "The Origin and Rise of the Republican Party in Indiana from 1854 to 1860," *Indiana Magazine of History,* XIII, No. 3 (September 1917), 211–269; No. 4 (December 1917), 349–412.

Zoellner, Robert H. "Negro Colonization: The Climate of Opinion Surrounding Lincoln, 1860–1865," *Mid-America,* XLII, No. 3 (July 1960), 131–150.

Index